CAPTAINS OF THE OLD STEAM NAVY

MAKERS OF THE AMERICAN NAVAL TRADITION
1840–1880

EDITED BY JAMES C. BRADFORD

NAVAL INSTITUTE PRESS
Annapolis, Maryland

CAPTAINS OF THE OLD STEAM NAVY

MAKERS OF THE AMERICAN NAVAL TRADITION
Edited by James C. Bradford

Command Under Sail, 1775–1850
Captains of the Old Steam Navy, 1840–1880
Admirals of the New Steel Navy, 1880–1930
(in preparation)

For Barbara and Bill Conrad

CONTENTS

LIST OF ILLUSTRATIONS

PREFACE

The middle decades of the nineteenth century constitute one of the great transitional eras in naval history. For three centuries ships and weapons had remained basically unchanged, and developments were evolutionary in nature. Then in only a few decades propulsion changed from sail to steam, hulls from wood to iron and steel, ordnance from muzzle-loading smoothbore cannon to breech-loading rifled guns, and projectiles from solid shot to exploding shells. The transformation was such that a virtual revolution in naval warfare occurred.

Developments of such magnitude appeared to demand changes in both strategy and tactics, but the nature of the changes required was unclear. The superiority of steam over sail, and the relatively short range of ships employing the new mode of power, seemed to render obsolete old blockade strategies; and tactics, which had previously been limited by considerations of wind direction and velocity, seemed similarly outdated.

The era was equally one of change for the American navy. The Continental Navy of the Revolution had actually been disbanded after the war. Its successor, the United States Navy, was established by Congress in 1794, but its first ships did not go to sea until four years later. From this uncertain beginning a sound basis was laid during the Quasi-War with France, the Barbary Wars, and the War of 1812. By midcentury the existence of the Navy was no longer in doubt; it had passed from infancy to adolescence. Indeed, some believed it had ossified.

During the Age of Sail men such as John Paul Jones, Thomas Macdonough, Oliver Hazard Perry, and Stephen Decatur exemplified courage and leadership under fire; William Bainbridge, Robert Stockton, and Isaac Hull established precedents for naval officers serving as diplomatic agents; and John Barry, Stephen Decatur, John Rodgers, and Isaac Hull set high standards of professionalism and loyalty to service and country.

These men had worthy successors. David Farragut's "Damn the torpedoes" joined John Paul Jones's "I have not yet begun to fight" and James Lawrence's "Don't give up the ship" in the lexicon of naval quotations. In the same vein, Franklin Buchanan, David Farragut, and David Porter assumed the mantle of decisive leadership and courage under fire. Solid administrators such as Isaac Hull and John Rodgers had their successors in Franklin Buchanan and John Rodgers, Jr., while Matthew C. Perry, Charles Wilkes, and Robert Shufeldt continued the tradition of naval diplomacy.

The legacy of the sailing navy was not entirely positive. Some of its problems were so persistent they could indeed be called "traditional." The nepotism and political favoritism that repelled John Paul Jones during the Revolution continued, exemplified by such "naval families" as the Perrys and the Porters. Problems of alcoholism, officer education, and career uncertainty persisted, retarding the development of a sense of professionalism by many officers. Leadership in the crusade for reform passed from such men as Richard Stockton to Matthew C. Perry, Franklin Buchanan, and Andrew Foote.

Although few officers questioned the value of tradition, most were keenly aware of the rapid changes in their profession, which led some to question just how applicable such traditions would be to the new era. The most obvious challenges brought by the age of steam were scientific and technological. John A. Dahlgren, Matthew Fontaine Maury, and Benjamin Franklin Isherwood were prominent among the pioneers in advancing scientific inquiry and solving technological problems.

The age of steam brought with it other difficulties, some of which were not solved during the era, and continue to affect the Navy to this day. Divisions within the officer corps between line and staff officers became apparent as soon as the Engineering Corps was formed. Its officers considered themselves "heralds and makers" of a new Navy, much like the aviators of the 1920s and 1930s and the nuclear power officers of the 1960s and 1970s.[1] None of these officers believed they were accorded their just place in the service. John A. Dahlgren was the preeminent ordnance expert in the Navy, but he longed for, and finally received, a command at sea that brought him recognition as a "regular" officer. Such recognition eluded Matthew Fontaine Maury, who was even forced temporarily into retirement by a board charged with recommending dismissal of "inefficient" officers. Benjamin Franklin Isherwood's promotion in the Navy through ship design and construction, rather than through service at sea, forecast Hyman Rickover's similar advancement by almost a century, and both men endured similar sniping from "regular" officers. Likewise, the problems Isherwood faced in dealing with civilian shipbuilders more closely resemble those of today's Navy than the problems encountered by earlier officers such as Oliver Hazard Perry and Thomas Macdonough.

The history of the old steam navy has rarely been dealt with as a unit. Works on the Civil War era abound, and many others address particular aspects of the age, such as the new technology, naval diplomacy, and administration, but no single volume spanning the era has surveyed all these fields. Our perspective, too, is a unifying force. For, as one modern naval leader has written, "Important as ships are, naval history is made by men."[2] The biographical approach of this volume brings that era to life. By viewing the old steam navy through the eyes and careers of its officers, one can more fully understand the strengths and weaknesses of the service and the variety of roles played by naval forces, in peacetime as well as in war.

These biographical studies, all written especially for this volume, are interpretive rather than merely descriptive. The authors have chosen which aspects of their subjects' lives to emphasize. Andrew Foote is generally best remembered for his conduct of riverine operations during the Civil War, but John D. Milligan emphasizes his intellectual makeup and his role as a reformer. David Dixon Porter and Franklin Buchanan are famous for their wartime leadership, but Charles Todorich and Tamara Moser Melia show that their direction of the Naval Academy probably had a more lasting effect on the Navy. One might question the inclusion of Admiral Raphael Semmes of the Confederate States Navy in a book such as this, but the American naval tradition fairly includes the Continental and Confederate Navies as well as the U.S. Navy, and even if it did not, Semmes was the practitioner par excellence of *guerre de course*, or commerce raiding, the traditional nineteenth-century American naval strategy. In a later period, Alfred Thayer Mahan might reject such a strategy, but he never denied its importance as a tradition.

These essays are not simply short biographies. Instead they assess the role of their subjects as establishers, practitioners, and exemplars of the American naval tradition. For this reason authors were selected whose knowledge extends beyond the individual about whom they write. Thus John C. Schroeder, a diplomatic historian, was invited to write on Matthew C. Perry; William Stanton, whose specialty is the history of science, to write on Matthew Fontaine Maury because of his knowledge of science during the era; and David Allison, a historian of naval technology, to write on John A. Dahlgren. Some of the authors have written on their subjects before, but all offer more than simple distillations of views presented elsewhere.

There has been no attempt to impose uniformity of interpretation upon the essays. Men such as David Dixon Porter and Benjamin Franklin Isherwood were sometimes at odds with one another during their careers; so if the authors writing about them are not in agreement, that is altogether appropriate. The authors' views are their own, and each contributor has provided suggestions for additional reading to guide those whose interest they kindle.

The choice of subjects for this volume was not easy. No doubt a case could be made for including other officers of the era, but considerations of length dictated selection of only these thirteen individuals, whose careers illuminate the American naval tradition. Every important type of military and diplomatic operation can be examined and the major problems of the era can be explored through them.

Lessons of seamanship, tactics, and strategy drawn from the lives of men who served a century ago may not be directly applicable to the modern era, but there are connections, however metaphysical, between the periods. No modern admiral is likely to be called upon to test his ships against land fortifications in the same way Samuel Du Pont and Andrew Foote did, but the experiences of those two Civil War officers clearly demonstrate the value of close cooperation between army and naval officers in joint operations. Du Pont, who did not establish good relations with his counterpart in the Army, failed at Charleston, while Foote, who worked closely with Ulysses S. Grant in the West, succeeded at Ft. Donelson. Officers of the old steam navy also provide role models in their dedication to their naval careers in trying circumstances. The antebellum Navy had more officers than appropriate billets, and an officer could expect several involuntary furloughs over the course of his career. He could also expect to be assigned to duty with the Lighthouse Board and the Coastal Survey, neither of which was particularly popular among officers. Not surprisingly, many officers felt unappreciated by their countrymen in such circumstances. Thus, their loyalty to a naval career is especially laudatory.

During the mid-nineteenth century, foundations were laid for two important naval institutions. The establishment of the Naval Academy is traced through the lives of two of its most important early superintendents, Franklin Buchanan and David Dixon Porter. The Navy also began to generate an institutional capability for research and development. John A. Dahlgren's ordnance work at the Washington Navy Yard led to the establishment of the Naval Gun Factory there and served as a precedent for similar institutions scattered across the country, from torpedo development and production facilities at Newport, Rhode Island, to ordnance testing grounds at China Lake, California.

Few would deny the crucial importance of leadership in naval affairs. Most of the qualities that stood an officer of the mid-nineteenth century in good stead would serve the modern officer equally well. Personal courage under pressure is as important now as it was then. David Farragut standing in the rigging of the *Hartford* as she steamed into Mobile Bay and Raphael Semmes coolly striding the deck of the *Sumter* as she dashed through the Union blockade symbolize such qualities. The diplomatic skills demonstrated by Matthew C. Perry and Robert Shufeldt, the technical expertise of John A. Dahlgren and Benjamin Franklin Isherwood, and the administrative powers of Franklin Buchanan and John Rodgers can be profitably studied.

All these officers had great self-confidence, a characteristic to be encouraged, but one that could lead to hypersensitivity or to impetuosity. Its inherent dangers are shown in Franklin Buchanan's overly hasty resignation from the U. S. Navy followed by an attempt to gain reinstatement at the beginning of the Civil War, and by Raphael Semmes's rash decision to pit his *Alabama* against the superior *Kearsage*, which had disastrous results for both ship and crew. Some qualities highly respected then would be highly criticized today. The belligerent imperialism of Andrew Foote in Hawaii, of Charles Wilkes in Somoa and the Gilbert Islands, and of Robert Shufeldt in Korea were applauded then but would find few defenders now.

The question of whether leadership is innate or learned is insoluble, and no attempt is made to answer it here.[3] The focus of this volume is on the Navy in transition and the men who guided it. Men, more than ships or administrative agencies, link today's Navy with its past. The U.S. Navy has never had a dominating figure like Horatio Nelson. Instead it has a group of symbolic heroes, including Matthew C. Perry "opening Japan," David Farragut "damning the torpedoes" at Mobile, and Robert Shufeldt destroying Korean forts.

The group of men who guided the Navy into the steam age, shaped its character, and set its course were a mixed lot. They lived in an age of adventure. Some met the challenge, others did not, but all were makers of the American naval tradition. This is their story. It is also the story of the old steam navy.

NOTES

1. Lance Buhl, "Mariners and Machines: Resistance to Technological Change in the American Navy, 1865–1869," 725.

2. James Calvert, *The Naval Profession*, 6.

3. Older studies include Alfred Thayer Mahan, *Types of Naval Officers* and Charles Benedict Davenport, *Naval Officers: Their Heredity and Development*. The subject of leadership continues to intrigue authors. See, for example, John Horsfield, *The Art of Leadership in War: The Royal Navy from the Age of Nelson to the End of World War II* and Oliver Warner, *Command at Sea: Great Fighting Admirals from Hawke to Nimitz*.

ACKNOWLEDGMENTS

This book is a joint enterprise, and its editor could not have had better partners. All bore with great equanimity the editor's cavils about phraseology and what must have seemed contradictory requests for elaboration on some points and pleas for compression of other sections. My debt to these authors is gratefully acknowledged. Dale T. Knobel and John H. Lenihan read the preface and made suggestions that improved it. The entire manuscript benefited from Craig L. Symonds's reading and advice. The volume has been made more attractive by the assistance of Patty M. Maddocks, Director of Library and Photographic Services at the Naval Institute, and Charles R. Haberlein, Head of the Photographic Section of the Naval Historical Center. At the Naval Institute Press, our editor Deborah Guberti, provided encouragement, and our manuscript editor, Constance M. MacDonald, not only exacted a high standard of consistency of usage, but also suggested numerous changes to improve the clarity of the essays. Loretta C. Doty, Carole R. Knapp, and Lauri V. Caldwell of the Texas A&M University Department of History typed the manuscript. Laurie V. Caldwell also assembled the bibliography and with Rosa B. Richardson assisted in reading the proofs. My wife, Judy, proofread the entire manuscript and, with our sons, John and Jim, provided less tangible, but equally important support. To them is due the greatest gratitude.

FROM SAIL TO STEAM

MATTHEW CALBRAITH PERRY: ANTEBELLUM PRECURSOR OF THE STEAM NAVY

BY JOHN H. SCHROEDER

B etween the War of 1812 and the Civil War, the peacetime role of the U.S. Navy expanded dramatically. The primary peacetime mission of the Navy continued to be the protection of American overseas commerce, but accelerating American economic activity around the world transformed the operational definition of that duty by creating an array of additional demands and pressures for increased naval support. In the years after 1815, the protection of commerce meant that the Navy combated pirates, policed smuggling, showed the flag in major ports around the globe, maintained a continuous presence on various overseas stations, and performed limited diplomatic duties. Government officials and most politicians, regardless of their partisan faction, believed the Navy should play a limited peacetime commercial role and defined that mission in a rather narrow and defensive manner. Americans also assumed that most of the Navy's activities would occur in the Caribbean, the Mediterranean, and the Atlantic. To perform its role, the Navy Department maintained a small, active force of fewer than two dozen wooden sailing warships and existed on a budget that averaged less than $4 million per year.

By the 1850s the protection of commerce had been redefined and meant a great deal more than it had three decades earlier. The Navy now played a positive and expansive role in the nation's burgeoning overseas commerce. It not only protected and defended American lives, property, and trade overseas; it now also helped identify new markets, collected valuable commercial and nautical information, concluded diplomatic agreements, and opened new areas to American enterprises. In the Navy, the Mediterranean Squadron continued to be the most prestigious duty station, but American naval forces in Latin America, the Pacific, and the East Indies now carried out activities that were more challenging and more valuable to American overseas commercial interests. The Navy's far-flung activities required an active force of steam as well as sail vessels numbering between forty and fifty, and an annual budget

3

Matthew Calbraith Perry. Portrait by William Sidney Mount in 1835. *Courtesy of the Naval Academy Museum.*

of more than $12 million per year. On the eve of the Civil War, the Navy still had fundamental problems, and it hardly resembled the modern naval force of the late nineteenth century; but the nation's staggering overseas commercial expansion had already transformed the Navy's peacetime mission. And in the process, the Navy had assumed an important diplomatic and commercial role in shaping the nation's overseas economic development.

The naval career of Matthew Calbraith Perry spanned this period, and he stands as a key transitional figure between the navy of the early nineteenth century and the new commercial navy that was beginning to emerge by the

Civil War. His early career embodied the values and the traditions of the old navy, dominated by its magnificent wooden sailing warships. At the same time, Perry was an early proponent of the type of technological innovation and naval reform that would transform the peacetime role of the Navy and the character of its warships by the end of the century.

Matthew Calbraith Perry was born into a distinguished American naval family. His father had been a naval officer in both the American Revolution and the undeclared Naval War with France; his four brothers also joined the Navy, and one, Oliver Hazard, became one of the fighting heroes of the War of 1812. Matthew himself entered the Navy at age fourteen and served under the legendary John Rodgers and Stephen Decatur in the War of 1812. He subsequently served on various duty stations, mastered the intricacies of seamanship in wooden sailing vessels, rose to the rank of captain, and eventually commanded the Africa Squadron. During the Mexican War, Perry commanded the Gulf Squadron and distinguished himself in battle during several engagements, including the expeditions against Tabasco and the capture of Vera Cruz. By 1850 Perry, or "Old Bruin" as he was known, had compiled an impressive record of command and service similar to other top naval officers in the Age of Sail.

Unlike most of his naval peers, however, Perry had long been an energetic proponent of technological innovation, improved education, and progressive reform within the Navy. In a navy of wooden sailing vessels, Perry had become an early advocate of steam power and explosive ordnance. Throughout his career, he had demonstrated a notable intellectual curiosity and wide range of educational interests. Perry had also compiled an exceptional record of diplomatic experience in different capacities. Yet these attributes might well have represented nothing more than interesting sidelights to an impressive and traditional antebellum naval career had Perry not been chosen to command the American expedition to Japan. His selection permitted him to combine and fully utilize his varied naval, diplomatic, and intellectual talents in commanding an undertaking that developed into a major diplomatic expedition. The dramatic success and far-reaching significance of the expedition captured the nation's imagination and elevated Perry to his place as one of the Navy's most distinguished nineteenth-century officers. In retrospect, Perry's understanding of the broad significance and implications of his Far Eastern exploits as much as the achievements themselves made the commodore an exemplary harbinger of a coming epoch when the Navy and its officers would play an instrumental role in forging an overseas colonial empire for the United States.[1]

Born on 10 April 1794, in Newport, Rhode Island, Matthew Calbraith Perry was one of the eight children of Christopher Raymond and Sarah Wallace Perry. Christopher Perry was a seafaring man who served in several ships and was taken prisoner four times during the Revolution. Later he served in the American merchant marine and, in June 1798, he entered the Navy as captain in command of the yet unfinished frigate *General Greene.* During the naval war with France, the warship helped suppress pirates, conveyed American merchantmen, and patrolled the Caribbean. In 1801, Perry returned to the merchant service, but he later received a temporary appointment as commandant of the Charlestown Navy Yard.

Matthew Calbraith was the fourth child and third son of the family. All five of the boys became naval officers, and two of the three daughters married naval officers. Matthew entered the Navy as a midshipman in January 1809 and served on the schooner *Revenge* under the command of his brother Oliver Hazard Perry. In the next six years, Matthew also served under Commodores John Rodgers and Stephen Decatur, but he was not involved in any of the dramatic naval engagements of the War of 1812. In fact, the British blockade bottled up Decatur's frigate *President* in New York and allowed Perry enough time ashore to court and marry Jan Slidell, the daughter of a prominent New York merchant, in December 1814. The marriage was a happy one, providing Perry with nine children as well as important political contacts through his brother-in-law John Slidell, an influential Jacksonian Democrat during the 1830s and 1840s. One of Perry's sisters, Anna Maria, provided another family tie of professional importance through her marriage to the younger brother of Commodore John Rodgers.[2] These family connections aided Perry's social stature and professional career. And later his social connections were further enhanced by the marriage in 1848 of his daughter Caroline to August Belmont, the wealthy, German-born financier who was active in New York Democratic Party circles.

After a brief tour of duty with the Mediterranean Squadron in 1815, Perry took a furlough from the Navy and commanded merchantmen owned by his in-laws, before returning to the Navy in 1819. In the next eleven years, Perry received several assignments, including his first two commands, and his career progressed steadily. He served with the naval squadron that escorted a group of free blacks to West Africa to found a free colony at the site of Monrovia at Cape Mesurado. He served with the West Indies Squadron in the effort to end piracy in the Caribbean. He also received valuable experience as first lieutenant or executive officer of the 102-gun *North Carolina.*

In 1830, the Navy Department ordered Perry to assume command of the new sloop *Concord.* This assignment proved to be a frustrating but worthwhile experience for Perry as he was first forced to deal with the personal demands of an eccentric politician and later allowed to view firsthand the effect that naval power could have on diplomatic disputes. Perry's initial assignment on board the *Concord* was to convey John Randolph of Roanoke to Russia as the republic's new Envoy Extraordinary and Minister Plenipotentiary. The cruise provided a trying but useful lesson in patience and self-restraint for the thirty-six-year-old officer. Randolph embarked with a mountain of luggage, an entourage of personal servants, and his well-known cantankerous personality. The new minister insisted that Perry make several stops en route, and once Randolph reached Russia, he remained there only briefly before having Perry convey him and his entourage back to England.[3]

When finally rid of Randolph, the *Concord* joined the Mediterranean Squadron where Perry served for the next two years. Here Perry was able to pursue his intellectual interests in the culture and history of the region as well as to play an instructive role in resolving a claims dispute with Sicily in 1832. When discussions stalled, Commodore Daniel T. Patterson entrusted temporary command of the squadron to Perry. In concert with the *Brandywine* and the *Constellation*, Perry sailed to Naples in July 1832, then departed, and reappeared in September in command of the *Concord*. With the sloop *John Adams* already in port, all this naval activity had the desired effect, and a treaty resolving the claims issue was signed in October 1832.[4]

By the mid-1830s, Perry found himself among a number of energetic and farsighted younger officers who wanted to introduce various progressive ideas into the Navy. Perry, his brother-in-law Alexander Slidell MacKenzie, Robert Stockton, and Franklin Buchanan were officers whose further advancement and ideas for change had been stifled by the Navy's seniority-based promotion system and by the number of officers in their sixties and seventies who clung to positions of power in the department because there was no retirement system. These senior officers dominated the Board of Navy Commissioners which directed naval affairs, and generally opposed progressive reform and technological innovation because they held very traditional ideas about the Navy and its role. For example, the board conceded a limited place for steam power in the Navy, but detested the very thought of a navy dominated by cumbersome steam vessels that did not demand a high level of seamanship and created endless noise and dirt.[5]

In contrast, the younger group of career naval officers advocated extensive changes to improve the Navy and urged the application of steam power and other technological advances. These officers admired the changes then beginning in Europe where serious experiments had begun with steam power, iron hulls, and explosive shells. Perry, Slidell, and others also sought a much expanded peacetime diplomatic and commercial role for the Navy. To protect and extend American commerce, they wanted more ships deployed overseas and engaged in an increased array of peacetime activities. Thus Perry, Charles Wilkes, Matthew F. Maury, and other officers actively supported the proposed naval exploring expedition to the South Seas. In endorsing the project, these officers emphasized that the gathering of scientific, commercial, and nautical information would immeasurably enhance the nation's overseas maritime and economic interests in the Pacific. In essence, they sought an active role for the Navy in the creation of an overseas American commercial empire.[6]

Perry soon emerged as a leader in the group. During a decade as second in command and then as commandant of the Brooklyn Navy Yard, Perry advocated an array of reforms and innovations. He sought improvement in the recruiting of seamen and in the education of officers. He had long taken the shipboard instruction of officers seriously and now supported the establishment of a naval academy. In 1833, he was instrumental in founding the United States Naval Lyceum, an organization formed "to promote the diffusion of useful knowledge, (and) to foster a spirit of harmony and a community interest in the service." For officers in New York, the Lyceum held regular meetings and lectures, recorded weather data, and maintained a library. Perry served as its first curator and later became its president. He also helped found the *Naval Magazine*, served on its editorial board, and contributed occasional articles. When the Naval Academy was founded in 1845, Perry served on the board of officers that organized the new institution and designed its first curriculum. During this period, Perry developed an interest in the improvement of coastal lighthouses as important aids to navigation. In 1837, he wrote a report that recommended improvements in navigational aids for the New York area. Then after a trip to Europe and England in 1838, he prepared a report recommending the creation of an independent lighthouse board and the application of the superior lens of Augustin-Jean Fresnel to replace the older reflectors then in use in American lighthouses. Although his recommendations were practical and well advised, they were not widely adopted in the United States until the 1850s.[7]

Perry had a more immediate impact in the area of naval technology. He had long been interested in steam power and wanted to develop a genuine steam warship rather than the harbor-bound floating steam batteries authorized by Congress and favored by some senior officers. After the construction of a steam warship was authorized in 1834, the Navy Department placed Perry in charge of construction of the *Fulton II*, which was launched in 1837. Although serious problems existed with the vessel, Perry worked hard to demonstrate the practicality of an ocean-going steam warship. In 1838, he sailed the *Fulton II* to Washington where the President and numerous congressmen toured the ship. Resistance to steam power remained intense in the Navy and the Van Buren administration, but this venture helped persuade numerous politicians of the potential of steam power and proved to be one factor in Congress's 1839 decision to authorize three war steamers, including two, the *Mississippi* and the *Missouri*, that followed Perry's designs. For his efforts, Perry has been credited with being the "father of the steam navy." Although the label is perhaps an exaggeration, Perry nevertheless deserves recognition as the founder of the Navy's engineering corps, whose organization he outlined and championed. In 1839 and 1840, Perry also experimented with different cannons and types of shells. As a result, he demonstrated the superiority of the Paixhans type 64-pound shell artillery and the comparative inaccuracy of grape shot. Perry also advocated the use of iron warships and endorsed construction of the propellor-driven, steam frigate *Princeton*, which was built under the supervision of Robert Stockton.[8]

Many of the ideas of the Navy's progressive young officers were embodied in an influential 1837 article "Thoughts on the Navy," published in the *Naval Magazine*. Although it bore the name of Perry's brother-in-law Alexander Slidell, the article was coauthored by Perry and expressed his ideas about the need for a more modern, efficient, and powerful American navy. Its authors asserted that "all of our misfortunes as a nation, from the day we became one," have proceeded from the "mistakes and disasters of the past," and the nation must establish the principle that attacks on our commerce and "our national honor shall be prevented at the time by a prompt display of power . . . ." To accomplish this, the United States needed to build a navy commensurate with the "extent and value" of its commerce in "relative proportion" to the navies that other maritime nations maintained to protect their respective foreign trades. The Navy could then "follow the adventurous trader, in his path of peril, to every sea with cruisers ready to spread over him the protecting flag of the republic!" The United States had the world's eighth largest navy, but to meet its peacetime responsibilities,the Navy would need to be expanded to three times its size, a goal that Slidell and Perry endorsed enthusiastically.[9]

In spite of Perry's vision and achievements, relatively little progress had been made in the movement for naval reform by the early 1840s. The Van Buren administration remained indifferent to the need for changes in the Navy. Secretaries of the Navy Mahlon Dickerson and James K. Paulding both held very conservative naval attitudes and opposed technological innovation. The administration also demonstrated little interest in the peacetime commercial and diplomatic potential of the Navy. For example, the United States Exploring Expedition, which had been authorized during Andrew Jackson's presidency, almost did not sail at all, owing to administration inertia and indifference, before finally departing in 1838.

In early 1843, orders to command the Africa Squadron ended Perry's term of shore duty. The assignment was a difficult one, not highly coveted by experienced naval officers, because service in African waters was characterized by bad weather, difficult conditions, the constant threat of yellow fever, and the absence of recreational or leisure outlets for the men. The squadron under Perry was dispatched to police the slave trade in accord with the recently negotiated Webster–Ashburton Treaty, to protect the black settlements established by the American Colonization Society, and to provide "all the aid and support" that lawful American trade required. "It is the chief purpose, as well as the chief duty of our naval power," wrote the Secretary of the Navy, "to see that these [commercial] rights are not improperly abridged, or invaded."[10]

In Africa, Perry attempted to police the slave trade in a conscientious manner, but the size of his four-ship squadron limited its effectiveness. The commodore had much better fortune in combating yellow fever among his crews. He instituted a number of measures that dramatically reduced the effect of the disease. All men were required to wash their bodies every week, to wear a flannel undershirt during nights as well as days, and to sleep in a cloth jacket and pants. In addition, fresh air was dried and circulated below the decks of the ships, and smudge pots were burned to repel insects.

Under Perry's leadership, the Africa Squadron provided effective naval support for American commerce along the West African coast. In previous years, legitimate American trade and black American settlements had been subjected to constant danger and periodic attacks by various native African tribes. In 1841, at the village of Little Berebee on the Ivory coast, the American schooner *Mary Carver*, carrying a cargo valued at $12,000, had been captured and her crew murdered. Although the Secretary of the Navy had issued instructions in August 1842 for Commodore William Ramsey to obtain reparation, it was Perry who finally took action. On 13 December 1843, Perry's entire squadron anchored off Little Berebee. Two hundred sailors and marines landed and pitched a tent on the beach so that the Americans would not have to enter the hostile village to hold a conference with the local ruler, King Ben Krako. Krako, a man of great size and strength, attended the meeting accompanied by several subordinates and an interpreter. In regard to the *Mary Carver* outrage, Krako provided an explanation that Perry found preposterous, and a general melee ensued. The American sailors killed the king and several natives in the scuffle and burned the village. The following day, Perry proceeded to Grand Berebee and held a conference with several other local chiefs, all of whom disclaimed any part in the *Mary Carver* attack and praised the killing of the feared King Krako. To appease Perry, local authorities signed a treaty specifying that natives in the area would not plunder trading ships or molest missionaries.[11]

In September 1845, several months after Perry returned to the United States from Africa, Secretary of the Navy George Bancroft informally offered Perry command of the Gulf Squadron. The deterioration in Mexican–American relations and the likelihood of war made this command highly attractive, but complications soon arose. The Secretary did not identify a specific date for the appointment to become effective, and indicated that Perry would take over as soon as Commodore David Conner relinquished his command of the Gulf Squadron. Since Perry sought additional time at home in 1845 and Conner was known to be in poor health, neither Perry nor the Navy Department anticipated any problem with the transition of commanders. However, in spite of his health, Conner had no intention of relinquishing his choice command and, in fact, remained as commodore of the squadron until he was finally removed in March 1847, more than eighteen months after Bancroft had first offered the command to Perry. In the meantime, Perry languished in the United States until August 1846 when he received command of the steamer *Mississippi* and joined the Gulf Squadron. Once on station, Perry flew the red broad pendant of vice commodore until he finally took full command of American naval forces in the Gulf in March of 1847.[12]

Once hostilities with Mexico began in May 1846, the U.S. Navy played an essential military role in the war. American naval forces prevented Mexican gunboats and privateers from disrupting American commerce, captured a number of Mexican seaports, transported troops, carried supplies, and provided additional logistical support for the American armies of Zachary Taylor and Winfield Scott. Although the enemy's weak naval forces proved to be no match for the United States, the U.S. Navy's achievement was rendered more impressive by the severe obstacles that had to be surmounted. In Washington, the Polk administration had not prepared for naval warfare and provided minimal support once hostilities began. The administration never assigned high priority to the Navy, and Congress responded to the Navy's needs in a piecemeal manner. Officers complained frequently of inadequate supplies, poor facilities, and long delays in the arrival of war material. The Navy also required more warships, and many of those provided were unsuitable for effective use in the shallow waters along the Mexican coast.[13]

After he joined the Gulf Squadron in September 1846, Perry assumed an active part in the war effort. In October, he led the first Tabasco expedition which produced the easy conquest of Frontera and a seventy-mile expedition up the Grijalva River to Villahermosa. Although he could have occupied the town, Perry withdrew after a brief truce and limited fighting because he lacked sufficient forces to occupy and hold the town. After participating in several other actions including the capture of Tampico, Perry returned briefly to Norfolk and Washington, D.C., in early 1847. This visit finally produced the Navy Department's decision to remove Conner and install Perry as commander of the Gulf Squadron. Although Conner had proved to be rather ineffective as a fighting commander, his removal produced bad feeling among his own partisans and criticism of Perry's presumed political machinations in Washington.

Conner's removal was especially controversial because it came in the midst of the American offensive against Vera Cruz on 20 March 1847. The overall operation was commanded by General Winfield Scott, who relied on the Navy for logistical support and control of the coast. In addition, Scott urgently needed artillery, but Perry insisted that naval forces would provide the guns that Scott required only if the gun crews came as well. In this way, Perry ensured a significant combat role for naval forces in the invasion and capture of Vera Cruz. His well-drilled gun crews fought valiantly and earned special praise from Scott himself. Subsequently, Perry's forces captured Tuxpan in April and then returned to Tabasco in June. There with the river approach blocked by enemy forces, Perry led a naval landing force that marched overland several miles and forced the surrender of the town of Villahermosa.[14]

By the end of the war, Perry had achieved a reputation as one of the Navy's

Capture of Tabasco. On 14 June 1847 Perry led nine ships and forty-seven boats up the Tabasco River (top). Two days later he personally led a naval brigade ashore (bottom) to occupy the city of Tabasco (present-day Villahermosa). These lithographs, published by Sarony & Major in New York in 1848, were based on watercolors by eyewitness Lt. Henry Walke, U.S.N. *Courtesy of the Naval Academy Museum.*

most capable officers. Known as "Old Bruin" for his gruff way of barking out orders, Perry was widely respected for his diligent, serious and efficient manner. "In many respects he is an astonishing man," wrote fellow officer Franklin Buchanan in 1847, "the most industrious, hardworking, energetic, zealous, preserving, enterprising officer of his rank in our navy. He does not spare himself or *anyone* under him. . . . his great powers of endurance astonish everyone; all know he is by no means a brilliant man but his good common sense and judgment, his sociable manner to his officers, no *humbuggery* or *mystery*, make him respected and esteemed." Never a dashing or romantic figure, "Old Bruin" inspired neither great love nor hero worship. Instead, he earned the respect and admiration of his contemporaries through hard work, sound judgment, and effective performance.[15] Although his family ties and political connections might have been resented, Perry's talent and achievements could not be denied.

After he returned to the United States and was honored for his wartime exploits, Perry relinquished command of the Home Squadron in the fall of 1848 and began more than three years of shore duty as general superintendent of mail steamers. Perry's most important responsibility in his new role was to supervise construction of government-financed mail steamers being built for several private steamship lines. Congress had approved subsidies for the steamers with the specification that the ships would be built in such a way that they could be converted to naval vessels in wartime. But Perry's instructions and authority were vague, and he exercised little control over the new steamships in spite of the energy and commitment he brought to the assignment. Although Perry was an enthusiastic proponent of steam warships, he doubted that the new mail steamers could ever be converted into effective steam fighting ships.[16]

Near the end of 1851, the Navy Department selected Perry to command the East India Squadron and to lead a major diplomatic mission to Japan. Although the East Asian assignment provided an opportunity that led to Perry's greatest professional achievement, Perry preferred command of the prestigious Mediterranean Squadron. An exotic, remote, secluded land in Asia, Japan had long held a fascination for Europeans and Americans. After initial contact with Westerners, the Japanese suppressed Christianity and excluded all foreigners during the seventeenth century. The only contact occurred at the small island of Deshima, off Nagasaki, where the Dutch maintained a small settlement that provided the few items Japan sought from the outside world. During the Napoleonic Wars, the Dutch chartered a number of American ships to fly their colors and visit Deshima, but this early and trifling American commerce with Japan ended once the Dutch resumed trade in their own ships in 1813. For the next three decades, Americans had virtually no contact with Japan.

During the 1840s, American interest grew in Asia and Japan in the aftermath of the signing of the Treaty of Wanghia with China. In 1845, the Polk administration dispatched Alexander H. Everett to exchange treaty ratifications with China and to negotiate a treaty with Japan. When Everett died en route, his naval escort, Commodore James Biddle, continued the mission, exchanged ratifications with China, and then proceeded to Japan in the 90-gun *Columbia* accompanied by the sloop of war *Vincennes*. Arriving in the Bay of Yedo (Tokyo) in July 1846, Biddle achieved little and committed a number of blunders in the process. He permitted dozens of armed guards to surround his ships and Japanese sailors to board and inspect them. Without an interpreter, he dealt directly with minor Japanese authorities, showed himself freely on board, and entrusted the President's official letter to one such minor official. The Japanese refused to accept the letter and ordered the American ships to depart with a curt note from a local official. To receive the reply, Biddle boarded a Japanese guard boat and in the process was rudely pushed or bumped by a Japanese sailor. Although the Japanese offered to punish the offender, the damage was done. Lacking explicit instructions that would have permitted retaliation, Biddle departed with the embarrassing assistance of a tow from the Japanese. In 1849, the Navy sent Commander Thomas Glynn to Nagasaki to pick up fifteen American whalemen who were being held there. Unlike Biddle, Glynn demanded respect for the American flag and the return of the Americans. He sailed his *Preble* through a cordon of guard boats and anchored within cannon shot range of the city. In subsequent negotiations, he threatened to bombard the city if the Americans were not released; and they were freed within two days.[17]

When he returned to the United States in 1851, Glynn urged the Fillmore administration to send another mission to Japan and in the process added his name to a growing movement to open relations with the Japanese. By this time, the United States had emerged as a Pacific power eager to expand its political influence in the Pacific Basin, increase its economic activity in the area, and establish close ties with the Far East. Although various factors were involved, the main pressures were economic and commercial as different American interests sought to protect the nation's extensive whaling fleet, expand existing trade, and open new markets. The Treaty of Wanghia had only quickened American commercial interest in Asia and whetted the American appetite for the fabled commercial wealth of the Orient. In response to active lobbying, the Fillmore administration agreed in 1851 to send a new mission to Japan and selected Commodore John H. Aulick for the assignment. With a squadron of three ships, Aulick experienced difficulties soon after his departure, quarreled with one of his captains, suffered a breakdown in health in Canton, and ended up being removed from his command in November 1851.[18]

Perry's selection as Aulick's replacement was exceptional. Perry's vision, initiative, experience, and influence transformed the mission into a major naval and diplomatic project of far-reaching significance for the United States. Although he would have preferred command of the Mediterranean Squadron, Perry informed the Navy Department that he would accept command of the East India Squadron if the sphere of action and size of the squadron were "so enlarged as to hold out a well grounded hope of its conferring distinction upon its commander."[19]

From the outset, Perry's command contrasted sharply with that of his predecessor Aulick because of the great care, time, and energy Perry devoted to preparations for the expedition. He also requested and received a much enlarged squadron with three additional ships assigned immediately and others to follow. Eventually, Perry would command ten ships, an American squadron of unprecedented size in Asian waters. He also selected first-rate officers whom he had known previously to assist him including Commanders Franklin Buchanan, Sidney S. Lee, and Joel Abbot, who commanded the *Susquehanna*, the *Mississippi*, and the *Macedonian*, respectively.

During 1852, Perry collected as much information and learned as much about Asia and Japan as he could. He met with naval officers who had sailed in the western Pacific and visited New Bedford, Massachusetts in April to talk to whaling captains familiar with the area. He read extensively and conferred with German scholar Philipp Franz von Siebold. As a result, Perry was exceptionally well versed in the history, culture, and customs of the Japanese by the time he sailed. Perry also took great care in purchasing various presents for the Emperor and other Japanese dignitaries. He selected gifts to demonstrate the culture and technological advancement of American civilization. In addition to volumes by John J. Audubon, Perry included an assortment of champagne, cordials, and perfumes. More important were the gadgets and machine products, including rifles, pistols, carbines, farming implements, a daguerreotype camera, a telegraph, and a quarter-size railroad complete with locomotive, tender, coach, and track.

Perry also reshaped the expedition by convincing the administration to make the mission to Japan his primary duty, in contrast to Aulick's instructions which specified that the Japan mission was supplemental to his regular duties as commander of the East India Squadron. After receiving general instructions in March 1852, Perry conferred with Secretary of the Navy John P. Kennedy and Secretary of State Daniel Webster, who suggested that the commodore be permitted to draft his own diplomatic instructions. When he departed, Perry carried detailed instructions from Kennedy, diplomatic instructions from the State Department, and a letter from the President to the Emperor of Japan.[20]

Most specific in regard to Japan were the instructions Perry himself had written for the State Department. Signed by Acting Secretary of State C. M. Conrad, this document outlined the background, three main objectives, and conduct of the mission to Japan. First, the treaty was to provide protection for American seamen and ships wrecked or endangered by weather in Japanese waters. Second, the agreement should permit American vessels to obtain provisions, water, and fuel, and, if necessary, to refit in Japanese ports. Third, the treaty should allow American vessels to use one or more Japanese ports to trade their cargoes. In addition, the squadron was instructed to explore and survey the coastal waters of Japan. To achieve these objectives, the Navy authorized Perry to use his "whole force" but reminded him that the mission was to be of a "pacific character." The commodore's conduct was to be "courteous and conciliatory, but at the same time, firm and decided." He would resort to force only in "self defense" or "to resent an act of personal violence" against himself or one of his men.[21]

In November 1852, after months of preparation, Perry sailed in his flagship, the *Mississippi*, and arrived at Hong Kong via the Cape of Good Hope route in April 1853 to find three of his ships already in port. To his chagrin, the *Susquehanna* had sailed to Shanghai to protect American merchants under the threat of violence from the Taiping Rebellion. When he reached Shanghai, Perry ignored pressure from the merchant community and the American minister to remain there with his squadron. Although he agreed to leave a sloop at Shanghai, Perry transferred his flag to the *Susquehanna* and departed for Naha on Great Lew Chew (Okinawa) in the Ryukyus in mid-May. Earlier, Perry had written to the Navy Department emphasizing the importance of establishing "ports of refuge and supply" as bases for the mission to Japan. Lew Chew seemed an ideal choice for such a base because the harbor was good, and it was accessible to Japan. Although nominally under Japanese control, the islands were semiautonomous. Moreover, the people were docile, unarmed, and backward, with their only defense being their considerable ability to evade, procrastinate, and ignore foreigners and their demands. The proximity of Lew Chew to Japan ensured that Perry's actions and the size of his squadron would be reported to the Japanese. Lew Chew, then, provided an excellent place for a dress rehearsal.[22]

At Naha, Perry refused to meet with natives or local officials who met the American ships. Only when the regent for the ruler of the island visited the *Susquehanna* did Perry receive him and announce that he would visit the royal palace at Shuri. The horrified officials of Lew Chew attempted without success to divert Perry. On the appointed day, Perry and an impressive entourage landed, rejected further attempts to divert them, and proceeded to Shuri. The commodore rode in an elaborate sedan chair constructed for the occasion to emphasize his exalted station. After visiting the palace and feasting at the regent's residence, Perry and his party returned to the American ships. In the next two weeks, the Americans visited Naha frequently, procured a shelter for

Americans on shore, and dispatched a party to explore the island while other Americans surveyed the coastal waters.

In early June, the *Susquehanna* and the *Saratoga* sailed for the Bonin Islands to the northeast. At Port Lloyd, Perry found a small colony of thirty-one residents headed by Nathaniel Savoy, a native New Englander who had settled the island with a small group from Hawaii. Although he had no intention of using the islands as a base for his Japanese operations, Perry understood the potential value of the port, which stood directly on the great circle route from Hawaii to the south China ports. Perry himself purchased a small tract of land to serve as a possible waterfront coal depot. He also raised the American flag, drew up a code of laws, and had Savoy elected chief magistrate. Later, Perry would assert an official American claim to the islands and recommend establishment of an open port for whalers, steamers, and merchant ships of all nations. Perry then returned to Naha, where he drilled American forces on shore and dispatched more parties to collect a range of information on the islands. As subsequent events would demonstrate, the commodore intended Lew Chew and the Bonins to serve as much more than a temporary base for his own mission. He believed that he had taken the initial steps in establishing two permanent American "ports of refuge and supply" for American whalers, merchantmen, transpacific steamers, and naval vessels.[23]

On 2 July 1853, the flagship *Susquehanna* and three other warships departed on a six-day journey to Japan. At the entrance to the Bay of Yedo, Japanese junks and guard boats immediately appeared and surrounded the American ships. But the Japanese ships were prevented from tying lines to the American ships, and Japanese sailors were not permitted to board. Only when a man identified as the vice governor appeared, was he permitted to board the *Susquehanna*, where he was received by Perry's subordinates rather than the commodore himself. The Americans informed the Japanese that Perry had a letter from the President for the Emperor, and they refused to deliver the document at Nagasaki as the Japanese specified. Operating through his subordinate officers, Perry insisted that the President's letter be delivered to appropriate authorities at Uraga, indicating that the American fleet would proceed directly to Yedo and the royal palace if the Japanese refused. To underline his claims, Perry had already initiated surveys of the area.

Finally, the Japanese agreed to receive the President's letter in special ceremonies at Kurihama near Uraga. At daybreak on 14 July, the *Susquehanna* and the *Mississippi* steamed into the bay at Kurihama, anchored, and positioned themselves to command the Japanese shore fortifications. Since thousands of Japanese troops congregated on shore, Perry sent 250 armed marines and sailors in several launches. Once they were ashore, the ceremony itself was brief. The American couriers opened the elaborate box containing the American document and received a Japanese scroll in return. The Japanese reply acknowledged receipt of the President's letter, explained that negotiations could not occur at this spot, and informed Perry that he could now depart. In response, the commodore explained that he would sail in two or three days and would be pleased to convey any messages to Lew Chew or Canton. When the Japanese did not reply, Perry explained that he planned to return the following spring with at least four naval vessels and possibly more. The conference then ended, the Americans returning to their ships without incident. The next day, Perry transferred to the *Mississippi* and steamed up the bay to the outskirts of Yedo before turning back. A final ceremony was held on 16 July, in which small presents were exchanged, and the American squadron departed for Naha the following day.[24]

Perry based his decision to return to Japan later rather than wait for the Japanese response to the President's letter on several considerations. By departing for China, Perry could reprovision his squadron, add warships, give the Japanese time for deliberation, and address any problems that might have arisen in China. When he left Japanese waters, Perry could take considerable satisfaction in his initial achievements. He had avoided Biddle's earlier mistakes and established contact with the Japanese on a basis of equality without provoking an incident or engaging in hostilities. He had insisted on proper respect for his official authority, refused to deal directly with lower Japanese officials, and delivered the President's letter in an appropriate ceremony. Perry had also refused to permit Japanese to swarm over his ships, insisted that all provisions be paid for, and exchanged gifts with the Japanese only on an equal basis. In addition, American forces had navigated the Bay of Yedo without hindrance, conducted surveys of the area, and approached the outskirts of the capital. His firmness, careful preparation, and conciliatory manner also left the unmistakable message that he was a determined man who would not be easily diverted by traditional Japanese tactics.[25]

Back at Naha, the reports he received displeased Perry. During his absence, provisions had proved difficult to obtain, and numerous spies and police plagued Americans on shore. At a dinner on 28 July, Perry insisted that a free market be established, that Americans be left unmolested on shore, that use of a rest house be continued, and that a coal shed be erected for use by Americans. When the regent demurred, Perry replied that he would again march to the palace at Shuri unless he received a satisfactory response within twenty-four hours. For effect, he dispatched a carpenter to inspect and repair the sedan chair he had used on his initial visit. However, the regent complied with each request the next day, and Perry departed for China on 1 August.

In China, the arrival of additional naval vessels strengthened Perry's forces, and by the end of 1852 his squadron numbered ten ships. Although he had originally planned not to return to Japan until the spring of 1854, rumors in China led Perry to fear that a Russian squadron was preparing to visit Japan before he returned, and he hastened his departure. By late January 1854, his entire squadron had assembled at Naha, where it remained for two weeks.

Perry found relations with the natives at Naha more amicable but protested to the regent about various difficulties. The commodore also recommended American occupation of Great Lew Chew should his mission to Japan fail. In February the squadron departed for Japan and anchored near Uraga where Perry prepared for a long stay.

Local Japanese officials welcomed the Americans hospitably and informed them that five Japanese commissioners had been appointed to negotiate with Perry at Uraga. Perry countered by suggesting the negotiations be held at the Japanese capital. Thus began several weeks of disagreement over exactly where the formal negotiations would be held. Finally, the Japanese proposed and Perry accepted Yokohama, fifteen miles south of the capital, as the site.

Formal negotiations began with an elaborate ceremony on 8 March 1854, after Perry with an entourage of three bands and 500 marines, sailors, and officers came ashore. In the initial meeting, the Japanese delivered the Emperor's reply and agreed to protect shipwrecked Americans and American ships in distress as well as to provide provisions, water, and coal to American ships at one designated harbor. According to the Japanese, preparation of the harbor would take five years, and, in the meantime, coal would be available at

"Comm. Perry meeting the Imperial Commissioners at Yokohama." On 8 March 1854 Commodore Matthew C. Perry led a party of 500 men ashore at Yokohama. Amid pomp and ceremony he received Japan's answer to the letter from President Millard Fillmore that he had delivered the previous year. Lithograph by Sarony & Company after a painting by W. Peters. *Courtesy of the Naval Historical Center.*

Nagasaki. The Japanese also agreed to sell or barter anything ships might want that could be furnished from their empire.

Negotiations continued through March as Perry and the Japanese differed on the extent of commercial privileges and the number of ports to be opened. On 13 March, Perry formally presented the American gifts to the Japanese and provided a full demonstration of the miniature railroad and telegraph. On the 24th, the Japanese reciprocated with gifts of their own as relations between the two groups continued to be cordial and free of hostility. Finally, on 31 March 1854, the Treaty of Kanagawa was signed in a formal ceremony. The agreement guaranteed protection for shipwrecked American sailors and American ships in distress and specified that the ports of Shimoda and Hokadate would be open to American ships to purchase wood, water, coal, and provisions at a fair price. At these two ports, shipwrecked American sailors were also permitted to reside temporarily and to move freely within designated areas. In addition, the treaty included a most-favored-nation clause and allowed the United States to send "consuls or agents" to reside at Shimoda anytime after eighteen months.[26]

Although the concessions granted in the treaty did not approximate those enjoyed by the United States in its relations with China, the agreement constituted a dramatic achievement. Not only had Perry accomplished the basic objectives outlined in his instructions; the commodore had also placed diplomatic relations between the two nations on a formal and equal basis. Such status had never been granted to the Dutch at Nagasaki or to any other nation. Subsequently, the commercial concessions would prove to be inadequate for the United States, but Perry's treaty nevertheless provided the basis for later expansion of commercial privileges.

As soon as the treaty was signed, Perry dispatched Commander H. A. Adams to the United States in the *Saratoga* with a copy of the treaty while the main body of the expedition remained in Japanese waters, continued to survey the coastline, and visited the treaty ports of Shimoda and Hokadate. In July, Perry returned to Naha and signed a treaty of friendship with the regent. The commodore then returned to Hong Kong before leaving for the United States in September 1854.

Although contemporary attention focused on the "opening" of Japan, Perry's own goals and achievements were not limited to the treaty with Japan. He himself conceived of his mission in broad strategic terms and attempted to provide the basis for an American commercial empire in the western Pacific. In addition to the concessions wrested from Japan and the substantial scientific and nautical activities of the expedition, Perry sought American maritime superiority in the area. In the Lew Chew Islands, he had insisted on a treaty that guaranteed water, wood, and provisions for American ships, native pilots to guide American captains safely into the harbor, land access for Americans on Great Lew Chew, an American burial ground there, and construction of an

American coal shed. In the Bonin Islands, Perry had formally asserted an American claim to the islands, helped establish a small independent community headed by a native New Englander, and purchased land at Port Lloyd to serve as a coaling station. He also dispatched two vessels to investigate reports that shipwrecked American sailors were being held captive on Formosa and to explore coal deposits there. Although no sailors were found, the coal proved to be abundant. The treaty with Japan, then, represented but a part of Perry's visionary Far Eastern program.[27]

Perry used the period after his return to the United States to outline his views on the nation's Far Eastern policy in two articles, as well as an address to the American Geographical Society. Like many other Americans of his time, Perry predicted a new era of commercial enterprise for the United States in the Pacific basin. The recent treaty with Japan represented only a "preliminary" step toward a more advanced commercial agreement that could be concluded once Japan was better prepared to enter the international community. To encourage American commerce, Perry urged formal diplomatic and commercial treaties with Siam, Cambodia, Cochin China, and parts of Borneo and Sumatra. Perry also endorsed creation of a government-supported steamship line from the Pacific ports of the United States to China, Japan, and the main islands in between. Finally, Perry emphasized the value of naval power in Asian diplomacy. "In all negotiations with China and other eastern nations," wrote Perry, "the display of a respectable armed force is necessary . . . in most cases, the mere presence of such force will answer the purposes desired . . . ."[28]

Although such views were popular during the 1850s, Perry went far beyond his contemporaries in advocating the creation of a European-style empire in the Pacific. He believed that the United States should take control of Lew Chew and the Bonin Islands, and he wanted the United States to take the initiative on the "magnificent island" of Formosa by establishing an American colony at the port of Kelung. Once established through a land grant, the American settlement would soon increase its area, wealth, and power until it rivaled the ports of Hong Kong and Singapore in importance. In addition to the rich coal deposits on Formosa, American settlement there would provide an "entrepot for American trade" in Asia and give the United States an excellent "naval and military position . . . directly in front of the principal ports of China." Like most other Americans of his day, Perry also embraced the idea of American intervention in the internal affairs of Asia as part of the "responsibilities which our growing wealth and power must inevitably fasten upon us." Because "the advance of civilization and the industrial arts" could only be achieved when the Asian peoples joined the "new family of commercial" nations, the commodore argued that military intervention might "be fully justified," to force "the empires of China and Japan into the family of nations."[29]

Perry envisioned continued American expansion in the Pacific as Americans reached for their ultimate destiny by settling the remote islands of the Pacific and creating their own governments there. But Perry well understood that the development of an American empire in the Pacific would not be a benign process. Forceful military and political action would be necessary to combat European rivalry and establish American supremacy. Eventually, the American people would extend "their dominion and their power until they shall have . . . placed the Saxon race upon the eastern shores of Asia." There, predicted Perry, the American "exponents of freedom" would eventually confront the Russian representatives of "absolutism" in a "mighty battle" that would determine "the freedom or the slavery of the world."[30] These visionary ideas placed Matthew Perry far ahead of his time and attracted little serious support in the 1850s. In this respect, the commodore's prescience made him much more an ideological contemporary of Alfred T. Mahan's generation than of his own antebellum era.

In the United States, Perry received a hero's welcome and lavish praise for the expedition's achievements. Congress gave Perry a vote of thanks and a $20,000 grant for serving as the diplomatic envoy as well as the naval commander of the expedition. The commodore received a gold medal from the merchants of Boston and a 381-piece silver service from the New York Chamber of Commerce. In a ceremony in June 1855 at Newport, the governor and the General Assembly of Perry's native Rhode Island presented him with a large silver salver. In the meantime, Perry had begun work on the official narrative of the expedition, with Volume I appearing in 1856 and Volume II in 1857. By the end of 1857, Perry seemed ready for a new assignment, and he was rumored to be the next commander of the Mediterranean Squadron. But in early 1858, Perry caught a severe cold, became seriously ill, and died on 4 March.

Although his death denied him the chance for further distinctions in the upcoming Civil War, Matthew Calbraith Perry's legacy was already secure. In nearly a half century of service, he had distinguished himself as a professional officer, wartime commander, naval reformer, and effective diplomat. The breadth of his achievements was unmatched in the antebellum Navy. As a professional naval officer and commander, Perry was one of the best of his day. He was courageous in battle, and during the Mexican War he proved to be an energetic and effective commander. But in addition to these attributes, Perry also distinguished himself as a naval reformer and diplomat. Throughout his career, he sought ways of modernizing and improving the efficiency of the Navy and better educating its men. Perry also became a skilled diplomat during his career, and the combination of his personal talent, energy, and intelligence was largely responsible for the spectacular success of the expedition to Japan. Equally important is the fact that Perry fully understood the long-term significance of his activities in the Far East. He realized that he was not merely opening formal relations with one island nation but was helping to shape a maritime empire as well. Thus representing the very best qualities of the old navy, Matthew Calbraith Perry also manifested the very attributes that would be demanded by the navy of the new American empire several decades later.

FURTHER READING

The standard scholarly biography of Perry is Samuel Eliot Morison, *"Old Bruin": Commodore Matthew C. Perry, 1794–1858*. In spite of some distracting digressions, Admiral Morison's biography is typically well written and extensively researched, and presents a full account of Perry's life. An old, still useful, but inaccurately titled study is William E. Griffis, *Matthew Calbraith Perry: A Typical American Naval Officer*. A more recent biography of little value is Edward M. Barrows, *The Great Commodore: The Exploits of Matthew C. Perry*.

Aspects of Perry's career have also been treated in a number of studies. His contributions to antebellum naval development are analyzed in John H. Schroeder, *Shaping a Maritime Empire: The Commercial and Diplomatic Role of the American Navy, 1829–1861*. Perry's service in the African Squadron is discussed in Donald R. Wright, "Matthew Perry and the African Squadron," Clayton R. Barrow, Jr., ed., *America Spreads Her Sails: U.S. Seapower in the 19th Century*. K. Jack Bauer, *Surfboats and Horse Marines: U.S. Naval Operations in the Mexican War, 1846–1848* is an excellent study that details Perry's role in the conflict.

On the development of steam power in the United States, see Frank M. Bennett, *The Steam Navy of the United States: A History of the Growth of the Steam Vessel of War in the U.S. Navy and of the Naval Engineer Corps*; see also, David B. Tyler, *Steam Conquers the Atlantic* and John G. B. Hutchins, *The American Maritime Industries and Public Policy, 1789–1914*.

On the expedition to Japan, an abundant literature exists, but good starting points are Morison's *Perry*, Schroeder's *Shaping a Maritime Empire*, and Arthur Walworth, *Black Ships off Japan: The Story of Commodore Perry's Expedition*. Perry's own account is found in the official narrative, F. L. Hawks, ed., *Narrative of the Expedition of An American Squadron to the China Seas and Japan*. Also insightful is Earl Swisher, "Commodore Perry's Imperialism in Relation to America's Present-day Position in the Pacific," in the *Pacific Historical Review*. Perry's difficulties in China are detailed in Curtis T. Henson, *Commissioners and Commodores: The East India Squadron and American Diplomacy in China*.

NOTES

1. Although the study is not directly cited in the notes, this article is based to a considerable extent on the research and material in John H. Schroeder, *Shaping a Maritime Empire: The Commercial and Diplomatic Role of the American Navy, 1829–1861*. For detailed treatments of Perry's life, see Samuel Eliot

Morison, *"Old Bruin": Commodore Matthew C. Perry, 1794–1858* and William E. Griffis, *Matthew Calbraith Perry: A Typical American Naval Officer.*

2. Detailed treatments of the Perry family and Matthew's early years are found in Morison, *"Old Bruin"* and Griffis, *Perry.*

3. Morison, *"Old Bruin,"* 104–17. Also, William Cabell Bruce, *John Randolph of Roanoke, 1773–1833: A Biography Based Largely on New Material,* I: 634–61.

4. Morison, *"Old Bruin"* 121–23.

5. W. Patric Strauss, "Mahlon Dickerson" and "James K. Paulding," in Paolo E. Coletta, ed., *American Secretaries of the Navy,* I: 160–62, 165–71.

6. *House of Representatives Report No. 94.* 23rd Cong., 2nd Sess. (1834–35).

7. Morison, *"Old Bruin",* 124–39.

8. Ibid., 127–32. Also, Frank M. Bennett, *The Steam Navy of the United States: A History of the Growth of the Steam Vessel of War in the U. S. Navy and of the Naval Engineer Corps.*

9. "Thoughts on the Navy," *Naval Magazine,* II (1837): 5–42.

10. Abel P. Upshur to Perry, 30 March 1843, Letters Sent by the Secretary of the Navy to Officers, 1798–1868, Naval Records, R.G. 45, National Archives, vol. 34.

11. Donald R. Wright, "Matthew Perry and the African Squadron," in Clayton R. Barrow, Jr., ed., *America Spreads Her Sails: U.S. Seapower in the 19th Century,* 80–99.

12. Morison, *"Old Bruin,"* 179–89.

13. K. Jack Bauer, *Surfboats and Horse Marines: U.S. Naval Operations in the Mexican War, 1846–1848.*

14. Ibid.; Morison, *"Old Bruin,"* 230–38.

15. Description by Buchanan as quoted in Charles Lee Lewis, *Admiral Franklin Buchanan: Fearless Man of Action,* 121–22.

16. David B. Tyler, *Steam Conquers the Atlantic,* 204–7.

17. David F. Long, *Sailor-Diplomat: A Biography of Commodore James Biddle,* 209–20; Merrill L. Bartlett, "Commodore James Biddle and the First Naval Mission to Japan, 1845–1846," *American Neptune,* 61 (1981): 25–35.

18. Charles O. Paullin, *American Voyages to the Orient, 1690–1865,* 123–24.

19. Perry to W. A. Graham, 3 December 1851, as cited in Griffis, *Perry,* 289–91. Perry's preparations for the expedition are described in detail in Morison, *"Old Bruin,"* 270–90. Also, Arthur Walworth, *Black Ships off Japan: The Story of Commodore Perry's Expedition.*

20. John P. Kennedy to Perry, 13 November 1852, C. M. Conrad to Kennedy, 5 November 1852, Fillmore to His Imperial Majesty, The Emperor, *Senate Executive Document No. 34,* 33rd Cong., 2nd Sess. (1854–1855), 2–11.

21. Conrad to Kennedy, 5 November 1852, ibid., 4–9.

22. Perry to Kennedy, 14 December 1852, ibid, 12–14. Perry's own account of the expedition is F. L. Hawks, ed., *Narrative of the Expedition of an American Squadron to the China Seas and Japan.*

23. Earl Swisher, "Commodore Perry's Imperialism in Relation to America's Present-day Position in the Pacific," *Pacific Historical Review*, 16 (1947): 30–40; "Extracts from the Rough Journal of Commodore Perry, 24 June 1853," *Senate Executive Document No. 34*, 33–39; "Report of an Examination of the Bonin Group of Islands," Hawks, ed., *Narrative of the Expedition*, II: 127–33.

24. "Notes Referring to . . . the preliminary negotiations of Commodore M. C. Perry with the authorities of Japan in July 1853," *Senate Executive Document No. 34*, 45–57.

25. Morison, *"Old Bruin,"* 336; Walworth, *Black Ships off Japan*, 115.

26. Perry to J. C. Dobbin, 25 January 1854, Dobbin to Perry, 30 May 1854, *Senate Executive Document No. 34*, 108–10, 112–13.

27. Hawks, ed., *Narrative of the Expedition*, I: 343–92; Perry to Dobbin, 1 April 1854, *Senate Executive Document No. 34*, 145–50. A copy of the treaty is contained in ibid., 174–75.

28. "Extracts from the Rough Journal of Commodore Perry, 24 June 1853," ibid., 39; Hawks, ed., *Narrative of the Expedition*, II: 153–54, 167–70, 180. Volume II of the *Narrative* contains various reports on aspects of the expedition including "Remarks of Commodore Perry Upon the Expediency of Extending Further Encouragement to American Commerce in the East," 173–82, and "Remarks of Commodore Perry upon the Probable Future Commercial Relations with Japan and Lew Chew," 185–87.

29. Ibid. 178, 180, 177, 176.

30. *A Paper by Commodore M. C. Perry, U.S.N., Read Before the American Geographical and Statistical Society . . . March 6, 1856.*

JOHN A. DAHLGREN: INNOVATOR IN UNIFORM

BY DAVID K. ALLISON

On 24 June 1863, Secretary of the Navy Gideon Welles issued the order. Rear Admiral John A. Dahlgren would relieve Rear Admiral Samuel F. Du Pont as Commander of the South Atlantic Squadron. Welles made the appointment reluctantly. President Lincoln, who lurked prominently in the background, considered Dahlgren among the most capable naval officers and strongly supported his advancement. Dahlgren's peers, however, deemed it an affront. They had witnessed his rapid rise from commander to rear admiral in less than a year without sea command. And now he was to be not just chief of the Bureau of Ordnance—a technical specialist—but a commander of a squadron! Were there not other officers who had demonstrated their courage and leadership under fire, and who were far more qualified than he was for this important job?

Dahlgren was ambitious. Perhaps nowhere is this clearer than in the diary entry he made on 27 February 1863, the day he became a rear admiral:

> To-night, about ten o'clock, I was confirmed by the Senate as Rear Admiral, not thinking of it at the time. So I am at last an Admiral of the Republic. There are five above me,—Farragut, Goldsborough, Dupont, Foote, and Davis. . . .[1]

This new rank and his selection as chief of the Bureau of Ordnance were crowning achievements for his remarkable accomplishments in improving naval ordnance in the 1840s and 1850s. Dahlgren had developed a standard series of naval guns that were the most powerful and reliable of the period and would be used effectively by both sides in the Civil War. He had carefully chosen the size and type of weapons he designed to make an integrated system of ordnance that would give warships maximum firepower. In addition, he had radically improved the Navy's in-house capability to design, develop, produce, and test its own ordnance. Yet these achievements, Dahlgren knew, would not bring glory in wartime. The parades would be for those who shot cannon, not for those who produced them. One can argue that Dahlgren's motive for operational command was simple patriotism, and surely that was part of it. His country was at war; the most courageous service he could perform was in battle. This indeed is what his widow later said in her loving biography of her husband, published in 1882. But at the time, Secretary Welles saw things differently. When first contemplating sending Dahlgren to Charleston in October 1862, he noted in his diary:

> It would be wrong to the service, and a great wrong to the country, for [Dahlgren] to leave the Ordnance Bureau, where he is proficient and can be most useful. His specialty is in that branch of the service; he knows his own value there at this time, and for him to leave it now would be detrimental to the object he desires to attain. He is not conscious of it, but he has Dahlgren more than the service in view.[2]

Although Welles questioned Dahlgren's motivations, he never disputed the terms of Dahlgren's dilemma. There was no royal road to glory for the innovator in Welles's Navy. Welles never doubted Dahlgren's contributions to ordnance, but at the same time, he would never even have promoted him to rear admiral had he not been pushed by Lincoln.[3] No matter how important the innovator's contributions, his was a supporting role. He provided weapons, but others determined when, how, and under what conditions they would be used. And if the weapons worked, others got the credit for victory.

Rarely in history has this dilemma been so personalized as it was in the case of Dahlgren. For he was both a brilliant innovator and a line officer. Innovation made his reputation, but like his peers he aspired to command at sea. His case, then, raises interesting issues. How did his training and orientation as a naval officer enhance his innovative ability? What limits did they impose? How did his dual roles as officer and innovator intertwine during his career? These questions are of more than mere historical interest, for the need to integrate effectively the work of technical experts and line officers is as important today as it was in Dahlgren's era.[4]

John Adolphus Bernard Dahlgren was born in Philadelphia on 13 November 1809. His father, a Swedish immigrant, had fled his native country in 1804 for political reasons. When the political climate changed, however, he came back into favor and was named Swedish consul in Philadelphia in 1806, a position he held until his death in 1824. Dahlgren's mother, Martha Rowan, was a daughter of James Rowan, who had served as an officer in the American Revolution.[5]

Taught at home by his father as well as in a Quaker school, Dahlgren was a good mathematical scholar, had studied navigation, and was proficient in Latin and Spanish.[6] He aspired to a naval career. Admission to the Navy in this era, however, was not simply a matter of merit. Midshipmen appointments were the prerogative of ship captains, the Secretary of the Navy, and the

John A. Dahlgren. Standing before a 30-pound Dahlgren rifle on board the USS *Pawnee* in Charleston Harbor, 1864. *Courtesy of the Library of Congress.*

President. Ultimately politics determined selections.[7] Dahlgren's first application, despite his being recommended by men of influence in Pennsylvania, was refused. Hoping that experience at sea might help, he joined the crew of the brig *Mary Beckett* for a cruise to Cuba. When in 1824 he applied again to the Navy, he was appointed midshipman and assigned to the frigate *Macedonian*.

Between 1826 and 1832, he completed his apprenticeship, on board the *Macedonian* and the brig *Ontario*. He then successfully passed his examination and was appointed passed midshipman. Following this cruise, he had seven years of shore duty at the United States Naval Station at Philadelphia. In his leisure, he studied law, an interest that he sustained and that resulted in a book on maritime law published posthumously.[8] Normally, he would have returned to sea in 1834. However, failing health prevented his doing so. Because of his mathematical ability, he was assigned to duty with the Coast Survey.

While there was no graduate training for naval officers interested in science and invention in the 1840s, service on the Coast Survey came close. The survey had first been authorized by Congress in 1807. Following a troubled early history, it finally became a major government effort in the 1830s. Rudolph Hassler, a scientifically trained Swiss geodesist, was then named its director for the second time. Hassler had headed the survey during its initial years, but had been removed in 1818 when the effort was turned over to the Army and the Navy. Though now in his sixties, he still had a keen mind, strong constitution, and unflagging commitment to his work. By congressional order, his professional staff was largely composed of army and naval officers serving on limited tours. Whatever restrictions this placed on Hassler's freedom to pick qualified assistants, it had the side effect of giving hundreds of military and naval officers excellent scientific training under an accomplished mentor. Other naval officers besides Dahlgren who worked under Hassler and later rose to prominence include James H. Gillis, Charles H. Davis, Charles Wilkes, and Franklin Sands.[9]

Hassler was a dedicated scientist, who demanded the newest technical methods, the best instruments available, and exactitude in measurement and calculations. His assistants watched him engage in long and often bitter struggles to uphold scientific integrity against calls for shortcuts, expedients, financial exigencies, and a faster pace. It was a lesson many of them, including young John A. Dahlgren, never forgot.

Dahlgren spent three years on the survey. In the summer, he performed field work, making triangulations and astronomical observations. In the winter, he engaged in exacting hand calculations of triangles and geographic projections. He soon won Hassler's respect for his abilities, and was given responsibility for verifying many of Hassler's own computations. Their relationship became close and personal.[10] The price was almost too high, however. In 1837, as a result of long hours of drawing and calculation, many of them in candlelight after a full day in the field, Dahlgren's eyesight failed. A trip to France for treatment by a world-renowned specialist brought only marginal improvements.

Dahlgren returned to the United States in 1839, and on his physician's advice retired to a country farm. He married Mary C. Bunker of Philadelphia, and fathered three children. She would later bear him four more. Fortunately for the Navy, he did not resign, but sought and was granted an extended leave of absence. Even more fortunately, farming did not satisfy his ambitions.

By early 1843, Dahlgren's eyes had recovered enough for him to return to naval service. In September, he was ordered to the steamer *Cumberland*, which was off for her maiden cruise to the Mediterranean. Her crew also included Andrew Hull Foote, who became one of his closest friends. [11]

If Dahlgren had not already been intrigued with naval ordnance, he soon became so. While in France he had learned about the shell guns of Henri-Joseph Paixhans. [12] Now he was given responsibility for four of them. Shells were still new in the fleet, and the sailors were leery of them. Dahlgren laid the first volleys himself, aiming them so they just grazed the surface of the water. He noted in his diary:

> The effect on the water was very pretty, the shells dashing the foam high into the air and bounding four and five times on the surface. Though I could not see as distinctly as the officers on the spar-deck, as the smoke so enveloped us after the discharge, I had the satisfaction of proving a plan for point-blank fire. [13]

Dahlgren was thirty-four. His training as a naval officer, apprenticeship under Hassler, and recovered health brought him to a turning point in his career. In his childlike fascination with the *Cumberland*'s Paixhans lay the beginning of a revolution in naval ordnance.

Dahlgren's voyage on board the *Cumberland* was followed by a tranquil year at his home in Wilmington, Delaware, after which he grudgingly reported to the Washington Navy Yard for ordnance duty on 27 January 1847. He would have preferred active service in the war against Mexico. Instead, he got the job of improving the experimental Hale rockets the Navy was using in the war. Despite his disappointment, Dahlgren's commitment was stronger than that of others around him. After three days at the Navy Yard, he scribbled in frustration:

> Got the mechanics to work making some rocket cases, heads, and tails. Time, time—the people here take no heed of it—three days gone and only a beginning made. And then very soon Rockets will be wanted. . . . [14]

Dahlgren did get production speeded up, and rockets were soon on their way to Mexico. [15] Within a year, however, he was forced to turn his attention from experimental weapons to the fleet's primary ordnance—guns.

In 1845, the U.S. Navy, largely following the British example, had decided to begin arming all ships with guns of a uniform caliber that fired standard 32-pound shot. [16] Standardization was supposed to bring economy in logistics and ease in training and use. To introduce this new ordnance system, however, the Navy had to sight and range the guns. This became Dahlgren's job. There was precious little to work with. Benjamin Franklin Coston, a young civilian inventor, ran a small laboratory at the Navy Yard, but it was devoted largely to experiments on fuses. Fuse stock, cannon, locks, and shells were not fitted out in an ordnance plant, but in the plumber's shop! [17] Of more immediate concern was that there was no gun range, nor indeed was there any available land on which one could be laid out.

Dahlgren's creative talent and specialized experience combined to solve this problem. Instead of land, he decided to use the Anacostia River for his range. For most naval officers, executing such a plan would have been impossible, but not for a graduate of the coast survey. To determine distances, Dahlgren could use the techniques of triangulation he mastered under Hassler's watchful eye. He even borrowed a good theodolite from the survey to lay out his grid. For measuring bars, he cut pieces from the rocket tubing he had recently been

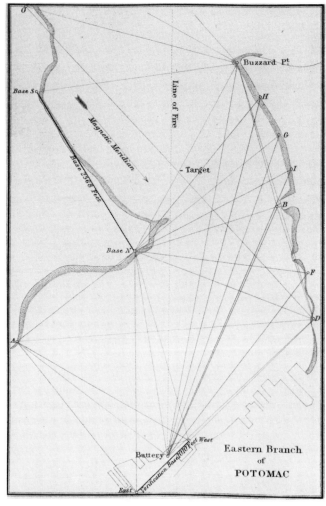

Gun range established by Dahlgren along the Anacostia River. From John A. Dahlgren, *Shells and Shell Guns* (1857).

stuffing with powder and shipping to Mexico. For accurately sighting the jet of water where the shot hit the water, he crafted his own alidade.[18]

The plan worked. Dahlgren ranged the guns and determined how to adjust the sights. But his testing led to a more important result: he concluded that adopting the 32-pounder uniform system was a grave error. The guns of this design were not only unreliable, they were also less powerful than those they were replacing. Their adoption would cause a diminution, not an increase, in firepower. This conclusion dictated Dahlgren's program for the next fifteen years. He would devise his own system of guns for naval ships, a system far superior to the 32-pounders. He would design them to be the most powerful, accurate, and safe guns in the world for their weight. Weight was the critical factor, for it affected both the speed of the ship and the ease of maneuvering the guns. Today we seek "more bang for the buck." Dahlgren's goal was "more bang for the pound."

Successful innovation is often less a matter of knowing more than others than of seeing things in a different way. The major technical problem with large guns in the mid–nineteenth century was bursting. The principal cause was defective materials. The detailed chemical structure of the metals used in gunmaking was unknown, and few mechanical tests were available to measure quality. Foundries generally judged metals only on the basis of appearance, density, and simple tensile strength of samples. In proofing guns, one or two of a lot were usually fired with increasingly large charges until they burst, but experience showed that this was not a reliable indication of the quality of the rest.

Given this state of affairs, Dahlgren might well have proposed research in metallurgy as the only path to progress in gunmaking. He did not, even though he fully appreciated the need for more knowledge. Instead he sought improvements that could be made in the face of ignorance. His method: distribution of metal. He thickened those areas of the gun near the breech, which were most subject to stress, and thinned those near the bore, least subject to it. Then if the gun *did* burst, it would burst near the bore, where the accident would be less likely to kill crew members. Thus he solved two problems at once. The gun was safer, less likely to burst at the breech, and lighter for a weapon of its caliber, because of the reduction of metal around the bore. All that was required to implement the plan was empirical testing that would establish the proper relations between breech and bore dimensions. This practical course in a sea of uncertainty was the foundation of Dahlgren's contributions to naval ordnance. It was the reasoning that led to the "soda-water bottle" shape of the heavy guns that soon came to be associated with his name.

Dahlgren's emphasis was always on heavy ordnance. But his broader goal was a system of guns for all naval ships that would give the fleet the most effective possible mix of weapons. Indeed his first innovative designs were not for heavy guns, but for light ones: boat howitzers.

In the Mexican War, the Navy had to attack along miles of coastline protected by shallow water. Large ships with big guns could not get close enough to shore; the Navy needed small armed boats. Unfortunately, it had no light howitzers in its inventory.[19] Initially, therefore, it had to rely on army guns, which were not well suited to shipboard use. Responding to the problem, Dahlgren designed a series of three light howitzers: one 24-pounder and two 12-pounders. All were bronze and similar in appearance.[20] Although the original designs were for smoothbores, Dahlgren eventually added rifled 12- and 20-pounder howitzers to his "system" of boat armament. In this innovation, he displayed another characteristic that contributed to his success: careful personal attention to detail in all parts of the design and production process.

Many naval officers were skeptical of his howitzers, but from the outset Dahlgren was supported by Commodore Lewis Warrington, the elderly chief of the Bureau of Ordnance and Hydrography. The howitzers soon proved their worth, and Dahlgren's initial success convinced Warrington to support him again in 1850, when Dahlgren submitted a plan for his first heavy weapon, a 9-inch shell gun weighing 9000 pounds. This time the criticism was far more intense, for the gun was much larger and heavier than anything in use. Dahlgren became worried enough to order also a 50-pounder of 8000 pounds to test against his design. Looking back later, he noted that once the guns arrived in May 1850, a single day's practice confirmed his preference for the heavier weapon.[21] Soon he was asking not only for more 9-inch guns, but for an 11-inch as well. His strategy was proving correct. By following it, the Bureau of Ordnance was moving ahead of Europe in naval gun design for the first time.

Linked to Dahlgren's preference for heavier guns was his preference for shell over shot. Experience proved time and again, he argued, that against wooden warships, shell was far more effective than shot. This was so because shell relied on the effect of an explosion after the projectile hit, rather than the effect of its kinetic energy, which friction constantly eroded. Thus his guns would not only be heavier than any previous weapon, they would use ammunition that many officers still viewed as dangerous and unreliable. This meant Dahlgren had two difficult cases to make: for weapons whose weight would slow ships down, and for filling magazines with explosive shell rather than shot.[22]

Dahlgren advocated a "systems approach" to gun development. However, his notion of systems was different from our current understanding. He thought of a system as a series of complementary weapons: howitzers, 9-inch guns, 11-inch guns. Our "systems approach" relates not to products, but to the development process. That process begins with a well-reasoned concept that meets a specific operational need. This concept is then exploited in a coordinated program that includes all aspects of the weapon: design, production, test and evaluation, training, logistics, and so on. Although Dahlgren did not think in these terms, the modern concept of systems development was inherent in his approach. To get his ideas implemented in the Navy, he became, in effect, the Navy's "heavy ordnance program manager." Besides conceiving the design of the 9- and 11-inch shell guns, he personally won support for their implementation, both within the Navy and in Congress. He proved their value not only on land but also in sea trials. He trained gun crews to operate them and devised proper techniques for their effective use. He determined the right mix of guns for each class of naval vessels. Dahlgren knew very well that getting a new form of technology accepted into the fleet took far more than simply designing and producing it.

Dahlgren's first chance to have his system adopted came in 1854, when the Navy began building the new *Merrimack* class of screw frigates. By now it was clear that continuing to use the 32-pound guns was absurd; so the Bureau of Ordnance and Hydrography agreed to try the new Dahlgren 9-inch guns. However, bureau leaders were too cautious to include the 11-inch guns as well. While Dahlgren protested that this compromise "mutilated" his ideas, it nonetheless was a major step forward. Here was a lead ship totally armed with heavy shell guns of his design.

Throughout the long years of struggle to get his innovations accepted, Dahlgren's personality worked both for and against him. He displayed unquestioned mathematical brilliance and dogged devotion to a field that, whatever its importance, attracted few as capable as he. He demonstrated a remarkably clear vision of what was needed in his chosen field, and of how much was possible given the state of the art. He also had the strong self-

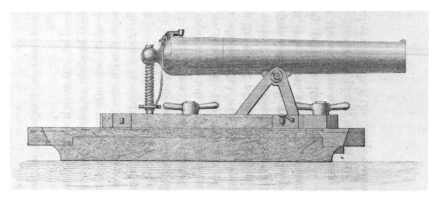

Dahlgren-designed boat howitzer. This illustration from Dahlgren's *The System of Boat Armament in the United States Navy* (1852) shows one of the most commonly used guns in the U.S. Navy.

discipline and self-confidence necessary to bring his vision to reality in the face of general indifference and occasional strong opposition. But Dahlgren was proud and vain. Tenacious in defense of his own ideas, he rarely acknowledged the contributions of others. When forced to convince skeptics, he inclined to be combative rather than diplomatic. Many who were subject to the sharp cut of his arguments did not become believers, but simply retreated to fight another day.

Recognizing that he would not be able to convince his opponents of the value of his 11-inch guns until they were tested, Dahlgren petitioned to get his own experimental ship to try them at sea. Although many in the Navy opposed this unusual idea, Secretary Isaac Toucey supported it, and the naval appropriations act of March 1857 provided funds for using the sloop-of-war *Plymouth* as an ordnance ship to test Dahlgren's guns and train crews.[23] Dahlgren armed her with an 11-inch pivot shell gun, four 9-inch shell guns, two 24-pound cannon, and one 12-pounder howitzer. Between June and December 1857, he sailed to Europe and back, firing over one hundred shells from the 11-inch gun without a failure. This successful voyage defiantly silenced his critics and brought the adoption of the 11-inch gun as a partner to the 9-incher. The frigates of the *Merrimack* class soon sported 11-inch guns on their spar deck.[24] Dahlgren's full system was now accepted.

During the Civil War, the value of Dahlgren's 11-inch shell gun would be dramatically proved in the battle between the *Kearsarge* and the English-built *Alabama* on 19 June 1864. The *Alabama* had then menaced Union commerce for a year and a half, capturing 68 vessels. But when the *Kearsarge* finally caught her and began blasting away with 11-inch Dahlgrens, the *Alabama*'s English guns proved no match. The most successful commerce raider of the Confederacy sank in defeat.

Complementing Dahlgren's work in the Navy were his books on naval ordnance. The two most important were *The System of Boat Armament in the U.S. Navy* (1852), in which he described his boat howitzers, and *Shells and Shell Guns* (1857), which argued for the superiority of shell over shot. The latter was his masterpiece. In it he demonstrated not only his knowledge of American naval ordnance, but also his familiarity with developments in Britain and France. In addition, he analyzed the ordnance implications of the naval battles of the Crimean War. The book was a milestone in his profession and established his international reputation as the leading spokesman on American naval ordnance.

Dahlgren's development of new guns in the 1850s led to his transforming the ordnance facilities at the Washington Navy Yard. The creation of a gun range and experimental battery have already been mentioned. These were greatly expanded and developed over the years Dahlgren was at the yard. Dahlgren also oversaw construction of a large, new ordnance building that opened in 1854. This soon grew to include a foundry for cannon, a mechanical department for finishing guns, and a gun-carriage shop.[25] It was here that Dahlgren howitzers were manufactured. In the long run, the development of this in-house naval capability in ordnance was a contribution at least equal to Dahlgren's gun designs, for the pattern Dahlgren established endured. Henceforth, the Navy would no longer be dependent on following the designs of Europe or accepting the products of American industry. It would have its own strong research, development, test, and evaluation capability. The ordnance specialty at the Washington Navy Yard grew to the extent that, by 1886, the yard's principal mission was gun manufacture, and it was renamed the Naval Gun Factory. After the Civil War, the Navy also established its own facilities for torpedo development and production in Newport, Rhode Island. Strong in-house capability was later developed in the field of smokeless powder production, mines, and other ordnance specialties. In 1918, at the suggestion of Rear Admiral Ralph Earle, Chief of the Bureau of Ordnance, the Navy commemorated Dahlgren's lasting institutional influence by naming its new proving ground in northeastern Virginia "Dahlgren." Although the naval facility has since changed titles, the surrounding town still bears the admiral's name.[26]

When the Civil War erupted in April 1861, Dahlgren held the rank of commander and was head of ordnance at the Washington Navy Yard. Captain Franklin Buchanan, a Southerner, was in charge of the yard. On 23 April, Buchanan resigned to join the rebels. Dahlgren thus inherited his first important operational command. The navy yard was a critical post, for it protected the strategic southern flank of Washington and the approach by river. The yard was also the chief arsenal for naval guns in the Union. With Norfolk already in Southern hands, losing the yard would have been a grave blow. Dahlgren rapidly moved to make his position secure. In addition, he assembled a small flotilla of ships that participated in operations around Washington, notably the assault on Alexandria.[27] Along with these new responsibilities, he still oversaw all ordnance activities.

In the harrowing early months of 1861, President Lincoln frequently visited the navy yard to confer with its commander. Lincoln quickly came to respect the views of Dahlgren, not only related to ordnance, but also to many questions of naval strategy. During the next several years, Dahlgren became one of Lincoln's most trusted technical advisors.[28]

Close association with the President gave Dahlgren's career a substantial boost. Lincoln ensured that the commander remained in charge of the navy yard, by law a captain's billet, until he was promoted to captain on 5 August 1862. When the promotion was approved, he pressured Secretary Welles to offer Dahlgren command of the Bureau of Ordnance and Hydrography. However, Dahlgren, hoping for sea duty, refused. Then in July 1862, the Navy's bureaus were reorganized from the existing five into eight.[29] The Bureau of Ordnance became a single entity. Dahlgren was the natural candidate to head it, but he recommended his friend Andrew H. Foote.[30] Welles appointed Dahlgren anyhow, and this time he accepted, realizing that his dream of a sea command might go unfulfilled. He was commissioned chief of the bureau on 18 July 1862.[31]

The ordnance problems that Dahlgren faced during the early years of the Civil War were the opposite of those of the 1850s. Officers who had been skeptical of his guns now wanted all they could get. Hence Dahlgren's main concern was increasing manufacture. To help maintain the quality of the increased production, he also expanded the testing facilities at the navy yard. During the war, the Navy produced around 800 guns of his design, 505 of which were 9-inchers.[32] Demand for guns of all sorts was so high that he was also forced to use some outmoded pieces.[33]

The greatest technical challenge to Dahlgren during the war came in the wake of the battle of the ironclads *Monitor* and *Virginia*, at Hampton Roads on 9 March 1862. As is well known, the arrival of the Union ironclad cut short the destruction the *Virginia* had wreaked the previous day. Although the battle ended in a draw, its effect was a Union victory, for the Union blockade was preserved. But if Secretary of the Navy Welles breathed a sigh of relief, he was still worried. The *Monitor* had been armed with two 11-inch Dahlgrens, the most powerful Union guns. These guns had been unable to destroy the iron-clad *Virginia*, despite many hits. Welles concluded that the Navy had to develop more powerful guns immediately. Why not follow the Army's lead and develop 15-inchers? The Secretary turned to his ordnance chief for advice.[34]

Surprisingly, Dahlgren, who had made his reputation by constantly pushing for ever heavier guns, was opposed. His reasoning in this case is as revealing of his character as an innovator as was his earlier program for developing a naval ordnance system. Metallurgical knowledge was still extremely limited. Dahlgren thus knew he could not design 15-inch guns based on scientific principles. On the other hand, there was no time for experimentation. He firmly believed that the threat posed by Confederate ironclads, no matter how serious, was not so great as that posed by a ship's own guns if they were likely to burst. Extreme caution was necessary. As an alternative to 15-inch guns, therefore, Dahlgren proposed 13-inchers, which he thought he could safely build following the same principles he used for his 9- and 11-inch guns.

Secretary Welles, relying on the advice of John Ericsson, angrily rejected the idea. He adamantly maintained that the new monitors being rushed into production needed the power of 15-inch guns, and he believed the Army's success directly contradicted Dahlgren's worries. He ordered Dahlgren to design and fabricate the 15-inch guns. Dahlgren consented, but haughtily insisted on being absolved of responsibility for the decision.

Dahlgren normally cast his guns solid, bored out the interior, and then shaped the exterior with metal lathes. But since he was treading on unfamiliar ground, he reluctantly decided to follow the casting method of his archrival in the Army, Captain Thomas J. Rodman. This involved hollow-casting the gun and cooling it from inside. The shape of the 15-inch gun Dahlgren designed was generally that of the earlier Dahlgren guns, scaled up to provide additional resistance to the larger charge.

The design turned out to be reasonably successful. True to his personality, Dahlgren would later argue at length that it was *his* design far more than *Rodman's* casting methods that was responsible for this achievement.[35] No 15-inch Dahlgrens burst in service causing a loss of life. However, several failed prematurely.[36] More problematic was their size. Dahlgren had made the guns so large that they did not fit through the portholes in the monitors. While this was consistent with the original plan, it resulted in smoke filling the gun turret and stifling the gun crew. One solution was to put a box around the muzzle of the guns so that the smoke would be directed outside. This helped, but was limited in its efficacy. After Dahlgren left the bureau, his successor decided to slim down later 15-inch guns so they could fit through the portholes. Because this also reduced their strength, the guns had to be fired with limited charges. After the war, Dahlgren emphasized these difficulties in passionately defending his earlier point of view. While admitting that the 15-inch guns had worked, he always claimed that his plan for 13-inch guns would have been both better and safer.

Dahlgren's stance on the 15-inch gun was similar to those he took on two other crucial ordnance issues: rifling and breech loading. In both cases, he generally opposed the innovations for large naval guns. While he recognized their potential, he said that experiments had shown the innovations to be still too experimental for introduction into the fleet. He too wanted improvement, but only when safety did not have to be sacrificed. Although some applauded this caution, many others bitterly opposed it, especially the innovators who stood to profit from the Navy's support of their ideas. In postwar investigations, they charged that Dahlgren had been unreceptive to any new ideas except his own. Given proper support, they said they could have provided the Navy with far more effective weapons. Dahlgren the innovator, they declared, had become an impediment to change.

Whether right or wrong, these charges indicate a serious flaw in Dahlgren's leadership of the bureau. He never mobilized the creativity of others effectively, but stuck rigidly to his own program. Yet beyond the 15-inch gun design he was forced to prepare, he contributed no significant new innovations during the war. It might have been, as Dahlgren argued later, that he had done all he could given the state of knowledge and the need for large-scale production. It is more likely, however, that his attention was directed elsewhere: to naval combat.

Dahlgren attained the rank of rear admiral in 1863 solely on the basis of his work in ordnance. Learning of his promotion, he went to thank Welles, but the Secretary, who had opposed it, told him to save his gratitude for the President.[37] However, Welles understood clearly the implications of the change. Now he would have difficulty refusing Dahlgren his greatest desire: an operational command. The new admiral's eye was on Charleston harbor.

Birthplace of the rebellion and defiantly free, Charleston stood out as an embarrassing breech in the Union blockade of Southern ports. Attempts to take it early in the war had been unsuccessful. In the development of the *Monitor* class of ships, however, Union leaders saw new hope. Early in 1863, a flotilla of seven new monitors was delivered to Admiral Du Pont to spearhead an attack on the city, and on 7 April 1863 he struck, only to suffer defeat in a fierce two-hour battle. In despair, Du Pont concluded that further attack was futile, and he notified the Navy Department that he had given up taking the city by sea.[38] Welles, unwilling to accept this position, clearly had to relieve Du Pont. Here was Dahlgren's chance. His could be the glory of conquering Charleston![39]

Although Welles knew that Lincoln supported Dahlgren's ambitions, he found the admiral vain, ambitious, and inexperienced. Welles desperately sought a compromise. Would Dahlgren be willing to go as second to his friend

Cross section of a 13-inch gun. The thickness of the breech relative to the barrel of a Dahlgren-type gun can be seen in this late-nineteenth-century photograph. The people have not been identified. *Courtesy of the National Archives.*

Foote? Dahlgren balked: two admirals to lead a single operation? But after discussions with Foote and an assurance that Foote would give him command of the ironclads, he finally agreed.[40] When Foote became critically ill in June, Welles reluctantly passed full command to Dahlgren.

Dahlgren took over the South Atlantic Squadron on 6 July.[41] The army forces had also received a new leader, General Quincy A. Gillmore. On 10 July, the combined Union forces attacked Confederate fortifications on Morris Island, a point guarding the southern end of the harbor. Dahlgren's ironclads pounded the rebels for four hours, until dusk. Gillmore, however, chose to delay his assault until the next morning. The attack failed, at a high cost in Union casualties. Thus the quick thrust under new leadership dissolved into a tedious program of siege and trench warfare. Day after day, Dahlgren directed his guns against the Confederate strongholds. But while shot and shell could destroy brick walls, they had little effect on mounds of rubble or sand, which provided equally good protection. Finally attrition took its toll; Morris Island fell on 7 September. Dahlgren followed up immediately on the 8th with an assault on nearby Fort Sumter. Although he and Gillmore had agreed on a joint attack, their efforts were not well coordinated. The attack was repulsed.

The long delay in taking Morris Island gave the Confederates the opportunity to strengthen the internal ring of fortifications around the harbor. Sumter's resilience meant that the evacuation of Morris Island had not weakened Confederate resolve. In addition, the Confederates proved to be remarkably innovative in their defense. They employed mines, semi-submersibles, and crude submarines against their foes.[42] Although not uniformly effective, and often causing loss of life among their users, these tactics helped discourage Dahlgren and his men from making a full-scale invasion. Like Du Pont before him, Dahlgren became acutely aware of the limitations of his ironclad fleet. Sadly, he too decided he could not take Charleston by sea. Unfortunately, Gillmore did not have the troops necessary to swing round behind the city and take it by land; so the two commanders glumly settled down to enforcing the blockade. The tedium of duty off Charleston broke briefly for Dahlgren when he personally led expeditions up the Broad, St. Johns, and Stone rivers in support of army forces. Charleston did not fall until General Sherman's advance up the coast forced its evacuation. When Dahlgren entered the city on 18 February 1865, he was a victor, but in a conquest far different from what he had imagined.

The years following the Civil War were trying ones for John Dahlgren. Even before the war ended, he was defending his actions off Charleston to Congress. Justifying his conduct and defending his reputation would remain major preoccupations until his death. After the war, even General Gillmore openly attacked him, charging that he had never given the Army enough support. Gillmore also argued that Dahlgren should have mounted an independent campaign with his ironclads against the inner harbor fortifications.

These criticisms deeply wounded the admiral and evoked his most impassioned rebuttals.[43]

Dahlgren was equally unhappy in his postwar assignments. He relinquished command of the South Atlantic Squadron on 12 July 1865, and returned to Washington, where he married his second wife, Madeleine Vinton, a congressman's daughter. She brightened his life over the next few years by bearing him three more children, including twins of whom he was very proud. His tour in the capital was short-lived, however, as he was ordered to assume command of the South Pacific Squadron on 1 December 1866. Dahlgren considered this rapid move out of Washington insulting.[44] In 1868, he came back, this time to his old post of chief of the Bureau of Ordnance. But if he expected a happy return to the field where he had achieved his most enduring accomplishment, he was disappointed once again. In 1867, Congress had appointed a Joint Committee on Ordnance to investigate the work of the Army and Navy in developing, manufacturing, and using heavy guns during the Civil War. After two years of work, the committee delivered a stinging indictment. Its report charged:

> The fact that the ordnance officers of the government find it necessary, at this late date, to return to the rudiments of their art and begin their experiments anew, as stated in the report of the Chief of Ordnance of the navy, shows a defect in the system upon which experiments have heretofore been conducted, and in the organization of the ordnance departments, calling for a remedy. The difficulty appears to have been two-fold: first, the ordnance officers, knowing their positions secure to them for life, have not felt the incentive to exertion and improvement which stimulates men not in government employ, and they have become attached to routine and to the traditions of their corps, jealous of innovation and new ideas, and slow to adopt improvements.[45]

Criticism in the press was bad enough, but from Congress it was devastating. Dahlgren had spent weeks compiling data for the committee and developing full explanations of his work over the years. The committee, however, proved to be uninterested in his early successes, focusing instead on his reluctance to design the 15-inch gun and his opposition to rifling and breech loaders. His critics had a field day. Dahlgren was not praised for circumventing the lack of knowledge of metallurgy and gun failure; he was blamed for not rectifying it.

The report broke what was left of Dahlgren's spirit. Under the circumstances, he felt he could not remain chief of the bureau. He petitioned for, and finally received, the post of commandant of the Washington Navy Yard, beginning on 10 August 1869. Although he replaced another admiral, he was returning to the same position he had held as a commander eight years before. The humiliation lasted less than a year. Dahlgren died on 12 July 1870.

Although Dahlgren's greatest contributions came in ordnance innovation rather than naval command, he always considered himself a naval officer first and an innovator second. He once wrote in a letter:

> My main purpose in seeking ordnance duty was to fit myself more fully for sea service. In so doing, I have become more interested in the pursuit than I intended at the outset, and identified with innovations, which, however viewed by others, seemed to be essential.[46]

Dahlgren's sensibilities as a line officer are what allowed him to achieve his remarkable successes. His major innovations, made during peacetime, were already being implemented when the war began. Unlike many other inventors, he never let peace lull him into focusing on technical progress rather than manufacturing products. Yet while this orientation had strengths, it also had limitations. It blinded Dahlgren to the need for continual support of innovation in wartime as well as peace, by others as well as himself. Even in the midst of a conflict, a Navy that is satisfied with the weapons it has is a Navy whose power is slipping away. It is ironic that the Confederates, who eagerly sought to capture and use Dahlgren guns, seemed to understand this point better than he did. Their effective use of wartime inventions was among the reasons that Dahlgren never achieved his greatest goal as a naval officer: capturing Charleston by sea.

FURTHER READING

Unlike many of his contemporaries, John Dahlgren has not had a modern biographer. The only major secondary source on his life and work is the uncritical *Memoir of John A. Dahlgren*, published by his second wife in 1882. The natural praiseworthy tone of this work was probably further enhanced by the fact that Mrs. Dahlgren was seeking substantial compensation from the government for her husband's ordnance inventions as she was writing. But if the volume is strong on Dahlgren's accomplishments and light on his weaknesses, it remains a very valuable source, in that it includes a wealth of direct quotations from Dahlgren's papers and much factual material available nowhere else. Most other biographical sketches are based largely on this work. An exception is the earlier article by J. T. Headley in *Farragut and Our Naval Commanders*, written soon after the Civil War. Taylor Peck's history of the Washington Navy Yard, *Round Shot to Rockets*, also has some unique material.

Historians who have discussed Dahlgren in a broader context have largely done so in writing about naval combat. I found Bern Anderson's *By Sea and by River* and V. C. Jones's multivolume *The Civil War at Sea* to be particularly useful. Several works have also been written just on the siege of Charleston. The most useful supplement to the general histories that I used was John Johnson, *The Defense of Charleston Harbor*, an 1890 account with good maps and detailed descriptions of the combat. Assessments of Dahlgren as an ordnance innovator are much rarer. Warren Ripley's *Artillery and Ammunition of the Civil War* was most helpful in analyzing Dahlgren's innovations in comparison to the work of other ordnance innovators of the time, particularly Thomas Rodman of the Army. The book also has many photographs of Dahlgren guns. Even more insightful, however, is the treatment of Dahlgren in a forthcoming book by Albert B. Christman, *Naval Innovators from Bushnell to Holland*. This work compares and contrasts Dahlgren to many other naval innovators of the nineteenth century and looks at both technical and administrative aspects of his work. It should be published by the Navy in 1986 or 1987. Robert V. Bruce's *Lincoln and the Tools of War* gives good coverage of the relationship between Dahlgren and the President. Biographies of Dahlgren's contemporaries such as Samuel Du Pont, Gideon Welles, and Andrew Foote provide a limited view of Dahlgren from the perspective of their subjects.

Dahlgren himself was the author of about a half dozen technical publications. His most valuable books for historians are *The System of Boat Armament in the United States Navy* (1852), which covers his howitzers, and *Shells and Shell Guns* (1856), which covers heavy ordnance. His *Memoir of Ulric Dahlgren, By his father, Rear Admiral Dahlgren* provides insight into his personality.

The major collection of Dahlgren's papers is in the Library of Congress and contains 10,000 items, including nineteen boxes of general correspondence and twelve boxes of ordnance papers. Although purchased by the library from a private dealer, these records were clearly the source of Madeleine Dahlgren's book. Other record collections, which I did not consult, include a small second group of papers in the Library of Congress and records at Syracuse University, the New York Public Library, and the Eleutherian Mills Historical Library. Copies of primary sources related to Dahlgren appear in many published collections of Civil War figures, most notably the *Diary of Gideon Welles* and the *Official Records of the Union and Confederate Navies*. Materials in the published papers of Abraham Lincoln and Samuel F. Du Pont are also useful.

NOTES

1. Madeleine V. Dahlgren, *Memoir of John A. Dahlgren*, 389.
2. Gideon Welles, *Diary*, I: 164.
3. Ibid., I: 239; Abraham Lincoln, *Collected Papers*, VI: 111–12.
4. The June 1985 issue of U.S. Naval Institute *Proceedings* has an article on exactly this issue: John L. Byron, "Warriors," 63–68.
5. "John A. Dahlgren," in Allen Johnson and Dumas Malone, eds., *Dictionary of American Biography*, III: 29–31.
6. Dahlgren, *Memoir of John A. Dahlgren*, 11–13.
7. Charles Todorich, *The Spirited Years*, 5–6.
8. John A. Dahlgren, *Maritime International Law*, 1877.
9. Albert B. Christman, "Naval Innovators from Bushnell to Holland" in preparation, Chapter 3.

10. Dahlgren, *Memoir of John A. Dahlgren*, 92.

11. Ibid., 82.

12. J. T. Headley, *Farragut and Our Naval Commanders*, 458.

13. Dahlgren, *Memoir of John A. Dahlgren*, 87.

14. Christman, "Naval Innovators from Bushnell to Holland," Chapter 4.

15. Headley, *Farragut and Our Naval Commanders*, 460.

16. John A. Dahlgren, *Shell and Shell Guns*, Chapter I.

17. Taylor Peck, *Round Shot to Rockets*, 105.

18. Document entitled "Printed," file 1862, box 27, Dahlgren papers, Library of Congress.

19. John A. Dahlgren, *The System of Boat Armament in the United States Navy* (1865 ed.), 10–14.

20. Warren Ripley, *Artillery and Ammunition of the Civil War*, 87–88.

21. Document entitled "Printed," file 1862, box 27, Dahlgren Papers, Library of Congress.

22. Dahlgren, *Shells and Shell Guns*, 1856.

23. "Isaac Toucey," in Paolo Coletta, ed., *American Secretaries of the Navy*, I: 307.

24. Dahlgren, *Memoir of John A. Dahlgren*, 314.

25. *Round Shot to Rockets*, 107–9.

26. Kenneth G. McCollum, *Dahlgren*, 1–8.

27. Peck, *Round Shots to Rockets*, 115–49.

28. Robert V. Bruce, *Lincoln and the Tools of War.*

29. The former bureaus were Ordnance and Hydrography; Yards and Docks; Construction, Equipment, and Repair; Provisions and Clothing; and Medicine and Surgery. Ordnance and Hydrography was split into the Bureau of Ordnance and the Bureau of Navigation; Construction, Equipment, and Repair was split into Construction and Repair, and Equipment and Recruiting. A new Bureau of Steam and Engineering was added.

30. Peck, *Round Shot to Rockets*, 145.

31. Headley, *Farragut and Our Naval Commanders*, 474.

32. U.S. Congress (38:2), Senate Report 142, section "Heavy Ordnance."

33. Christman, "Naval Innovators from Bushnell to Holland," Chapter 5.

34. U.S. Congress (38:2), Senate Report 142, section "Heavy Ordnance," 126–29.

35. U.S. Congress (40:3), *Report of the Joint Committee on Ordnance* (Senate Report 266), 130.

36. Ibid., 137.

37. Welles, *Diary*, I: 239.

38. Bern Anderson, *By Sea and by River*, 163–68.

39. Dahlgren, *Memoir of John A. Dahlgren*, 390.

40. Welles, *Diary*, I: 317. See also, U.S., Department of the Navy, *Official Records of the Union and Confederate Navies in the War of the Rebellion*, I: 14.

41. This account of the fall of Charleston relies on Bern Anderson, *By Sea and by River*; Dahlgren, *Memoir of John A. Dahlgren*; and V. C. Jones, *The Civil War at Sea*, III.

42. Christman, "Naval Innovators from Bushnell to Holland," Chapter 5.

43. An account of his defense is in Dahlgren, *Memoir of John A. Dahlgren*, 532–50.

44. Ibid., 623.

45. U.S. Congress (40:3), *Report of the Joint Committee on Ordnance* (Senate Report 266), 4.

46. Dahlgren, *Memoir of John A. Dahlgren*, 176.

MATTHEW FONTAINE MAURY: NAVY SCIENCE FOR THE WORLD

BY WILLIAM STANTON

Matthew Fontaine Maury never commanded a vessel. Yet he enjoyed an international renown beyond that accorded any other American naval officer of his generation. Born the son of a failed farmer in Spotsylvania County, Virginia, 14 January 1806, and growing up in Tennessee in near privation, young Maury early displayed the vein of personal ambition that was to mark his career and with it a compensating pride in his Huguenot ancestry. With little opportunity for formal training, he was largely self-educated, displaying an early enthusiasm for mathematics. Appointed midshipman in 1825 at the age of nineteen, Maury first saw blue water on a voyage to England on board the *Brandywine,* Captain Charles Morris, then returning Lafayette at the conclusion of his farewell visit to the republic. In the course of the voyage Maury learned seamanship from the bos'un and navigation from the schoolmaster, George Jones (1800–70), who later became an accomplished astronomer. Jones introduced Maury to the Navy's longtime textbook, Nathaniel Bowditch's *New American Practical Navigator* (1802); and on later voyages, particularly while serving on the Brazil Station, Maury prepared himself in mathematics.

There, as in the *Brandywine,* enthusiasm for formal learning was thought distinctly quirky. But ignoring shipmates' sidelong glances, Maury assumed that authorship of a new textbook on navigation, one that presented theory as well as practice, would win him promotion "over the heads of many," while filling a gap in the education of midshipmen. Bowditch said he thought such a book "would be very useful to those who have a taste for the subject," and though himself having chosen to present only practice, he must have known how few those were. Alexander Dallas Bache, future head of the Coast Survey and ever the apostle of the theoretical, offered warmer encouragement, in what was Maury's first, and an utterly misleading, contact with a man later to play a fateful role in confining both his ambition and his posthumous reputation.[1]

46

When Maury's first book, *A New Theoretical and Practical Treatise on Navigation,* appeared in the spring of 1836, it met with acclaim from Edgar Allan Poe, who was pleased to see "science . . . gaining votaries" from the Navy; from officers who would command the Navy of the future; and not least from the schoolmasters ("Professors of Mathematics") at naval stations and on board ship who sought to launch a little learning onto the sea of indifference. By an 1844 order of Secretary of the Navy John Y. Mason, Maury's fellow Virginian, the book replaced Bowditch for some years. Not least in Maury's eyes, it won him promotion to lieutenant, though not to the lieutenant of ten years' standing (with corresponding back pay) he had hoped for.[2]

Organization of the United States Exploring Expedition in the years 1836–38 revealed yet another vein of Maury's ambition. An unprecedented undertaking by the U.S. government in support of science, the expedition was designed specifically to upgrade the reputation of American science in world opinion. Maury probably had met J. N. Reynolds, tireless promoter of the expedition, in 1833 when both men sailed from Callao to the United States on board the *Potomac.* If so, their mutual interest in science must have led them to discuss an expedition, and Reynolds to tell Maury how he deplored those skeptical of the practical benefits of such an enterprise. Three years later, to skeptics in Congress, Reynolds would bluntly observe that in matters of science, "utility cannot be computed in advance," and "scientific research ought not to be thus weighed." Reynolds asked Congress to display unwonted liberality in preparing an expedition to be conducted "By an enlightened body of naval officers, joining harmoniously with a corps of scientific men."[3]

When Congress finally approved the enterprise in 1836, the prospect of joining it was appealing to Maury, a young lieutenant with ambitions in science both for himself and for his service, and it seemed for a time that he would have a place. In November 1837 he was appointed astronomer to the expedition. But in the widely publicized struggle between the Secretary of the Navy, Mahlon Dickerson, who hoped to kill the enterprise, and the expedition's commander, Captain Thomas ap Catesby Jones, Maury brushed up against another lieutenant with similar ambitions. In an appointment as unprecedented as the expedition itself, Lieutenant Charles Wilkes—who shared both Maury's interest in science and his determination to keep civilian scientists out of the Navy, and promised as well to explore on the cheap—was given the command. Maury, who had hoped that somewhere in the labyrinthine ways of Washington the command might fall to him, refused to serve in any capacity with Wilkes (who would have refused his services anyway), and in the summer of 1838 found himself left with only "my integrity."

The two years of preparation were a national scandal and a great embarrassment to the Navy. Though determined to make the expedition exclusively a naval affair and so arrogating to himself the duties in physical science, Wilkes, despite diligent search, failed to find a body of naval officers enlightened in

Matthew Fontaine Maury. This salt print photograph was taken circa 1856. *Courtesy of the National Portrait Gallery.*

science and was obliged to fall back on Reynolds's original plan of employing a corps of civilian scientists and artists. Maury was humiliated, both for himself and for the service, and the humiliation continued to rankle for years after the expedition's return. It rankled the more as the expedition proved to be a grand success for American science, giving rise to the important government institutions of science—the National Museum, the Naval Observatory, the U.S. Botanic Garden—and winning the acclaim of a skeptical world.[4]

What Maury himself acquired from the experience was an abiding hatred of Charles Wilkes (fully reciprocated), a renewed determination to limit the instruction of naval officers to naval officers, and the conviction that the Navy, as exemplified by its rejection of his talents, was badly in need of reform. Idle now, "awaiting orders," in the late summer of 1838 he gave vent to his frustrations, first as "Harry Bluff," then as "Will Watch," in a spate of twelve articles in the *Richmond Whig and Public Advertiser*. Lambasting the treatment accorded the Navy in organizing the expedition, these essays presented the first of Maury's proposals for overhauling the service.

When orders finally came in the fall of 1839, he hurried off to Washington, only to be injured in a stagecoach accident that left him permanently lame. A man less determined and less bitter, perceiving the handwriting on the wall, might have turned his back on the service to accept an instructorship in mathematics at one of the colleges. Instead, lying abed in Fredericksburg, Maury mused on the character of a navy that kept most of its officers on shore, kept the ablest of them in subordinate ranks, mistrusted science, contemned learning, and in consequence sailed by the charts of other nations. Writing in the *Southern Literary Messenger*, "Harry Bluff" widened his critique of the service to include charges of administrative incompetence, waste and fraud in ship construction and repair, poor administrative and officer promotion procedures, and a narrowness of vision. Maury proposed several reforms to correct these deficiencies, including the addition of more ranks to the service to supplement the existing three, and an increase in the number of ships. These would solve some of the problems of promotion. Further, he argued, there must be a school ship for the training of midshipmen in a four-year curriculum that would include such exotic subjects as foreign languages, chemistry, natural history, astronomy, and mathematics, as well as naval architecture, gunnery, and tactics, all to be taught by naval officers. The list lengthened as the articles grew in number, and the school ship came to be supplanted by a naval academy. Still another article proposed replacing the Board of Navy Commissioners with a system of bureaus.

Having got this much off his chest, Maury, feeling his way, applied for sea duty. Rejection on medical grounds only served to reinvigorate his pen, and "Union Jack" urged enlargement of the steam merchant marine by means of a government subsidy after the manner of France and England, the vessels to be built in commercial yards and available to the government in time of war. In a remarkably short time, most of these reforms would be adopted and Maury hailed as their prophet, for he had been at no great pains to preserve anonymity once an approving audience appeared.[5]

One early indication of popular approval was his election to membership in the National Institute for the Promotion of Science, a short-lived Washington organization got up by "friends of science" in the hope of its being chosen to administer both the Smithson fund and the soon-to-be-returned natural history collections of the exploring expedition. In one of the first papers presented before the institute, Maury proposed that the West Indies Squadron chart the ocean bottom by means of "drags."[6]

The frustrating years of inactivity came to an end, and Maury's true career began when in June 1842 Secretary of the Navy Abel P. Upshur, a fellow Virginian, appointed him superintendent of the Depot of Charts and Instruments. Established twelve years earlier under Lieutenant Louis Goldsborough, the depot had become in 1833 an astronomical observatory of sorts under its second superintendent, Charles Wilkes, who, entirely on his own initiative, mounted a 3½-inch telescope in order to test chronometers and other apparatus. The nascent observatory assumed a more ambitious role when the expedition sailed, for it was necessary that Wilkes's successor, Lieutenant James M. Gilliss (1811–65) make continuous observations—astronomical, magnetic, meteorological—during the squadron's absence. (Gilliss claimed that his own impulse to pursue an active career in science came when as a passed midshipman he heard "remarks to the effect that there was not an officer in the navy capable of conducting a scientific enterprise.") With Gilliss's four years of unremitting labor, his extraction from Congress of an appropriation of $25,000, and his purchase in Europe of the best instruments obtainable came realization of the hopes of a generation of scientists and cultural patriots for the national observatory that Congress, for political reasons, had so many times refused to provide. In the eyes of the scientific community, an institution devoted to the "queen of the sciences" would effectively give the lie to the

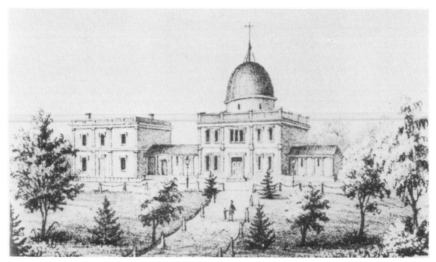

The U.S. Naval Observatory and Hydrographical Office. The height of the dome is exaggerated in his sketch of the facility as it appeared during Maury's tenure as superintendent, 1844–61. The building on the left was the superintendent's house added in 1847. *Courtesy of the Virginia State Library.*

charge that the American republic was committed to the merely useful and indifferent to basic research.

Thus while the appointment gave Maury his chance in science as well as in the Navy, it also set the pattern of his relations with his scientific contemporaries, a pattern that his superintendence of the institution would soon confirm. Gilliss, then preparing for publication both his four years' observations and a star catalogue—which would be the first American works of their kind—was an accomplished astronomical observer, while Maury, whose training in astronomy was largely confined to what he had learned at the hand of Walter Johnson while with the Exploring Expedition in Philadelphia, was still at nurse. That Gilliss should be supplanted by a man with little training in and less taste for astronomy left the scientific community astonished and dismayed.[7]

In view of the emphasis Maury had long placed on confining science in the Navy to the Navy's own officers, the priority he accorded astronomy became clear when he staffed the observatory with civilian observers, though to be sure there were able men among them, some—Sears C. Walker, James Ferguson, Joseph S. Hubbard, John H. C. Coffin—astronomers of considerable distinction. Maury at first displayed great energy in directing his staff, and the observatory's future seemed promising, though Maury himself published few papers in astronomy, and those were purely observational. Other opportunities drew Maury's attention, opportunities that astronomer Simon Newcomb would knowingly call "from a practical standpoint, the vastly more important work" of investigating ocean winds and currents. In consequence the observatory fell into disarray. Astronomical observations came to lack direction; instruments became obsolete.[8]

It soon appeared that such neglect could do astronomy positive harm. When in 1847 a new determination of the solar parallax was proposed, James Gilliss, now with the observatory's chief rival, the Coast Survey, organized an expedition to Chile for observing Venus and Mars. Many in the scientific community agreed with the American Philosophical Society that the expedition would "confer honor on our country," which had "hitherto contributed but little . . . to astronomy and navigation." Though Maury pronounced the expedition a useless affair (having supplanted Gilliss, he was never to forgive him), Secretary of the Navy Mason assigned him the task Gilliss had performed for the Wilkes expedition, conducting parallel observations. However, Gilliss found on his return that the Naval Observatory had executed only nineteen such observations, nearly half of them valueless, and had scuttled the enterprise. For such neglect, whether born of indifference or animus, the astronomers of the country, and with them the champions of disinterested science, never forgave Maury.[9]

Maury had early interested himself in the movement of winds and currents. It was a subject of vital importance to the seafarer, but one curiously little

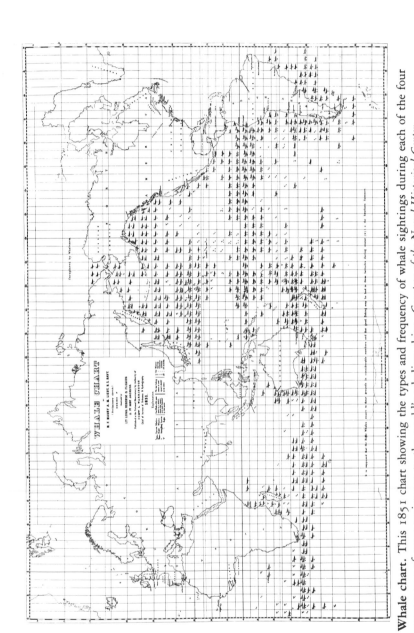

Whale chart. This 1851 chart showing the types and frequency of whale sightings during each of the four seasons was of great assistance to the world's whaling ships. *Courtesy of the Naval Historical Center.*

investigated in view of the belief, common in the Western world of the nineteenth century, that, as Maury put it, "There is no colonizer, civilizer, nor Christianizer like commerce." And as Britain had discovered two centuries before, extensive commerce is dependent upon a large navy. Moreover, Maury was an expansionist, especially a Southern expansionist.

Shortly after assuming his new post, Maury discovered that a great deal of useful information on the subject lay at hand in the depot itself in the accumulated bundles of logbooks of naval voyages over the years. Perhaps he had learned of their utility from the meteorologist William C. Redfield. Five years earlier, for the benefit of the Exploring Expedition, Redfield had prepared "a series of maps and charts" showing "the predominating systems of winds and currents in different oceans, derived from the logbooks of voyagers and other sources." (Redfield's work was lost in the wreck of the expedition's *Peacock* in 1842.) Many of the logbooks at the depot covered the frequently traveled route from New York to Rio and contained data on wind force, current, fog, rain, and day's run. On working up the data, Maury concluded that there was a "natural" path along which nature herself would aid the navigator. No doubt there were similar "natural" paths through other seas. To acquire more information than the depot contained, he took up the common-sensical device, much used by meterologists and natural history men, of distributing a questionnaire; he dispatched to ship captains an abstract log for the recording of force and direction of winds, currents, temperature of air and water, and the like. In return for filling in the blanks, merchant mariners would receive copies of the charts and sailing directions that Maury derived from the data. Captains of naval vessels would simply obey orders—or be reported to the Secretary.[10]

Collation of data over a five-year period from the store of logbooks and the abstract logs, as well as the blank charts he also distributed to naval captains, revealed that ships had been making outrageously long detours on the route from New York to Rio in an attempt to escape purely imaginary currents. It was estimated that some had sailed far enough out of the way to have crossed the Atlantic three times. With the new body of information, Maury was enabled to lay out the "Fair Way to Rio," specifying the position at which ships could cross the equator at various times of the year. The first ship to follow his sailing directions (1848) effected a saving of thirty-five days on the round trip.

In the merchant service, where time indeed was money, Maury's *Wind and Current Charts* quickly came into demand, the Navy offering them free of charge to those who would record their observations in the abstract log and return them to the observatory. Gradually, sufficient data accumulated for charts of the Atlantic, Indian, and Pacific oceans and for more specialized charts depicting trade winds, ocean temperatures, storm and rain charts, and finally a whale chart.

The gold rush to California brought Maury's charts into their own, for by 1851 they had shortened the six-month voyage round the Horn by forty-odd days. Sailing the path Maury had found, the clippers reduced the passage still further, the *Flying Cloud* making the run in just under ninety days in 1851. The clipper, "the noblest work that has ever come from the hands of man," Maury observed, could thus "astonish the world" because it had been "guided by the lights of science, to contend with the elements." The astonished world responded with praise for him who had made such speed possible.[11]

Maury's hydrographical investigations had led a man of local allegiances (Virginia, the South, the Navy) to think in global terms. And when in 1851 Britain proposed to cooperate with the United States in making standard meteorological observations, Maury responded by organizing an international conference on marine meteorology. At Brussels in 1853 delegates from nine European nations agreed on a standard set of observations and a standard abstract log to be kept on warships of the participating nations. Maury found the conference "a sublime spectacle." He rejoiced in the assurance that "Every ship that navigates the high seas, with these charts and blank abstract logs on board, may henceforth be regarded as a floating observatory, a temple of science." With the new volume of information (other nations joined the program from time to time) Maury brought out more charts.[12]

In the meantime, the indefatigable little superintendent interested himself in a variety of exploring enterprises. His unhappy experience with the Wilkes Expedition had not soured him on naval exploration, nor was his pointed nonparticipation in Gilliss's expedition an indication of indifference. To expeditions more in accord with his own enthusiasm, scientific and otherwise, Maury gave unstintingly. He wrote a glowing report on the 1847–48 expedition to the Dead Sea that his old naval friend William F. Lynch conducted in an attempt to fix its level in relation to that of the Mediterranean. (Whether the superintendent shared the pious Lynch's hope of dredging up bits of Sodom and Gomorrah is unclear.) He took greater interest in exploration of the Amazon basin. Persuaded that the currents of the Atlantic decreed a direct commerce between the South and the Amazon region, he was sure that exploration of the area would serve the South as well as science. Not only was Brazil rich in resources, as a slave country she would surely welcome the slaves of the Southern states (their masters, too, he would later assume) when slavery should be abolished in the United States. As it was unthinkable that the erstwhile slaves should become citizens, Brazil would be the South's "safety valve." Maury therefore encouraged—indeed informally sponsored—the expedition to the Amazon and its tributaries conducted in 1851–52 by two Southern officers, his brother-in-law Lieutenant William L. Herndon and Passed Midshipman Lardner Gibbon. For similar reasons he supported Lieutenant Thomas Jefferson Page's expedition of 1853–56 to the Rio de la Plata. Because they promised to yield yet more meteorological and hydrographical data as well as evidence in support of his conviction—shared with many others—that an open sea lay about the North Pole, the Ringgold–Rodgers Expedition of 1853–56 to the North Pacific and the Grinnell expeditions of 1850–55 to the Arctic won his enthusiastic cooperation as well.[13]

Investigating the ocean's winds and currents was no more than Maury's entrée into the field of hydrography, the whole of which he was to claim as his domain—both intellectually and administratively. In 1849 he had begun to plumb the oceans, dispatching the schooner *Taney* to take soundings across the Atlantic at 200-mile intervals, and as part of his *Sailing Directions* for 1853 he published a relief map of the sea bed along approximately the thirty-ninth parallel, the first such effort completed for the deep sea. The *Taney*'s line of soundings revealed a shallow plateau at a depth of 1,500 to 2,000 fathoms, extending the 1,600 miles from Newfoundland to Ireland. With an eye on the transatlantic telegraph service that Cyrus Field was promoting, Maury labeled it the Telegraphic Plateau.[14]

Effective mapping of the ocean bed became possible through an ingenious device invented in 1852 by one of Maury's assistants at the observatory, Lieutenant John Mercer Brooke: a sounding lead that brought up samples of the ocean floor. The samples both confirmed that bottom had been reached (hitherto a matter difficult to determine) and revealed its nature. Their examination by Jacob Whitman Bailey at West Point, the country's pioneer microscopist, revealed them to consist of unbroken calcareous and silicious shells. Characteristically, Maury promptly discerned the practical significance of Bailey's findings: as the shells were unbroken, the bottom was calm, and a telegraph cable might lie along it undisturbed. When the first, if short-lived, cable was laid in 1858, it was laid along the route Maury had proposed and at the season he indicated.[15]

It may truly be said—and it regularly was—that Maury's researches revolutionized ocean communications. But for one of his ambition and energy, merely gathering data to nourish the theories of "closet men of science" was not enough. He aspired to revolutionize the whole domain of knowledge about the sea. (And much of the land as well; in 1854 and 1855 he was campaigning with politicians and agricultural societies to wrest control of land meteorology from the Smithsonian by making scientists of farmers as he had seafarers.) Reminded by his publisher that his *Sailing Directions* were unprotected by copyright and might be appropriated by any enterprising hack, he hastily assembled sections of them, together with various of his articles published in scientific and popular journals over the years, and in the summer of 1854 completed his "magnum opus," as he called it, *The Physical Geography of the Sea.*[16]

The book was his attempt to present his science to the general reading public. For a scientific treatise in a time of increasing specialization it was immediately and immensely popular. And for good reason. Like "Call me

Ishmael," its opening sentence disarms: "There is a river in the ocean." Then follow phrases cadenced like the ocean's own waves. "In the severest droughts it never fails, and in the mightiest floods it never overflows. Its banks and its bottom are of cold water, while its current is of warm. The Gulf of Mexico is its fountain, and its mouth is the Arctic Seas. It is the Gulf Stream."

Admittedly, Maury addressed the book, not primarily to men of science, but to a popular audience; but because he was presenting his science as it had matured in his hands, he inevitably invited the judgment of the international scientific community. And for its members the cadences held fewer charms. Unaccustomed to this sort of thing now, they found it disconcerting—overblown and superfluous. To entice them into his chapter on the influence of ocean currents on the climate of the land, it was necessary to inform them "How the Washington Observatory is warmed" by the gravity flow of hot water. And repeated reference to the "One Intelligence" and "the Almighty hand" that salted the oceans (the same that "cares for the sparrow") struck contemporaries in the scientific community as so many substitutes for sound thinking.[17] Reviewers in the European scientific journals complained of the lack of organization, but the most frequent criticism, in the words of the *Edinburgh Review,* was that the author "theorizes too largely and hazardously, and does not clearly separate the *known* from the *unknown.*"[18]

The few American scientific reviewers were still less kind. The country's premier scientific journal, *Silliman's,* for which Maury had written his first scientific paper, was cursory and cold: "While the work contains much instruction, we cannot adopt some of its theories, believing them unsustained by facts." Less laconic, the reviewer for the *Southern Quarterly Review* agreed. In his "true province as an observer and recorder of facts, and as a discoverer of the currents and prevailing winds of the ocean," Maury showed promise of becoming "a benefactor of mankind." Outside that province, he produced "such crude ideas" as left "true men of science" embarrassed that they "should go forth as specimens of American science."[19]

It was Maury's misfortune to bring out his book at a time when the scientific community was never more exclusive, more jealous for the advancement of science and of science in America. Though few were so exclusive, so jealous, or so imperious as Alexander Dallas Bache, Bache had expressed the sentiments of many of the emerging professional scientists of his and the following generation in his farewell address as president of the American Association for the Advancement of Science in 1851. He warned the members that the great danger in America lay in "a modified charlatanism, which makes merit in one subject an excuse for asking authority in others, or in all, and, because it has made real progress in one branch of science, claims to be an arbiter in others." Then more pointedly, "In a country where everything is free, and every one may obtain a hearing, notoriety is often dearly purchased by the sacrifice of some portion of real reputation." Not least among the merits of the specialization he and they championed was that it obliged the investigator to confine his pronouncements to his competence. "True men of science" had thus observed Maury's career with mounting apprehension, had watched as, unschooled in astronomy, he sought the post of astronomer at the national observatory only to neglect astronomy and sabotage Gilliss's expedition to Chile. They had been obliged to look to their defenses when, placing the interests of the Navy above the advancement of science, he sought to extend the Navy's jurisdiction over Bache's Coast Survey and the observatory's over Joseph Henry's Smithsonian network in land meteorology. They quite appreciated the useful work he had done, but, a distinction the public seemingly failed to grasp, useful work was not true science, nor were ships and barns its palaces.[20]

A distinguishing mark of "true men of science" was their willingness to submit their work to the judgment of their peers, and to them alone, for as the *Southern Quarterly Review*'s man observed, they are "the only tribunal by which its merits can be judged; none other is competent." As peers perhaps foresaw, Maury showed little in the way of submission. In advancing from the known to the unknown, he had not hesitated to march up to the cannon's mouth. In opposition to Sir John Herschel, he denied (and with some reason) any role to the winds in influencing ocean currents, and in response to both Herschel and the courteous objections of James P. Espy (1785–1860), the "Storm King," he clung to his own scheme for the circulation of the earth's atmosphere—winds coverage toward the poles, currents of air in vertical motion cross one another near the equator—notions unsupported by observation. (His *idée fixe* that magnetism controlled the winds made no known converts either within or without the scientific community.)

While little of Maury's theorizing served to advance the science of the seas, his theory of the general circulation of the atmosphere did result in advance, but only by way of its refutation. Attracting the exasperated notice of William Ferrel (1817–91), then with the Nautical Almanac Office and later the Coast Survey, it provoked the latter to a formulation of his own. By reversing the direction Maury had assigned surface winds near the poles and introducing the effects of the earth's rotation on the circulation of both the atmosphere and the oceans, Ferrel was able to account for phenomena that resisted Maury's theory. "None of Maury's theoretical generalizations," says the most recent editor of the *Physical Geography*, "approaches in significance the effect of his scheme of atmospheric circulation on Ferrel, who was sufficiently outraged by it to apply his knowledge of theoretical mechanics to the motions of the atmosphere." Yet Maury took no notice of Ferrel or his theory in the next (and last) edition of his book. Other criticisms he ignored or responded to with a touch of the old "Harry Bluff" polemics. It was a stance that only served to substantiate the suspicion that Maury was submitting not to the judgment of his peers but to the public, a public whose acclaim perhaps had persuaded him that he had no peers.[21]

The Navy was no more ready with acclaim than were "true men of science," and Maury would leave its service a lieutenant still. Denial of promotion, officially rationalized on the ground that lameness incapacitated him for command at sea, only further vexed a temperament that made for a tetchy colleague and a tyrannical superior, a temperament that perhaps as much as the game leg (or the widely resented and well remembered, if finally realized, demands for naval reform; or the Navy's traditional indifference to the cause of science) forever foreclosed to Maury the high command he craved.

The rest of Maury's history as a scientist is soon told. When Virginia seceded, Maury resigned his commission. (To his fury Secretary Welles recorded him as "dismissed the service," and, a further insult, gave Gilliss his place at the observatory.) His welcome South was only lukewarm, for in Congress Jefferson Davis had long ago aligned himself with Bache and Henry, and Maury had once reported the Confederacy's ranking naval officer, Franklin Buchanan, to the Secretary for failing to fill in one of the abstract logs. But appointed commander in the Confederate Navy, he worked at devising submarine mines. Dispatched to England as a Confederate naval commissioner to see to the purchase of warships, he busied himself for the duration with petitioning Palmerston to put a stop to the war in America and by experimenting with land mines. He was at Havana, returning with a supply of mine equipment when he learned the news from Appomattox. "Vox populi," as he contemptuously put it, having won out at home, the disillusioned democrat sought out the nearest monarch and settled in Mexico with the intention of persuading several thousand Virginia slaveowners to join him. Maximilian welcomed him warmly, but there was not much for Maury to do. In 1866 he returned to England, where Cambridge awarded him (and Alfred Tennyson) an LL.D., and friends got up a purse to relieve his want. He finally came home in 1868, when the Virginia Military Institute offered him a professorship in physics. There, once again evoking the vox populi (agricultural now in place of maritime), he resumed the old battle with Joseph Henry over who should administer land meteorology, wrote geography books for children, and planned an inventory of the state's natural resources. Maury died at Lexington on 1 February 1873.[22]

It has been suggested that Maury did not command mathematics well enough to understand William Ferrel's theory. Few did, and there was the rub. The emergence of scientific professionalization and specialization made for difficulty in the equalitarian society. There was something profoundly undemocratic about this clique of scientists conferring with one another in Latin. (Compare Charles Wilkes's determination to publish the exploring botanists' descriptions in English in place of the accustomed Latin.) Mistrust was inevitable. As champions of American science before a skeptical world, the circle about Bache and Henry were forever on guard against the charlatan. Wrong-headedness was one thing, and as secretary of the Smithsonian, Joseph

Henry time and again patiently sought to entice village cranks out of their cracked pots; but wrong-headedness persisted in, wrong-headedness boosted onto the shoulders of the multitude—that was charlatanism. No doubt Maury's critics rejoiced that their old enemy had written a book. But his attempts at theory would hardly have attracted the concern they did had it not been for the position he had assumed in the public mind. They saw notoriety in his celebrity, infamy in his fame. As the acclaim mounted, so in proportion did the threat he posed. They watched as he assumed the mantle of the scientist to posture before a nation in which science was dependent on public support. As a benefit performance it might have been excusable, but the man seemed consistently to act for the advancement, not of science—what science he had was dismayingly casual—but of the Navy, the South, commerce, the observatory, himself. To Henry, whose researches in electromagnetism produced the first telegraph but who refused to interrupt his investigations to patent the contraption, Maury could only be the interested investigator and so no true man of science.[23]

What Maury saw in his antagonists was an aristocratic cabal of Northern "scientifics" (also a favorite epithet with Charles Wilkes, who had his troubles with these people, too); would-be high priests of science who sought to control scientific endeavor in the nation by their influence over the federal patronage; "closet men of science" who disdained the practical and preached the necessity of academic training and specialization. Their enmity, their interference, he could only lay to jealousy of one justly recompensed in popular acclaim for his contributions to the public welfare. To their consternation the self-educated Tennessee farm boy (albeit of respectable Huguenot ancestry) had achieved distinction in the world of science yet remained the good democrat withal, at home with seafarers and farmers and faithfully asking the permission of Congress for each decoration a monarch sought to bestow.[24]

With some eloquence, Maury put his case (in the third person) to Belgium's Astronomer Royal in 1860. His position at the observatory, he explained, obliged him to seek "practical results" that would benefit navigation. "He is therefore compelled to work by stealth, as it were, and to treat questions of science merely as questions that are incidental to the main object." And that was not the only restriction: "He has to work for and with a class of men—'old salts'—most of whom hate what is called science and feel a sort of contempt for your so-called man of science. His success depended upon interesting these men in his labours, and in inducing them to become, almost without their knowing it, themselves active and efficient laborers in the cause of science . . . . Moreover, in treating the questions of science as they arose, he had to treat it in a way that would most interest his fellow labourers at sea." And, he poignantly asked, "Has he not therefore . . . rendered better service to the cause of science than he could have done by following the rigid reserve and cold formulae of calculating analysis?"

Even in this century, when the line between the pure and the practical in science is less distinct than it appeared to the "scientifics," the historian can only agree with that argument. Neither by temperament nor ability was Maury equipped for calculating analysis. But the historian must assent, too, with the physicist Henry Rowland at the century's end (as well as with Bache in his address and the anonymous reviewer in the *Southern Quarterly Review*) that "He who makes two blades of grass grow where one grew before is the benefactor of mankind; but he who obscurely works to find the laws of such growth is the intellectual superior as well as the greater benefactor . . . ." It does his career no disservice to conclude that, with even less taste for obscurity than for calculating analysis, Maury could only attain the lesser success.[25]

FURTHER READING

In his time and since, Matthew Fontaine Maury has been the popular ideal of the American scientist: humble birth, practical accomplishment, international celebrity. There even hovers the aura of the Lost Cause. In some degree the folklore has colored nearly all the biographies, from the admiring daughter's (Diana Fontaine Maury Corbin, *A Life of Matthew Fontaine Maury, U.S.N. and C.S.N.*) to Charles Lee Lewis, *Matthew Fontaine Maury, the Pathfinder of the Seas,* to the latest and by far the most ambitious, Frances Leigh Williams, *Matthew Fontaine Maury: Scientist of the Sea.* The exception is Patricia Jahns, *Matthew Fontaine Maury and Joseph Henry: Scientists of the Civil War.*

Though the paucity of documentation is exasperating, the Jahns book derives from considerable research. Henry is its hero, to whom the resentful, self-righteous, ever scheming Maury is a considerable nuisance in their continuing administrative warfare. In playing Maury against the champions of the new science, she rightly perceives the significance of Maury's career in American science.

The Williams biography, with its nearly exhaustive documentation and its excellent bibliography of Maury's writings, is unlikely to be outdone in covering the facts of Maury's life. Interpretation is another matter, for like its predecessors it tends to the worshipful and so fails to explain its subject's turbulent relations with the scientific community. In the same year there appeared John Leighly's edition of Maury's *Physical Geography of the Sea.* In his introduction Leighly examines the reception accorded the book both by the public and by European and American scientists. His own view is that Maury's attempts at theory "fell below the level of the best contemporary knowledge" and have had a pernicious influence on popular understanding. Leighly thinks no better of Maury's prose.

In a perceptive essay reviewing the Williams and Leighly volumes, "Two Views of Maury . . . and a Third," Nathan Reingold, editor of the Joseph Henry Papers, dismisses Maury as an important theoretician and sees him as the survivor of an older tradition rapidly being supplanted by the new professionals, whose abomination of Maury derived from their own exaggeratedly clear notion of the line between their disinterested science and Maury's merely utilitarian. Future volumes of *The Papers of Joseph Henry* promise to enlarge our understanding of Maury's relations with his scientific contemporaries.

Edward L. Towle's long dissertation, "Science, Commerce and the Navy," finds that Maury displayed a commonsense understanding of the relation between the pure and the applied, and that in consequence his researches effectively stimulated contemporary investigations in both natural history and the physical sciences.

For more on the new "scientifics" (who were to be the founders of the National Academy of Sciences), see Lillian B. Miller, *The Lazzaroni: Science and Scientists in Mid-Nineteenth Century America* and Sally G. Kohlstedt, *The Formation of the American Scientific Community* (on National Institute, pp. 54–57). Essential to understanding the emerging role of science in government is A. Hunter Dupree, *Science in the Federal Government, a History of Policies and Activities to 1940*.

NOTES

1. Frances Leigh Williams, *Matthew Fontaine Maury*, 53–54, 107; Bowditch to Maury, 21 April 1835, and Bache to Maury, 14 April 1835: both quoted in Maury, *A New Theoretical and Practical Treatise on Navigation*, 337.

2. Edgar Allen Poe, "Maury's Navigation," *Southern Literary Messenger*, II (1836): 454–55; Maury to Richard L. Maury, 29 October 1835 (quoted in Williams, *Maury*, 107–8); Williams, *Maury*, 110–11, 157.

3. William Stanton, *The Great United States Exploring Expedition*, 31–32; J. N. Reynolds, *Address on the Subject of a Surveying and Exploring Expedition*, 22, 72.

4. Williams, *Maury*, 115, 118–19; Stanton, *Great United States Exploring Expedition*, 63, Chapter 23.

5. Williams, *Maury*, 119, 121, 133–37.

6. Maury, Letter to National Institution for the Promotion of Science.

7. Nathan Reingold, ed., *Science in Nineteenth-Century America*, 135; Williams, *Maury*, 148; Ruth Shepard Granniss, "James Melville Gilliss," *Dictionary of American Biography*; J. M. Gilliss to Elias Loomis, 18 October 1844, in Reingold, ed., *Science in Nineteenth-Century America*, 138–39.

8. Williams, *Maury*, 163–65; Simon Newcomb, *The Reminiscences of an Astronomer*, 102–6. Walker, who had died at the early age of forty-eight, pioneered in the application of telegraphy to astronomical observations. Coffin and Hubbard would be elected to membership in the National Academy of Sciences.

9. "Astronomical Observations," *H. R. Report 470*, 30th Cong., 1st Sess., 5–6 (American Philosophical Society's resolution; that of the American Academy of Arts and Sciences appears on 43–44). On Maury's disapproval: Maury to F. P. Stanton (Chairman, House Committee on Naval Affairs), 21 March 1848, in ibid, 52–53; and Gilliss to Benjamin Peirce, 22 October 1847, in Reingold, ed., *Science in Nineteenth-Century America*, 139–40. On Maury's neglect: ibid., 135–36, and F[razer, John F.], "The U.S. Naval Astronomical Expedition to the Southern Hemisphere, during the years 1849–1852."

10. M. F. M[aury], "The Commercial Prospects of the South"; William C. Redfield, "On Tides, and the Prevailing Currents of the Ocean and Atmosphere"; Williams, *Maury*, 149, 150, 151, 181.

11. Williams, *Maury*, 149–51, 181.

12. Ibid., 219, 221.

13. M. F. Maury, "The Dead Sea Expedition"; M. F. M[aury], "The Commercial Prospects of the South"; [James Henry] H[ammond], "Maury in South American and Amazonia"; Williams, *Maury*, 202; Edward L. Towle, "Science, Commerce and the Navy on the Seafaring Frontier (1842–1861): The Role of Lieutenant M. F. Maury and the U.S. Naval Hydrographic Office in Naval Exploration, Commercial Expansion and Oceanography before the Civil War," 437–68 and Chapter VII.

14. Williams, *Maury*, 228.

15. George M. Brooke, Jr., *John M. Brooke: Naval Scientist and Educator*, 54–59; Williams, *Maury*, 230–31, 245.

16. Ibid., 213–24, 259; John Leighly, Editor's Introduction to Matthew F. Maury, *The Physical Geography of the Sea and Its Meteorology*.

17. [Henry Holland?], "The Physical Geography of the Sea"; Williams, *Maury*, 264; Leighly, Introduction; Maury, *Physical Geography of the Sea*, 63, 69.

18. [Henry Holland?], "The Physical Geography of the Sea," esp. 380.

19. "The Physical Geography of the Sea," *American Journal of Science*; "The Physical Geography of the Sea," *Southern Quarterly Review*.

20. A. D. Bache, "Address of Professor A. D. Bache"; Williams, *Maury*, 204; Reingold, ed., *Science in Nineteenth-Century America*, 146.

21. Maury, *Physical Geography of the Sea*, 40–41, 149–51; James P. Espy, "Fourth Meteorological Report," *Sen. Exec. Doc. 65*, 34th Cong., 3rd Sess. (1859), 159; Leighly, Introduction; William Ferrel, "An Essay on the Winds and the Currents of the Ocean."

22. Williams, *Maury*, Chapter XVIII, n. 108, 372; Patricia Jahns, *Matthew Fontaine Maury and Joseph Henry: Scientists of the Civil War*, 187–88, 271; Williams, *Maury*, 473.

23. Leighly, Introduction; Stanton, *Exploring Expeditions*, 334; Arthur P. Molella, "At the Edge of Science: Joseph Henry, 'Visionary Theorizers,' and

the Smithsonian Institution," *Annals of Science* 41 (1984): 445–61; Reingold, ed., *Science in Nineteenth-Century America*, 146.

24. Williams, *Maury*, 223 and Chapter XI, n. 150.

25. Maury to Adolphe Quetelet, 7 December 1860, quoted in ibid., 324–25; Henry A. Rowland, "The Highest Aim of the Physicist."

CHARLES WILKES:
THE NAVAL OFFICER AS
EXPLORER AND DIPLOMAT

BY GEOFFREY S. SMITH

More than most naval officers in the nineteenth century, Charles Wilkes exerted a significant impact upon his nation's growth. The contributions of this ambitious officer, who expected much of himself and more of his subordinates, touched American diplomacy, commerce, scientific development, and exploration. Wherever Wilkes went, it seemed, achievement and controversy followed in his wake. Best known for his provocative role in precipitating the *Trent* affair in 1861, which brought the United States and Great Britain to the verge of war, he also allows historians to examine the connection between naval exploration and antebellum expansionism within the larger context of American responses to the outside world.

In the years before the Civil War, American naval officers often initiated and resolved crises on their own. Even prior to the emergence of what Peter Karsten dubbed "the naval aristocracy," several officers grasped the relationship between commercial expansion, scientific achievement, and the strength of republican government.[1] Yet during Wilkes's lifetime, with the exception of the Civil War, most of his fellow citizens did not appreciate— indeed, they railed against—the need for a strong naval establishment. Antimilitarism, combined with frugality in government, resulted in jeers at Yankee cockboats trailing in the wake of British men-o'-war. Most Americans considered the Atlantic Ocean (and the Royal Navy) adequate for coastal defense. But this narrow view minimizes the nonmilitary and diplomatic functions executed by the U.S. Navy, for during much of the century, especially in peacetime, the service became a sharp cutting edge of American diplomacy. Its explorers played prominent roles in various parts of the world, especially the Pacific, the Far East, and the diplomatic maneuvers for control of the Pacific Northwest.

The ways in which a single naval officer—a scientist, publicist, explorer, naval commander, and self-appointed definer and defender of the national interest—thought about these roles indicate Wilkes's importance to an understanding of the dynamics of American expansion and, not incidentally, the shift of the Navy from wood and sail to iron, steel, and steam. A transitional figure whose discipline and sternness exemplified the "old navy," Wilkes nonetheless displayed support for scientific exploration, technological efficiency, intraservice reform, modernized strategy during war, and the commercial and political destiny of the United States. In these and other ways he foreshadowed contributions by such post–Civil War navalists as Robert Shufeldt, Stephen B. Luce, and David D. Porter—those influential but still underrated forerunners of Alfred Thayer Mahan.

A grandnephew of the famous English dissenter John Wilkes, Charles Wilkes was born on 3 April 1798. His youth coincided with America's naval war with France and with the successful acquittal of national seapower during the War of 1812. His death on 8 February 1877, came during an era when the republic's naval strength touched its nadir. The son of an erstwhile Loyalist whose mercantile connections focused his family's attention upon the Atlantic, young Charles grew to maturity with a keen interest in scientific and maritime topics. An able student with private tutors, he concentrated upon mathematics, navigation, and draftsmanship. While in his teens he idolized an older brother who served in the War of 1812 and also joined in celebrations held in New York to commemorate naval successes during that conflict. At the age of seventeen, against his father's wishes, he joined the merchant marine and got his first whiff of salt air on a voyage to Europe. A second journey placed him under the command of a former officer in the French navy—a contact that led to Wilkes's appointment as a midshipman in the U.S. Navy on 1 January 1818.

The need for greater national attention to the scientific aspects of navigation and naval technology engrossed Wilkes's attention early in his career. From 1824 to 1826, while preparing for his lieutenant's examination, he worked with Dr. Ferdinand Hassler, a Swiss immigrant who in 1802 founded what became the United States Coast and Geodetic Survey. From that encounter, and from later surveys of Narragansett Bay and St. George's Shoal, Wilkes learned to apply principles of geodesy, hydrography, and astronomy to navigation. Hassler's disorganization and primitive surveying instruments also provided a source of irritation, pricking Wilkes's desire to see the nation jettison its dependence upon European equipment and expertise.

In 1833 Wilkes put his ideas to work when he became superintendent of the Naval Depot of Charts and Instruments. To attract the attention of Congress and to facilitate his astronomical experiments, he soon transferred the depot from the western part of Washington, D.C. to Capitol Hill. He became the first American to build an observatory and use fixed astronomical instruments.

Charles Wilkes. Engraving by A. H. Ritchie. *Courtesy of the Naval Academy Museum.*

He also used this office to stress the point that by expanding the charting of Atlantic ports and coastal waterways, naval surveys and exploration would aid commercial interests and produce America's nautical independence.

The advisability of a global exploring expedition assumed priority in Wilkes's assessment of the needs of the Navy. When President John Quincy Adams proposed such an expedition in 1825, Wilkes had agreed that such a voyage might strengthen the interdependence of the scientific community and the Navy and augment the reputation of both. In addition, he realized that the project would require an experienced commander. Already a surveyor of ability and a budding naval scientist, Wilkes felt himself uniquely qualified for the post.

Yet before the Navy could further national scientific prestige, shipboard behavior of captains and crew alike had to change. Wilkes's introduction to life at sea left him unhappy with naval mores. Although nautical efficiency required discipline and order, he also felt that life in the old navy left much to be desired. "No school could have been worse for the morals and none so viciously constituted," he wrote. Younger men could hardly view the Navy as an institution of national prestige when older officers, in the absence of a merit system, stood above the law and made others "subservient to their pleasures, caprices, and gratifications." Neither the Navy's nor the nation's interests were served by "debauching and drunken blackguards" masquerading as captains and lacking any understanding of the potential of scientific advancements to navigation. Troubled by petty bickering among officers, debilitated by a lack of pride, and hamstrung by an uneducated officer corps, the Navy needed reform. Wilkes proposed to meet these problems through creation of a naval academy, but he also stressed that officers should first secure practical experience through a sea cruise. Naval midshipmen might be reasonably well educated, but their understanding of shipboard etiquette was often abysmal. [2]

Wilkes's feelings about the Navy were similar to his general outlook toward politics. A social aristocrat in Jacksonian America (albeit a Democrat as well), he criticized political patronage as demoralizing and felt that good men should be above it. Too often, party harmony dictated sacrificing one's personal integrity. Wilkes's antipolitical animus was understandable: institutional politics had stifled naval reform in the early nineteenth century; sectional and personal politics in 1825 undercut Adams's proposed exploration of the Pacific Ocean and Northwest Coast; and when Congress created a Navy-directed scientific expedition in May 1836, interdepartmental and individual jealousy combined with mismanagement by the Secretary of the Navy to jeopardize the undertaking.

Impressed by Wilkes's scientific reputation, Secretary of the Navy Mahlon Dickerson had proposed that Wilkes command one of the expedition's smaller vessels. Commander-designate Thomas ap Catesby Jones balked at the proposal, however, and argued in unabashed old-navy rhetoric that Wilkes's attainments were of a "peculiar nature."[3] Jones explained that Wilkes's competence extended to caring for instruments and surveying, but was not, under any circumstances, to be considered "as [befitting] a commander, or for any other performance of regular navy duty."[4] What was needed, he believed, was an experienced officer who could command respect on the quarterdeck.

Wilkes, in turn, berated Jones's lack of interest in science and ridiculed the proposal that twenty-one civilian scientists accompany the expedition. Anticipating later navalists who zealously guarded their control over scientific matters related to navigation, Wilkes argued that the civilian presence would transform naval regulars into inconsequential "hewers of wood and drawers of water."[5] To protect his reputation, Wilkes quit the expedition and returned to New York, resuming his scientific work.

In his absence, the exploring expedition ran aground on administrative shoals. Congress's plan for a voyage of exploration to facilitate trade with Latin America, aid Pacific whaling interests, and augment the reputation of national science became instead an albatross for President Martin Van Buren. Even John Quincy Adams, the spiritual father of the voyage, announced that he hoped only to hear that the expedition had sailed. Blame for the delay was primarily Dickerson's: after contacting several scientific groups to find men competent to accompany the voyage, the Secretary hesitated to convene them, failed to pay them, and proved unable to provide necessary equipment. The delay made it appear that rival French and British expeditions, then preparing to sail, might steal the thunder of the U.S. Navy.

Jones quit his post as superintendent of the Depot of Charts and Instruments in November 1837 because of poor health. When Dickerson failed to name a suitable replacement, Van Buren transferred supervision of the undertaking to Secretary of War Joel R. Poinsett. The latter, a capable administrator and leading advocate of government science, quickly named Lieutenant Wilkes to head the expedition. Wilkes's relative youth did not prejudice his qualities as a navigator and seaman; indeed, his scientific ability made him one of the few officers qualified to command.

Nevertheless, Wilkes's appointment in April 1838 threatened once more to upset preparations for the expedition. The two-year delay in mounting the expedition—and Wilkes's inexperience at sea—sparked renewed criticism from many quarters. Moreover, the new commander's well-known temper and impulsiveness, together with his earlier resignation, rankled the feelings of colleagues and politicians alike. Lieutenant C. K. Stribling, who equaled Wilkes in rank, called the appointment "highly injurious" to the morale of senior officers; a congressman wondered how a junior officer could command respect on so difficult a journey; and another lawmaker suggested that ships assigned to the expedition be transferred to the coast squadron for routine duty.[6] One highly respected officer, Captain Beverly Kennon, succeeded in forcing the administration to divest the expedition of its military character. He did so to avoid what he termed a dangerous precedent, and his plan prevented departure from the custom of selecting commanding officers from senior ranks of the Navy.[7]

The most vitriolic criticism of Wilkes, however, came from Lieutenant Matthew Fontaine Maury, another naval scientist, whose hydrographic skill rivaled his adversary's. Maury scorned Wilkes as "a cunning little Jacob" who had campaigned assiduously for the position. Wilkes, Maury asserted, lacked the experience necessary to master simple shipboard routine. He was merely a

The South Seas Exploring Expedition, 1838–42. Wilkes's flagship, the USS *Vincennes*, in Disappointment Bay, Antarctica. Painting after a sketch by Charles Wilkes. *Courtesy of Captain Glenn Howell.*

shore-bound sinecurist—an armchair admiral—who clearly did not merit his position.[8]

For the moment, Wilkes ignored these attacks. With Poinsett's support he moved swiftly to take charge of the project. Wilkes oversaw personally the repair, equipping, and final selection of ships assigned to the cruise; he reassigned sailors and soothed their dissatisfactions; and he named his old Brooklyn friend, Lieutenant William L. Hudson, second in command. He also reduced the number of civilian scientists assigned to the voyage, explaining that the Navy was fully qualified to execute scientific tasks related to navigation. Finally, he tested and calibrated his instruments at the Naval Observatory in Washington to check their accuracy. Late in July, when Van Buren, Poinsett, and new Secretary of the Navy James Kirke Paulding visited the squadron at Hampton Roads, Virginia, the project received what appeared to be an official blessing.

Nevertheless, a serious and potentially damaging problem remained. That difficulty stemmed from Wilkes's abrasive personality and from his dissatisfaction that promotion had not accompanied his new command. Named to a post of high responsibility, charged with a mission of international scientific import, and representing the nation and the Navy before the world, he felt

sharply the lack of power and prestige that came with professional advancement. His crew's carping reference to their "lieutenant-commodore" did
nothing to assuage his wounded self-image. He brought this situation to Van
Buren's attention and reminded the President that a failure to rectify the
existing state of affairs would do "great injustice" to the expedition and its
commanding officers.[9] Patriotism alone, Wilkes later wrote, prevented him
from again quitting the voyage.

Unwilling (or unable) to see that the administration's failure to raise his
rank resulted at least partially from its desire to prevent further controversy,
Wilkes became obsessed with the successful execution of his mission. This
presumed "slight" no doubt contributed to his subsequent transformation into
a shipboard martinet. Pique also led him to hide a commodore's uniform and
pennant on board the flagship *Vincennes* for later use. Characteristically, he
would resolve the problem himself.

The United States Exploring Expedition of 1838–42 illustrated the broad
functions executed by naval officers in the 1840s and 1850s. Instructed to
"extend the empires of commerce and science; to diminish the hazards of the
ocean and [to] point out to future navigators a course by which they might
avoid dangers and find safety," Wilkes assumed command of a squadron of six
ships, 83 officers, and 342 enlisted men.[10] The last global voyage dependent
entirely upon sail, the flotilla departed Hampton Roads on 8 August 1838—
three months after Matthew C. Perry crossed the Atlantic in the *Fulton*, the
maiden transoceanic voyage of a steam-powered vessel.

One of numerous contemporary episodes pitting civilized man against
primitive nature, the Wilkes expedition encompassed human elements of
courage, tragedy, and humor as it completed an arduous journey of nearly four
years. The American seafarers ranged waters from the Antarctic and the South
Pacific to the Juan de Fuca Strait, surveying approximately 280 islands, about
800 miles of coastline and contiguous territory in Oregon and Alta California,
and some 1,500 miles along the Antarctic continent. While the expedition
made few discoveries in the Pacific, the maps and charts resulting from the
voyage anticipated Matthew Fontaine Maury's *Physical Geography of the Sea*
(1855) in providing American merchantmen new certitude as they plied
maritime routes.

The expedition helped clarify and augment the Navy's role in American
diplomacy. At midcentury the Navy's major tasks, aside from showing the
flag and protecting American citizens and property (private interests predominated over strictly "national" interests abroad), centered upon commercial, scientific, and political reconnaissance. As collators and interpreters of
reams of information—anthropological and ethnographic as well as strategic
and economic—Wilkes and his cohorts helped lay a foundation upon which
later navalists built a new service that became a powerful ally of the republic's
thriving network of global trade.

A key part of Wilkes's work was a series of warnings to the Navy Department of the need to strengthen the American presence in Polynesia and the Pacific Northwest. In addition to recommending and publicizing points of commercial and strategic interest, surveying maritime channels, and stressing the need to increase American power throughout the Pacific, the voyagers also served as unofficial diplomats in such remote places as Brazil, New South Wales, Manila, and Singapore. The expedition proved that during the 1840s Manifest Destiny was as much a maritime as a territorial force. Indeed, the personnel of the expedition became "maritime frontiersmen," mirror images of the thousands of mountain men, traders, pioneers, adventurers, and army surveyors who trekked across the continent to the Pacific.

The expedition played an important part in the diplomacy of westward expansion. The voyage enabled Wilkes to point out the hazards of crossing the bar at the entrance to the Columbia River (which resulted in the destruction of one of his ships), and to publicize the inadequacies of Columbia Bay as an ocean harbor. More important, Wilkes underlined the strategic importance of territory adjoining forts Walla Walla and Tacoma, the commercial potential of the Juan de Fuca Strait and Puget Sound, and the magnificence of the harbor at San Francisco. These descriptions—appearing in a special confidential report to the government and in Wilkes's five-volume *Narrative*—affected various Anglo–American boundary discussions in the 1840s and generated subsequent official interest in California.

The Wilkes Expedition also coincided with important advances in transportation and technology. These intensified the desire of Americans to subdue their "half-known country."[11] Less an end in itself than a means to several specific ends, the project provided "a public purpose which the democratic society could properly patronize."[12] For the first time in American history, civilian scientists used the Navy to carry out scientific objectives. While the Lewis and Clark Expedition of 1804–6 marked the first marriage of science and military, the Wilkes voyage fixed scientific exploration as a province of government, and it established the scientists' dependence upon the military for transport and logistical services.

Yet if this ambitious undertaking in government-sponsored science stimulated the growth of scientific agencies, it also posed problems. A prototype of the close, uneasy alliance of government, science, and the military in the twentieth century, the expedition foreshadowed an equally modern concern— securing and maintaining cooperation between civilians concerned with "pure" science and regular naval personnel who stressed improvements in naval technology and architecture. Of necessity, Wilkes spent much time mediating between civilian demands and the mundane needs of his sailors. Though he did not always reconcile these differences, he was able to ensure that they did not jeopardize the objectives of the voyage. To this end he ordered each officer to keep a journal, remained aloof from shipboard politics, and worked to prevent the formation of cliques. An indefatigable worker, Wilkes personally supervised all work in geodesy, geography, hydrography, astronomy, physics, and surveying. If he expected much of his subordinates, he also drove himself mercilessly.

In addition to its other objectives, the expedition sought to protect whalers and traders in the Pacific by initiating relations with aboriginal tribes through "wood-and-water treaties" and, if necessary, force. Though usually restrained in his dealings with native peoples, when Wilkes felt that power would have a salutary effect, he acted with dispatch. Crew members once imprisoned a native chief implicated in a prior murder of sailors from an American brig, and on another occasion, after natives pilfered supplies from a disabled cutter, Wilkes ordered their village razed. On the island of Malolo, after the murder of two of his crew (including his nephew), Wilkes ordered the destruction of two more villages. These early instances of gunboat diplomacy marked a step toward Western law and order and were designed to impress natives with the consequences of harm to American vessels and visitors.

When Wilkes appointed agents to represent American whalers and traders at Upolu and the main island of Fiji, he also exercised quasi-diplomatic powers. The agents earned their posts by arranging with native chieftains for the safety of visiting ships and crews (and the protection of the natives from the sailors); but because few American ships visited these outposts, the agents had little to do. Still, Wilkes's early attempts to establish binding agreements with native chiefs in Samoa and Fiji illustrated the growing interest of naval commanders in protecting American overseas property and in preserving order and stability. Anticipating similar agreements between army officers and Indians after the Civil War, Wilkes's accords also foreshadowed executive agreements of the sort naval commander William T. Truxton concluded with chieftains in the Marianas, Gilberts, and Marshalls in the 1870s.

Three incidents during the expedition, in New Zealand, Hawaii, and Oregon, illustrated some of the prime themes of nineteenth-century naval diplomacy. Like many of his countrymen, Wilkes was an Anglophobe, and events during the journey exacerbated that sentiment, strengthened his cognizance of the relationship between economic progress and political sovereignty, and revealed him as an ardent advocate of the republic's Manifest Destiny.

The first of these episodes took place in 1840—shortly after England established a measure of sovereignty in New Zealand by negotiating the Treaty of Waitangi with some five hundred Maori chiefs—a pact that ceded North Island to the crown. Wilkes arrived in New Zealand a few days after the signing and determined that James R. Clendon—an Englishman who a year earlier had become the first American consul for the important trading post of the Bay of Islands—had used his diplomatic post to force the chiefs to agree. Clendon quit his office in 1841, but not before new import laws and tonnage duties severely damaged the profitable Yankee whaling and shipping trade.

These new regulations forbade American whalers from hunting in their favorite waters and curing their oil on North Island. Between 1840 and 1841, the number of American vessels calling at the Bay of Islands dropped by 50 percent, and Wilkes estimated that the loss from the annual oil yield would reach three hundred thousand dollars. The Treaty of Waitangi, Wilkes averred, transformed the Maori into prey for "the hosts of adventurers flooding in from all parts," and he found in Clendon's role proof of the need for American citizens to serve as commercial representatives abroad.[13] Although Wilkes did not contest the treaty (and thereby jeopardize the expedition), he considered the agreement as pointing to a deficiency in American diplomacy. Clearly, commercial connections counted for more in becoming a diplomatic representative than either ability or sympathy for U.S. interests.

When the expedition reached Hawaii in late September 1840, Wilkes praised the enterprise and culture of its inhabitants. He also noted with interest the strategic promise of ports at Lahaina and Pearl River, and the commercial future of such island products as coffee, cattle, indigo, and sugar. Wilkes expressed surprise at the apparent empathy between local American missionaries and merchants, but realized soon that this cordiality signified less a community of interest than a defensive drawing together in the face of British and French challenges to American trade and religious interests. The years 1840 and 1841 witnessed a sharp, though temporary, statistical increase in British trade with the islands.

In addition, as several Protestant clergymen warned, France had adopted an aggressive Hawaiian policy. In 1837 and 1839, French naval officers forced King Kamehameha III to sign treaties guaranteeing extraterritoriality to French citizens, the free importation of French wines, and the toleration and protection of Catholicism. Wilkes shared the Protestant clergy's view that French wine would accelerate the physical and spiritual decline of sailors and natives alike, but he took no action beyond forwarding his impressions to Washington. With no specific orders, he rejected Kamehameha's suggestion to renew and strengthen the agreement that Captain Thomas ap Catesby Jones had concluded a decade earlier.

A theoretical devotion to global liberty and equality infused the rhetoric of many Americans at midcentury. But navalists did not always share these feelings. Wilkes's rejection of a petition for a territorial constitution presented by American settlers in the Willamette Valley of Oregon indicates that he responded to pragmatic rather than ideological pressures. His refusal, which was similar to his government's response to Hungarian rebel Louis Kossuth a decade later, underlined Wilkes's appreciation of the danger of a premature action that might jeopardize the national interest by placing the nation in a situation it could not handle. American interests in New Zealand and Hawaii did not warrant positive action, but in the Pacific Northwest conditions necessitated a different kind of response. There, the presence of the British

Hudson's Bay Company made Oregon a contentious issue in Anglo–American relations, as borne out in Wilkes's instructions to pay close attention to the Columbia River, the Northwest Coast, and San Francisco Bay.

While colleagues carried out scientific and surveying duties in the Puget Sound area in May 1841, Wilkes and a party of men traveled to Astoria where they encountered the remnants of the former headquarters of the Hudson's Bay Company. Although American settlers had charged the organization with "avarice, cruelty, despotism, and bad government," Wilkes found the corporation's representatives amenable and helpful.[14] Wilkes praised Sir George Simpson and Dr. John McLoughlin for their hospitality, and his remarks led to the notion that the voyage commander had succumbed to English blandishments while ignoring "the wants of the infant settlement at Oregon."[15] In stressing this theme, however, Anglophobic settlers (and subsequent local historians) missed the mark. When necessary, the expedition leader could subordinate his own hostility toward Britain to the demands of his mission. In this case Wilkes needed the aid of the company to carry out plans to explore the northernmost reaches of Oregon. He thus refused to be drawn into the controversy and suggested, in fact, that the Willamette settlers acted from selfish motives in seeking to induce new settlement and thereby hoping to augment the value of their farms and livestock. The settlers, Wilkes concluded, enunciating the "ripe fruit" theory, should wait for Washington to throw its mantle over them.

His public statements on the Oregon issue reflected Wilkes's skill as a naval diplomat, for his true sentiment was different. The removal of the Hudson's Bay Company headquarters to Vancouver struck him as the harbinger of a brilliant American future. He praised the commercial and agricultural character of the Willamette Valley and looked forward to the day when the area would belong to the United States. He sensed that he and his men "were not strangers on the soil," and explained that they "could not but take great interest in relation to its destiny, in the prospect of its one day becoming the abode of our relatives and friends."[16]

Such sentiments actually prevented Wilkes from filing a special report on Oregon until 13 June 1842, three days after he returned to New York. The forty-four–page document remained confidential because Secretary of the Navy Abel Parker Upshur felt its release might threaten concurrent diplomatic negotiations between Secretary of State Daniel Webster and British diplomat Lord Ashburton. The two men had hoped to include the Oregon question on their wide-ranging agenda, but the return of the explorers prevented this. A hint of the report's contents became public on 20 June when Wilkes lectured on some of his findings at the National Institute in Washington. There, he mentioned the dangers of the mouth of the Columbia as a potential port and reported the wreck of the *Peacock* as she crossed the bar. "Mere description can give little idea of the terrors of the bar of the Columbia," he wrote. "All who have seen it have spoken of the wildness of the scene, and incessant roar of the waters, representing it as one of the most fearful sights that can possibly meet the eye of the sailor."[17]

This description contrasted with Wilkes's positive assessment of more northerly harbors, upon which the future security and prosperity of the nation depended. Praising the safety of Juan de Fuca Strait, Admiralty Inlet, Puget Sound, and Hood's Canal, he stressed that no area in the world afforded "finer inland sounds or a greater number of harbors . . . capable of receiving the largest class of vessels, and without a danger in them that is not visible."[18]

Even these views were moderate when compared with the expansionist tone of the confidential report. By surrendering the disputed area north of the Columbia, Wilkes wrote, the United States would relinquish a cornucopia of natural resources that in time would buttress "an extensive commerce on advantageous terms with most parts of the Pacific."[19] The report also argued strongly for a boundary at 54°40′. Such a division would decrease the value of territory south of that line. The nation that dominated land adjoining Juan de Fuca Strait would control Vancouver Island and enjoy access to the heart of the Oregon country.

In addition to pointing out the practical difficulties of locating a boundary at the forty-ninth parallel, Wilkes showed concern that land held by the Hudson's Bay Company might become a sanctuary for brigands and Indians to attack Americans in the Willamette Valley. Wilkes felt certain that the Hudson's Bay Company already had moved "to secure permanent settlement in the area" by "asserting its rights to the soil north of the Columbia." In his view, procrastination by Washington would enable the company "to obtain such a foothold as will make it impossible to set aside British sovereignty in it."[20]

The precise effect of Wilkes's report and other expedition publicity upon subsequent American acquisition of Oregon and California remains moot. Certainly no evidence suggests that Wilkes's call for 54°40′ led to a similar cry two years later.[21] Nonetheless, when Upshur released the portion of the report that extolled the immense value of the western part of Oregon, late in 1842, he stimulated what shortly became the "Oregon fever." Even Webster, who earlier termed Oregon "a land of deserts, eternal snows, of shifting sands, and sagebrush, fit to be inhabited only by the jack-rabbit and the coyote," admitted that inland waters adjoining the Juan de Fuca Strait contained all the good harbors between Russian Alaska and California.[22]

Wilkes did not mention California in his special report, an omission reflecting Washington's overriding concern with Oregon; but his subsequent *Narrative* rhapsodized on the strategic significance of San Francisco Bay. That port—located on a major trade route linking China, Manila, Hawaii, India, and outlets in Mexico and South America—promised to become "one of the finest, if not the very best in the world—sufficiently commodious that the combined fleets of all the naval powers of the world might moor in it."[23] Convinced that the dearth of Mexican authority at Yerba Buena promised an imminent American windfall, Wilkes added that possession of both San Francisco and the harbors of Puget Sound would establish a transpacific triangle and facilitate national commerce.

The exploring expedition thus wrote an important chapter in the opening of the West, generating much reliable intelligence about climate, land forms, commercial prospects, and navigational problems. Americans trekking westward after 1842 no longer had to depend for information upon the sketchy reports of Lewis and Clark and Lieutenant William Slacum, the fiction of Washington Irving and James Fenimore Cooper, or the oft-contradictory accounts of missionaries and mountain men. Beyond cavil, Wilkes's report and *Narrative* deserve a place in the transformation of the context of the Oregon question.

Yet during the voyage Wilkes quarreled with several of the expedition's civilian scientists and naval officers. Within a week of his return to New York he requested courts-martial for several of the officers and a court of inquiry into his own conduct. In so doing, he anticipated a request from some of his officers that he be court-martialed for illegally punishing several sailors. On 7 September he was found guilty of the charge and sentenced to a public reprimand by the Secretary of the Navy. This was the lightest penalty possible and did not reflect great displeasure with Wilkes, who was promoted to commander during the following July.

In August 1842 the Joint Library Committee of Congress asked Wilkes to prepare a history of the exploring expedition. A year later he took charge of the collections and reports resulting from the voyage, and over the next few years he devoted much of his time to editing the narrative volumes, the first of which appeared in 1845. That work led to the refusal of his request for service in the Mexican War. In 1855 he was promoted to captain. His active career would have ended on land, had not the Civil War intervened.

Wilkes's place in American diplomatic history—as every midshipman since knows—stems from the events of 8 November 1861, when on his own initiative he removed two Confederate envoys from a British ship. What became "the gravest foreign crisis of the Civil War and the most perilous development in Anglo–American relations between the War of 1812 and the Venezuelan crisis of 1895" was not a chance occurrence.[24] In May 1861 Wilkes was ordered to go to Africa, take command of the *San Jacinto*, and bring the ship back to American waters. While cruising the Caribbean in search of Raphael Semmes in the *Sumter*, Wilkes visited Havana where he learned that James Mason and John Slidell planned to elude the Union blockade and take passage on the mail packet *Trent*. Working with U.S. chargé d'affaires Robert Shufeldt, Wilkes decided to lie in wait in the Bahama Channel. When the *Trent* appeared, Wilkes fired a shot across her bow, removed the Confederate agents, and took them to Boston where he was received as a hero. British protests led President Abraham Lincoln and Secretary of State William H. Seward to free the men and let them continue on to Europe, but not before a major diplomatic storm arose.

Historians have interpreted the importance of the *Trent* affair in several ways—from the vantage point of international law, as an example of the way public opinion complicated presidential decision making, as a chapter in Anglo–French diplomacy, and as a way of assessing the character of British politics during the early Civil War.[25] The delicate relationship between military necessity and civilian command of foreign policy has of course taken on great importance in the twentieth century. In stressing this motif as it emerged during the *Trent* crisis, however, scholars have failed to emphasize an unexpected by-product of the incident. Although Wilkes provoked a situation that pushed Great Britain to the brink of war, that question turned on one variable: whether Washington would sanction the seizure. And that possibility, as even the most ardent Anglophobe admitted, was remote.

Collaborators against the *Trent*. Consul General Robert W. Shufeldt and Captain Charles Wilkes in Havana, November 1861. *From a private collection.*

Britain did not enter the war for many reasons, including the problem of defending Canada, the fortuitous advice (and death) of the Prince Consort at the height of the imbroglio, and doubts about the motives of Napoleon III of France. The martial bluster from both sides of the Atlantic, therefore, fortunately comprised nothing more than a rhetorical equivalent of war. In light of these factors, Wilkes's role in the affair was ironic: what struck many contemporaries as a *casus belli* became a strong force for peace. The *Trent* incident forced Britain and the United States to establish earnest diplomatic relations early in the war, and the episode also created channels of communication that proved invaluable during the ensuing years. Had the incident not occurred when it did, the parameters of Anglo–American relations would have remained murky; in November 1861, however, each nation was forced to assess publicly and soberly the motives of its adversary.

The *Trent* affair, and Wilkes's subsequent Civil War record, suggest the ways (not always salutary) in which naval vessels served as "floating embassies," supplanting distant or nonexistent State Department authority. Certainly Lincoln and Navy Secretary Gideon Welles found Wilkes next to impossible to restrain. In turn, the latter's ability to influence national policy resulted from the primitive communications network that left naval officers on their own for weeks at a time. In any event, the *Trent* incident featured Wilkes in the combined role of international lawyer and prize court judge. Reports of the seizure of the Confederate envoys Mason and Slidell reached Northerners at the nadir of Union fortunes and had an impact similar to the Battle of Saratoga in 1777 and Andrew Jackson's triumph at New Orleans in 1815. Overwhelming popular support accorded Wilkes was reflected in Unionist denial that his act violated the principles of maritime neutrality that the United States defended against France in the late 1790s and England in 1812.

This Northern reaction focused attention upon Alexis de Tocqueville's warning, three decades earlier, that "foreign politics demand scarcely any of those qualities which a democracy possesses; and they require, on the contrary, the perfect use of almost all those faculties in which it is deficient."[26] The response of Lincoln and Seward, however, like that of most policymakers in the nineteenth century, was circumspect. The two men rightly hesitated to extend national interests into areas where the country might prove unable to exercise commensurate power.

It was a good thing that Lincoln was, in historian Jay Monaghan's words, a "diplomat in carpet slippers," for Wilkes's behavior during the Civil War underlined the ease with which an isolated, self-righteous naval officer might involve his country in a crisis. Wilkes's zeal was a product largely of his own ambition—thwarted during the previous twenty years by several frustrating occurrences. After his return from the exploring expedition, while other naval explorers carried the flag to Asiatic, North Pacific, and Latin American waters, Wilkes remained on shore, confronting the indifferences of President John

Tyler's Whig administration, enduring a highly publicized court-martial, and waging an arduous fight with Congress for appropriations to support work connected with the expedition. A further blow came when British explorer James Clark Ross denied the validity of Wilkes's greatest accomplishment, proving the continental dimension of Antarctica, by claiming to have sailed directly over the "discovery." Wilkes's surveys of the Sacramento Valley of California also ended in a bitter dispute when John C. Frémont, the famed pathfinder of the West, located mistakes in Wilkes's map and suggested that it had been copied from a discredited English chart.

These problems contributed to Wilkes's aggressive conduct and his growing tendency to ignore the rights of nations and feelings of individuals with whom he dealt. During the war he came into conflict with the Navy Department, and—because of his contempt for international law while intercepting blockade runners and chasing Confederate commerce destroyers in the West Indies—with diplomatic and naval representatives of Britain, France, Spain, Denmark, and Mexico. Far from being an apostle of understanding during the Civil War, Wilkes was nothing short of a seagoing bull in a maritime china shop.

Wilkes's "heroism" in the *Trent* episode led to his appointment in July 1862 to command the newly formed James River Flotilla, and later, after a nine-day stint heading the Potomac River Flotilla, to command the West India "Flying" Squadron. In the first position he earned the reputation of a headstrong commander, on one occasion disobeying a Navy Department order to detach two men from his squadron, and on several others entreating the department to allow him to combine his forces with those of General George B. McClellan's Army of the Potomac to storm the Confederate stronghold at Richmond. Even after General Henry W. Halleck ordered McClellan's troops to withdraw to defend Washington, Wilkes persisted, writing Welles that the mundane chore of reconnaissance did not sate his desire to turn the tide of war.

In August Wilkes was promoted to commodore. A month later, in appointing Wilkes to lead the West India "Flying" Squadron, Lincoln issued a thinly veiled warning to the European powers—especially Britain—to honor the requirements of maritime neutrality. The appointment was paradoxical, but the President and his advisers could count upon Wilkes to follow an aggressive course. They knew he would do all he could to capture the *Alabama,* the *Florida,* and the many contraband carriers that outwitted the Union blockade. Soon, though, it appeared that Wilkes was determined to extend the blockade into West Indian waters. Foreshadowing Alfred Mahan's view that the Navy's major wartime task consisted of locating and destroying the enemy, Wilkes ignored Welles's oft-repeated counsels of caution and acted as if existing conditions excused breaches of maritime law and naval custom. Convinced that European colonial officials had forfeited their rights as neutrals by aiding Confederate vessels, Wilkes literally transformed Havana into a base of Union operations as he searched for Southern cruisers. To extend the sailing capacity of his own vessels, he illegally established and employed coaling stations on Spanish, French, Danish, and British soil; to capture blockade runners, he allegedly placed spies on British soil and instructed his ships to "hover" in waters off the Danish port of St. Thomas; and to augment the strength of his command, he unilaterally detached vessels from the squadrons of C. H. Baldwin and David G. Farragut.

Exacting and vain, Wilkes was unable to capture the Confederate raiders— and this failure provoked widespread criticism of Welles and his department. Hostility between the Secretary and his subordinate grew when Wilkes charged that the department had failed to provide the ships and manpower necessary for him to execute his mission. Wilkes's charge that these measures would have allowed him to capture the *Alabama* or the *Florida* had some merit, but the Union commander never mastered the myriad reefs, inlets, and cays dotting the Caribbean. This ironic shortcoming, compared with the geographical expertise, nautical skill, and desperation of his Confederate adversaries, contributed significantly to Wilkes's failure to capture his quarry.

Wilkes managed to collect substantial prize money from the vessels he did capture—a point that galled Welles. And although its scope made halting the contraband trade impossible, the Flying Squadron did upset the continuity of Confederate transactions, force shifts in bases of operation, and compel Southern vessels to ply Caribbean and Gulf waters with greater caution. Yet Wilkes's arrogance and disrespect for maritime law made him a symbol of Anglo–Amerian rancor. His detention of several British ships spawned legal and diplomatic squalls across the Atlantic, and his zealous pursuit of duty left Britons bothered by what the Liverpool *Mercury* termed "an ill-formed and violent naval officer."[27]

In June 1863, Welles recalled Wilkes from active duty as a gesture toward securing improved Anglo–American relations. Having shown its toughness by appointing Wilkes, the administration could now reap the rewards of conciliation by retiring him. His removal from command marked a bitter end to a stormy career. The *Trent* affair was now all but forgotten: Union victories at Vicksburg and Gettysburg would supply a pantheon of new heroes. His reputation tarnished by failure, Wilkes returned to New York, believing that he had been sacrificed to Navy Department incompetence and British diplomatic pressure.

There remained a denouement, a second court-martial that convened in March 1864. The list of particulars had a familiar ring: Wilkes had contravened orders and engaged in conduct unbecoming an officer. By publishing a letter critical of Welles's *Annual Report,* he had disobeyed a general naval regulation and showed disrespect toward his superiors. Found guilty on all counts, the hero of the *Trent* affair received a public reprimand and a three-year suspension—a sentence that Lincoln later shortened to one year.[28] In July

1866, Wilkes did achieve a measure of honor when he was named rear admiral, albeit on the retired list. Though he was recalled to special duty to continue work on the exploring expedition records, by 1870 his active duty with the Navy was essentially over. In 1871, at the age of seventy-three, Wilkes began writing his autobiography. In its 2,800 pages he both recalled his life and sought to bring his old opponents to account. If he hoped to see his memoirs published during his lifetime, he was to be disappointed. He no doubt remained bitter until his death in 1877.

Throughout his career Wilkes displayed attitudes that characterized commanders of the old navy. Imperious toward both associates and civilian superiors, single-minded in his execution of duty, and devoted to God and country, he epitomized those contemporary navalists who harbored an enduring faith in America's political, commercial, and spiritual mission—a mission, not incidentally, in which several cast major roles for themselves. Duty addressed Wilkes in severe terms, and he in turn expected as much of subordinates as he did of himself. His egotism—a mix, at worst, of Captains Ahab and Bligh—led him to make decisions often based on impulse and ambition, to ignore naval etiquette when regulations or orders contravened what he defined as the proper course of action. Welles often despaired of his underling's contumacy while heading the James River Flotilla. In Welles's view, Wilkes was "very exacting toward others, but [was] not himself as obedient as he should be." Possessing talent "but not good judgment in all respects," Wilkes might "rashly assume authority, and do things that might involve himself and the country in difficulty."[29] Wilkes, meanwhile, considered Welles "entirely incompetent to fill the position" of Secretary of the Navy.[30]

Wilkes's zealous actions during the Civil War leave the impression that his contribution to the American naval tradition was negative—in short, the unwarranted assumption of power over the formulation of national policy. Such an interpretation is one-sided. Certainly there was danger in Wilkes's "my country right or wrong" attitude, but as an explorer and scientist he displayed ability and courage; as a cartographer, surveyor, and discoverer, he contributed to growing national prestige. Given the primitive communications and technology of the late 1830s, his confirmation of the continental dimensions of Antarctica compares favorably with the complex systems supporting American space efforts in the post-Sputnik era. Similarly, his maps of the Pacific did not end up in dusty archives: those charts facilitated naval operations on Wake Island, the Makins, and Tarawa a century later, during World War II.

James Dwight Dana accompanied the exploring expedition and knew well its commander's acerbic tongue. But Dana concluded that Wilkes's caustic nature and conceit did not detract from his "wonderful degree of energy." Nor did Dana miss the mark when he told Asa Gray of Harvard that "no more daring or driving officer" existed in the Navy.[31] As Wilkes's son John recalled after his father's death, the rear admiral was "a fearless, energetic, and unflinching officer, never afraid to assume responsibility."[32] These characteristics, of course, tossed Wilkes into choppy waters as a wartime commander; yet they also contributed to his scientific achievement. His positive legacy emphasized, understandably, the admonition that the national interest depended upon strong and continuous government sponsorship of scientific research and exploration. Wilkes participated in organizations such as the American Philosophical Society; he wrote on such diverse subjects as the zodiacal light, the Oregon Territory, and the character of meteors and Native Americans; and the expedition that bears his name contributed to the development of the Smithsonian Institution and several other government agencies. All of these things advanced the expansionist *Zeitgeist* that permeated the United States at mid-century.

The general strategic importance of naval exploration in antebellum America, together with Wilkes's personal caution during the expedition, necessitate another look at the diplomatic era usually analyzed within the rubric "Young America." Certainly the movement for all of Mexico, the Ostend Manifesto, and the ill-fated filibustering expeditions of William Walker into Nicaragua and Narciso López into Cuba illustrate some uncoordinated muscle flexing by an adolescent nation seeking to elbow its way into the international political arena. But in contrast to these episodes in bumptious diplomacy, the government and the Navy showed their appreciation of the need to acquire systematic knowledge of the globe and its ports, products, and peoples. Matthew C. Perry's epochal voyage to Japan was the best known of several other expeditions; but other voyages, including one led by Lieutenant William F. Lynch to the Dead Sea area by 1847 and another led by Lieutenant William L. Herndon and Passed Midshipman John Rodgers to North Pacific waters off China and Japan, suggest that Manifest Destiny influenced spheres of activity far removed from the domestic emphasis on westward continental expansion.

Next to his scientific work, Wilkes expressed his greatest concern for the international image of the Navy. Although as commander of the exploring expedition he in no way spoke as a captive of special economic interests, he did conceive of the Atlantic and especially the Pacific as maritime highways rather than barriers. In this he anticipated the post-1865 vision of Secretary of State Seward, arguing that knowledge of the seas would consolidate control over global waterways. Even if the United States could not wrest maritime supremacy from Great Britain, the Navy might stabilize oceanic routes so that American political and trade interests would profit. Well before Mahan systematically articulated the strategic variables that comprised modern navalism, Wilkes stressed the continuing need to employ sea power in peacetime as an instrument of technological, scientific, and economic advancement.

Wilkes also favored extending to aboriginal peoples the benefits of republican, Anglo-Saxon government and Protestant religion; but his Anglophobia ruled out kinship with the naval aristocracy of the late-nineteenth and twentieth centuries. Though rejecting Rousseau's portrait of "noble savages" enjoying idyllic bliss in a Pacific paradise, several passages in his *Narrative* and *Autobiography* (especially those dealing with the expedition's contacts with native peoples) makes clear that Wilkes, too, used a yardstick of idealized American culture values to measure the civilization of the aborigines he encountered. Like most navalists he criticized missionaries and commercial agents who failed to execute with sufficient seriousness their respective spiritual and material commissions.

As an explorer, Wilkes demonstrated what historian Richard W. Van Alstyne termed "a mariner's sense of distance from the United States."[33] Wilkes's earnestness in stressing the strategic and economic potential of Puget Sound and the harbor at San Francisco presaged an American mercantile empire on the Pacific. In this sense the naval scientist possessed a "Pacific consciousness" long before Seward, the first great apostle of that doctrine. Wilkes's *Narrative*, though written in stodgy prose and printed in limited number, made him a prophet. Not only in his view that Oregon, California, and Hawaii would eventually come under the dominion of the republic did he foresee future developments; Wilkes also predicted that San Francisco Bay and the Juan de Fuca Strait possessed "everything to make them increase, and keep up an intercourse with the whole of Polynesia, as well as the countries of South America on the one side, and China, the Philippines, New Holland, and New Zealand on the other." From these venues would come "materials for a beneficial exchange of products and intercourse that must, in time, become immense, while this western coast," he indicated, "is evidently destined to fill a large space in the world's future history."[34]

Wilkes was neither a first-rate naval officer nor a diplomat of distinction. Nonetheless, through his work in naval science for utilitarian ends, he both contributed to, and reflected, the restless activity of a people on the move. His work in the fields of meteorology, hydrography, and geodesy ensured the safety of vessels traversing maritime routes; his compilation of charts and surveys during the expedition facilitated coastal and international trade; and his maps of California and Oregon (despite errors) buoyed confident Americans heading for these destinations in the late 1840s and 1850s. Above all, Wilkes's career suggests that if the pseudoscience of Social Darwinism contributed heavily to the distinctiveness of the new Manifest Destiny of the 1890s (and to the *raison d'être* of the new naval aristocracy), midcentury expansionism contained a genuine scientific concern—to which the Navy made a signal contribution.

FURTHER READING

Like many other naval officers, Wilkes left scattered records pertaining to his life, in depositories in the United States and several other countries. The most complete manuscript collection is available at the Library of Congress. The only full-length biography, Daniel Henderson's *The Hidden Coasts: A Biography of Admiral Charles Wilkes*, exemplifies the hagiography that colored so much naval biography until recent years. Satisfactory in few areas, its unabashed tone of admiration leaves the impression that Wilkes still awaits his biographer. Wilkes's *Autobiography*, published in 1978, will aid this quest, although the volume is as heavy as a frigate, marred by Wilkes's faulty memory, and dominated by its author's desire to use it as a vehicle to hit back at the many enemies he encountered during his life. Still, the volume is valuable.

Turgid and overwritten, yet revealing its author's driving ambition, zeal, and scientific and diplomatic interests, Wilkes's *Narrative of the United States Exploring Expedition during the Years 1838, 1839, 1840, 1841, 1842* also reveals the ethnocentrism that influenced his world view. The best scholarly analysis of the exploring expedition is also a delight to read—a combination that is all too rare these days. William Stanton's *The Great United States Exploring Expedition of 1838–1842* limns well the human frailties and professional successes (and jealousies) that attended the voyage. Vincent Ponko, Jr.'s *Ships, Seas, and Scientists: U.S. Naval Exploration and Discovery in the Nineteenth Century* and David Tyler's *The Wilkes Expedition: The First United States Exploring Expedition (1838–1842)* are also helpful.

The author's "The Navy Before Darwinism" and "An Uncertain Passage: The Bureaus Run the Navy, 1842–1861" place Wilkes and his work in broad context.

NOTES

1. For examples of officers whose vision encompassed an augmented role for the Navy in the nation's affairs, see Karsten, *The Naval Aristocracy: The Golden Age of Annapolis and the Emergence of Modern American Navalism*; Vincent Ponko, Jr., *Ships, Seas, and Scientists: U.S. Naval Exploration and Discovery in the Nineteenth Century*; Geoffrey S. Smith, "The Navy Before Darwinism: Science, Exploration, and Diplomacy in Antebellum America," *American Quarterly*, XXXVIII (Spring, 1976): 41–55; and Smith, "An Uncertain Passage: The Bureaus Run the Navy, 1842–1861," in Kenneth J. Hagan, ed., *In Peace and War: Interpretations of American Naval History, 1775–1984*, 79–106.

2. William James Morgan et al., eds., *Autobiography of Rear Admiral Charles Wilkes, United States Navy, 1798–1877*, 44–46, 68–69.

3. Jones to Dickerson, 22 August 1836; Dickerson to Andrew Jackson, 31 October 1836; 25 Cong., 2 sess., *House Executive Document 147*, 139–47.

4. Ibid.

5. Quoted in David B. Tyler, *The Wilkes Expedition: The First United States Exploring Expedition (1838–1842)*, 17.

6. Stribling to Martin Van Buren, 3 April 1838, in Letters Pertaining to the Preparation of the Wilkes Expedition, National Archives, Vol. IV.

7. Kennon to Dickerson, 8 April 1838, ibid.

8. Quoted in Charles Lee Lewis, *Matthew Fontaine Maury, The Pathfinder of the Seas,* 33.

9. Wilkes to Van Buren, Charles Wilkes Papers, Box 11, Library of Congress.

10. The instructions are quoted in G. S. Bryan, "The Purpose, Equipment, and Personnel of the Wilkes Expedition," *Proceedings* of the American Philosophical Society, LXXXII (June 1940): 560.

11. For other examples of this spirit, see Daniel J. Boorstin, *The Americans: The National Experience,* 223ff.

12. George H. Daniels, *Science in American Society: A Social History,* 176.

13. Charles Wilkes, U.S.N., *Narrative of the United States Exploring Expedition During the Years 1838, 1839, 1840, 1841, 1842,* II: 376–81.

14. Ibid., V: 136–37, 147.

15. Helen Ramage, "The Wilkes Exploring Expedition on the Pacific Slope, 1841," 42–44.

16. Wilkes, *Narrative,* IV: 321.

17. Ibid., IV: 243. See also Wilkes to Alexander Dallas, 20 April 1843, Wilkes Papers, Box 2, Library of Congress.

18. Wilkes, *Narrative,* IV: 305.

19. Wilkes's confidential report is contained in *Congressional Record,* 62 Cong., 1 sess., XLVII (15–20 July 1911): 2977–85.

20. Ibid., 2982.

21. For the origins of that demand as a campaign slogan, see Hans Sperber, "Fifty-four Forty or Fight; Facts and Fictions," *American Speech,* XXXII (February 1957): 5–11.

22. Quoted in Ramage, "Pacific Slope," 161.

23. Wilkes, *Narrative,* V: 157. See also Norman A. Graebner, "American Interests in California, 1845," *Pacific Historical Review,* XXII (1953): 24–25.

24. Gordon H. Warren, *Fountain of Discontent: The Trent Affair and Freedom of the Seas,* 222.

25. On these aspects see Stuart L. Bernath, *Squall Across the Atlantic: American Civil War Prize Cases and Diplomacy;* David P. Crook, *The North, the South and the Powers, 1861–1865;* Norman B. Ferris, *The "Trent Affair": A Diplomatic Crisis;* Lynn M. Case and Warren F. Spencer, *The United States and France: Civil War Diplomacy;* and Frank J. Merli, *Great Britain and the Confederate Navy, 1861–1865.*

26. Alexis de Tocqueville, *Democracy in America,* II: 243.

27. Liverpool *Mercury,* 23 March 1862.

28. Charles Wilkes, *Defense of Com. Charles Wilkes, U.S.N., Late Acting*

Rear Admiral, in Command of the West India Squadron, Read Before a General Court Martial, on Charges Preferred by the Secretary of the Navy.

29. Gideon Welles, *Diary of Gideon Welles,* I: 73.

30. Quoted in Morgan et al., eds., *Autobiography of Wilkes,* 755.

31. Quoted in Daniel C. Gilman, *The Life of James Dwight Dana,* 149.

32. John Wilkes's praise of his father, along with other encomiums, may be found in Wilkes Papers, Box 11 (Family Correspondence), Library of Congress.

33. Richard W. Van Alstyne, *The Rising American Empire,* 127.

34. Wilkes, *Narrative,* V: 171–72.

FRANKLIN BUCHANAN: SYMBOL FOR TWO NAVIES

BY CHARLES M. TODORICH

Friday, 5 August 1864, dawned hot and humid in Mobile Bay. The heavy rains of the past few days had subsided the evening before, and a light southwesterly gulf breeze creeping over the peninsular and island forts at the entrance to the bay stirred small ripples on waters soon to be churned by the fury of desperate battle. Just outside the mouth of the bay a powerful Union flotilla of eighteen ships totaling 159 guns had mustered in the early morning hours and set a northerly course on a flood tide through the 150-yard-wide channel. Opposing the Union flotilla, which included four ironclad monitors, was a Confederate force of three light gunboats and the mighty, though untested, ironclad ram *Tennessee*.

The commanding figure of Admiral Franklin Buchanan strode the deck of the *Tennessee*. Compactly built and of slightly below-average height, with the iron gray hair on the sides of his head brushed upward toward a balding crown, the admiral gave the appearance of both physical and moral strength. In his younger days, he had been considered the third strongest man in the Navy.[1] Now, in his sixty-fourth year, he could look back on a career of professional accomplishment surpassed by very few naval officers of his time. As a junior officer, he had made a reputation for physical courage, temperance, and discipline. As a commander, he had helped launch the Naval Academy as its first superintendent; distinguished himself in the Mexican War; been the first American naval officer to set foot on Japanese soil during the epic Perry expedition; and helped reform officer promotion on the famous Star Chamber Board in 1855. At the height of his career, he had cast his lot with the South and commanded the *Merrimac* in that first ironclad's destruction of the Union fleet at Hampton Roads in 1862. What Buchanan did, he did "with all his might."[2]

Mobile Bay was to be the last battle for this officer who embodied the daring, dash, and discipline of the old navy along with the professionalism of the new. As he took the measure of the wood and iron behemoths plowing toward him, Buchanan resolutely addressed his officers and crew:

> Now men, the enemy is coming and I want you to do your duty; and you shall not have it to say when you leave this vessel that you were not near enough to the enemy, for I will meet them, and then you can fight them alongside of their own ships; and if I fall, lay me on one side and go on with the fight, and never mind me—but whip and sink the Yankees or fight until you sink yourselves, but do not surrender.[3]

Franklin Buchanan. Photograph of Buchanan as a commander, taken shortly before the Civil War. *Courtesy of the Library of Congress.*

The old navy fighting spirit that Buchanan displayed at Mobile Bay was evident from the first days of his career. Born on 17 September 1800 in Baltimore into a well-educated and politically prominent family, Buchanan joined the Navy less than fifteen years later during the waning days of the War of 1812 when patriotism was at fever pitch. At the time, Buchanan was living in Philadelphia where his father, a doctor and an abolitionist, had moved the family in 1806. Ordered to the still unfinished frigate *Java* in April 1815, Buchanan found his desire to see action against the British thwarted by delays in the *Java*'s completion and by the war's end. Rather than languish in Baltimore where the *Java* was being built, Buchanan signed on with a merchant brig, the *Acme*, for a West Indies cruise. The experience was valuable preparation for midshipman service in the *Java*, to which he was again ordered after the *Acme*'s two-month cruise. Buchanan first went on board the *Java* in Annapolis. She was commanded by Captain Oliver Hazard Perry, one of the few old navy captains with enlightened views on midshipmen education. According to Alexander Slidell Mackenzie, one of Buchanan's fellow midshipmen in the *Java*, Perry's shipboard library was "well selected" and

> . . . freely placed at the disposal of the curious . . . . On every occasion he manifested that most ardent zeal and persevering interest in the improvement of the younger midshipmen. They were compelled to devote a given portion of each day to studies connected with the profession, under his own eye, in the cabin, the forward part of which he relinquished to them for this purpose. A competent teacher was always on board to teach them French and Spanish; and a good swordsman to render them skillful in the use of arms. Even the lighter accomplishment of dancing was not neglected.[4]

The *Java*'s mission was to deliver a newly ratified treaty with Algiers to the American consul there, William Shaler. Arriving off Algiers on 8 April, the *Java* found a twelve-vessel English squadron attempting to negotiate a treaty with the Dey similar to that of the Americans. The Dey used this as an excuse to reject the treaty carried by the *Java*, whereupon the Americans commenced secret preparations to attack. The plan was called off when a French frigate tipped the Dey. During the summer the *Java* protected American shipping and performed routine diplomatic functions in a host of Mediterranean ports. In November she returned to Algiers where a new treaty was negotiated. In January 1817, the *Java* was ordered home.

Thus, on his first midshipman cruise Franklin Buchanan had visited the great ports of the Mediterranean, been witness to old navy diplomacy, encountered the British Navy and the Barbary corsairs, and enjoyed the good fortune of serving under one of the old navy's great sea captains.

Buchanan's thirteen-month stint in the *Java* was followed by a cruise on board the brig *Prometheus*, which was surveying the Atlantic coast. This has been called "the first practice cruise for midshipmen in the history of the

United States Navy,"[5] since the mostly-midshipmen crew performed all of the duties of enlisted seamen. Thus, on each of his first two old navy men-of-war, Buchanan was exposed to progressive approaches to professional education that portended a new navy struggling to be born.

Buchanan's career over the next twenty years, like that of other officers of his period, was marked by slow promotion and lengthy service in men-of-war on distant stations. He made three more Mediterranean cruises; three cruises to the Gulf and Caribbean; a China cruise as second officer on board a merchantman; and a cruise to Brazil in which he personally delivered a Baltimore-built 64-gun ship to that country's emperor.

Of particular significance was his 1829–31 cruise in the frigate *Constellation*, for it was here that Buchanan began to make his reputation as a disciplinarian. It nearly cost him his life after the ship's return to Norfolk in November 1831. While traveling in a small boat up the Chesapeake en route to Philadelphia to see his family, Buchanan was surrounded on deck by a group of the *Constellation*'s seamen in a scene described thus by an eyewitness:

> There he stood, with form erect, both hands resting on his cane; the expression of his countenance calm, resolute, and defiant. The seamen gathered around him, and gave vent to their feelings in blasphemous oaths. One man remarked that he had been more than twenty years in the service; that he had fought at Tripoli, and had never been punished until ordered by Lieutenant Franklin Buchanan. Another said he was a tyrant; another that he was no seaman; another that he should be driven out of the service. But there he stood in statue-like repose, not a word escaping his lips. He seemed rooted to the deck. For full five minutes or more he braved the tempest, but not a man dared lay the weight of his finger upon him. Quietly and gracefully he turned upon his heel, and passed down the stairway through the long passage into the after cabin and went to bed.[6]

Later, on a canal boat between the Chesapeake and the Delaware Bay, these same seamen so frightened the other passengers that the captain put several of the worst of them ashore. Franklin Buchanan at once interceded on their behalf, begging that they not be left to suffer in the cold after years in the moderate Mediterranean climes and taking responsibility for their future actions. Buchanan's judgment was vindicated when, on this same eventful trip to Philadelphia, the steamer to which they had transferred ran down a sloop. In a commanding voice Buchanan cried, "Where are the men of the *Constellation?*" They soon appeared and assisted in the rescue of those on board the sinking sloop. When later that evening the *Constellation* sailors invited him to their cabin, Buchanan went, a pistol in each overcoat pocket. But the sailors' intentions were conciliatory and they proposed a toast to his health. "With all my heart," was Buchanan's reply.[7]

Buchanan's rise in rank was slow. In 1822 he completed the examinations for promotion to the rank of passed midshipman. The examinations, first held in 1819, were an early step toward establishing professional standards in the officer corps. They covered seamanship, gunnery, navigation, and higher mathematics. Passing them meant that Buchanan was qualified to be a lieutenant, but promotion would have to wait until there was a vacancy in the ranks, which could be years. In Buchanan's case an opening occurred in 1825. It would be sixteen years before his next advancement. Such a slow promotion system that rewarded longevity and mixed bearded men and young boys in the same rank stifled the upward climb of officers and doubtless caused many to leave the service.

On 19 February 1835, Buchanan, still a lieutenant, married Anne Catherine Lloyd in St. Anne's Church in Annapolis. The union was in the Buchanan family tradition of "marrying well." Anne Catherine's father was the recently deceased Edward Lloyd, who had been governor of Maryland, a congressman, and a U.S. senator. Coincidentally, her brother-in-law was Francis Scott Key, whose "Star Spangled Banner" contributed to the patriotic fervor that two decades earlier had helped entice Franklin Buchanan into the Navy. Buchanan's new fervor was Anne Catherine, and over the next three years she bore him three daughters. The purchase of a two-story brick home on Scott Street in December 1836 strengthened Buchanan's ties to Annapolis.

Perhaps because of his family, Buchanan requested duties less arduous and distant than in the past. From July to November of 1836 he served as assistant inspector of ordnance and was the only lieutenant on a board composed of a commodore and four captains charged with testing various medium and light guns. From the end of 1836 until 1839 Buchanan commanded the receiving ship in Baltimore. When in 1839 the Maine boundary dispute threatened war with Britain, Buchanan requested and received orders as Commodore Alexander Claxton's flag lieutenant on board the *Constitution*. Diplomacy defused the crisis, and Buchanan got a Pacific cruise instead. One of the *Constitution*'s sailors wrote a book on the cruise describing frigate life. Published in 1841, it praised Buchanan for his "prompt and energetic action" in rescuing men who had fallen overboard.[8]

Buchanan made waves of another sort in Callao, Peru, when he brought charges against Captain John H. Clack of the USS *Lexington* that resulted in a court-martial. Buchanan charged Clack with drunkenness, "scandalous conduct tending to the destruction of good morals," and not repaying money he had borrowed to cover his gambling debts, thereby, in Buchanan's words, "disgracing his own character as an officer, and bringing odium and contempt on the American Navy abroad."[9] The incident strengthened Buchanan's reputation as a temperance man of strict moral character. It may also have contributed to Commodore Claxton's approval, on grounds of ill health, of Buchanan's request to return to the states in the sloop *Falmouth*. This was his last service at sea as a lieutenant, for on 8 September 1841, after twenty-six years of service, he was promoted to commander.

Buchanan's next orders, to the steam frigate *Mississippi*, placed him square-ly in the camp of a small group of officers determined to force steam propulsion upon a Navy still intoxicated with the romance of the age of sail. The *Mississippi*'s design had been approved by a board headed by Matthew C. Perry, who visited the ship when she was outfitting in New York. Perry's biographer, Samuel Eliot Morison, claims that Perry, along with David Stockton and Franklin Buchanan, led the "devoted band" of officers who could see that "steam propulsion and the shell gun were fast making sailing navies obsolete."[10] Interestingly, Buchanan's biography, by Charles Lee Lewis, has no real information regarding this. It is clear, however, that Buchanan had a strong interest in steam propulsion. His scrapbook contains numerous news-paper clippings about foreign steamers, and even an article and drawing of an "aerial steam carriage."[11]

In his service on board the *Mississippi* from April to November of 1842, Buchanan gained invaluable experience in the logistics and engineering of steam propulsion and what it demanded in the education of naval officers. His views were likely influenced by two other officers in the *Mississippi*, Surgeon John A. Lockwood and Professor of Mathematics William A. Chauvenet. The three would serve together again three years later on the first staff at the United States Naval Academy.

In December of 1842 Buchanan took command of the sloop *Vincennes*. His selection caused a brouhaha, eventually aired in the press, among the fifty-four commanders and twenty-eight lieutenants passed over by Navy Secretary Abel P. Upshur. Buchanan's scrapbook contains a newspaper clipping of a letter against his appointment signed "A Friend to Justice and the Navy," as well as a retort in his defense signed "A Friend to the Service."[12] The reaction to his command selection likely shaped Buchanan's thinking on the whole system of officer seniority and promotion and may bear on his performance with the Star Chamber Board in 1855.

Of particular significance during Buchanan's *Vincennes* command was his system of discipline, especially with regard to drunkenness. "The crime of drunkenness," he wrote to Navy Secretary David Henshaw in December 1843, "causes all the insubordination and consequent punishment to officers and men. My experience has convinced me of this fact, and hence my determination never to overlook such an offense when committed under my command."[13] Buchanan had at least a few opportunities to exercise his "no quarter" philosophy, most notably in Pensacola where "insubordinate," "turbulent," "outrageous," and "extremely riotous" were the words used in letters he received describing the conduct of two of his inebriated crewmen.[14] These, however, appeared to be the exception to a fine system of discipline, as noted by the *Pensacola Gazette*:

> There is nothing on board of [the *Vincennes*] which indicates the martinet. On the contrary, there seems to be just the amount of ease and freedom of

manner which ought to be exhibited where every man feels satisfied, interested, and protected. By which art it is that Buchanan and his officers have been able to perfect and maintain so admirable a system, we are not able to explain. But we do know that his men have proved themselves to be the most orderly and sober of any crews . . . which have ever been in this port . . . .[15]

When Buchanan brought the *Vincennes* into Norfolk in August 1844, he had vindicated Abel Upshur and proved himself worthy of further responsibility. A petition from the officers of the *Vincennes* for the establishment of naval schools ashore hinted at the direction those future responsibilities might take.[16] Awaiting orders, Buchanan repaired to "The Rest," his home on Maryland's Eastern Shore.

These officers were not the first to lobby for naval schools ashore. Those of the *Constitution* and the *Vandalia* had done so in 1836, and theirs were but a pair of over two dozen such proposals by naval officers, naval secretaries, and others between 1800 and 1840. To be sure, there were shore schools at Boston, Norfolk, New York, and the Philadelphia Asylum, but these were little more than temporary way stations where midshipmen could cram a few months for exams, perhaps with the assistance of a chaplain or schoolmaster. Attendance was voluntary, instruction haphazard, and learning beyond rote memorization rare. It was worse on board ship, where a schoolmaster, usually the chaplain, had to contend with his own lack of knowledge, the ship's lack of facilities, the midshipmen's lack of interest and time, and the distractions of a man-of-war under sail. Instituted in 1802, the year West Point was founded, the school-master program worked against the establishment of a naval academy, for it enabled opponents of such an institution to argue that a system of officer education already existed. And academy opponents were numerous among old-time officers and conservative congressmen, who felt that you could no more train naval officers ashore than "teach ducks to swim in a garret."[17] Moreover, claimed opponents, formal education ashore was aristocratic and would produce effeminate officers lacking the high degree of personal courage that had long been the Navy's hallmark. These flimsy arguments torpedoed academy proponents for decades.

Steam propulsion changed all of that. As "part of the greatest revolution in naval technology since the galley age had given way to sail,"[18] steamships demanded officers with technical and scientific training unobtainable on board ship. But steam was only one element in a larger picture of naval reform led by progressive officers "determined to improve the service and their own fortunes."[19] Matthew Fontaine Maury's oceanographic research and agitation for improved officer education and promotion; Matthew C. Perry's foresight in founding the Naval Lyceum and in establishing the apprentice system; John A. Dahlgren's genius in naval ordnance; Charles Wilkes's exploration of the Pacific Basin; Robert F. Stockton's campaign against flogging; the temperance efforts of Chaplain George Jones—all of this was part of what Samuel Huntington has called the American Military Enlightenment of the 1830s and 1840s, the technological, scientific, humanitarian, and professional elements of which argued strongly for a naval academy.[20]

In 1842 two events occurred that would lead directly to the establishment of the Naval Academy. One was a near mutiny on board the brig *Somers* commanded by Alexander Slidell Mackenzie, brother-in-law of Matthew C. Perry and Buchanan's old shipmate in the *Java*. The mutiny was ostensibly led by Midshipman Philip Spencer, who hoped to turn the *Somers* into a pirate. Spencer, a bad-apple whose father was Secretary of War John C. Spencer, was hanged at sea along with his two enlisted cohorts, at Mackenzie's order. The affair caused an uproar and focused attention on the dismal state of naval education at sea.

The second 1842 event was the appointment of Professor William A. Chauvenet to head the Naval Asylum School in Philadelphia. Chauvenet totally revamped the asylum's program, making it so successful that naval officials added Lieutenant James Harmon Ward, Professor Henry H. Lockwood, and Passed Midshipman Samuel Marcy to the staff in an effort to concentrate all shore schooling there. In 1844 Chauvenet drew up a plan for a two-year asylum course to be funded from monies already appropriated for schoolmasters. Chauvenet had shown how an academy could be founded without congressional approval. He sold the idea to Secretary of the Navy Henshaw, but Henshaw's successor, John Y. Mason, scrapped it at the behest of senior officers.

When scholar-politician George Bancroft became Secretary in March 1845, Chauvenet sent him his once-rejected 1844 plan. Bancroft seized upon it, eliciting the views of the rest of the asylum staff and dispatching Samuel Marcy and Henry Lockwood to West Point to study its program. Marcy also prodded his father, Secretary of War William L. Marcy, to approve Bancroft's request for the transfer of Fort Severn to the Navy. Already, Bancroft had requested the views of the Board of Examiners, then meeting in Philadelphia, on locating a naval school at Annapolis. The board, which included Franklin Buchanan's friend Matthew C. Perry and Annapolis resident Isaac Mayo, made its report on 25 June. Besides Annapolis as the site, it recommended:

1. That a grade of naval cadets from thirteen to fifteen years of age be created and appointed in the same manner as West Point cadets.
2. That a practice frigate and a small steamer be located at the school.
3. That the program include two years of study at the school followed by three years at sea and then a year at the school on board the practice frigate before the lieutenant's exam.
4. That, except for the abstruse study of calculus, the course of study be almost identical to that of West Point.
5. That the school's academic board, assisted by three persons appointed

by the Secretary of the Navy, conduct annual examinations of the midshipmen.[21]

The report of Lockwood and Marcy, just returned from West Point, reinforced the Board of Examiners' proposals.

Buchanan's name first appears in connection with the school as a member of a three-man board that also included Commanders Samuel F. Du Pont and William W. McKean (a cousin) and was formed by Bancroft to pass judgment on Annapolis as a site. The board's report was positive. On 7 August, two days after the transfer of Fort Severn to the Navy, Bancroft selected Buchanan to be the school's first superintendent and charged him with drawing up plans for its establishment. American naval officers, Bancroft wrote, should:

> . . . make themselves as distinguished for culture as they have been for gallant combat.
>
> To this end it is proposed to collect the midshipmen who . . . are on shore, and give them occupation . . . in the study of mathematics, nautical astronomy, theory of morals, international law, gunnery, use of steam, the Spanish and French languages, and other branches essential to the accomplishment of a naval officer.[22]

A week later, Buchanan submitted his plan of organization to Bancroft. It drew heavily on the asylum program for curriculum and on the West Point model for organizational matters. It also conformed to the basic concepts, though not the exact wording, set down by the Board of Examiners in June.

The Naval Academy at Annapolis. Old Fort Severn is in the foreground of this 1855 view of the Naval Academy. Engraving after an oil by W. R. Miller. *From the collection of James C. Bradford.*

Bancroft approved this plan with only minor revisions on 28 August, and on 3 September Buchanan officially assumed command. Soon thereafter, Bancroft appointed Chauvenet, Lockwood, Marcy, and Ward as the first instructors, and ordered some forty-nine midshipmen and seven acting midshipmen to the school. On 10 October 1845 at 11:00 A.M. Buchanan gathered the midshipmen and faculty in one of the recitation rooms and in "sharp, vigorous tones"[23] delivered remarks formally opening the Naval School.

Buchanan's opening charge laid down the precepts of obedience, moral character, and temperance that remain goals of Naval Academy education. "The regulations of the navy," Buchanan warned,

> require you to pass through a severe ordeal before you can be promoted; you must undergo an examination on all branches taught at the naval school before you are eligible for a lieutenancy; your morals and general character are strictly inquired into. . . . By carefully avoiding the first step toward intemperance, shunning the society of the dissolute and idle, and by cherishing a wish to deserve and the hope of receiving the approbation of your country you alone can render yourselves able to occupy with honor the high standing in the Navy to which you are destined. . . .[24]

To enforce his high standards, Buchanan promulgated the school's first regulations. They placed the school under the governance of naval law; established a midshipmen watch organization; required midshipmen to "obey the commands of the Professors"; prohibited midshipmen from bringing intoxicating liquors onto school grounds or smoking cigars in the mess hall, classrooms, or their quarters; required midshipmen to get the superintendent's approval before leaving school grounds; warned against vandalism; compelled all of the school's officers, professors, and midshipmen to report breaches of regulations to the superintendent; and enjoined the midshipmen to "abstain from all vicious, immoral, or irregular conduct" and to "conduct themselves with the propriety and decorum of gentlemen."[25] While Buchanan wanted shipboard-like discipline, the school lacked the essential accoutrements of military life. There was no midshipmen leadership organization, marching, formations, or drill. These omissions may have been purposeful so as to make the break from the asylum program less marked, thereby allowing Bancroft to maintain the veneer that he had not violated the will of Congress by establishing an academy. Thus, it would not be structure and routine but the forceful character of Franklin Buchanan that would maintain discipline at the school.

Buchanan's impact on the academic program was less pervasive. He appointed Lieutenant Ward president of the school's first Academic Board and charged it with developing and implementing the course of studies. William Chauvenet was the leading force on the board, and the course of study bore close resemblance to the one he had proposed to Secretary Henshaw in 1844.

While Buchanan delegated academic details, he established the school's overall academic tone. Reflective of the dominant influence of Bancroft and Chauvenet in establishing the school, the course of studies Buchanan approved devoted only eight hours (out of sixty-one) to what might be called professional subjects (ordnance, gunnery, steam engineering, and chemistry), thirteen hours to the liberal arts (history, English, composition, geography), twenty hours to mathematics and natural philosophy (science), and twenty hours to French and Spanish. The short shrift given to steam propulsion may indicate that in the minds of some academy proponents, raising the educational level and moral tone of the service was a stronger argument than new technology. That Buchanan aimed for high academic standards was shown in his response to a group of midshipmen who complained that their physics test was too difficult. "Professor Henry of Princeton College has adapted this work for his classes," he explained, "and I know not why the standard of education at Princeton should be superior to that at the Naval School."[26]

Still, Buchanan would eventually opt for a practical emphasis, as shown in his October 1846 instructions to the Academic Board:

> Natural philosophy is an important branch of education . . . but as the School was established with a view to make useful, practical officers first, I wish that branch confined principally to Mechanics, and illustrated as far as possible by experiments.[27]

Buchanan may have been influenced by a 13 August letter from Lieutenant Ward recommending that the school have only three courses—mathematics, French, and gunnery and steam—and criticizing the faculty for "spoiling men capable of making good navigators in the frequently abortive attempt to make them good mathematicians."[28] Whether Buchanan's "practical emphasis" reflected Ward's letter, George Bancroft's recent departure as Secretary, or his own maturing views is not known. What is significant is that from its earliest days the question of education versus training, or Athens versus Sparta as more recently phrased, has faced the Naval Academy. Franklin Buchanan tilted toward the latter.

Of greater immediate concern to the school's personnel was Buchanan's work in transforming the dilapidated buildings and "rickety white washed barracks of Fort Severn"[29] into classrooms and homes. He personally oversaw the renovating, furnishing, and equipping of the new school. Eighty iron camp bedsteads were bought for $8 each in Georgetown; furniture for the superintendent and faculty, a stove for the mess, and matting for the classrooms were bought in Baltimore; chronometers, sextants, and a telescope came from the Naval Asylum; muskets and a 24-pound gun came from the Bureau of Ordnance; and gun carriages came from the Washington Navy Yard. The Army left the powder behind. Midshipmen supplied their own bureaus, candles, and wood and coal for heat. Many slept on the floor during the school's early months.

Fort Severn's dreary surroundings had consequences beyond discomfort, for "so long as it was in a certain sense ragged and unprovided with suitable appliances . . . so long were the Midshipmen reckless, inattentive, and turbulent."[30] In truth the discipline problem that flared up after the New Year could also be traced to a heavy academic workload, too little recreation, the lack of military routine and formality, and the mixing of "youngsters" and "oldsters" at the school. The youngsters were the newly appointed acting midshipmen, boys between thirteen and sixteen years of age, fresh from puberty, who would be at the school for a year prior to being sent to sea. The oldsters were senior midshipmen, between eighteen and twenty-seven years old, who were sent to the school for a year's study prior to the lieutenant's exam. Though pupils in theory, they "regarded themselves . . . as officers on leave of absence from sea duty. Consequently, the most military exercise was duelling, the most popular uniform dressing gowns, and the favority study researches into the spiritual possibilities of barley and the grape."[31] Midshipmen drinking clubs like the Spirits and the Ballsegurs sprang up and met regularly in some of the more seedy establishments of antebellum Annapolis, such as Harry Matthews's tavern. Initially winked at by school authorities, the midshipmen antics soon became too numerous and serious. In February, Buchanan recommended dismissal for Midshipman Nones, who had left the yard while restricted for academic deficiencies. Bancroft discharged Nones within three days. Later that month, Buchanan suspended two midshipmen for smoking in their rooms and reported three others to Bancroft for intoxication. Writing to Bancroft on the drinking problem, Buchanan said:

> dissipation is the cause of all insubordination and misconduct in the Navy, and will, if countenanced by me under any circumstances at this School, ruin its usefulness to the service . . . and injure its character with the country.[32]

Bancroft dismissed one of the midshipmen and officially reprimanded the other two, and discipline improved markedly. With Bancroft's support, Buchanan had reined in his midshipmen.

From the start, the best families in town welcomed the midshipmen into their homes. These good relations reflected Annapolitans' esteem for Buchanan and his wife. In January 1846, the midshipmen reciprocated with a grand naval ball that became an annual event. Because Annapolis was the state capital, many Maryland politicians visited the school and were welcomed by Buchanan. "I am desirous that the institution should be seen and understood by Marylanders," he wrote.[33] In its still fragile state, it was important for the school to win friends.

In 1846, the Board of Examiners came to Annapolis to scrutinize not just the midshipmen but the whole system of education at the Naval School. Forty-three of the forty-nine oldsters who took the exams, which emphasized practical knowledge, passed. So, too, did the Naval School. The Examiners praised Buchanan's administration and supported his recommendations for new quarters and recitation rooms; spending $200 to $300 a year for experimental apparatus and additions to the library; and stationing a practice ship at the school.

In August, Congress appropriated $28,200 "for repairs, improvements, and instruction at Fort Severn, Annapolis, Maryland,"[34] and in October 1846, when classes began again, construction was under way on a new building that would house the kitchen, mess hall, lyceum, and library.

In January of 1847, this new building was the site of the school's second naval ball. In attendance were the House and Senate Naval Affairs Committees and John Y. Mason, who had recently succeeded George Bancroft as Secretary of the Navy. Mason and the congressmen had other things on their minds than the Naval School, for war had erupted with Mexico eight months earlier. Secretary Bancroft had refused Buchanan's request then for sea duty "because of the important business in which you are at present engaged."[35] Buchanan's 2 February 1847 request, however, was honored, and on 9 March he detached from the school to a nine-gun salute.

No Naval Academy superintendent has ever faced a greater challenge than did Franklin Buchanan. His was not the challenge of providing a blueprint for circumventing Congress or of being the prime mover in acquiring senior officer approval and old Fort Severn to formally establish the school—these were the work of Chauvenet and Bancroft. Buchanan's challenge was to combine old Fort Severn, a disparate band of midshipmen, the asylum faculty, a little money, and some general guidelines with elements of the West Point system, Chauvenet's asylum program, and the recommendations of the Board of Examiners to create, on less than three months' notice, something resembling a college. That he succeeded was attested to in an article in *Niles' National Register* of January 1846, barely three and a half months after the school's opening: "The police and discipline of the establishment are conducted by the Superintendent in person. He has already given to the institution a consolidated character which would render it difficult for an observer to detect evidences of its recent origin."[36] If Buchanan's early career established his credentials as an exemplar of old navy courage and discipline, his year and a half at the Naval School made his reputation as an energetic, hard-driving organizer and manager. That he possessed the qualities of both the old navy and the new, and had a home in Annapolis besides, had made him an excellent choice for superintendent. With Franklin Buchanan at the helm of the Naval School, the idea that it would graduate weak, timid officers waxed preposterous. Reformers like Chauvenet and Bancroft needed a symbol who could administer and lead. Franklin Buchanan was perfect.

The school, however, was not, and by 1849 its supporters felt strong enough to push for a major reorganization. Buchanan served on a special Board of Revision that recommended a four-year course (a pair of two-year stints at the Naval School separated by three years at sea); the removal of the school from the daily control of the Secretary of the Navy; strengthening the Academic Board; tightening discipline; introducing mandatory formation; establishing a midshipmen hierarchy; and renaming the school the Naval Academy. These changes were instituted in 1850. Buchanan also served on the 1851 Board of Examiners that established the four-consecutive-year course with summer cruises which has endured to the present. Without question, Franklin Buchanan had more impact on officer education during the Naval Academy's first two decades than any other line officer.

On 15 March Buchanan departed Norfolk for Mexican waters in command of the 900-ton sloop *Germantown*. Two weeks later the *Germantown* arrived off Vera Cruz, which had fallen to Perry a week earlier, and on 10 April she made for Tuxpan, one of the few remaining Gulf towns not under American control. As Tuxpan was some eight miles inland, Perry anchored his ships at the mouth of the Tuxpan River, loaded their barges with the landing force, and towed them upstream with three steamers and three sloops. Buchanan was in one of the *Germantown*'s boats towed by Perry in the steamer *Spitfire*. Coming under fire from a Mexican battery at La Pena, Perry cast off the landing force, which rowed for shore through a shower of grape and cannister. Buchanan and the *Germantown* detachment won the race, and at Perry's orders he leaped ashore and led his foot soldiers in the charge up the hill. The Mexicans' flight was as wild as Buchanan's advance was determined, and the *Germantown* party soon raised the stars and stripes over La Pena. Tuxpan fell by day's end.

Buchanan participated with Perry in a similar upriver expedition against Tabasco. The force was ambushed at Devil's Bend on the Tabasco River some twelve miles from the town, and Perry decided to anchor his ships and march overland to Tabasco. Buchanan selected the landing spot and commanded a detachment as part of Perry's thousand-man force. Aided by his naval forces which finally broke through river obstructions, Perry's overland force took Tabasco, destroyed its military stores and fortifications, and carried off its cannons, three of which were sent to the Naval School at Annapolis to honor the role of its first graduates and Buchanan in their capture.[37]

This was the last major naval engagement of the war. In February 1848 the *Germantown* returned to Norfolk where Buchanan relinquished command. For his services Buchanan received the "high commendation"[38] of Secretary Mason, a resolution of praise from the Maryland legislature, and 160 acres of land in Iowa from Congress.

The deserved approbation of his countrymen was a strong motivating factor in Franklin Buchanan's career. This was reflected in his successful opposition to the incorporation of officers of the Texas Navy into the U.S. Navy. Along with Commanders Samuel F. Du Pont and George A. Magruder, Buchanan addressed a pamphlet to the House of Representatives that recounted the naval glories of the recent war and continued:

For these achievements the sole reward of its officers has been the melancholy privilege of stepping into the vacant place of their brethren whom the sword or the more deadly pestilence had removed; and the consoling consciousness of having done their duty to their country.

Is it then unreasonable for us to complain that these gentlemen having left that country and its flag to seek fame elsewhere, should now mount over the shoulders of their seniors and former superiors in command—stop up the crowded avenues of promotion—and reap the rewards of services they did not perform and dangers they did not encounter.[39]

While the expansionist impulse underlying the Mexican War would lead to disunion by 1861, in the early 1850s it spawned the epic Perry mission to Japan which involved Buchanan in another historic event of the antebellum Navy. Buchanan's selection in January 1852 to command the nine-gun steam frigate *Susquehanna* during the expedition, and Perry's decision to make her his flagship, spoke eloquently of Old Bruin's regard for Old Buck. Buchanan's views on Perry were set forth in a letter written in July of 1847 that reveals the qualities Buchanan admired in a man. "Industrious," "energetic," "persevering," and "enterprising" wrote Buchanan of Perry. "He does not spare himself, or anyone under him . . . he is by no means a brilliant man but his good common sense and judgment, his sociable manner to his officers, no humbuggery or mystery, make him respected and esteemed."[40] This description could have fit Buchanan well, too.

While humbuggery was foreign to their character, Buchanan and Perry would have to exercise a fair amount of it to unlock the mystery of Japan. Because image and bearing were crucial in dealing with the Japanese, American crews had to be disciplined and well mannered. And since flogging had recently been abolished, "moral suasion"[41] would have to be the major governing force. Using language taken nearly verbatim from his October 1845 speech opening the Naval Academy, Buchanan's regulations for the *Susquehanna* established strict guidelines for midshipmen training and discipline. "As the Regulations of the Naval Academy prohibit midshipmen . . . from chewing and smoking tobacco," Buchanan concluded, "I direct that those regulations be conformed to in this ship."[42]

During his two years commanding the *Susquehanna*, Buchanan showed skill and patience in representing Perry in the "tedious and long winded"[43] negotiations leading to the historic Treaty of Kanagawa, signed in March 1854, that opened trade relations between the two countries. Buchanan enjoyed the distinction of being the first American ashore in the initial landing at Kurihama in July 1853, and, unlike Perry's other captains who "spent their thoughts in criticizing what he did and wishing they were going home,"[44] he was supportive of the commodore. Only on one occasion is it reported that they clashed, when Perry mitigated to life imprisonment the punishment of one of the *Susquehanna*'s coal heavers convicted of mutiny for assaulting a master at arms and resisting arrest. Buchanan had sentenced the man to be hanged, and he reportedly denounced Perry's lenience to his crew.[45]

Detached from Perry's command following the treaty signing, Buchanan remained in Asian waters for several months. In May 1854 he took the *Susquehanna* up the Yangtze River to Nanking where he attempted to open communications with the Tai-ping rebels. When they demanded tribute, Buchanan steamed the *Susquehanna* sixty miles upriver, a feat that "created the greatest astonishment among the Chinese,"[46] for no foreign ship had ever gone farther than Nanking. In September the *Susquehanna* departed Hong Kong for her voyage home. She reached San Francisco in November, having completed the first steamship crossing of the North Pacific.

The triumphs that marked the 1845–55 period in Buchanan's career were tragically absent from his last decade of naval service. In June 1855 he was ordered to serve on a board of some fifteen senior and junior officers who were to cull the officers corps of its dead wood. The board, which came to be called the Star Chamber Board, recommended that 49 officers be dropped from the rolls and that 152 be placed on the "reserved list." An uproar ensued, and over half of the decisions were later reversed by a special court of inquiry, but the affair left a residue of bitter feeling in the Navy for years. That may explain why Buchanan, promoted to captain in September 1855, did not see active service until May 1859 when he was ordered to command the Washington Navy Yard. It may also have sown seeds of the bitterness that would play a role in the most fateful decision of Buchanan's career—to fight for the Confederacy in the Civil War.

Buchanan's decision reflected the tortured logic that seized normally clear-headed men when they dealt with the questions of slavery, secession, and states' rights. But until the moment he resigned his commission, Buchanan performed his duties to the fullest in preparing the Washington Navy Yard for anticipated attacks from a mob of secessionists who wanted its armory and magazine. In instructions to Commander John A. Dahlgren, Buchanan ordered: "This yard shall not be surrendered . . . except by an order from the Honorable Secretary of the Navy, and in the event of an attack I shall require all officers and others under my command to defend it to the last extremity, and should we be overpowered by numbers, the armory and magazine must be blown up. . . ."[47] Buchanan would later be accused of breathing an "impure moral atmosphere"[48] at the Navy Yard because of strong secessionist sentiment there. By April of 1861 secessionist sentiment in Maryland had convinced Buchanan that his native state would join others that had left the Union, and on 22 April he personally delivered to Secretary of the Navy Gideon Welles a letter resigning his commission. Later that day, Welles detached Buchanan from the Navy Yard command in a communique that stated, "Your resignation is yet under consideration."[49] Buchanan's farewell address urging navy yard personnel to be faithful to their flag while still in its service brought tears to the workers' eyes and won him three lusty cheers.

When it became apparent that Maryland would not secede, Buchanan tried to withdraw his resignation. Writing to Welles on 4 May, he pleaded, "The circumstances which induced me . . . to tender my resignation, no longer exist, and I cannot voluntarily withdraw from a service in which I have passed nearly forty seven years of my life."[50] That same day he wrote to a friend that he had acted "very hastily," "never was a secessionist,"[51] and was miserable out of the service. Welles replied, "By direction of the President your name has been stricken from the rolls of the Navy."[52]

Buchanan's actions stunned many long-time friends. On 8 May 1861, Samuel F. Du Pont wrote to a friend, "Buchanan's resignation is looked upon as most incomprehensible and unjustifiable—yet he brings himself down with nine children to eleven hundred dollars a year, which is all his income. Thank God [he is not] going to serve."[53]

But Buchanan *would* serve, and his letters over the spring and summer showed increasing bitterness, despair, and militance. Writing to his nephew on 29 May, Buchanan once again forswore secession, but admitted the "right of revolution." He claimed that if his resignation had not been accepted, he would have requested foreign duty, and that his intention was to "remain neutral." But "if all law is to be dispensed with . . . and coercive policy continued which would disgust barbarians; and the South literally trampled upon, I may change my mind and join them."[54] Buchanan's ire had been raised by a group of Northern soldiers who trespassed on his property, threatened to arrest him, and took several of the shells he had won as trophies in the Mexican War. When Buchanan demanded of the colonel in charge that his trophies be restored, the colonel asked, "Who are you?" Buchanan replied, "I am a gentleman and the owner of the property your men are stealing, that is enough for you to know." The colonel and his men, described by Buchanan as "of the lowest order of mankind, and of all nations," returned the shells.[55] Buchanan's mind-set was shown in a lengthy letter writen to Du Pont in July, in which he said, "The Negro is the cause of it all, and the rascally Northern interference with the institution of slavery . . . ." He said it was a war of races, expressed his disgust with the Lincoln administration, predicted that Northern peace sentiment made acknowledgment of the Confederacy inevitable, and said that the flag under which he had served "no longer exists; it has been degraded, disgraced, and torn to pieces by those who rule the country."[56] Buchanan's vituperations seemed to bear out Du Pont's characterization of him as "a man of resolute will, [who] never had the intellect to grapple with political issues."[57] Buchanan had not always championed states' rights. In 1845 he had argued that federal authority should supersede a Maryland law that prohibited the hiring of a free black man he had brought to the Naval School. Nor was he a champion of Negro rights, for Franklin Buchanan, the son of an abolitionist, was a slaveowner.

By the end of August, Buchanan realized that war passion had overwhelmed peace sentiment. As he had from the first day of his career, Buchanan sought action. He legally assigned all of his property and slaves to his family and made for the southern Chesapeake and then Richmond where, on 5 September, he donned the gray uniform of a captain in the Confederate Navy.

Buchanan served as chief of the Office of Orders and Details during his first six months of service and became one of Confederate Secretary of the Navy Stephen Mallory's most trusted advisors. He participated in the erection of batteries along the Potomac, in strengthening river defenses near Richmond, and, after old friend Samuel F. Du Pont had captured Port Royal in South Carolina, in the improvement of defenses at Savannah. Buchanan also had the job of recommending officers to be assigned to the Confederate ironclad *Merrimac*.

Scuttled by Union forces on the night of 20 April 1861 as they withdrew from the Norfolk area, the *Merrimac*, a 3,500-ton steam frigate, was raised in May, cut down to the berthing deck, and converted into an ironclad. When completed, she sported a seven-foot-high, 170-foot-long casemate, covered with four inches of iron and two feet of wood, that sloped at thirty-five degrees and which was built on the original deck. She was armed with two seven-inch Brooke rifles at bow and stern, and two 6.9-inch Brookes and six nine-inch smoothbore Dahlgren's in broadside. A 1,500-pound wedge-shaped ram two feet under water projected like a dagger two feet from the prow. She had a top speed of seven knots, drew twenty-two feet of water, took more than a half hour to turn around, and steamed with her 263-foot deck awash.

On 24 February 1862, Secretary Mallory ordered Buchanan to command the Naval Defenses of the James River, and on 4 March Buchanan raised his flag over the *Merrimac*. Besides the *Merrimac*, Buchanan's 27-gun squadron included two steamers and three gunboats. It was opposed by a Union squadron of eleven vessels mounting over 200 guns. Buchanan's orders from Secretary Mallory were advisory. Tactically he recommended the use of the ram at night against an anchored enemy. Strategically he suggested that a raid on Washington "would be important to the cause."[58] Buchanan's strategic vision was defensive. Because of her twenty-two-foot draft, he informed Mallory, a raid up the Potomac was impossible. His tactical vision, however, was offensive, for he aimed at defending the James River through the destruction of Union naval forces at Newport News.

At 11:00 A.M. on the morning of 8 March, the *Merrimac* and two gunboat escorts got under way and made for the enemy. As the battle neared, Buchanan addressed his men, saying, "Men, the eyes of the country are upon you . . . . You must not be content with only doing your duty, but do more than your duty."[59] Shortly after 2:00 P.M. the *Merrimac* opened fire on the *Cumberland* and fifteen minutes later rammed her, backed off, and directed fire on the *Congress*. The *Cumberland* sank at 2:40, and the *Congress*, after an hour and a half of withering fire, hoisted the white flag at around 4:00 P.M., whereupon Buchanan gave orders to cease fire. When Union forces opened fire on his gunboats attending to the *Congress*'s surrender and evacuation, an enraged Buchanan grabbed a rifle from a crewman, fired it at the *Congress*, and ordered her destroyed by hot shot and incendiary shell. Soon thereafter, Buchanan was wounded in the thigh by shore fire, and he turned over command to Lieutenant Catesby Jones. After an attack on the *Minnesota*, an ebbing tide and waning daylight forced the *Merrimac* to retire. Shortly after midnight the burning *Congress* exploded. She had lost 136 men, including her commanding officer, Lieutenant Joseph B. Smith, who had been a midshipman at the Naval School when Buchanan was superintendent. One member of the *Congress*'s crew who survived was its paymaster, McKean Buchanan, Franklin's brother.

The next day, while Buchanan was recovering from his wound, the *Merrimac* and the *Monitor* fought their famous duel. The resulting stalemate did little to dampen the South's wild hopes for the *Merrimac*. A week after the battle, Mallory suggested a raid into New York harbor to shell and burn the city and its shipping. He hoped this would prompt bankers to withdraw financial support from the government and force the North to sue for peace. Buchanan's reply made clear that he thought the unseaworthy *Merrimac* would be lucky even to get to New York, let along return from a foray into the harbor. "I consider the [*Merrimac*] the most important protection to the safety of Norfolk," he wrote.[60] The *Merrimac*'s strategic role remained defensive. Buchanan's gallant service made him a hero in the South, and on 26 August he was promoted to admiral. A week earlier he had been ordered to command the Confederate naval defenses at Mobile, Alabama.

The two years between his arrival at Mobile and the Battle of Mobile Bay were the most frustrating of Franklin Buchanan's career. His nemesis was fellow Southerner David Farragut. Each commander feared attacks by the other that, for the most part, never materialized. Farragut could not get the needed forces from Secretary Welles, while Buchanan was assisting in the building and fitting out of several ironclads without which he could not seriously threaten the blockade.

On 22 May 1864, Buchanan finally took command of the recently completed ironclad ram, the *Tennessee*. Built at an estimated cost of just under $900,000, the ship featured an armament and sloping casemate design similar to that of the *Merrimac*. Though it was quite an achievement that she had been built, the *Tennessee* had serious design defects. Her engines could only drive her at six knots (thereby making ramming difficult), her gunport shutters were prone to jamming in battle, and her rudder chains were exposed on deck and subject to being shot away.

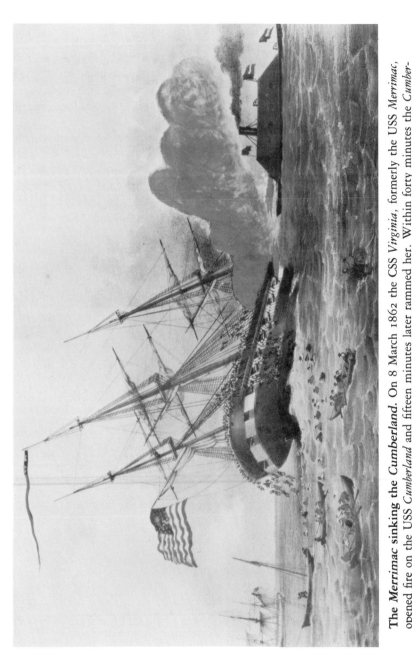

The *Merrimac* sinking the *Cumberland*. On 8 March 1862 the CSS *Virginia*, formerly the USS *Merrimac*, opened fire on the USS *Cumberland* and fifteen minutes later rammed her. Within forty minutes the *Cumberland* sank, and the *Virginia* turned her guns on the *Congress*. Contemporary lithograph by Currier and Ives. *Courtesy of the Naval Historical Foundation.*

The summer of 1864 saw the strengthening of Union forces, and by early August Farragut's eighteen-ship, 159-gun squadron was ready to force Mobile Bay. On 4 August, Union forces laid siege to Fort Gaines which guarded the entrance to the bay from the west side. Fort Morgan on Mobile Point guarded the channel from the east. Between the two forts were hundreds of underwater mines (torpedoes) and obstructions. To get to Mobile, some thirty miles to the north, Farragut had to pass Fort Morgan, penetrate the mines and obstructions, and defeat Buchanan.

Led by four ironclad monitors and followed by fourteen wooden ships lashed together in pairs, Farragut's squadron got under way at 5:40 A.M. on 5 August, and shortly after 7:00 A.M. the battle was joined. Buchanan had stationed his ships just north of the mine field, and his guns and those of Fort Morgan raked the Union fleet. It was a mine, however, that claimed the first Union ship, the *Tecumseh*. This disaster caused the rest of Farragut's force to slow, whereupon he issued his famous order to "Damn the torpedoes. Full speed." His squadron steamed unscathed the rest of the way through the mines, which months of immersion had rendered harmless.

The *Tennessee* fired on the Union ships as they passed and attempted to ram them, but their speed was too great. After an hour and a half of this, Farragut anchored about four miles up the bay and prepared for breakfast. His three gunboats out of action, Buchanan had only the *Tennessee* left. Instead of anchoring under the protection of Fort Morgan and making Farragut come to him, Buchanan unexpectedly—but not uncharacteristically—charged into the midst of Farragut's seventeen ships. The action may have been prompted by criticism he had received of late from a Mobile newspaper for not rushing out and destroying the federal blockade. Buchanan's plan was to do whatever damage he could with his remaining ammunition and steaming time and then retreat to the cover of Fort Morgan. Farragut considered the action reckless. "I did not think Old Buck was such a fool," he exclaimed.[61] In the wild melee that followed, the *Tennessee* was several times rammed and reduced to helplessness by raking fire and broadsides at ten feet that jammed her gunports and cut the steering chains. One of these salvos, from the *Chickasaw*, seriously wounded Buchanan in the leg, and he turned command over to Captain Johnston. The *Tennessee* was soon rendered immobile and impotent, absorbing concentrated fire for some thirty minutes without firing a shot. Apprised of the situation by Johnston, Buchanan ordered: "Fight to the last! Then to save these brave men, when there is no longer any hope, surrender."[62]

At 10:00 A.M. Johnston surrendered. Ironically, Confederate losses were light (only 12 killed from Buchanan's squadron) and Union losses heavy (145 dead). With Union command of the bay, Mobile was cut off from blockade runners and effectively isolated, though the city did not fall until after Lee's surrender the next spring. Buchanan was taken to Pensacola where excellent treatment saved his leg from amputation, and thence, at the end of November, to Fort Lafayette in New York where he was imprisoned. He faced the situation with typical resolve. "I never despair," he wrote to his nephew, "and trust in God to carry me through my present humiliating, degrading position."[63] Released in early March 1865 as part of a prisoner exchange, Buchanan returned to Mobile and assisted in its defense until its fall on 14 May. Twice vanquished in Mobile, Buchanan ended a fifty-year naval career.

Franklin Buchanan spent his remaining years rebuilding his home at "The Rest," which in 1863 had been destroyed by a fire; serving for a year as president of the Maryland Agricultural College, now the University of Maryland; working in Mobile for nearly a year and a half with an insurance company; and enjoying the admiration of his family, friends, and many others in the South to whom he had been the Nelson of the Confederacy. He died of pneumonia on 11 May 1874.

A newspaper epitaph described Buchanan as ". . . a thorough sailor, a strict disciplinarian, born to command, bold and venturesome, impetuous and brave to a fault, of sound judgment, kind and affable to subordinates, . . . an accomplished gentleman, and the soul of honor. . . ."[64] It might have included the words, ambitious, stubborn, iron-willed, principled, and excitable. While his name figures prominently in the various reforms, and some of the battles, of the early steam navy, he embodied the values of the Jones and Decatur era as a man of action willing to challenge long odds. Making single-ship charges like a knight of old in the *Merrimac* and the *Tennessee* was in keeping with the romantic warrior ideal that seemed to drive him.

His ethic was professional advancement through dedicated—preferably dangerous—service. These qualities, along with his skills as a leader and an organizer, made him something of a walking role model, the "beau ideal"[65] officer that the Naval Academy was supposed to produce. He combined the qualities of Athens *and* Sparta, both of which condoned slavery. Politically well connected but not politically astute, he made an ill-reasoned decision to fight for the South, guaranteeing a tragic end to a naval career that could have made him a national hero under the Stars and Stripes. Having always sought it, Franklin Buchanan would die without the approbation of his countrymen.

His enduring contribution, however, had been made years earlier at the Naval Academy, where his emphasis on discipline, practical education, and character gave strong impetus to the professionalization of the Navy's officer corps. In the process, he had forged the sword of his own undoing, as was noted by Admiral David Dixon Porter after the Civil War. "It was owing to the practical teaching of the Naval Academy," Porter wrote, "that we were able during the late war to rapidly build up so large a Navy, and in a short time drill the hardy officers of the mercantile marine into good practical naval officers."[66] Like his mentor, Matthew C. Perry, Buchanan was a transitional figure in the nineteenth-century Navy whose noncombat service has echoed more loudly over the years than the sound of round shot on armor. When the Naval Academy celebrated its centennial anniversary on 10 October 1945, the ceremony began with a reading of the address Buchanan had delivered at the opening of the school. He would have been pleased with its progress.

FURTHER READING

Despite his prominence among naval officers of the period, Franklin Buchanan has been the subject of only two biographies. The first of these was *Admiral Franklin Buchanan: Fearless Man of Action*, by Naval Academy professor Charles Lee Lewis. Published in 1929, Lewis's account is well-researched, drawing on papers made available by the Buchanan family, manuscript materials at the Naval Academy, and various secondary sources in the field. The narrative is fast-paced and well-written, but adulatory. Lewis covers the "man of action" side of Buchanan well, but, aside from his chapter on the early Naval Academy, offers little on how Buchanan fit in with the general naval reform movements of the period. The other biography is *Daring Sea Warrior: Franklin Buchanan*, by George Fielding Eliot. Published in 1962, Eliot's work is aimed at a younger, nonscholarly audience. It is unfootnoted and full of fictitious dialogue that would not be found in the dozen general sources listed in its bibliography.

Most of the articles in which Buchanan appears deal with the events he was involved in, that is, the founding of the Naval Academy and his Civil War service, rather than with Buchanan himself. An exception is Oretha Swartz's article, "Franklin Buchanan: A Study in Divided Loyalties," which details his decision to fight for the Confederacy.

Original Buchanan papers in the form of scrapbooks, ships' journals, diaries, and miscellaneous materials can be found at the Maryland Historical Society; the Special Collections Division of the Nimitz Library at the Naval Academy; the Naval Academy Museum; and the Southern History Collection of the University of North Carolina Library. Buchanan letters can be found in the Naval Records Collection of the Office of Naval Records and Library (Record Group 45), in Records of the Naval Academy (Record Group 405), and in John D. Hayes's *Samuel F. Du Pont: A Selection from His Civil War Letters*.

Buchanan's Naval Academy service is covered in Charles M. Todorich's *The Spirited Years: A History of the Antebellum Naval Academy*; Jack Sweetman's *The U. S. Naval Academy: An Illustrated History*; William D. Puleston's *Annapolis: Gangway to the Quarterdeck*; and Park Benjamin's 1900 work, *The United States Naval Academy*. Samuel Eliot Morison's biography of Matthew C. Perry, *"Old Bruin,"* offers good material on Buchanan's service with Perry during the Mexican War and the Japan Expedition. Buchanan's Civil War service is covered in a host of books dealing with the ironclads *Merrimac* and *Tennessee* at the battles of Hampton Roads and Mobile Bay, respectively.

NOTES

1. Charles Lee Lewis, *Admiral Franklin Buchanan: Fearless Man of Action*, 270.

2. Franklin Buchanan Scrapbook, Maryland Historical Society, Baltimore (hereafter cited as Buchanan Scrapbook).

3. Lewis, *Buchanan*, 228, quoting from J. T. Scharf, *History of the Confederate States Navy*, 560.

4. Ibid., quoting from Alexander Slidell Mackenzie, *The Life of Commodore Oliver Hazard Perry*, II: 140–41.

5. Ibid., 31.

6. Ibid., 69, quoting from William H. Hexall in the Richmond *Dispatch*, 13 May 1883.

7. Lewis, *Buchanan*, 70.

8. Ibid., 79.

9. Buchanan Scrapbook.

10. Samuel Eliot Morison, *"Old Bruin": Commodore Matthew Calbraith Perry*, 131.

11. Buchanan Scrapbook.

12. Ibid., also Lewis, *Buchanan*, 84.

13. Lewis, *Buchanan*, 89–90, quoting from Buchanan to Henshaw letter, 8 December 1843.

14. Letters to Buchanan, 2 October 1843 and 21 November 1843, Commander's Letters, R.G. 45, National Archives.

15. Lewis, *Buchanan*, 90.

16. Jack Sweetman, *The U. S. Naval Academy: An Illustrated History*, 9.

17. Ibid., 10.

18. Charles M. Todorich, *The Spirited Years*, 12.

19. Harold D. Langley, *Social Reform in the United States Navy, 1798–1862*, 25.

20. Samuel P. Huntington, *The Soldier and the State: The Theory and Politics of Civil–Military Relations*, 217.

21. Todorich, *The Spirited Years*, 17.

22. Mahlon S. Tisdale, "A Cruise Through the First Academic Journal and Some Modern Analogies," U.S. Naval Institute *Proceedings*, 50 (1924): 355.

23. Lewis, *Buchanan*, 100.

24. Tisdale, "A Cruise," 356–57.

25. Lewis, *Buchanan*, 101–3.

26. Henry F. Sturdy, "The Establishment of the Naval School at Annapolis," U.S. Naval Institute *Proceedings*, 71 (1945): 14.

27. Tisdale, "A Cruise," 358.

28. Ward to Buchanan, 13 August 1846, R.G. 405: Records of the Naval Academy, National Archives.

29. Thomas G. Ford, "History of the Naval Academy," U.S. Naval Academy Library, Special Collections Division, Annapolis, Chapter 10, 1 (hereafter cited as Ford Manuscript).

30. Ford Manuscript, Chapter 12, 18.

31. Carol H. Foster, "The United States Naval Academy," *Scribner's Magazine* 64 (July 1918): 3–21.

32. Buchanan to Bancroft, R.G. 405.

33. Buchanan to the President of the Maryland Senate, 4 February 1847, R.G. 405.

34. Todorich, *The Spirited Years*, 34.

35. Lewis, *Buchanan*, 112.

36. Ibid., 113, quoting from *Niles' National Register*, 31 January 1946.

37. K. Jack Bauer, *Surfboats and Horse Marines: U. S. Naval Operations in the Mexican War,* 1846–1848, 118.

38. Lewis, *Buchanan*, 123.

39. Franklin Buchanan File, U. S. Naval Academy Library, Special Collections Division, Annapolis.

40. Morison, *"Old Bruin,"* 237.

41. Edward M. Barrows, *The Great Commodore: The Exploits of Matthew Calbraith Perry*, 358.

42. Lewis, *Buchanan*, 129.

43. Ibid., 136.

44. Morison, *"Old Bruin,"* 406.

45. Ibid., 403.

46. Lewis, *Buchanan*, 148.

47. Oretha D. Swartz, "Franklin Buchanan: A Study in Divided Loyalties," U.S. Naval Institute *Proceedings*, 88 (1962): 61.

48. Samuel F. Du Pont to Franklin Buchanan, 26 May 1861 in John D. Hayes, ed., *Samuel Francis Du Pont: A Selection from His Civil War Letters*, I: 72.

49. Lewis, *Buchanan*, 162.

50. Swartz, "Divided Loyalties," 65.

51. Lewis, *Buchanan*, 164.

52. Swartz, "Divided Loyalties," 66.

53. Samuel F. Du Pont to Henry Winter Davis, 8 May 1861, in Hayes, *Du Pont*, 69.

54. Lewis, *Buchanan*, 166–67.

55. Buchanan to Du Pont, 9–11 July 1801, in Hayes, *Du Pont*, 97.

56. Ibid., 95, 98.

57. Du Point to Davis, in Hayes, *Du Pont*, 69.

58. Lewis, *Buchanan*, 178.

59. Ibid., 185, quoting from Scharf, *History of the Confederate States Navy*, 154.

60. Lewis, *Buchanan*, 194.

61. E. B. Potter and Chester W. Nimitz, eds., *Sea Power: A Naval History*, 320.

62. Lewis, *Buchanan*, 238, quoting from Dr. D. B. Conrad in Southern Historical Society Papers, XIX: 78.

63. Lewis, *Buchanan*, 249.

64. Buchanan Scrapbook.

65. James D. Johnston, "The Battle of Mobile Bay," *United Service*, VI: 108.

66. Ford Manuscript, Chapter 29, 19.

THE OLD STEAM
NAVY AT WAR

ANDREW FOOTE:
ZEALOUS REFORMER,
ADMINISTRATOR, WARRIOR

BY JOHN D. MILLIGAN

Though perhaps not so well known as some of his naval contemporaries, Rear Admiral Andrew Hull Foote was surely one of the more fascinating personages of the old steam navy. He was a fighting commander who seemed genuinely to enjoy battle, but he was also a man of parts. He was to a fair degree a capable technician; he was to a consummate degree an able administrator. Yet, as much as any of these, Foote was an ardent social reformer. And in each of these roles he contributed to the traditions of the U.S. Navy. Still more, Foote as a driven personality elicits considerable interest.

"There is a risk," James Ford Rhodes once warned his fellow historians, "in referring any historical event to a single cause." So, too, the biographer must be wary in referring the actions of his historical subject to a single impulse. Still, his warning notwithstanding, Rhodes, having weighed the evidence concerning the coming of the Civil War, one of the most profound events in American history, proceeded to announce that "it may safely be asserted that there was a single cause. . . ."[1] In similar fashion, recognizing the risk but weighing the evidence, one can attribute the many activities of Andrew Foote and his near fanaticism in pursuing them, if not solely at least primarily to a single impulse, his determination to serve God.

Men of strong faith were not, of course, uncommon among the commanders of the old steam navy; nevertheless, after experiencing a religious transformation, Foote seems to have stood apart. Already made receptive by a puritanic New England rearing, he, as a twenty-one-year-old midshipman in 1827, underwent that experience on the West India station. While standing night watch, he was approached by one of his ship's lieutenants, apparently a deeply devout man. Perhaps the beauty of that moonlit scene and the gentle swell of the Caribbean added their influence; Foote responded to the man's entreaties, and the two knelt in prayer. For the next fourteen days, the midshipman spent every spare moment pouring over his Bible. The result seemed conclusive.

Andrew Foote. A photograph taken during the Civil War. *Courtesy the Naval Historical Foundation.*

Henceforth, he wrote to his mother, he would "under all circumstances . . . act for God."[2]

Later, when he was troubled to reconcile his dedication to the Almighty with his career in a service prepared to use force to achieve national objectives, his father, former state governor and U.S. senator from Connecticut, put to him two questions. First, was a navy necessary? "Certainly, the seas must be policed." Then, "Should the navy be in charge of good or bad men?" "Of good men," came the reply; and after that, as much as any naval officer of his time,

Andrew Foote seemed convinced that he was God's agent and that the service must be made God's instrument.[3] This conviction persuaded him to give first priority to principle as he perceived it, even at times to the point of acting independently of authority and at some risk to his professional career. The man seems to have been a reasonable facsimile of that nineteenth-century type whom David Riesman and his associates have characterized as "inner-directed."[4]

Reformation under Foote came to mean three things—support for Protestant missionary activity, support for temperance, and suppression of the African slave trade. To understand the directions Foote's reforming energies took is to remember that his was the generation of the Great Reform Movement, of that antebellum epoch when many Americans stood ready to eliminate those conditions that they believed hindered the perfectibility of man and his society. Thus, it was during those years, when Protestant evangelicals were sending missionaries overseas and doing battle with Catholicism at home, that Foote took abroad his urge to help these missionaries in their quest to convert the infidels and to preserve the converts from the influence of Romanism.[5] In October 1839, he, now a lieutenant, arrived in the Sandwich (Hawaiian) Islands. If his official duty was as executive officer on the sloop of war *John Adams*, when he learned what had been happening ashore, Foote gave equal weight to what he manifestly saw as his God-given duty.

The islands and their people were ostensibly independent and ruled by a native monarch; but citizens of the United States, England, and France were active in them. American missionaries had been particularly energetic in proselytizing among the indigenous population and, according to the tiny community of resident French Catholics, had been influencing the local king to take measures against them, their religion, and his subjects who practiced that religion. The resulting clash had brought a French frigate to the islands in July. Its captain threatened that, unless the king signed a treaty that among other things extended to Catholics the same religious "privileges granted to Protestants," he would make war on the natives and, in that event, treat the American missionaries as natives. In the circumstances the king signed, and the frigate sailed away.[6]

One can readily imagine Foote's dismay when he learned of these events. Though the teachings of the American missionaries seemed indeed to have been swaying the king against Catholicism, the lieutenant probably thought it proper that they should; and, as neither the American consul nor the commander of the East India Squadron, Commodore George Read, evinced any inclination to act, Foote, himself, took action. Supported by a like-minded lieutenant from the *John Adams*, he persuaded the missionaries to ask Read to establish a naval court of inquiry to investigate the whole matter. When Read refused, the two lieutenants framed a letter calling on their national government to protect the missionaries as U.S. citizens, and solicited signatures for the letter from other officers in the squadron. By the time the French consul had got wind of the lieutenants' activity and had brought it to Commodore Read's attention, the letter carried sixteen signatures. Doubtless exasperated by the unauthorized action of his two officers, Read at first refused even to read the missive. Foote then used his persuasive abilities, which, as demonstrated then and later, were considerable, to convince his commander that the letter made no direct attack on the French government but simply called on the U.S. government to shield its citizens. Subsequently, the letter, together with correspondence relating to the affair and an article written by one of the missionaries to exonerate the mission, was published as a pamphlet. Moreover, when he returned to the mainland, Foote spoke out publicly about the case.[7]

If his objective had been to further the American missionary effort, Foote may have had some success. True, the native monarch would presumably still honor his pledge to the Catholics; but at the very least the American East India Squadron had unofficially made known that violations of the rights of the American mission, whether by local officials or foreign representatives, would not go unnoticed. This episode and Foote's role in it also stressed something familiar to anyone who has a nodding acquaintance with the diplomacy of the period and the character of relations between people of European descent and native peoples. Even before social Darwinism provided a rationale, the former felt free to manipulate native rulers and to assume over their subjects the roles of military, political, and even moral and spiritual guardians.[8] Thus, tensions, as in the affair just described, were frequently between caucasians, who, representing different national or religious interests, sparred for dominance. Only when indigenous peoples offered serious resistance, as in the case of Foote's later experience in China, did Westerners pay first consideration to them.

Though the treaty that the French captain had forced on the native monarch had also provided for the importation of French brandy into the Sandwich Islands, this provision did not seem to cause Foote particular anguish. He had not yet formed strong convictions on the subject of temperance. During his early years in the Navy, he would later tell a brother, he had assumed that he "could not be a temperance man." Meeting "with persons of all nations," he explained, he would be "obliged to conform to their customs."[9] It was while stationed ashore after the cruise in the *John Adams* that he changed his mind.

In 1841, Lieutenant Foote was appointed to the Naval Asylum in Philadelphia, and in time he took charge of it. The asylum was part hospital and part naval school. It also provided quarters for elderly naval pensioners who, according to Foote, seized every opportunity to become intoxicated. Watching this spectacle, and undoubtedly influenced by the temperance movement, which at that period seemed to be moving from strength to strength, Foote, like many reformers, came to the conclusion that from the consumption of alcohol flowed social and moral evil.[10] The problem, as he saw it, was that the Navy, by its tradition of regularly issuing a whiskey or "grog" ration to enlisted men, including his pensioners, was in effect putting its official imprimature on the general consumption of spirits. The alcoholism among seamen that this tradition encouraged was, Foote believed, destroying their lives in both this world and the next. It debauched them, made them, in Foote's phrase, easy prey for "land-sharks," and hastened their deaths in this world; and, because drunkenness was itself a sin, it condemned them to eternal damnation in the next. Far more important, then, than the favorable impression that he might make on foreign nationals by indulging with them in strong drink was the influence that he could exert for sailors' welfare by supporting temperance.[11]

Thus, while commanding the asylum, Foote set a precedent by signing "the pledge" of abstention. The pensioners in time followed his example, no doubt convinced by their commander's moral suasions liberally couched in warnings of hell-fire and brimstone. Subsequently, they drew up a petition expressing their gratitude.

> [Lieutenant Foote] has done us a great deal of good in making us all sober men. We once thought that old sailors could not do without grog. Now there is not a man in the house who draws his grog, and we feel like human beings, and hate the sin of getting drunk.[12]

Not surprisingly, when in 1843 he was again ordered to sea, Foote took with him his zeal against alcohol and his desire to win converts. Almost immediately he had the opportunity to indulge both. He had been assigned as executive officer to the USS *Cumberland*, a frigate with officers and crew numbering over 250 men. Even before the ship departed Boston harbor for the Mediterranean, a few of the crew broke into her store of whiskey. Becoming drunk, they assaulted an officer and were heavily flogged. To Foote, it seemed ludicrous that, on the one hand, the Navy with its "grog tub" encouraged addiction, but, on the other, it punished those who, breaking rules to sate that addiction, got out of hand. Being the man he was, he would once more have to act.

Foote began with the ship's officers. Encouraged by his close friend, Commodore Joseph Smith, whose flag flew in the *Cumberland*, he again demonstrated his talent for making proselytes by persuading them to found a temperance society. Soon his influence was felt by the crew as well. In time all of the sailors agreed to accept a cash payment in lieu of their whiskey ration. It had taken a year into the voyage to achieve this, but the *Cumberland* became a temperance ship, the first in the history of the U.S. Navy. If Foote is to be believed, during the second year of her cruise the frigate's sober crew did superior duty in getting her under way, keeping her snug and clean, exercising her guns, and bringing her to anchor. Moreover, upon the completion of the voyage, her crew and all her officers petitioned the U.S. Congress to abolish the whiskey ration throughout the Navy.[13]

The causes of missionary endeavor and temperance did indeed recruit many supporters; yet, of all the social issues that in Foote's era evoked sentiment for reform, none was more compelling than slavery, and in the United States the movement against it had already achieved some impressive results. The Revolution had started the institution on its way to extinction in every state north of Maryland; Congress in 1808 had prohibited U.S. citizens from participating in the African slave trade; and by the 1830s and 1840s the antislavery movement was gaining new strength in the Northern states.[14]

Foote, himself, was not an abolitionist. If he condemned England for having "imported and grafted" slavery on the American colonies when they were subject to its authority, he did not condemn Southern slaveholders. He seems to have viewed the peculiar institution as relatively benign. On the other hand, Foote was ready to admit that blacks, even free blacks, could not progress in the United States. Partly he attributed this fact to innate character-istics; but he also acknowledged that white racial attitudes stood in the way. Free blacks, too, were still in bondage, because, Foote stated, the white American "is not, and never has been disposed . . . to unite himself with a caste, marked by so broad a distinction as exists between the two races."

The solution to the problem seemed obvious to Foote. Apparently never entertaining the thought that whites should alter their attitudes, he argued instead that blacks should be colonized in Africa. There, Liberia, the Amer-ican Colonization Society's recently founded settlement for free blacks on the west coast, would not only provide them with superior opportunities unim-peded by persecution but would enable them to bring to the "dark continent" the "light and faith" of "Christian truth and civilization."[15] In these thoughts, Foote may have been somewhat more enlightened than many of his coun-trymen; but, in common with the intellectual and scientific communities of his day, he deemed the white as the superior race whose responsibility was to guide the inferior races, whether Polynesian, Negro, or other.[16]

If Foote was not strongly opposed to slavery, he was adamantly opposed to the African slave trade, which persisted even though England and the United States both officially condemned it, their national legislatures both declared it illegal, and units of both their navies cruised the African coast to suppress it. The rewards were so high that Americans and other nationals continued to carry the trade to those places in the New World where slavery survived—Cuba, Brazil, and the southern United States.[17]

Having served for three years as executive officer of the Boston Navy Yard after his cruise in the *Cumberland*, Foote was delighted in 1849 to be ordered again to sea—and doubly delighted when he learned that he was to command his own ship, the brig *Perry*, and with her to join the small American squadron on the west African coast to help suppress the slave trade. *Africa and the*

American Flag, the book that Foote would write upon his return from this cruise, dwells on the horrors to which the "matured villainy of the world" subjected its victims during the "middle passage." In words that eloquently reveal its author's persuasiveness, the book expresses Foote's bitterness against those who profited from the trade and his conviction that ultimately they would be judged sinners before God. Observing the "graceful" lines and "gallant bearing" of a ship putting out from the African coast, Foote would write, the casual observer could hardly divine that this "deceitful beauty may conceal . . . the theft of living men, the foulness and corruption of the steaming slave-deck, and the charnel-house of wretchedness and despair." Nor, looking down into the sapphire sea, reflecting "the blue sky in these tragic regions," might one realize that this "transparent abyss . . . for ages has sunk the dark-skinned sufferer from 'the horrors of the middle passage' . . . to rest until 'the sea shall give up its dead,' and the slaver and his merchant come up from their places to be confronted by their victim."[18]

During their two years on the West African station the *Perry* and her crew under Foote worked not only to suppress the offending trade but to guard ships legitimately flying the American flag against search by the Royal Navy. To be sure, the Americans and British were cooperating to interdict the trade; but the U.S. government, mindful of past British violations of the flag, and aware of the American slaveholder's fear that too vigorous an attack on the slave trade might portend an attack on slavery itself, insisted that only American warships could search American commercial ships. Knowing this and hoping to gain immunity from the Royal Navy, non-American slavers not infrequently raised the American ensign. This custom encouraged British captains to board anyway, gambling that the vessels they were investigating were hiding their true nationalities.[19] Out to put a stop to this British practice, Foote challenged it at every opportunity and finally made a test case of the British detention of an American ship that was not a slaver and whose papers were in order. In 1851, Parliament published his lengthy correspondence with the British squadron commander, who in the end asked pardon of the ship's master and proposed remuneration.[20]

Foote's efforts might also have resulted in an increase in the slave trade by ships illegally flying the American flag, had he, within his cruising ground, not been so vigilant in stopping vessels that flew it. In a typical encounter, the *Perry*, purposely not flying her own colors, overhauled a large, three-masted ship, the *Martha*, displaying the American ensign. Suddenly realizing the nationality of the *Perry*, the ship's crew replaced the American with the Brazilian ensign, but the truth—that her owners and her captain were U.S. citizens—was revealed in papers that Foote's sailors recovered from a desk that the *Martha*'s crew had hastily thrown overboard. If the boarders found no slaves, they did find all the paraphernalia—water, food, and a "slave deck" with irons—needed to ship a cargo of captives. Instead, it was the ship's

The USS *Perry*. While commanding the African Squadron, Andrew Foote, in the *Perry*, stopped the American slave ship *Martha* off Ambriz on 6 June 1850. Lithograph by Sarony & Company. *Courtesy of the Naval Historical Center.*

company whom the righteous Foote put in irons. He then dispatched the vessel under a prize crew to New York, where she was condemned as a slaver, the largest such ship captured off Africa in a number of years.

In truth, the *Perry* captured few vessels actually engaged in the slave trade. Her mission, though, was as much to deter as to interdict; and the fact that during her cruise her sailors boarded some seventy vessels must have established a considerable deterrent. In a private letter, Sir George Jackson, the British commissioner at Laonda, later told Foote that the American squadrons' being "prepared to confront [slavers and] to vindicate the honor of their insulted flag [has] struck [such] terror into those miscreants" that since Foote's "very opportune captures, not a vessel illicitly assuming American colors has been seen on the coast."[21]

Foote attempted further reform, not only in his official duties as a naval officer but as an author and lecturer. After his cruise with the *Perry*, while again stationed ashore, he wrote his only book to achieve two ends: to persuade the national government to continue to suppress the African slave trade and to persuade the reading public of the merits of the colonization experiment in Liberia. At the same time, Foote initiated a practice that would become his stock in trade when he was ashore. He began giving regular public lectures to extol the virtues of temperance, overseas Christian missions, and colonization. If the Navy brought forward other reformers in his time, few if any exceeded Foote in the catholicity of his concerns or the fervor of his commitment.[22]

On the other hand, as a capable technician and an able administrator, Andrew Foote has to some extent been misunderstood. While he made contributions to naval tradition in both roles, praises of Foote the technician have sometimes been oversung and praises of Foote the administrator understated. For instance, Foote has on occasion been described as the individual who early in the Civil War virtually single-handedly gave technological life to the federal naval squadron in the upper Mississippi Valley.[23] Perhaps the extollers have taken their cue from Lincoln's Secretary of the Navy. Certainly Gideon Welles, who could never forget that he and Foote "were school boys together," seldom missed an opportunity to praise Foote's abilities and to credit the Mississippi Squadron mainly to his genius. The Secretary indeed claimed that he was the one who first recognized the man's singular qualities.[24]

Two points should be made respecting Foote's part in the building of the river navy. First, the initial units of that navy were operational before Foote took command of the force on 6 September 1861. Naval Constructor Samuel Pook and naval Commander John Rodgers, working with western boat builders, had already put in commission three wooden-bulwarked gunboats converted from conventional river steamers. Second, there are even misperceptions concerning the seven ironclad sister-gunboats, the first true American ironclads, which made up the core of the squadron and for which Foote commonly receives much credit. Almost every important decision about their conception, design, and construction had been made earlier by Pook, Rodgers, and contractor James B. Eads. Further, plans for the conversion of two commercial steamers into still larger ironclads and for the construction of thirty-eight mortar rafts had been consummated and the work on them begun by the time Foote took command.[25]

Nevertheless, as the ironclads neared completion, Foote did make some important decisions respecting final alterations. In the sister-vessels, he saw to the correction of a list to the boilers; and to the elevation of the steam drums from the holds, where their location caused water as well as steam to enter the engines, to the tops of the boilers. To give more speed and maneuverability to the *Benton*, one of the converted steamers, he had the paddle wheel raised, the rudder broadened, and an auxiliary water pump added. With these changes and with what engineer Eads had already built into her, the *Benton* became the most formidable ironclad on the interior waters. Foote also oversaw some alterations to the mortar-boat hulls that made them more river-worthy.[26]

If Gideon Welles exaggerated Foote's technological contributions, the Secretary did indeed have in his subordinate a splendid administrator. Whether commanding a ship, a squadron, or a shore installation, the man evinced a fine talent not merely for running a "tight" unit but for advancing it to its next logical stage. When Foote was at the Philadelphia Naval Asylum, the method of instructing midshipmen was in transition, from the use of schoolmasters in ships at sea to teachers in classrooms ashore. Advances in nautical science and engineering, in particular the application of steam to warships, mandated the Navy's giving its future officers more formal and thorough training. Initially, the classrooms were established at navy yards, but these schools were uncoordinated and functioned irregularly. Not until 1839, when, at the urging of Commodore James Biddle, the naval school was founded at the asylum, were midshipmen provided with an institution where they could spend a full academic year preparing for their examinations. The school was in fact the precursor of the U.S. Naval Academy, which was established some years later.[27]

Foote had come to the Naval Asylum in 1841; and according to his biographer, James Hoppin, he was "especially assigned the care and education of midshipmen." Foote seems to have clearly understood the transitional role that the school was meant to play. Charles Paullin credits him with securing his charges more adequate accommodations; and Hoppin writes that, notwithstanding opposition from more traditional salts, Foote actively defended the proposition that midshipmen should be exposed to theoretical instruction by professional teachers as well as practical instruction by men who had been to sea. Perhaps one can conclude that to his other reforming bents Foote had added pedagogy.[28]

That his superiors appreciated his administrative abilities was demonstrated in 1855 when Foote was appointed to the Navy's efficiency board, an agency charged with recommending means for increasing the efficiency of the service.

Throughout his career as an administrator—which also included effective terms as executive officer of both the Boston Navy Yard (1846–49) and the Brooklyn Navy Yard (1858–61), at which latter station he helped fit out the expeditions for Forts Sumter and Pickens—Foote, as always, put faith in his Maker to guide him right. Especially when confronted by seemingly insuperable obstacles did he call upon Him.[29] And Foote must have frequently found it necessary to do so, once he had been posted by Gideon Welles to the assignment that would provide the last and most difficult test of his executive skills—to take charge of that federal naval force forming on western waters. Never mind that this squadron was still officially under the aegis of the War Department, necessitating Foote's successively taking orders from those jealous and incompetent generals John C. Fremont and Henry W. Halleck, and still worse, until he was given the nominal title of flag officer, from army officers down to the level of lieutenant colonel, the rank the Army then equated with his grade of captain.[30] Never mind that the government was far in arrears in paying the boatbuilders, that much of the ordnance for his vessels had not arrived, that sufficient recruits to man the craft seemed unobtainable, and that because of this last he could only deploy four ironclads in each of his first two battles. Never mind all this—Foote was expected to overcome every obstacle; and, amazingly, for the most part he did.

To maintain close contact with the generals who had their headquarters in St. Louis and to hurry work on the ironclads and mortar boats that were under construction nearby, Foote stationed himself in the Missouri city and put a subordinate in charge of the woodclad gunboats downriver at Cairo, Illinois. Only when the new vessels were well on their way to completion did Foote move them to Cairo and make that riverside town his naval depot in the west.[31] In the meantime, when the contractors threatened to stop work on the ironclads and mortar vessels unless they were paid, Foote's persistent cajoling of them to continue their labors and of Washington to produce funds had its effect: the work went on to completion and the contractors were eventually paid.[32]

To secure the ordnance he required, Foote fired off demands to the War Department, the Washington Navy Yard, the arsenal at Erie, and the Fort Pitt Foundry, and he dispatched personal representatives to the latter two facilities to prod people into action. Even so, when they arrived, the guns frequently proved old and defective, especially the rifled pieces, which, being simply reamed-out, army smooth bores, were given to bursting when fired.[33] To push recruitment, Foote added shipping rendezvous to those already established by Rodgers and hired private individuals to enlist men along the rivers. Yet, by 19 October he had only one hundred of the 1,700 men he needed. The problem was that the Navy Department had not only depleted the area's pool of volunteers by shipping men for sea duty but would permit Foote to offer recruits only about half the going wages of civilian boatmen. So, Foote resorted to other measures. For one thing, he pleaded with the department to send him crews from the east, and in this way by mid-November raised the number of his recruits to 650. For another, he persuaded Washington to authorize General Halleck to discharge soldiers who would volunteer to reenlist in the Navy. However, when army officers discouraged their men from volunteering, Foote again turned to Washington. By the time he took his squadron into action, the eastern Army of the Potomac was preparing to send Foote enough men to fill out his complement.[34]

Though Foote was finally to have his men, they would be a motley crew of landlubbers and former river and lake deck hands, leavened with a sprinkling of seasoned sailors and the few officers the Navy Department had sent out to command the gunboats, provide gunnery training, and fill administrative positions. The subordinate officers were often neophytes. If one were "ignorant" of his duties, wrote a young, freshly appointed officer, "it is nothing more than is the case with *everyone*, with the exception only of the captains and a few eastern officers holding positions . . . ."[35] Just two months after this statement was penned, Foote took these men into what for many of them was their baptism in battle.

None of the naval parts played by Andrew Foote better illustrated his conviction that duty to country and duty to God were one and the same than

Attack on the barrier forts. In November 1856 the USS *Portsmouth*, commanded by Andrew Foote, and the USS *Levant* bombarded Chinese forts, after which Foote personally led a force of marines and sailors ashore to capture the four forts. A contemporary lithograph by J. H. Buffords. *Courtesy of the Franklin Delano Roosevelt Library.*

his part as fighting commander. It made him one of the most militarily aggressive officers in the service. That is, it did so until one desperate February day on the waters of the Cumberland River that seemed to drain him of his passion.

Foote's 1856 service on the China station exemplifies his aggressiveness. At the time, the British were making war on the Chinese. Foote, commanding the sloop of war *Portsmouth*, had brought his vessel up the Canton River to Whampoa and from there with eighty of his men had proceeded in boats to Canton City. Having made up his mind to protect American property and resident American merchants (though there seems to have been little of the former and not much peril for the latter), Foote would not easily be deterred. He resolved to stay where he was though the local Chinese commissioner, hoping to avoid an incident, asked him and his men to leave. He intended to stay even though East Indian Squadron Commander James Armstrong, calling for strict neutrality, had asked him to bring his ship to Shanghai. To emphasize his intention, Foote ordered the sloop of war *Levant* to join the *Portsmouth* at Whampoa and her commander to join him in Canton with reinforcements.

While the British were storming Canton's defenses, Foote regularly drilled his 150 men and their two light cannon to impress the Chinese. When an American steamer reported that the Chinese had fired upon her near Macao, Foote urged the U.S. consul to give the Chinese commissioner exactly forty-eight hours to redress the grievance. It was only when Commodore Armstrong—who had brought his flagship to Whampoa and apparently concurred with the commissioner that the American naval force in Canton was provocative—ordered his subordinate to withdraw his men that the latter reluctantly began the process.[36] And then came the opportunity Foote so obviously was seeking—a fine illustration of how a perceived insult to his country's flag automatically cast him in the role of avenging agent, and of how a success in that role automatically elicited his thanks to Almighty Beneficence.

Between Canton and Whampoa lay the four "Barrier Forts" manned by the Chinese. As Foote was being rowed past, they fired several rounds at his boat. The shots missed, but the American ensign at his boat's stern had been dishonored, and that was sufficient. Urged on by the indignant Foote, the commodore ordered his two sloops of war towed upriver to chasten the offenders. On 16 November, only Foote and the *Portsmouth* could open fire, however, because the *Levant* had grounded downstream. That the forts were of formidable European design and disposed 176 guns, some of large caliber, did nothing to deter the bold Foote. By sunset, his ship, while taking several hits, had temporarily silenced one of the forts. Before the attack was resumed four days later, the commodore, who had come upriver and had observed the earlier action from the *Portsmouth*, returned to his flagship to open negotiations with the Chinese. He left Foote in charge with the caveat that he was not "to take aggressive action without sufficient cause." Unfortunately for the Chinese, Armstrong added the qualifier that Foote could capture the forts, if he deemed it necessary to prevent their being strengthened. Foote naturally deemed it necessary.[37]

On the 20th, both sloops opened fire on two of the forts. When the return fire fell off, a landing party of marines and sailors led by Foote disembarked in boats and in three columns made for the bank. Once ashore and with the marines in the van, the force overran the first fort and employed its guns to soften up the second. The next day the essence of this scenario was repeated, and two more forts came into American hands. The last fort fell the following morning. Chinese casualties may have reached several hundred; the American came to thirty-five.[38]

The local American commissioner and the Secretary of the Navy would later claim that the attack had been justified to oblige the Chinese to respect the flag. Some disagreed. A lieutenant on board the *Portsmouth* thought Foote had deliberately provoked the affair, and a naval chaplain evidently concurred. Criticism from a man of the cloth not surprisingly brought a scathing reply from the righteous Foote, who was convinced that "merciful interposition of a kind Providence" had carried the day, and who after the battle had sung His praises at religious services both on board ship and in one of the captured forts.[39] It also seems clear that Foote had come to a conclusion that flew in the face of traditional naval wisdom: properly fought warships, if properly inspired, were a match for fixed fortifications.

Certainly as commander of the Mississippi Squadron during the Civil War, Foote initially evinced no trepidation in leading his force against land-based works. To understand the technological significance of these engagements is to appreciate that seven of the ironclads under Foote were the first in America built as such, and that all nine of his ironclads were the first in America to combine armor, steam propulsion, rifled cannon, and shell guns. Each of these vessels—with her thick, rectangular wooden casemate squatting on a broad, shallow hull; her two high-pressure steam engines turning a single, stern-located paddle wheel; her iron plates meant to cover the most vulnerable surfaces; and her mixed battery of rifles, shell guns, and smoothbores—seemed, even before her trial by fire, to be a formidable weapon.

On the other hand, some caution might have been advised. True, the casemate sides of the two converted ironclads were heavily armored; but those of the seven sister-craft not only carried lighter armor but no armor at all on their quarters and sterns, and none of the "ironclads" carried iron on her hurricane deck. Furthermore, whereas the sails and rigging of the ships Foote had customarily commanded could absorb considerable punishment from enemy fire, the delicate steam machinery in any of his new ironclads might be disabled by a single, well-placed shot. And finally the ironclads mounted fragile, extempore rifles.[40]

Caution had no place in Foote's plans, however. He and Brigadier General Ulysses S. Grant, commanding local army units, seemed convinced that the four ironclads that Foote could adequately man would be sufficient to attack the two forts—Henry on the Tennessee River and Donelson on the Cumberland River—that the Confederates had built just south of Kentucky to block federal ingress into Tennessee. So confident was Foote of the outcome of the attack on Fort Henry that even before it took place he issued orders to the commander of his woodclad gunboats: as soon as the fort capitulated, that officer was to take his vessels on a sortie up the Tennessee deep into enemy territory. Thus, though Foote only learned after the battle that Grant's troops had been unable to cooperate because recent rains had washed out roads, earlier knowledge of that fact would hardly have curbed his confidence. Time spent praying prior to the engagement gave him all the assurance he required.

The outcome of the 6 February 1862 naval attack on Fort Henry seemed to confirm Foote's and Grant's faith in the ironclads. After ninety minutes of close-range battering by the bow guns of these vessels, supported by longer-range shelling from the woodclads, the Confederate work—with most of its twelve cannon that bore on the river silenced—surrendered. Nevertheless, there were omens. The armor of all the ironclads had withstood the blows of the fort's fire; but some balls had penetrated their unsheathed quarters, causing casualties, and the effect of a particular shot should have given even Foote pause. In the advance on the fort, one of the ironclads had suddenly slowed as live steam began pouring out of all her ports. The steam was soon followed by men, flinging themselves overboard. For several unspeakable moments the vessel lay stationary, seemingly a giant steam cooker; and then she drifted downstream. The fateful shot had exploded one of her boilers.[41]

This calamity, of course, did not daunt Foote. The Lord, he characteristically wrote to his wife after the battle, "has given me this victory"; and the next Sunday, in the absence of the minister, the flag officer entered a Cairo pulpit to offer up more thanks and preach from the text, "ye believe in God, believe also in me."[42] Never doubting the moral absolutes that impelled him and his command to victories in China and on the Tennessee and being so convinced of the Source that conferred them, it is perhaps no surprise that he misjudged or simply discounted other factors that contributed to his triumphs.

In China, even though his ships had fought at anchor, one such factor had been the poor marksmanship of Foote's opponents. On the Tennessee, a combination of factors, not likely to be repeated, had contributed to his success. Fort Henry had been defended by only one artillery company because before the battle General Lloyd Tilghman, the fort's commander, had become

Bombardment and capture of Fort Henry. Foote's capture of Fort Henry on 6 February 1862 and the capture of Fort Donelson later in the month forced the withdrawal of Confederate forces from Kentucky and opened western Tennessee to invasion. Currier & Ives lithograph. *Courtesy of the Naval Historical Center.*

convinced that the work's lowly, partially flooded site was virtually indefensible and had sent most of its garrison to Fort Donelson. When he surrendered, Tilghman told Foote that nevertheless "he would have cut [the ironclads] . . . all to pieces had his best rifle not burst and his 128-pounder been stopped in the vent." In his official report, the Confederate general wrote that the "weak points in all their vessels were well known to us and . . . our firing developed them, showing conclusively that this class of boats, though formidable, cannot stand the test of even the 32-pounders. . . ." To cap his critique, Tilghman pointed out perhaps the most serious weakness in each ironclad, the vulnerability of her unarmored hurricane deck or, as he put it, "the immense area forming what may be called the roof." Given a higher site from which his guns could have rained down a plunging fire, he had no doubt of the outcome.[43]

With the reduction of Fort Henry, the woodclads, following Foote's orders, ranged up the Tennessee to Florence, Alabama. En route they burned or seized enemy steamers and captured one unfinished ironclad.[44] This operation demonstrated the flag officer's acute appreciation of the strategic importance of river control. He knew that by neutralizing Fort Henry, he had laid open a highway directly into the western Confederate heartland, a highway that, unlike a road or railroad, could not be torn up by the enemy. He would now move on Fort Donelson to open a second highway.

Grant's army was ready to cooperate. Having invested Fort Donelson but obviously impressed with the Navy's solo feat against Fort Henry, it delayed assaulting Donelson's land side until the gunboats had been given their opportunity on its waterside. Foote's order of battle duplicated that which had earlier brought success, and, ostensibly, the situation along the river at Donelson did look comparable to, even in some ways more promising than, that at Henry. The number of enemy guns that bore on the Cumberland was the same. The weight of their combined fire was somewhat less. And as soon as the action commenced, the Confederate's only rifled piece was disabled when a priming wire jammed its vent. In one way only was the enemy's riverside position superior: its guns, sited on a bluff forty feet above the Cumberland, were poised to pound the ironclads with the kind of plunging fire that General Tilghman had predicted would be decisive.

And on 14 February, decisive it was. No sooner had Foote's four ironclads steamed within range than the storm of Confederate shot and shell began. It carried away boat davits and parts of smokestacks, crushed iron plating, smashed pilot and wheel houses, pierced casemates and hulls, inflicted heavy casualties, and soon had all four vessels shipping water. On top of these injuries came specific blows that forced the ironclads to retire. Cut tiller ropes, an incapacitated paddle wheel, and shots below water sent three out of the fight. In the flagboat's case, when a ball entered her pilot house and carried away her helm, killed her pilot, and wounded the flag officer in the left foot, she too drifted downstream. Federal casualties were high and added to by the bursting of one of those weakened rifles. The Confederates, in sharp contrast, had not lost a man or a gun to naval fire. When Fort Donelson fell, it was entirely to pressure from Grant's army.[45]

Though the Army was responsible for the reduction of the work, the knowledge that the Navy could now make flanking incursions and convoy troop transports up both the Cumberland and the Tennessee, caused the Confederates to evacuate Bowling Green, Kentucky; Nashville, Tennessee; and Columbus on the Mississippi. In fact, before the meddling Halleck had stopped them, Grant and Foote were preparing to move upriver directly to Nashville. When the federal naval squadron, finally near full strength, next closed with the enemy in March 1862, it was not on the Tennessee but on the Mississippi at Island No. 10, the outpost that the Confederates had retained when they fell back to a new defense line.[46] By that time, however, the flag officer no longer seemed the same man.

It is difficult to imagine the Andrew Foote of the Barrier Forts or Fort Henry actions being intimidated by Island No. 10, even with its fifty-two cannon. Had his setback at Donelson—"I will not go so near [enemy batteries] again"—shaken his faith? Was his wound, which refused to heal and kept him on crutches, sapping his energy? Was the recent death of his thirteen-year-old son, in his phrase, "draw[ing] off my mind from my duties"? Or was it the simple realization that fighting downriver meant that an incapacitated gunboat would be carried directly under the enemy's guns? Whether any or all of these factors were undermining his resolve, Foote displayed great caution in testing the defenses of Island No. 10. Excepting one attack at medium range by three of his ironclads lashed together to facilitate their maneuvering down current, an attack that suffered its only casualties when another of those fragile rifles exploded, Foote kept his gunboats and mortar rafts bombarding the enemy from long range. The damage effected was negligible.[47]

The strategy to which the Confederate bastion would eventually succumb was nevertheless in process of formulation. Below Island No. 10 a federal army under General John Pope had driven the Confederates away from the Missouri side of the river. Pope's engineers then cut a shallow canal through the swampy peninsula abreast of the island. Although it could not accommodate the gunboats, it did allow transports to bypass the enemy's position and reach Pope's army. The general now wanted Foote to send down two of his ironclads directly through the fire of the island's many guns. Following their passage, these vessels could neutralize the rather weak Confederate batteries on the Tennessee shore opposite Pope and allow the transports to carry his troops across the river and disembark them in Tennessee. By cutting its communications to the south, the federal soldiers could then force the surrender of Island No. 10.

This, in fact, was the script that was played out. After considerable delay,

Foote sent two of his ironclads and their crews in a dash past the island. Accomplished on separate nights, each time under a howling storm without injury, this success set Pope's plan in motion; and on 8 April, Island No. 10 capitulated.[48] Although the Navy's daring passage through the Confederate fire and the joint operation that followed established precedents for the future, Andrew Foote had virtually no part in initiating the strategy and had procrastinated before abetting its execution. If the truth be known, he had to be persuaded by Halleck and others to put his ironclads at risk.[49]

In the last analysis, Foote's judgment very likely had been adversely influenced by the many pressures on him and by the effects of his wound, which, after the surrender of Island No. 10, went on draining away his health. As the Union forces continued to press down the Mississippi, the flag officer seemed to lose what little was left of his old zeal. Reading Foote's dispatches, Secretary Welles must have sensed the problem because he sent Captain Charles H. Davis to assist Foote in the execution of his duties. Finally, Foote, too, came to acknowledge his condition. On 9 May, following the advice of his physician, he turned over his command to Davis and went on sick leave. In recognition of his achievements, he was promoted to rear admiral.

Both Foote and his old schoolmate Welles expected him to return to the Mississippi Squadron, but his continued bad health sent that hope aglimmering. The admiral lived on for another year. In the latter months of his life he seemed, in fact, to be recovering, so much so that he was able to take charge of the newly authorized Bureau of Equipment and Recruiting and, just before his final relapse, was actually on his way to assume command of the South Atlantic Blockading Squadron. Then his health suddenly and irreversibly collapsed. He died in New York City on 26 June 1863.[50]

If Foote's death was mourned in the service, the reason is not difficult to find. He had generally got on well with his fellow officers, no small achievement considering the disparate and idiosyncratic personalities of, say, a Samuel Du Pont, a David D. Porter, or a John Dahlgren, all of whom he had considered his friends. Perhaps it was because the man never seemed to allow ambition to manifest itself in jealousy or envy; he appeared genuinely happy in the success of others.[51]

Furthermore, appreciation of Foote's contributions to American naval tradition was expressed at the time, though it would, of course, require historical perspective to make them entirely manifest. His espousal of the rights of missionaries in Hawaii underscored the precept that U.S. citizens should be protected even when they reside beyond the official jurisdiction of their government. His temperance proselytizing ashore and afloat did more than the efforts of anyone else to achieve in 1862 the abolition of the spirit ration in the Navy. His zeal in suppressing the African slave trade while protecting American ships from British search set a humane standard for the service and indubitably emphasized the inviolability of the American flag. His work at the Naval Asylum facilitated the pedagogic transition in preparing the Navy's future officers. If his technological expertise was exaggerated, his administrative acumen, when added to what John Rodgers had already achieved, organized the nucleus of the federal inland navy. Equally important to the western campaign, Foote established relations with army commanders that were significant for the future. To be sure, his connections with Halleck and Pope were at times strained, but his relations with Grant were at all times excellent; and even regarding Pope, Foote's final cooperation with him, when added to that which he had already exercised with Grant, started a working partnership between the services that would be continued by Foote's successors, Davis and particularly David Porter. Without this close Army–Navy cooperation, the final campaign to open the Mississippi River, divide the Confederacy, and complete the blockade of the Old South "could not," in Ulysses Grant's words, "have been successfully made . . . ."[52]

Yet, granting Foote's contributions to the service and tradition, one can still ask the question, did his friendship with Secretary of the Navy Welles further his Civil War career? The answer is, almost assuredly, yes. In his diary Welles as much as states that Foote was his personal choice to command first the Mississippi Squadron and later the South Atlantic Blockading Squadron. But Welles says more than that: "Had any other man than myself been Secretary of the Navy, it is not probable that . . . Foote would ever have had a squadron." Foote had initially been brought to his notice, Welles explains, by the simple fact that "[he] and myself [had been] youthful companions." That Welles worked to further Foote's career does not, on the other hand, necessarily prove that Foote worked on him to do so; in fact, there is some evidence that he did not. Welles complained to his diary that, whereas he hoped his relations with Foote might return to the "friendly and social intimacy of earlier years," the naval officer insisted that Welles's office decreed that their relationship must be on a formal, superior–subordinate basis. Moreover, Welles intimates that Foote was at first reluctant to supersede Du Pont in command of the South Atlantic Squadron. Welles, who seems to have nurtured a strong aversion to Du Pont, attributed Foote's reluctance to his being under that officer's spell. Given Foote's demonstrated independence of mind, a more likely explanation would seem to be that Foote was simply loyal to his friend Du Pont. Not until he had learned that the latter was to be relieved in any event, did Foote agree to accept the command. His biographer seems correct when he writes of his subject: "He did not pull down others to build up his own reputation."[53]

Only when one comes to Foote, the fighting commander, do serious doubts about the man intrude. Had he not been so supremely confident, he might have perceived that his victories in China and on the Tennessee River were not solely owed to his aggressive tactics. Fort Donelson had laid bare that truth. Had it, however, pushed Foote in the other direction of excessive caution? Certainly at Island No. 10 he overestimated the perils of running ironclads past fixed batteries. Yet ironically even his new-found wariness may have proved salutary in the end. Had Foote forced a stand-up fight with the island's strong defenses, he could well have lost some of his original ironclads, vessels that continued throughout the war to form the backbone of the river service. Later, once Foote had been persuaded to cooperate with General Pope, the Navy and the Army quickly felled Island No. 10 and, in doing so, set one more example of the kind of joint operations that General Grant would later extol. Given these facts and the habit of his faith, might not Andrew Foote, had he lived, have come retrospectively to see God's hand even in the repulse he had suffered at Fort Donelson?

FURTHER READING

Though collections of Andrew Hull Foote's correspondence are in the Library of Congress and the New Haven (Connecticut) Colony Historical Society, and many of his letters are scattered among the holdings of the National Archives and some few of them can be found elsewhere, there is no printed edition of his papers. The two best published sources for Foote's Civil War correspondence are the U.S. Navy Department's *Official Records of the Union and Confederate Navies in the War of the Rebellion* (especially vol. XXII); and the *Confidential Correspondence of Gustavus Vasa Fox, Assistant Secretary of the Navy, 1861–1865* edited by Robert Means Thompson and Richard Wainwright (especially vol. II). Foote's own book, *Africa and the American Flag* (1854), and his pamphlet, *The African Squadron: Ashburton Treaty: Consular Sea Letters: Reviewed in an Address by Commander A. H. Foote* (1855), are, of course, primary sources. Both are valuable for his African cruise, his views on the slave trade, and his proselytizing zeal.

Other printed primary sources that touch on Foote were written by men who knew him. The *Diary of Gideon Welles, Secretary of the Navy under Lincoln and Johnson* edited by Howard K. Beale and Alan W. Brownsword is effusive with praise. On the other hand, the writings of Commander (later Rear Admiral) Henry Walke, who had charge of an ironclad under Foote, convey mixed signals. His *Naval Scenes and Reminiscences of the Civil War in the United States . . .* , published in 1877, is critical of, even hostile to, Foote as a naval chieftain; however, ten years later his two essays in Robert Underwood Johnson and Clarence Clough Buel, eds., *Battles and Leaders of the Civil War* (I: 358–67, 430–52) are considerably more positive in their evaluations. No such inconsistency is found in the articles that James B. Eads, the contractor who built the early river ironclads, and John A. Foote, the admiral's brother, contributed to *Battles and Leaders* (I: 338–46, 347). They tell only of Andrew Foote's determination and fortitude. And in his *Personal Memoirs* (vol. I), Ulysses S. Grant describes the flag officer's enthusiastic cooperation in the campaign against Forts Henry and Donelson.

If primary materials on Foote are accessible in a number of places, comprehensive secondary treatments of him are not—a rather surprising fact given the breadth of the man's reformational and naval activities. Perhaps the explanation lies in his rather short Civil War career. In any event, only one full-length biography of Foote has appeared, and that one over a century ago. *The Life of Andrew Hull Foote, Rear-Admiral United States Navy* (1874) was written by Yale professor James M. Hoppin, who, notwithstanding the romantic *zeitgeist* of Victorian America, presents a fairly factual account and is even in a few places mildly critical of his subject, albeit only implicitly. Still, the general interpretive bias of the book—the author's frank hope was "that young men in the [naval] service might be led to emulate [Foote's] example" (v)—is very much in Foote's favor. That the biographer had to rely for data on two of the late admiral's staunch friends may also have had a bearing. In his preface, Hoppin thanks both Gideon Welles for placing "valuable letters" at his disposal and Rear Admiral Joseph Smith for giving him "access to the files and records of the Navy Department" (vi).

Beyond sketches in such biographical anthologies as the *Dictionary of American Biography* and *The National Cyclopedia of American Biography*, there are three short studies of Foote. All of them emphasize his Civil War career, and none of them hides the author's affection for the subject. This last should perhaps not be surprising of two of these pieces. J. T. Headley's treatment of Foote in his *Farragut and Our Naval Commanders* (151–81) was published soon after the Civil War, when victory's glow still suffused the North. It is replete with adulation and romantic exaggeration. Allan Keller's forty-six-page essay, *Andrew Hull Foote, Gunboat Commodore, 1806–1863*, was published almost a century later as part of the Civil War Centennial. It too is understandably full of praise for its principal. Clarence Edward Macartney's chapter on Foote in his *Mr. Lincoln's Admirals* (78–115), published in the 1950s, is also entirely positive.

Secondary studies of Foote may not be plentiful, but other secondary works shed light on aspects of his naval career. For example, George Verne Blue's article "The Project for a French Settlement in the Hawaiian Islands, 1824–1842," *Pacific Historical Review* (II [1933]: 85–99), Jean Ingram Brookes's *International Rivalry in the Pacific Islands, 1800–1875*, and Bradford Smith's *Yankees in Paradise: The New England Impact on Hawaii* provide the context for the Hawaiian episode. Or again, Hugh G. Soulsby's *The Right of Search and the Slave Trade in Anglo–American Relations, 1814–1862* gives the history of that controversy including Foote's opinions on the matter. Though one must rely mainly on Hoppin's biography for Foote's part in the education of midshipmen, the importance of the Philadelphia Naval Asylum to that end can be found in David Foster Long's *Sailor-Diplomat: A Biography of Commodore James Biddle, 1783–1848* (173–80) and in articles in the U.S. Naval Institute *Proceedings* by Charles O. Paullin ("Beginnings of the United States Naval Academy") and Henry Francis Sturdy ("The Establishment of the Naval School at Annapolis").

For the roles of Foote and the Navy in China, Robert Erwin Johnson's *Far China Station: The U.S. Navy in Asian Waters, 1800–1898* and Curtis T. Henson, Jr.'s *Commissioners and Commodores: The East India Squadron and American Diplomacy in China* are invaluable, though the authors disagree on the suitability of Foote's response. Johnson, correctly I believe, is disapproving, Henson generally approving. A short article holding that, in storming the Barrier Forts, Foote raised nineteenth-century American amphibious warfare to its apogee is Neville T. Kirk's "Commander Foote at the Barrier Forts," U.S. Naval Institute *Proceedings*.

Finally, several secondary sources give close scrutiny to the creation and operation of the Mississippi Squadron. *Rear Admiral John Rodgers, 1812–1882* by Robert Erwin Johnson describes that officer's role in its genesis. *Battle Flags South: The Story of the Civil War Navies on the Western Waters* by James M. Merrill and *Gunboats Down the Mississippi* by John D. Milligan also cover Rodgers's role, as well as telling the story of the squadron while it was under Foote's command. Both are generally approving of the flag officer. A recent study by Milligan, in which he is more critical of Foote's battle sagacity, is his "From Theory to Application: The Emergence of the American Ironclad War Vessel," *Military Affairs*.

NOTES

1. James Ford Rhodes, *Lectures on the American Civil War*, 2. Earlier, in the first volume of his massive study *History of the United States from the Compromise of 1850*, he argued that slavery was the sole cause of the war.

2. Quoted in James M. Hoppin, *Life of Andrew Hull Foote, Rear-Admiral United States Navy*, 32.

3. This conversation was recalled by Foote's brother in John A. Foote, "Notes on the Life of Admiral Foote," in Robert Underwood Johnson and Clarence Clough Buel, eds., *Battles and Leaders of the Civil War: Being for the Most Part Contributions by Union and Confederate Officers*, I: 347 (hereafter cited as *B&L*).

4. David Riesman, Nathan Glazer, and Reuel Denney, *The Lonely Crowd: A Study of the Changing American Character*, 23, 29–30.

5. Ray Allen Billington, *The Protestant Crusade, 1800–1860: A Study of the Origins of American Nativism* is a standard work on Protestant activities in the period.

6. Hiram Bingham, *A Residence of Twenty-one Years in the Sandwich Islands . . . ,* 311ff., 535–50; George Verne Blue, "The Project for a French Settlement in the Hawaiian Islands, 1824–1842," *Pacific Historical Review*, II (1933): 85–99; Jean Ingram Brookes, *International Rivalry in the Pacific Islands, 1800–1875*, 86–89.

7. Hoppin, *Foote*, 43–47. The lieutenants' letter is quoted herein. See also Bingham, *Sandwich Islands*, 551–55; and J. T. Headley, *Farragut and Our Naval Commanders*, 158–59.

8. For example, in his study of American naval explorers and scientists of the 1840s and 1850s, Geoffrey S. Smith concludes that in their racial attitudes they bore "striking similarities" to the later naval Darwinists. See his "The Navy Before Darwinism: Science, Exploration, and Diplomacy in Antebellum America," *American Quarterly*, XXVIII (1976): 41–55.

9. Quoted in Hoppin, *Foote*, 56.

10. For a study of American temperance thought, see Norman H. Clark, *Deliver Us from Evil: An Interpretation of Prohibition*.

11. Foote's ideas on temperance are given in his speech of 1 November 1845, and his letter to George P. Rockwell, 15 June 1847, both quoted in Hoppin, *Foote*, 59–60, 62–63.

12. Quoted in Hoppin, *Foote*, 57. See also J. Foote, "Admiral Foote," in *B&L*, I: 347.

13. Hoppin, *Foote*, 58–60. See also Clarence Edward Macartney, *Mr. Lincoln's Admirals*, 83–84.

14. Dwight Lowell Dumond, *Anti-slavery: The Crusade for Freedom in America*.

15. Foote's views on black people, slavery, and colonization are expressed in his *Africa and the American Flag*, 14, 52, 103–5, 109, 178–79, 196–99.

16. For the racial attitudes of American antebellum educated classes, see William Stanton, *The Leopard's Spots: Scientific Attitudes Toward Race in America, 1815–59*.

17. W. E. B. Du Bois, *The Suppression of the African Slave-Trade to the United States of America, 1638–1870*, Chapter 9; Daniel P. Mannix, *Black Cargoes: A History of the Atlantic Slave Trade, 1518–1865*, 191ff.

18. Foote, *Africa*, 15.

19. Hugh G. Soulsby, *The Right of Search and the Slave Trade in Anglo–American Relations, 1814–1862* is a thorough treatment of the subject. See also George M. Brooke, Jr., "The Role of the United States Navy in the Suppression of the African Slave Trade," *American Neptune*, XXI (1961): 28–41.

20. Foote, *Africa*, 311–18. See also Foote, *The African Squadron: Ashburton Treaty: Consular Sea Letters: Reviewed in an Address by Commander A. H. Foote*.

21. Quoted in Hoppin, *Foote*, 86. The capture of the *Martha* is described in Foote, *Africa*, 287–91.

22. Foote, *Africa*, 14–15; Foote, *The African Squadron*; Hoppin, *Foote*, Chapter 9.

23. Macartney calles Foote "the creator of the western flotilla," and Headley describes him as "superintend[ing] the creation of an inland navy." See Macartney, *Lincoln's Admirals*, 86; and Headley, *Farragut and Our Naval Commanders*, 161.

24. Howard K. Beale and Alan W. Brownsword, eds., *Diary of Gideon Welles, Secretary of the Navy Under Lincoln and Johnson*, I: 74–75, 167, 335–36; II: 135; Welles to Hoppin, 8 October 1873, quoted in Hoppin, *Foote*, 391–97.

25. For the genesis of the river navy, see Robert Erwin Johnson, *Rear Admiral John Rodgers, 1812–1882*, 156–68; James M. Merrill, *Battle Flags South: The Story of the Civil War Navies on the Western Waters*, 24–38; John D. Milligan, *Gunboats Down the Mississippi*, 3–19; and Milligan, "From Theory to Application: The Emergence of the American Ironclad War Vessel," *Military Affairs*, XLVIII (1984): 126–32.

26. James B. Eads to Montgomery C. Meigs, 27 January 1862, James B. Eads papers, Missouri Historical Society, St. Louis; U.S. Navy Department, *Official Records of the Union and Confederate Navies in the War of the Rebellion*, XXII: 463, 525 (hereafter cited as *ORN*); G. D. Wise to Foote, 18 December 1861, Area 5 File, 1861–1865, R.G. 45, National Archives; Foote to Gustavus V. Fox, 11 January 1862, and Henry E. Maynadier to Charles H. Davis, 2 August 1862, Andrew H. Foote Papers, Library of Congress.

27. Henry Francis Sturdy, "The Establishment of the Naval School at Annapolis," U.S. Naval Institute *Proceedings*, LXXI (1945): 1–17; David F. Long, *Sailor-Diplomat: A Biography of Commodore James Biddle, 1783–1848*, 173–80.

28. Hoppin, *Foote*, 54–55, 143; Charles O. Paullin, "Beginnings of the United States Naval Academy," U.S. Naval Institute *Proceedings*, L (1924): 173–94. For documents on the subject, see K. Jack Bauer, ed., *The New American State Papers: Naval Affairs*, VIII: 223–56.

29. Foote's correspondence and journals are filled with invocations, testimonies, resolves, and prayers.

30. Foote to John A. Dahlgren, 23 October 1861, in Letter Book, S. Ledyard Phelps Papers, Missouri Historical Society; *ORN*, XXII: 390, 429; U.S., *Statutes at Large*, XII: 329.

31. *ORN*, XXII: 432–33, 441; *Annual Report of the Secretary of the Navy, 1863*, ix–x.

32. Eads to Edward Bates, 10 November 1861, Eads Papers; Foote to Phelps, 23 October 1861, Phelps Papers; Meigs to H. A. Wise, 13 November 1861, and 17 June and 3 July 1862, Letter Books, Office of the Quartermaster General, R.G. 92, National Archives; Thomas A. Scott to Edwin M. Stanton, 6 March 1862, Edwin M. Stanton Papers, Library of Congress.

33. *ORN*, XXII: 330–31, 338, 341, 356; Merrill, *Battle Flags South*, 49–50, 56–57.

34. Milligan, *Gunboats*, 25–27.

35. Quoted in ibid., 27. See also Henry Walke, "The Gun-Boats at Belmont and Fort Henry," in *B&L*, I: 358–59; "Annual Report of the Quartermaster General, 1862," in U.S. Congress, *House Exec. Docs.*, 37 Cong., 3 Sess., No. 1, IV: 66; and James Edwin Campbell, "Recent Addresses," in *Ohio Archaeological and Historical Quarterly*, XXXIV (1925): 58.

36. Foote to Armstrong, 8 November 1856, in Letter Book, Foote Papers; Foote to "My dear Bradford," 27 June 1858, quoted in Hoppin, *Foote*, 125–26; Johnson, *Far China Station: The U.S. Navy in Asian Waters, 1800–*

1898, 82–84; Curtis T. Henson, Jr., *Commissioners and Commodores: The East India Squadron and American Diplomacy in China*, 129–31.

37. Armstrong's orders are quoted in Foote to Armstrong, 26 November 1856, in Letter Book, Foote Papers.

38. Ibid.; Johnson, *Far China Station*, 84–88; Henson, *Commissioners and Commodores*, 131–33.

39. Hoppin, *Foote*, 123–24, 126–27; Johnson, *Far China Station*, 90.

40. Milligan, "American Ironclad," *Military Affairs*, 126–28.

41. U.S., War Department, *The War of the Rebellion: A Compilation of the Official Records of the Union and Confederate Armies*, IV: 528 and VII: 131–33, 146, 561 (hereafter cited as *ORA*); Foote's Special Orders No. 3, 2 February 1862, Phelps Papers; Foote to his wife, 6 February 1862, Area 5 File; Foote to Welles, 6, 7, and 10 February 1862, and Walke to Foote, 8 February 1862, Letters Received by the Secretary of the Navy from Commanding Officers of Squadrons: Mississippi, 1861–1865, R.G. 45, National Archives (hereafter cited as Mississippi Squadron Letters); *ORN*, XXII: 314, 541, 568–69, 601–4.

42. Foote to his wife, 6 February 1862, Area 5 File; James B. Eads, "Recollections of Foote and the Gun-Boats," in *B&L*, I: 343. Milligan, ed., *From the Fresh-Water Navy, 1861–64: The Letters of Acting Master's Mate Henry R. Browne and Acting Ensign Symmes E. Browne*, 6.

43. Foote to his wife, 6 February 1862, Area 5 File; *ORN*, XXII: 553–61.

44. Phelps to Foote, 10 February 1862, Mississippi Squadron Letters.

45. Foote to Welles, 15 February 1862, and Walke to Foote, 15 February 1862, ibid.; Egbert Thompson to Foote, 17 February 1862, Area 5 File; *Chicago Tribune*, 19 February 1862; *Missou Democrat* [St. Louis], 18 February and 4 March 1862; *ORA*, VII: 277, 28ⵁ-81, 388–401; *ORN*, XXII: 591, 594, 606.

46. Scott to Stanton, 1 and 6 March 1862, Stanton Papers; William T. Sherman to Halleck, 4 March 1862, William T. Sherman Papers, Library of Congress; *ORN*, XXII: 618, 626–30; *ORA*, VIII: 418–26, 436–38, 633.

47. Foote to his wife, 16 February 1862, quoted in Hoppin, *Foote*, 228; Foote to Welles, 17, 19, and 20 March and 8 April 1862, Mississippi Squadron Letters; Foote to his wife, 17 and 19 March 1862, Area 5 File; *Missouri Republican* [St. Louis], 21 March 1862; *ORN*, XXII: 660, 739, 745–48, 769–71, 773–77; *ORA*, VIII: 153–57, 159–61, 170–71.

48. Pope to Foote, 26 March 1862, Area 5 File; Scott to Stanton, 30 March 1862, Stanton Papers; Walke to Foote, 8 and 25 April 1862, Mississippi Squadron Letters; *ORN*, XXII: 692, 712–24; *ORA*, VIII: 85–90, 133, 135, 158–59, 175–76, 625, 629.

49. Scott to Foote, 4 April 1862, Area 5 File; Foote to Welles, 7 April 1862, Mississippi Squadron Letters; Scott to Stanton, 16 April 1862, Stanton Papers; *ORN*, XXII: 703, 714–15.

50. Physicians' report, 15 April 1862, and Foote to Welles, 9 May 1862, Mississippi Squadron Letters; Foote to Welles, 15 May 1862, Gideon Welles Papers, Library of Congress; *Diary of Welles*, I: 74ff., 311ff.; Hoppin, *Foote*, 314ff.

51. Foote's papers contain numerous letters from naval officers expressing their friendship and warm regard. See also Walke, "The Gunboats," in *B&L*, I: 360.

52. Ulysses S. Grant, *Personal Memoirs*, I: 574.

53. *Diary of Welles*, I: 311–15, 317, 346; II: 135; Hoppin, *Foote*, 388.

SAMUEL FRANCIS DU PONT: ARISTOCRATIC PROFESSIONAL

BY K. JACK BAUER

Occasionally, because of his ability or otherwise, the nineteenth-century American navy singled out a younger officer as worthy of special consideration and destined to rise above his contemporaries. Samuel Francis Du Pont was such an individual. He was better educated than most antebellum officers, with political and family connections as strong as those of any officer except perhaps Robert F. Stockton. More important for his standing within the service, Du Pont early established a large and active correspondence with other officers, including such powerful superiors as W. Branford Shubrick and Matthew C. Perry. Yet his would be a bittersweet career, its generous successes and early advancements ultimately tempered with deep disappointment and unanticipated pain.

Samuel Francis Du Pont was the fourth, and second surviving, son of Victor Marie Du Pont and his wife Gabrielle Josephine de la Fite de Pelleport. His grandfather, Pierre Samuel du Pont de Nemours, a moderate leader of the French Revolution, subsequently fled to the United States where he became a confidant of many leaders of the new nation. Victor Du Pont served as French consul at Charleston, South Carolina, before moving to New York in 1800 to establish an import house.

Samuel Francis, called "Frank" by his family and friends, was born 27 September 1803 at Goodstay, Bergen Point (modern Bayonne), New Jersey. Two years later his father's firm failed, and the family migrated to a Du Pont–backed settlement in Genesee County, New York. That too failed, and in 1809 they moved to Delaware where Victor established a woolen textile mill. Between 1812 and 1817, Frank Du Pont attended Mount Airy College, an academy near Germantown, Pennsylvania.[1]

During the War of 1812 young Du Pont developed an interest in the Navy, and his parents agreed to his entering the sea service. Their tapping of the family's considerable political connections, which included Caesar Rodney and Thomas Jefferson, produced both a midshipman's warrant and an appointment to the Military Academy. The youngster chose the former, which was dated 19 December 1815.[2]

Finally, on 18 February 1817, long anticipated orders assigned him to the 74-gun ship-of-the-line *Franklin*, the flagship of Commodore Charles Stewart in the Mediterranean. Later Du Pont transferred to the sloop of war *Erie* (18). The cruise not only introduced the young midshipman to the rudiments of his profession, but it permitted visits to Italy and Algiers and the opportunity to meet such dignitaries as the future Napoleon III.[3]

Returning home in early 1820, Du Pont resumed his studies at Mount Airy, before sailing to the Mediterranean again the following year, this time in the frigate *Constitution* (44).[4] Du Pont spent the summer of 1822 at home preparing for his promotion exams, only to learn that a reduced promotion zone excluded him. He soon joined the frigate *Congress* (44) assigned to the West Indies Squadron.[5] It was not a comfortable cruise, since he came under "that selfish little viper" Captain James Biddle.[6]

In July 1824, Du Pont received orders to the spanking new ship-of-the-line *North Carolina* (74), bound for the Mediterranean as flagship for Commodore John Rodgers. It was an educational cruise, since Rodgers was both the senior officer in the service and its leading practitioner of taut discipline. Moreover, much of the cruise was spent in the eastern Mediterranean as negotiations were initiated for an American–Turkish commercial treaty through the Turkish fleet commander.[7] Du Pont received his promotion to lieutenant effective 26 April 1826, but could not convince the commodore to relieve him of his onerous responsibilities as the flagship's sailing master until the end of the year. Then Rodgers sent him to the schooner *Porpoise*, in which he cruised until he returned home the following spring.[8]

While ashore on waiting orders, the new lieutenant became engaged to his first cousin Sophie Madeleine Du Pont, the daughter of Eleuthere Irenee Du Pont, who had founded the family's powder firm. She was a woman of great character, intellect, and charm, who became her husband's closest confidante. A devout Episcopalian, known for her compassion, she soon drew her husband into the activities of the church. In 1848 he joined in founding Christ Church, Christiana Hundred, Delaware and remained its principal financial supporter as long as he lived. Mrs. Du Pont was stricken with an illness soon after her marriage and thereafter lived a restricted life. As a result, Du Pont regularly refused shore assignments distant from Wilmington.[9]

In June 1829, Du Pont joined the sloop-of-war *Ontario* (18) bound for the Mediterranean, on a cruise that introduced him to a pair of officers who would figure significantly in his later career: Passed Midshipman Charles Henry Davis and Midshipman John A. Dahlgren. Du Pont returned home in 1832 and went on waiting orders.[10] During his stay ashore Du Pont demonstrated his interest in the intellectual aspects of a service gradually shifting from

Samuel F. Du Pont. Engraving from a photograph taken while Du Pont commanded the Union fleet off Charleston. From *Harpers Weekly*, VII, 257.

rough-hewn, merchant seaman—militia leadership to a professional, technically competent officer corps. In 1833 he joined the U.S. Naval Lyceum that Commander Matthew Calbraith Perry had established in New York. Du Pont's rising status in the service was demonstrated by his writing testimonials for both the first and second editions of Matthew F. Maury's *A New Theoretical and Practical Treatise on Navigation*.[11]

Offered a new assignment to the *Erie* in 1834, Du Pont refused it because he would have gone out in a billet he believed beneath his seniority. In November of the following year he accepted orders as first lieutenant of the sloop-of-war *Warren* (18). Her cruising ground in the Gulf of Mexico exposed Du Pont to a pair of problems that plagued American leaders for better than a decade: the Seminole Indians in Florida and the American settlers in Texas. Commodore Alexander J. Dallas, the squadron commander, moved Du Pont about, assigning him to command of the schooner *Grampus* (10), the *Warren*, and later the flagship *Constellation* (36). Du Pont returned home during the fall of 1836.[12]

Both Commodore W. Branford Shubrick, the new commander in the West Indies, and Perry, now commander of the experimental steamer *Fulton*, urged him to return to sea with them, but he refused because of his wife's health. A growing concern about administrative problems in the service began to appear in Du Pont's correspondence during 1838. He complained that "I have never known Navy matters at a lower ebb," and he embarked on a letter-writing campaign aimed at replacing the Board of Navy Commissioners with a bureau system.[13]

During the autumn of 1838 Du Pont again secured active service and joined the new ship-of-the-line *Ohio* (74), the flagship of War of 1812 hero Commodore Isaac Hull in the Mediterranean. When Hull, contrary to regulations, brought his wife and sister-in-law on board for the trip, they displaced Du Pont and three other lieutenants from their quarters. The officers' protests brought them a reprimand from the Secretary of the Navy and a dismissal from the squadron by Hull.[14]

During 1842, Du Pont served on the court trying the cases that grew out of the conflicts of the Wilkes Exploring Expedition. Although excused from some of the proceedings because of potential conflicts of interest, Du Pont still had to remain in New York during most of the summer and autumn.[15] Close on the heels of the Wilkes trials came the *Somers* mutiny uproar. Du Pont, like many other naval officers, strongly supported the actions of Commander Alexander Slidell Mackenzie in hanging a midshipman and two enlisted men for plotting a mutiny on board the training brig.[16] The two incidents sharpened Du Pont's conviction of the need for extensive reform of the service.

Receiving his promotion to commander on 10 January 1843 (with a date of rank of 28 October 1842), Du Pont requested assignment as an assistant inspector of ordnance, a role he filled until September. Then he commissioned the new brig *Perry* (10) with orders to the Orient, but he became sick during the voyage and was forced to surrender his command and return home in January 1844.[17]

Until then, Du Pont had spent a disproportionate share of his sea time in the highly desirable waters of the Mediterranean and on board flagships. While this service undoubtedly assured him recognition, it offered a young commander, now in midcareer, little opportunity to demonstrate his competence. The situation changed in 1845 when Du Pont joined Commanders Franklin Buchanan and William M. McKean in recommending the site and curriculum for the Naval School that Secretary George Bancroft established at Annapolis.[18]

On completion of the Annapolis assignment, Bancroft rewarded Du Pont with command of the frigate *Congress* (44), flagship of Commodore Robert F. Stockton, commander-designate of the Pacific Squadron. Having departed Norfolk on 30 October 1845, the frigate dropped anchor off Monterey, California, on 15 July 1846. By then the Mexican War had begun. Du Pont shifted to command of the sloop of war *Cyane* (18), and in her seized the port of San Diego late in July. He then took his vessel into Mexican waters to establish a blockade along the west coast and off Baja California. The *Cyane* attacked Mexican defenses, seized vessels, and blockaded Guaymas and Mazatlan, remaining on station until November. The sloop then headed north to California, arriving in time to join the mixed army–navy expedition to Los Angeles at the start of 1847.[19]

Du Pont sailed south again in April to resume the blockade. Except for a visit to Hawaii to replenish supplies, the *Cyane* remained in the Gulf of California for the rest of the year. When Commodore W. Branford Shubrick, who had replaced Stockton, occupied Mazatlan in November, Du Pont was one of the commissioners who worked out its capitulation. He also saw action on Baja California, where in February 1848 he personally led a landing party that raised the siege of San José. Du Pont subsequently landed a second detachment to aid in the capture of the last Mexican force on the peninsula. The *Cyane* returned home in the autumn of 1846.[20]

Du Pont's activities in the Gulf of California were important in that they brought him under the approving eye of Commodore Shubrick. That reinforced professionally a long-standing personal friendship between the two men. Their partnership brought substantial benefits to the Navy in the decade of the 1850s.

Following a long leave, Du Pont in late 1849 embarked on a decade of shore duty during which he played an increasing role in the naval reform movement, which made possible much of the Navy's effectiveness during the Civil War. He first joined a board headed by Shubrick to draw up a new curriculum for the Naval School, following which he would be named superintendent. The board's far-reaching proposals included expansion of the course of study from one to four years; establishment of six departments of instruction; a new marking system; and a name change to the Naval Academy. But Du Pont did not implement the reforms—because of Mrs. Du Pont's health, he requested cancellation of his orders as superintendent.[21]

In 1850 Du Pont assumed command of the Philadelphia receiving ship *Union*, essentially a sinecure for officers the department could not or did not want to send to sea. It made him available for special assignments, such as the one that occurred in 1851 when frequent complaints about the quality of American aids to navigation led Congress to order an investigation of the Lighthouse Establishment. A board consisting of Shubrick, Du Pont, Brigadier General Joseph G. Totten of the Army Engineers, Lieutenant Colonel

James Kearney of the Topographical Engineers, Professor Alexander Dallas Bache of the Coast Survey, and Lieutenant Thornton A. Jenkins undertook the study. They spent seven months in a careful investigation of the lighthouse organization and recommended the creation of a Lighthouse Board composed of naval officers to administer the service. When Secretary of the Treasury Thomas Corwin appointed that group in October 1852, Du Pont joined Shubrick as a member, serving until 1857.

Membership on the Naval Academy and Lighthouse boards clearly signaled Du Pont's acceptance into the circle of officers, collected around Branford Shubrick, who constituted the professional leadership of the Navy. Moreover, Du Pont's frequent visits to Washington brought him into contact with the political and service leaders upon whom his continued rise depended.

While on the Lighthouse Board, Du Pont undertook occasional special assignments. During 1851 Secretary of War Charles M. Conrad requested his comments on proposals for a new coast defense system. Du Pont responded with a paper, published the next year as *Report on National Defences*, that stressed the impact of steam on naval tactics while arguing that it was the Navy's function "to carry the 'sword of the state' upon the broad ocean" and "to contend for the mastery of the seas . . . ." The essay attracted attention in both the United States and Britain.[23] In 1853, he served as superintendent of the New York World's Fair as well as one of its official American representatives. Two years later, he was on the board of officers that rewrote the naval disciplinary code to offset the abolition of flogging. That code remained in effect with little change for a century.[24]

Along with many other officers, Du Pont had long argued the need to purge the officer ranks of those who were over age, in poor health, or otherwise incapable of further service. In January 1855, he drafted a bill to create a reserve list of officers unable to perform active duty, arguing that without such legislation an officer would spend twenty-five years as a lieutenant. With other supporters of the legislation he successfully lobbied Congress, which in February 1855 enacted a law establishing a "Naval Efficiency Board" to report those officers no longer able to perform their duties promptly and efficiently.[25]

For membership on the board, Secretary James C. Dobbin selected a strong, knowledgeable group under Commodore Shubrick. The board was to designate those officers to be placed on the Reserved List at half or furlough pay; those to be placed on the list, but who "for service rendered and for fidelity in the discharge of duty" deserved to draw full or leave-of-absence pay; and finally those so incompetent as to be dropped. The board acted decisively and with dispatch. Between 20 June and 26 July, it considered 712 officers and recommended the removal of 201: 49 by outright dismissal, 81 to be placed on the Reserved List with furlough pay, and 71 to be retired on leave-of-absence pay. The board complicated the acceptance of its findings by neither ascribing reasons nor hearing appeals. On balance the results were positive. Most of the officers removed deserved it, although some of the individual actions, such as the retiring of Matthew F. Maury, were extremely controversial. Much of the animosity centered on Du Pont, who was correctly perceived as the promoter of the scheme, but incorrectly portrayed as a ruthless assassin of the character of men who had devoted their lives to the service of their country. It also fell to him to attempt to smooth the indignation of men who believed they had been cast into "official disgrace."[26]

The wholesale departure of senior officers reopened promotions, and one of those for whom the way to captain was cleared was Du Pont. His commission carried the date of 14 September 1855. Although confirmation of the new captains, especially that of Du Pont, produced a heated debate in the Senate, they all were confirmed. The Texan Sam Houston led the attack, probably because of Du Pont's role in opposing the integration of ex-Texas officers into the Navy following annexation.[27]

Du Pont continued his Lighthouse Board duties until April 1857. Then he drew a prize command, the powerful and beautiful new steam frigate *Minnesota*, assigned to special duty in the Far East. Du Pont placed her in commission on 21 May and reached Hong Kong on 5 November. In May 1858 he observed the Anglo–French attack on the Taku forts below Tientsin. The impact of the massed fire of the allied guns on the Chinese forts convinced him that steamers armed with heavy guns could pound most forts into submission. After visits to Japan, Shanghai, Hong Kong, Malaya, and India, he brought his vessel home via Arabia and South Africa, reaching Boston on 16 June 1859.[28] Participation with William B. Reed in the negotiation of the Treaty of Tientsin and his visit to Japan caused his assignment as the senior escort for a Japanese delegation that visited the United States during May–July 1860.[29]

When Southern officers began to speak openly of following their states out of the Union upon the election of a Republican president in 1860, Du Pont was appalled. He immediately threw himself into a campaign to prevent their departure. Especially important to him was Branford Shubrick, a North Carolinian with great influence as the second ranking officer in the Navy.[30] Shubrick remained loyal. In December Secretary Isaac Toucey appointed Du Pont to command the Philadelphia Navy Yard.[31] It was a critical assignment, since the Philadelphia commandant, as head of the northern yard closest to Washington, was responsible for keeping water communications with the capital open in the event Virginia left the Union.

In April 1861, worry became reality. The passage of a Massachusetts regiment through Baltimore prompted a riot and the burning of the bridges that connected Washington with the Northeast. Du Pont promptly rushed a vessel to Annapolis to cover the departure of the Naval Academy for Newport, Rhode Island, and to support the landing of troops. He also provided a vessel to ferry other troops down the Chesapeake Bay to Annapolis, from whence they could reach Washington without passing through Baltimore. The quick action saved the capital and preserved Maryland for the Union.[32]

Once Washington was safe, the administration began to consider the steps necessary to put down the rebellion in the South. Some of Du Pont's political supporters, notably the Maryland radical H. Winter Davis, sought to have him appointed to lead the Office of Detail. Because it controlled the assignment of officers, the post was the most powerful uniformed administrative billet in the service. Secretary of the Navy Gideon Welles, who feared Du Pont's ambition and influence within and without the service, vetoed the assignment. He acceded, however, to the appointment of Du Pont to head a board to study the blockade of the Confederate coast.[33]

The committee, variously called the Blockade Board, Strategy Board, or Committee on Conference, first met on 27 June. It was composed of Du Pont, Alexander Dallas Bache, and Major John G. Barnard of the Army Engineers, with Commander Charles Henry Davis as secretary. Du Pont served as chairman. Although initially asked to select a point in South Carolina and another in Georgia or Florida for use as a coal depot for the blockading squadrons, the board enlarged its considerations to include naval strategy. Between 5 July and 3 September it issued seven reports, which not only catalogued the known hydrographic conditions along the Confederate shore but identified points to be seized and the steps to be taken by the blockading squadrons to close the coast to trade.[34] Since the recommendations fixed the strategy that followed throughout the war, the effectiveness of the blockade owned much to the insight and sagacity of Du Pont's board. Its recommendations pointed the way to the subsequent seizure of Hatteras Inlet, Port Royal, and New Orleans.

On 25 July, the board briefed Secretary Welles and Assistant Secretary Gustavus V. Fox on its initial recommendations for operations along the South Atlantic coast. They, in turn, gained the approval of the cabinet and the President. General Winfield Scott also agreed, and appointed Brigadier General Thomas W. Sherman to command the army element of what had to be a joint operation. Du Pont was the natural choice as naval commander.[35]

Welles, on 18 September, followed the recommendations of the board and split the Atlantic blockading force, with Du Pont (now authorized the square flag of a flag officer) commanding the squadron assigned to the area south of the border between the Carolinas. In acknowledging his orders, Du Pont asked for four light-draft screw sloops of war and three or four screw gunboats for use against the Confederate shore defenses, as well as a 300-man Marine Corps battalion, 500 landing craft, and several shallow-draft ferry boats to permit amphibious assaults.[36]

On 10 October, Du Pont hoisted his flag in the screw frigate *Wabash*, a sister to the *Minnesota*. Commander C. Raymond P. Rodgers commanded the flagship, and Charles Henry Davis served as chief of staff. Du Pont picked his

Samuel F. Du Pont on board the USS *Wabash*. The steam frigate *Wabash* was Du Pont's flagship during his first year as commander of the South Atlantic Blockading Squadron, September 1861–July 1863. From *The Photographic History of the Civil War*, vol. 6.

other subordinates with equal care. His command was the largest fleet yet assigned to a single American commander.[37]

The expedition sortied from New York with the target still unsettled. Although Port Royal Sound, South Carolina, was potentially the most useful base because of its unmatched deep-water anchorage and security from attack by Confederates on the mainland, it had been excluded during the Washington discussions because of the strength of its defenses. The final decision to attack it did not come until after Du Pont conferred with Fox at Hampton Roads. There additional regiments joined to bring Sherman's command up to 14,000 men. During the afternoon of 31 October as they sailed off Cape Hatteras, hurricane winds and rising seas scattered the vessels. They reassembled off Port Royal on 4 November.[38]

Although Confederate intelligence had determined that Port Royal was the target of the expedition, too little time remained for Brigadier General Thomas F. Drayton to strengthen his defenses adequately. They consisted of two earthworks—Fort Walker on Hilton Head Island mounting 23 guns and Fort Beauregard on Bay Point Island with 20 more—backed by Flag Officer Josiah Tattnall's squadron of three small river steamers.

On 4 November, a Coast Survey party marked the channel into Port Royal

Sound. The following day a division of gunboats drove off Tattnall's squadron and tested the forts. The plan of attack clearly drew on Du Pont's observations of the Taku attack and his coast defense monograph. The tactics, which stressed the weight of fire made possible by modern naval ordnance and the mobility introduced by steam, were Du Pont's most significant contribution to the plan. Moreover, the expanse of Port Royal Sound allowed the bombardment vessels to steam in an ellipse so as to keep up a heavy continuous fire. The attacking force would enter the harbor in two columns. The heavier line would attack the two forts, concentrating primarily on Fort Walker, while smaller craft shielded it from the Confederate squadron.

The actual attack did not go according to plan. Commander Sylvanus W. Godon in the *Mohican* inexplicably led most of the bombardment column into an enfilading position off Fort Walker. Nevertheless, at about 1:00 P.M., after less that three hours of heavy firing during which Du Pont and the vessels with him passed between the two forts three times, the garrison at Fort Walker abandoned the post. The defenders at Fort Beauregard soon followed suit.[39]

Because forts had rarely surrendered to ships, the victory was widely applauded. It proved to skeptics that wooden vessels could successfully attack forts and thus open the way for the assault on New Orleans. As for Du Pont's performance, the brilliance of his plan and the ease of the victory obscured the failure of Godon and other commanders to understand or execute it properly. That was clearly a failure of communications, for which the ultimate responsibility must rest with Du Pont. He had not ensured that his subordinate understood the plan. Here Du Pont's limitations as a senior commander began to be evident. He failed to spell out plans and responsibilities in a way that could be understood by men to whom the planning assumptions were not self-evident. In the long run, even more devastating was the public's assumption that the seizure of Port Royal would ensure the rapid fall of Savannah and Charleston—neither could be attacked immediately because the squadron had seriously depleted its coal and ammunition. The time needed to correct those logistic shortcomings allowed a new Confederate commander, General Robert E. Lee, to reorganize and strengthen the defenses in the region by withdrawal from exposed posts.[40] Thus Du Pont could occupy Beaufort and tighten his blockade of the South Carolina and Georgia coasts without having to seize secondary objectives such as Fernandina or St. Augustine.[41] The victory at Port Royal, along with Flag Officer Silas H. Stringham's occupation of Hatteras Inlet, came at a time when Union armies had yet to win a major battle. They earned the Navy masses of favorable publicity and a congressional vote of thanks for Du Pont.

Du Pont moved rapidly to establish Port Royal as a base for his blockaders. Its importance is hard to overstress. Before its seizure, blockaders lacked a coal depot between Hampton Roads and Key West, a limitation that could not be offset by employing sailing craft because of the shoal coastal waters. Only at

Charleston did blockaders patrol the approaches outside the bar. At Savannah and the ports south of it, light-draft steamers could operate in the calm waters inside the bars. Du Pont, an excellent organizer, directed ships on fourteen blockading stations. Except at Charleston, where their effectiveness was disputed by the Confederates, the blockaders easily accomplished their mission. Their captures earned Du Pont at least $75,000 in prize money.[42]

Du Pont had witnessed the effectiveness of the British floating repair facilities in China and knew of those in the Crimea. He immediately asked for a similar installation at Port Royal.[43] It proved to be invaluable in maintaining the squadron, and it demonstrated Du Pont's breadth of understanding of the complexities of mid-nineteenth-century naval warfare, in which he stood in advance of his contemporaries.

Du Pont's correspondence with the Navy Department constantly stressed a steady flow of coal. The failure to include provisions for it in the initial planning for the expedition undoubtedly reflected the limitations of his Mexican War experience. Had he served in the Gulf of Mexico instead of the Pacific, he would have been acutely aware of the need to arrange for a constant flow of fuel.

During December, Du Pont and Sherman began tightening the noose around Savannah. Army engineers concluded that Fort Pulaski, which commanded the approach to the Georgia port, could be reduced by batteries on Tybee Island or bypassed by vessels operating on the waterways north and south of it. Naval probes ventured up Wassaw Sound to within sight of Savannah and checked both St. Helena Sound and the North Edisto River, but no assault followed because Sherman lacked enough men to attack Savannah and also protect Port Royal.[44]

Because of the multiple entrances to its harbor, Charleston was much more difficult to close than Savannah. Early in the planning it had been decided that the approaches could be blocked by scuttling hulks in the channels leading into the port. As a result, the Navy purchased a fleet of old whalers and other bone yard relics, loaded them with stone, and sent them to Port Royal. The bulk of the "Stone Fleet," as the vessels came to be known, was sunk in the main channel at Charleston on 5 December. The effort did not close the port because the current soon cut a bypass channel, but it did restrict the passages available to blockade runners, and so reduced the demands on Du Pont's squadron. Other vessels were scuttled off both Savannah and Charleston later in the winter.[45]

Since Charleston appeared to be closed, and since Wassaw Sound seemed to offer a usable approach to Savannah, Du Pont concentrated on seizing the Georgia port. Only ten thousand men, he estimated, would be needed, but he soon found that the Washington authorities seemed to have no intention of dispatching them. Shortly after the arrival of the new year, Du Pont began a systematic reconnaissance of the approaches via the Savannah River. Fort

Pulaski, built on firm ground on the south side of the river, blocked the way. It had to be eliminated or bypassed by any attacking force. Both sides of the river were low marshlands, broken only occasionally by solid ground capable of supporting siege artillery. Thus the fort would be difficult to attack. A network of waterways, some of them large enough to float light-draft vessels, crisscrossed the marshlands. Army and naval planners first thought of using waterways in the marshes north of the river to bypass Fort Pulaski. When that proved impractical, the two commanders shifted to a strategy of interdicting supplies bound for Fort Pulaski in the hope of starving out the defenders while constructing a heavy battery to pound them.[46]

Unable to assail Savannah and lacking support by enough troops to consider an attack against the seaward defenses of Charleston, Du Pont had little choice but to turn to Fernandina. Between 3 and 12 March, Union forces occupied St. Mary's in Georgia and Fernandina, St. Augustine, and Jacksonville in Florida, as well as the coastal islands south of Charleston.[47]

While Du Pont had found General Sherman sometimes to be a difficult colleague, the two men worked together with relatively little friction. That changed on 31 March with the arrival of Major General David Hunter as commander of the newly created Department of the South. Although the Army's bombardment and capture of Fort Pulaski on 11 April effectively closed Savannah, Hunter soon negated some of the successes of his predecessors by abandoning the posts around Jacksonville.[48] Faced with an uncooperative army commander, Du Pont became petulant. On 3 April, he complained to Secretary Welles that "my force is not adequate to the work I have in hand."[49]

Conflicting with Du Pont's growing concern about the strength of his force was the consuming desire of both Welles and Fox for early seizure of Charleston by a solely naval expedition. In Washington the mechanism to achieve that victory appeared self-evident—the new ironclads, whose capabilities after Hampton Roads seemed unlimited. To Welles and Fox the wish was the fact, but they failed to appreciate, as Du Pont did, that a successful attack by a naval force alone was unlikely.

Du Pont viewed the repulse of the ironclads at Drewry's Bluff in May 1862 as proof that they could not overcome well-sited fortifications such as those at Charleston. He proposed instead to establish a siege base on James Island along the south side of the harbor entrance, from which land forces could begin dismantling the defenses. Although his squadron successfully landed an army brigade there in May 1862, the operations ashore failed. Nevertheless, Du Pont gained some personal satisfaction in July when he was promoted to rear admiral in recognition of his earlier successes. In September, Hunter was relieved by Major General Ormsby Mitchell, who shortly succumbed to yellow fever.[50] Further planning had to await the arrival of his successor, the very competent Major General John G. Foster, but the two commanders could not agree on an assault plan.[51] A different problem for Du Pont was the open interest of Captain John A. Dahlgren in replacing him. This undoubtedly inhibited Du Pont in communicating his growing conviction that a naval strike alone could not subdue the South Carolina port.[52]

In September, Welles called Du Pont to Washington to discuss the projected Charleston operation. During 1–18 October, he met with Welles and Fox but failed to make clear to them the strength of his reservations about a purely naval assault. Instead of offering a plan to seize the South Carolina target, he contented himself with recounting the difficulties he faced, the dangers of a premature move, and the necessity for army participation. To his wife he added the interesting complaint that he had no instructions for the attack. Since Welles and especially Fox had accepted the myth of the invulnerability of ironclads, Du Pont's warning fell upon deaf ears. On his part, Du Pont failed to grasp the political imperative for a quick and spectacular Union victory such as the seizure of Charleston. Nor did he accept the parochial argument that the assault should be a purely naval affair. Thus the visit did little to clear the air.[53]

This was perhaps the most controversial period in Du Pont's career. Fearful of replacement if he did not execute the attack quickly, but increasingly convinced of its impracticality, Du Pont contented himself with frequent calls for reinforcements. He apparently never considered a threat of resignation, but it is doubtful whether that would have diverted the officials in Washington. An attack on the cradle of secession was simply too politically significant to be dropped.

The defenses of Charleston, commanded by General Pierre G. T. Beauregard, were strengthened during the autumn and winter of 1862–63. They consisted of Fort Moultrie and Battery Beauregard on Sullivans Island at the northern entrance to the harbor, Fort Sumter commanding the entrance channel, and Fort Johnson on James Island on the southern shore. The Confederates had strung a boom between Fort Sumter and Sullivans Island and had mined the channel leading to Sumter and the city.[54] British officers who visited the port reported that its defenses were stronger than those of Sevastopol during the Crimean War. It was certainly the most strongly defended port with which the Union Navy would have to contend during the war. A further complication arose at the end of January when the two Confederate ironclads at Charleston attacked and severely damaged two of Du Pont's blockading vessels.[55]

On 6 January 1863, since nine of the Navy's ten available ironclads had been allotted to Du Pont, Secretary Welles directed Du Pont to launch an attack on Charleston without delay. It should be remembered that the winter of 1862–63 was the bleakest of the war for the Union. Despite their defeat at Antietam, in the east Confederate strength appeared undiminished; in the west Ulysses S. Grant's thrust southward had been checked at Shiloh, Braxton Bragg's invasion of Kentucky had yet to be diverted, and the initial effort

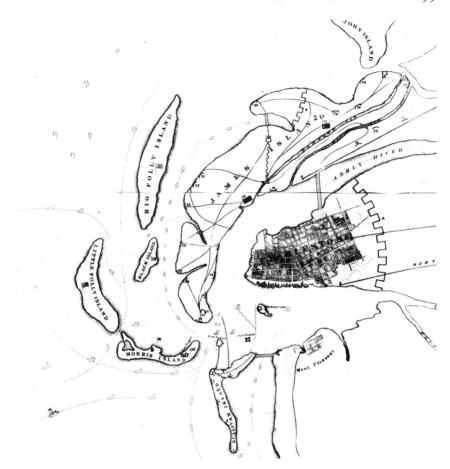

Charleston Harbor. Charleston was the most strongly defended Confederate port. On 7 April 1863 Du Pont's ships attacked the forts at pointblank range for almost an hour before they withdrew. This map shows the disposition of forces in the harbor followng the Confederate's 6 September 1863 withdrawal from Battery Wagner. *From the collections of the Geography and Maps Division of the Library of Congress.*

against Vicksburg had failed. The Union government was close to bank-ruptcy, desperately needing a military victory, and the capture of Charleston seemed to offer the best opportunity to restore public confidence. Moreover, from Welles's perspective the Navy also suffered from poor press over the failure to capture Charleston, the successful attack by the Confederate iron-clads on the blockaders, and rumors of extensive blockade running from the South Carolina port.[56]

Before launching his attack, Du Pont naturally wanted to test the ironclads. On 27 January he sent the monitor *Montauk* to bombard Fort McAllister on Ossabaw Sound south of Savannah. The attack, hampered by suspected torpedoes, proved the defensive strength of both the ironclad and the fort. Nor were the subsequent attacks by the *Montauk* on 1 February or the *Passaic, Nahant,* and *Patapsco* on 3 March any more effective. The monitor command-ers, some of the best young officers in the service, complained that the rate of fire of their big guns was too slow to be effective against well-built defenses.[57]

By early April the pressure for action had become irresistible; so Du Pont ordered his attack. On 4 April he issued his plan. It called for the nine armored vessels (the broadside ironclad *New Ironsides,* seven monitors, and the tower ironclad *Keokuk*) to pass the outer defenses without firing, but to open fire on Fort Sumter "when within easy range" while moving to positions about 600 to 800 yards north and west of it. Sumter was a brick and mortar fort that Du Pont believed more vulnerable to cannon fire than the other forts with their earthen ramparts. A reserve squadron of five wooden steamers stood by to assist when needed. The assault on 7 April did not go according to plan. An anti-torpedo raft fitted to the monitor *Weehawken* fouled her anchor and delayed the departure for two hours. The *New Ironsides* proved too clumsy to maneuver in the confined space of the harbor entrance and had to anchor twice, once atop a torpedo, to keep from running aground. She could not bring her broadside to bear on Fort Sumter and so fired only eight shots before Du Pont ordered a withdrawal. The monitors worked into their assigned positions but could accomplish little because of their miserable rate of fire. After less than two hours, Du Pont ordered their recall. The whole Union force fired only 1,140 rounds, while the Confederates rained over 2,200 projectiles on the attackers. The *Keokuk* sank after ninety hits, and the monitors took such a pounding that their commanders to a man recommended against renewing the attack.[58]

Du Pont had not expected victory and had only launched the attack because he was ordered to do so. With five of his monitors severely damaged before they could even pass the outer ring of Confederate defenses, he reasoned that pushing the attack without a land force to occupy the works would result in the loss of vessels that could later be raised by the defenders and used against the blockading squadron. He therefore canceled a resumption of the attack.[59]

On the heels of the decision to halt the attack, Du Pont received orders to send as many monitors as possible to the Gulf of Mexico for operations against Vicksburg and Mobile. Du Pont promised five, half of those on hand. Even so, Lincoln and the Navy Department unrealistically directed the depleted squad-ron to maintain its position within the Charleston bar so as to prevent any Confederate troops there from being sent to the Army of Northern Virginia.[60]

Du Pont's mind was poisoned by the running controversy with Washing-ton that had preceded the attack, the ego-numbing defeat, and his declining health. He interpreted Lincoln's message as a rebuke and was not mollified by a second letter that arrived late in the month. Nor was his temper improved by the letters written by Welles and Fox after they had recovered from the initial shock of the defeat, although both men attempted to soothe the disgruntled Charleston commander. In this charged atmosphere, Du Pont naturally assumed that a bitter account of the Charleston attack printed in the Baltimore *American* was part of a scheme by Fox and other proponents of the monitors to destroy him. The suspicion was further enhanced by Welles's refusal to publish Du Pont's report of the attack because it pointed out too graphically the shortcomings of the monitors. In these circumstances, Welles concluded that Du Pont must be replaced.[61] After considering possible replacements, Welles settled upon Andrew H. Foote. Unfortunately, Foote died suddenly in New York on 26 June while en route to take command. The choice then fell to Dahlgren, who relieved Du Pont on 6 July.[62]

Du Pont had been asked to do the impossible, he had failed, and the new commander did no better. Charleston was simply too strongly defended to be taken by naval assault alone, finally falling in February 1865 only when the advance of Major General William T. Sherman's armies through South Carolina rendered it indefensible. This is not to say that Du Pont's relief was inappropriate. After his failure at Charleston his relations with Washington had deteriorated too far for him to work in harness with Welles and Fox. Yet his treatment by the department was shabby. He received scant recognition for his undoubted accomplishments in seizing Port Royal and fixing a tight blockade on the South Carolina, Georgia, and northern Florida coasts and little understanding of the difficulties that he faced in trying to force his way into Charleston. Following his return, the Navy Department treated him like a leper. In the politically charged atmosphere of Washington, that was probably not surprising, since in no element of the Lincoln administration was bunker politics more clearly the order of the day than in the Navy Department. Moreover, in Du Pont that department was faced with a disgruntled officer whose champion, Henry Winter Davis, was one of the acknowledged leaders of the congressional opposition.

During the summer and autumn the admiral and the Secretary exchanged barbed letters over the refusal to publish Du Pont's report and the degree to which he had misled the department about his support of the attack. There the matter should have died, but Winter Davis saw political advantage in attacking the administration over the ironclad issue. He secured a joint resolution calling for Du Pont's reports on the Charleston attack. Welles surprised Davis and Du Pont and effectively turned the tables on them by supplying the correspondence. As a result, during the congressional investigations that followed, Du Pont was virtually on trial, as proponents of the monitors charged that he had misused them at Charleston.[63] Yet Welles was not vindictive. In June 1864 he allowed Fox to sound out Du Pont about taking command of the Pacific Squadron. Du Pont declined it until the department dropped what he saw as its allegations of duplicity.[64] Welles and Fox failed to satisfy him, and Du Pont did not again command at sea.

Du Pont's health deteriorated following his return from Charleston but it remained sufficiently robust for him to testify before the Committee on the Conduct of the War during the summer and attend an Episcopal Church gathering in Boston in October. In March 1865, at the insistence of Admiral David G. Farragut, he joined the board formed to consider promotion for officers who had performed outstanding service during the war. While in Washington, he caught a cold that developed into a bronchial condition. Du Pont considered a trip to Europe to improve his health, but on 23 June died suddenly while on a trip to Philadelphia with his wife.[65]

Du Pont was an outstanding peacetime leader. A thoughtful reformer and a student of naval affairs, he was an excellent administrator and a demanding superior to whom the privileges of rank were important. Most of the naval officer corps clearly regarded him as the service's leading professional following the death of Matthew Perry. He collected around him a cadre of able and loyal supporters such as Charles Henry Davis and Percivial Drayton, as well as Raymond Rodgers, who would follow in his footsteps as leader of the service. But for other officers and some of the civilians who staffed the Navy Department, he was a stiff and often haughty figure.

Du Pont is one of the more tragic figures in American naval history. Like his Army contemporaries Edwin V. Sumner and Henry W. Halleck, he had earned a service reputation in the years before the Civil War that he could not sustain on the field of battle. His failure occurred on two levels. The first was military. Du Pont lacked the self-confidence and drive of successful battle leader: the ability to push ahead at the critical moment when the enemy, as well as one's own forces, are tired and on the verge of collapse. The second level was political. Despite possessing the foresight to understand both the possibilities and the limitations of attacking land fortifications from the sea, Du Pont failed at his greatest opportunity, an attack in which he never believed and one in which no other leader succeeded. That experience illustrates the problem faced by military leaders forced to undertake operations for political reasons when they seriously question them from a military standpoint. Du Pont's failure to ensure that his political superiors understood his reservations guaranteed his disgrace and stands as a fundamental lesson for future commanders. Moreover, as far as the Navy Department was concerned, his presumed animosity and subsequent involvement in Washington politics destroyed any possibility of further significant service.

That Du Pont suffered the worse defeat of any Union naval commander during the Civil War does not erase his leading role in the promotion of naval reforms that allowed the Navy to prosecute so successfully the varied roles assigned it during the war. Success as a combat commander requires sound strategic and tactical planning, the ability to explain the military setting to one's superiors and to convey intentions to one's subordinates, as well as flexibility in the face of changing conditions. These qualities differ drastically from those required of a peacetime administrator. Du Pont's pre–Civil War career, his organization and execution of the blockade along the Confederate South Atlantic coast, and the seizure of Port Royal demonstrate his considerable abilities as an officer. They, not the unfortunate events at Charleston, illustrate the contributions of Samuel Francis Du Pont to the American naval tradition.

FURTHER READING

The basic source for any study of Samuel Francis Du Pont is the collection of his papers at the Eleutherian Mills Historical Library. They are extensive and well arranged, and frequently contain annotation by Mrs. Du Pont. Much of Du Pont's official correspondence is preserved in the National Archives.

There is only one book-length biography of Du Pont, the uncritical account by his nephew Henry A. Du Pont, *Rear Admiral Samuel Francis Du Pont, U.S. Navy*. This will be corrected with the publication of James M. Merrill's forthcoming study. The most balanced extended study is the sketch in John D. Hayes, ed., *Samuel Francis Du Pont: A Selection from His Civil War Letters*. Shorter accounts by Charles Oscar Paullin and Jeffrey M. Dorwart appear in the *Dictionary of American Biography* and *Dictionary of American Military Biography*.

Little has been written about Du Pont's career before the Mexican War, and he appears only fleetingly, if at all, in the memoirs or biographies of officers of that period. His extensive activities in the conflict with Mexico are described in Samuel F. Du Pont, *Official Dispatches and Letters, 1846–'48, 1861–'63* and "The War with Mexico: The Cruise of the U.S.S. *Cyane* during the Years 1845–48," U.S. Naval Institute *Proceedings*, VIII (1882): 419–37, as well as K. Jack Bauer, *Surfboats and Horse Marines*. There is no good study of the Naval Efficiency Board, but Harold D. Langley, *Social Reform in the United States Navy, 1798–1862* sets forth some of Du Pont's reform proposals in their broader context.

Admiral Hayes's collection of Du Pont's Civil War letters is the underpinning for any study of his activities during the war. It must be supplemented by the collateral material in *Official Records of the Union and Confederate Navies During the War of the Rebellion, The Confidential Correspondence of Gustavus Vasa Fox*, and the personal accounts in *Battles and Leaders of the Civil War*. Most of Du Pont's more important wartime reports also appear in *Official Dispatches and Letters* and in the *Report of the Secretary of the Navy in Relation to Armored Vessels*. Three studies of Civil War naval operations have been most valuable for this account: Daniel Ammen, *The Atlantic Coast*, Bern Anderson, *By Sea and by River*, and Rowena Reed, *Combined Operations in the Civil War*. Du Pont's tortured relations with the Navy Department can only be understood by reading *Diary of Gideon Welles*, preferably in the Beale edition, and John Niven, *Gideon Welles*. Richard S. West, Jr., *Gideon Welles: Lincoln's Navy Department* is balanced but allots little space to the "unlucky South Altlantic force."

NOTES

1. H. A. Du Pont, *Rear-Admiral Samuel Francis Du Pont U.S. Navy: A Biography*, 3–5; John D. Hayes, ed., *Samuel Francis Du Pont: A Selection from His Civil War Letters*, I: xlvii–xlix, li, cix.

2. C. A. Rodney et al. to B. W. Crowninshield, 1815, in Samuel Francis Du Pont Papers, Eleutherian Mills Historical Library, W9-3415; Du Pont, *Du Pont*, 6; Hayes, *Du Pont*, I: lii–liii.

3. Crowninshield to Du Pont, 18 February 1817, Stewart to Du Pont, 18 November 1818, Du Pont Papers, W9-3419, 3426; Du Pont, *Du Pont*, 7; Hayes, *Du Pont*, I: liii, cix; George F. Emmons, *The Navy of the United States, From the Commencement, 1775, to 1853*, 10–11, 86–87.

4. Smith Thompson to Du Pont, 21 March 1821, in Du Pont Papers, W9-3446.

5. In 1821 and 1822 the full year's group of midshipmen were not examined. Du Pont was not tested until 1825 and would not catch up in rank with his contemporaries until 1843. Du Pont to G. J. Pendergrast, 7 September, to Secretary of the Navy, 23 September, to David Porter, 23 September 1822, John Rodgers to Du Pont, 14 December 1841, in Du Pont Papers, W9-138-40, 3496, 687.

6. David F. Long, *Sailor-Diplomat: A Biography of Commodore James Biddle, 1783–1848*, 121.

7. Rodgers to Du Pont, 27 July 1824, 25 July, 3 September 1825, in Du Pont Papers, W9-3488, 3492, 3493; Du Pont, *Du Pont*, 11; Hayes, *Du Pont*, I: liii, cx; James M. Merrill, "Midshipman Du Pont and the Cruise of the *North Carolina*, 1825–1827," *The American Neptune*, XL (1980): 211–25.

8. Southard to Du Pont, 4 May, Rodgers to Du Pont, 11 December 1826, 17 April 1827, in Du Pont Papers, W9-3503, 3507, 3509.

9. Du Pont, *Du Pont*, 14–15.

10. Branch to Du Pont, 5 June 1829, in Du Pont Papers, W9-3538; Du Pont, *Du Pont*, 11–14; Hayes, *Du Pont*, I: lv–lvi.

11. H. J. Miller to Du Pont, 31 December 1833, Du Pont to C. H. Davis, 24 October 1844, in Du Pont Papers, W9-3884, 851; Francis Leigh Williams, *Matthew Fontaine Maury: Scientist of the Sea*, 110.

12. Du Pont to Pendergrast, 14 November 1835, to Dallas, 27 July 1836, Dallas to Du Pont, 27 April, 18, 23, June, 29 August 1836, in Du Pont Papers, W9-377, 443, 3737, 3744, 3747, 3756; Du Pont, *Du Pont*, 15; Emmons, *Navy of the United States*. 110–11.

13. Perry to Du Pont, 6, 11 September, Du Pont to Shubrick, 5 June 1837, to Pendergrast, 23 March, 28 July, 23 August, to C. H. Davis, 31 May 1838, to *Naval Chronicle*, 1838, letter on Steam Frigate Fulton, n.d., Du Pont Papers, W9-464, 3791, 3792, 488, 489, 491, 494, 520.

14. Du Pont to James K. Paulding, 29 August, Paulding to Du Pont, 13 September, Du Pont, Pendergrast, Missroon, and Godon to Secretary of the Navy, 10 October 1838, Hull to Du Pont, 31 March, Du Pont to Paulding, 5 June, to C. H. Davis, 26 June 1840, in Du Pont Papers, W9-496, 3817, 584, 3884, 613, 623; Gardner Weld Allen, ed., *Papers of Isaac Hull, Commodore United States Navy*, 140, 154–59. The other lieutenants were Garrett J. Pendergrast, John S. Missroon, and Sylvanus W. Godon. Though found guilty and given varying sentences, all appealed to Secretary of the Navy Abel Upshur, who overturned all the sentences and returned all three to the squadron, where they served until the summer of 1841.

15. Du Pont to Abel P. Upshur, 7 July, 25 August, to C. H. Davis, 29 July, to H. E. Ballard, 5 September 1842, in Du Pont Papers, W9-718, 735, 725, 738; William Stanton, *The Great United States Exploring Expedition of 1838–1842*, 283–88.

16. The Du Pont Papers contain extensive correspondence with both Mackenzie and his brother-in-law Matthew C. Perry, showing Du Pont's concern over service and popular opinion. The midshipman involved, Philip Spencer, was the son of the Secretary of War.

17. Upshur to Du Pont, 10 January, 7 March, commission, 9 January, Du Pont to Upshur, 30 January 1843, to Daniel Turner, 24 January 1844, David Henshaw to Du Pont, 30 August 1843, Turner to Du Pont, 27 January 1844, in Du Pont Papers, W9-4125, 4126, 776, 4165, 880, 4238, 4324; Henshaw to Du Pont, 22 November 1843, in Record of Confidential Letters, I: 17, Record Group (R.G.) 45, National Archives.

18. Hayes, *Du Pont*, I: lxii, cxi; Charles Lee Lewis, *Admiral Franklin Buchanan, Fearless Man of Action*, 93–94.

19. Du Pont to Bancroft, 6, 17 October 1846, in George Bancroft Papers, Massachusetts Historical Society; Du Pont to Stockton, 29, 31, July, 23 September 1846, in Samuel F. Du Pont, *Official Dispatches and Letters 1846–48, 1861–'63*, 1–6, 8–11; Du Pont to Stockton, 12 October, 1 December 1846, in Pacific Squadron Letters, R.G. 45; Samuel F. Du Pont, "The War with Mexico: The Cruise of the U.S.S. *Cyane* During the Years 1845–48," U.S. Naval Institute *Proceedings*, VIII (1882): 420–25; K. Jack Bauer, *Surfboats and Horse Marines*, 166–67, 170–73, 183–84, 192.

20. Du Pont to Shubrick, 26 September 1847, in Du Pont, *Official Dispatches*, 20; Du Pont to Shubrick, 25 March 1848, in 30th Cong., 2nd Sess., House Executive Document 1, 1149–50; Du Pont, "Cruise of the *Cyane*," 425–26; Bauer, *Surfboats and Horse Marines*, 208–9, 229–30; Du Pont, *Du Pont*, 48–56.

21. Du Pont to C. H. Davis, 11 September, to W. B. Preston, 24 September, Preston to Du Pont, 5, 21 September, 16 October 1849, in Du Pont Papers, W9-1135, 1136, 5511, 5518, 5537; Charles M. Todorich, *The Spirited Years: A History of the Antebellum Naval Academy*, 68.

22. Preston to Du Pont, 21 May 1850, William Hoge to Du Pont, 28 April, Shubrick to Du Pont, 7 November 1851, in Du Pont Papers, W9-5781, 6085, 6200; Du Pont, *Du Pont*, 58–59.

23. Samuel F. Du Pont, *Report on National Defences*; Hayes, *Du Pont*, I: cxii.

24. Hayes, *Du Pont*, I: lxvi, cxii; Du Pont, *Du Pont*, 58; Harold D. Langley, *Social Reform in the United States Navy, 1798–1862*, 174–75, 202–4.

25. Du Pont to Pendergrast, 31 May 1849, to C. H. Davis, 14 January 1855, draft of bill, n.d., in Du Pont Papers, W9-1114, 1569, 1576.

26. Dobbin to Du Pont, 5 June 1855, Du Pont to Maury, 16 November 1855, notes and tables concerning the Retiring Board, letter to *National Intelligencer* [May 1855], in Du Pont Papers, W9-7379, 1663, 1692, 1631; Dobbin to Shubrick et al., 20 June, Shubrick to Dobbin, 26 July 1855, in K. Jack Bauer, ed., *The New American State Papers: Naval Affairs*, VII: 121–28; Du Pont, *Du Pont*, 63–73; Hayes, *Du Pont*, I: lxii–lxiii.

27. Dobbin to Du Pont, 8 October 1855 and commission, Du Pont to C. H. Davis, 20 July 1855, in Du Pont Papers, W9-7539, 7540, 1806.

28. Du Pont to Isaac Toucy, 11 April 1857, to Andrew H. Foote, 11 April, 23 June 1858, in Du Pont Papers, W9-1887, 1965, 1982; Du Pont, *Du Pont*, 87–97; Hayes, *Du Pont*, I: lxiv, cxiii.

29. Robert Erwin Johnson, *Rear Admiral John Rodgers 1812–1882*, 148; Hayes, *Du Pont*, I: xlvi, cxiii.

30. Du Pont to Shubrick, 5 December, to Louis M. Goldsborough, 14 December 1860, in Hayes, *Du Pont*, I: 3–5, 9–10. See also Du Pont to Duncan N. Ingraham, 24 January, to Foote, 25 January 1861, in ibid., 26–28.

31. Toucy to Du Pont, 19 December 1860, in Du Pont Papers, W9-10568.

32. Du Pont, *Du Pont*, I: 105; Bern Anderson, *By Sea and by River*, 35.

33. Fox to Du Pont, 22 May, Du Pont to Bache, 30 May 1861, in Hayes, *Du Pont*, I: 71, 73–74. Howard K. Beale, ed., *Diary of Gideon Welles*, II: 157–58.

34. Du Pont to wife, 28 June 1861, in Hayes, *Du Pont*, I: 85–86; Welles to Barnard, 26 June 1861, in *Official Records of the Union and Confederate Navies in the War of the Rebellion* (hereafter *ORN*), ser. 1, XII: 295. Valuable commentaries on the activities of the board are to be found in Rowena Reed, *Combined Operations in the Civil War*, 8–9; Herman Hattaway and Archer Jones, *How the North Won*, 135; and Anderson, *By Sea and by River*, 39–40. The individual

reports are reprinted in *ORN*, ser. 1, XII: 195–206, XIII: 67–73, and XVI: 618–30, 651-55.

35. Du Pont to wife, 26 July 1861, Welles to Du Pont, 5 August 1861, in Hayes, *Du Pont*, I: 113–14, 126–27; Beale, *Diary of Welles*, I: 134, Daniel Ammen, "Du Pont and the Port Royal Expedition," in Robert U. Johnson and Clarence C. Buel, *Battles and Leaders of the Civil War* (hereafter *B & L*), I: 672.

36. Welles to Du Pont, 18 August, Du Pont to Welles, 18 August, to Goldsborough, Du Pont, and McKean, 5 October 1861, *ORN*, ser. 1, XII: 208–9, VI: 293. Sherman's orders were issued 14 October. Ibid., 220.

37. Du Pont telegram to Fox, 11 October, Welles to Du Pont, 12 October 1861, in *ORN*, ser. 1, XII: 213–14; Beale, *Diary of Welles*, II: 118; Daniel Ammen, *The Atlantic Coast*, 105–6.

38. Du Pont to Welles, 16 October, General Order, 23 October, Goldsborough to Welles, 18, 29 October 1861, in *ORN*, XII: 218, 224–25; Du Pont to Fox, 25 October 1861, in Robert Means Thompson and Richard Wainwright, eds., *Confidential Correspondence of Gustavus Vasa Fox, Assistant Secretary of the Navy 1861–1865*, I: 59; Ammen, "Du Pont and Port Royal," 674–75; Reed, *Combined Operations*, 24–25.

39. The account of the Port Royal attack is based upon: Du Pont to Welles, 6, 8, 11 November, Drayton to L. D. Walker, 24 November 1861, in *ORN*, ser. 1, XII: 259–65, 300–307; Du Pont to H. W. Davis, 6 November, to wife, 13 November 1861, in Hayes, *Du Pont*, I: 218–19, 239; Du Pont to Fox, 9 November 1861, in Thompson and Wainwright, *Correspondence of Fox*, I: 65–67; Ammen, *Atlantic Coast*, 18–33; Ammen, "Du Pont and Port Royal," 67–87; Anderson, *By Sea and by River*, 54–57; Du Pont, *Du Pont*, 122–40; Johnson, *Rodgers*, 174–79; Reed, *Combined Operations*, 28–31. Godon's explanation of his maneuver is in Beale, *Diary of Welles*, III: 217.

40. Douglas Southall Freeman, *R. E. Lee: A Biography*, I: 608–19; Anderson, *By Sea and by River*, 58–69; David Dixon Porter, *The Naval History of the Civil War*, 61.

41. Ammen to Du Pont, 9 November, Du Pont to Welles, 25 November, Drayton to Du Pont, 28 November 1861, in *ORN*, ser. 1, XII: 336, 320–23, 325–26. The capture of Port Royal earned Du Pont a congressional vote of thanks and permanent appointment as a flag officer. *Cong. Globe*, 37th Cong., 2nd Sess., 940, 1339; Lincoln to Senate, 4 February 1862, in Roy P. Basler, ed., *The Collected Works of Abraham Lincoln*, V: 127.

42. Du Pont, General Order No. 1, 24 October 1861, in *ORN*, ser. 1, XII: 225; Hayes, *Du Pont*, I: lxxvi, xcv.

43. Du Pont to Fox, 12 November 1861, in *ORN*, ser. 1, XII: 341.

44. Du Pont to Welles, 1 December, to wife, 5 December 1861, in

Hayes, *Du Pont*, I: 266, 270–72; Du Pont to Welles, 4, 6 December 1861, in *ORN*, ser. 1, XII: 382, 384–85; Du Pont to Fox, 6 December 1861, in Thompson and Wainwright, *Correspondence of Fox*, I, 76–77; Du Pont, *Du Pont*, 147–48.

45. Bache to Du Pont, 4 September, Du Pont to Welles, 23 December, to Fox, 19 October 1861, in *ORN*, ser. 1, XII: 207, 417, 421–22; Du Pont to wife, 12 December 1861, in Hayes, *Du Pont*, I: 273–79; Ammen, *Atlantic Coast*, 41–42; James Russell Soley, "Minor Operations of the South Atlantic Squadron Under Du Pont," *B & L*, IV: 27–30. For a general account of the Stone Fleet, see Arthur Gordon, "The Great Stone Fleet: Calculated Catastrophe," U.S. Naval Institute *Proceedings*, XCIV (December 1968): 72–82.

46. Du Pont to wife, 5, 12 December 1861, in Hayes, *Du Pont*, I: 270–79; Du Pont to Fox, 16 December 1861, in Thompson and Wainwright, *Correspondence of Fox*, I: 79: Ammen, *Atlantic Coast*, 46–47; Du Pont, *Du Pont*, 148; Johnson, *Rodgers*, 186; Reed, *Combined Operations*, 53–54.

47. Du Pont to Welles, 4, 9, 12, 13 March 1862, in *ORN*, ser. 1, XII: 573–75, 588–89, 595–99; Ammen, *Atlantic Coast*, 48–51; Du Pont, *Du Pont*, 143–44; Hayes, *Du Pont*, I: cxiv–cxv; Reed, *Combined Operations*, 55.

48. Du Pont, *Du Pont*, 149; James Russell Soley, *Blockade and the Cruisers*, 109; Du Pont to Fox, 3 April, in Thompson and Wainwright, *Correspondence of Fox*, I: 115–18; to wife, 4 April 1862, in Hayes, *Du Pont*, I: 401–2.

49. Du Pont to Welles, 3 April, 9 May 1862, in *ORN*, ser. 1, XII: 706–7, 803–4; Du Pont to Fox, 31 May, Fox to Du Pont, 3 June 1862, in Thompson and Wainwright, *Correspondence of Fox*, I: 121–24, 126; John Niven, *Gideon Welles: Lincoln's Secretary of the Navy*, 424–25.

50. Du Pont to Welles, 31 May, 3 July 1862, in *ORN*, ser. 1, XIII: 53–54, 166–67; Du Pont, *Du Pont*, 168; Reed, *Combined Operations*, 267. On 16 July Du Pont became one of the Navy's first three rear admirals. He broke his flag in the *Wabash* on 9 August.

51. Beale, *Diary of Welles*, I: 236–37; Fox to Du Pont, 16 February 1863, in Hayes, *Du Pont*, II: 443–44; Reed, *Combined Operations*, 272–75; Nevin, *Welles*, 433.

52. Beale, *Diary of Welles*, I: 158; Du Pont to Fox, 8 October 1862, in Thompson and Wainright, *Correspondence of Fox*, I: 160; Du Pont to Welles, 25 October 1862, in Hayes, *Du Pont*, II: 268; Reed, *Combined Operations*, 270.

53. Welles to Du Pont, 10 September 1862, in *ORN*, ser. 1, XIII: 322; Du Pont to wife, 16, 17, 18, 20 October 1862, in Hayes, *Du Pont*, II: 246–51; Beale, *Diary of Welles*, I: 160.

54. Pierre G. T. Beauregard, "The Defense of Charleston," in *B & L*, IV: 1–4; Du Pont to C. H. Davis, 4 January 1863, in Hayes, *Du Pont*, II: 340; Fox to Du Pont, 7 October 1862, in Thompson and Wainright, *Correspondence of Fox*, I: 157.

55. Du Pont to Welles, 3 February 1863, in *ORN*, ser. 1, XIII: 577–78;

Paul D. Lockhart, "The Confederate Naval Squadron at Charleston and the Failure of Naval Harbor Defense," *The American Neptune*, XLIV (1984): 265–66.

56. Welles to Du Pont, 6, 31 January 1863, in *ORN*, ser. 1, XIII: 503, 571; Beale, *Diary of Welles*, I: 216; Niven, *Gideon Welles*, 430.

57. Du Pont to Welles, 24, 28 January, 3, 27 February, 2, 3 March 1863, in *ORN*, ser. 1, XIII: 535, 543–44, 626, 692, 712–13, 716; to wife, 4 March 1863, in Hayes, *Du Pont*, II: 466–67, 474.

58. The description of the attack on Charleston is drawn from: Du Pont to Welles, 8, 15 April 1863 (with enclosures), in *ORN*, ser. 1, XIV: 3–27; Du Pont to wife, 8 April, to H. W. Davis, 8 April 1863, in Hayes, *Du Pont*, III: 3–4, 10; Ammen, *Atlantic Coast*, 94–104; Anderson, *By Sea and by River*, 163–66; Beauregard, "The Defense of Charleston," 10–12; Porter, *Naval History*, 373–79; C. R. P. Rodgers, "Du Pont's Attack at Charleston," in *B & L*, IV: 35–40.

59. Rodgers, "Du Pont's Attack," 40–41. See also Porter, *Naval History*, 375.

60. Welles to Du Pont, 2 April 1863, Du Pont to Welles, 11 April 1863, Lincoln to Du Pont, 13, 14, April 1863, in *ORN*, ser. 1, XIII: 803 and XIV: 124, 132–33.

61. Welles to Du Pont, 11 April, 14 May 1863, Du Pont to Welles, 22 April, 27 May 1863, in *ORN*, ser. 1, XIV: 51–56, 63–67, 123–24, and Percival Drayton to Du Pont, 8, 12 May 1863, in Hayes, *Du Pont*, III: 92, 110–11; Beale, *Diary of Welles*, 309–10; Madeleine Vinton Dahlgren, *Memoirs of John A. Dahlgren*, 390; Hayes, *Du Pont*, I: lxxxv–vi; Niven, *Welles*, 435–38, 472–73.

62. Welles to Du Pont, 3, 24 June 1863, in *ORN*, ser. 1, XIV: 159–60, 296; Beale, *Diary of Welles*, I: 309–14, 317, 320–21, 344; Welles to J. M. Hoppin, 8 October 1873, in James Mason Hoppin, *Life of Andrew Hull Foote*, 395–96; Dahlgren, *Memoirs*, 391–95.

63. Welles to Du Pont, 26 June, 4 November 1863; Du Pont to Welles, 22 October 1863, in Hayes, *Du Pont*, III: 184–86, 253–57, 257–71; Beale, *Diary of Welles*, I: 476–77, 531; II: 7–8, 30, 321; Niven, *Gideon Welles*, 472–78; *Report of the Secretary of the Navy in Relation to Armored Vessels*.

64. C. H. Davis to Du Pont, 5 June 1864; Du Pont to Davis, 11 June 1864, in Hayes, *Du Pont*, III: 353–54.

65. Du Pont to W. K. Hall, 13 October 1864, to H. W. Davis, 4 February, 31 March, to Percival Drayton, 5 March, 22 June, to Thomas Turner, 14 April 1865, all in ibid., 406, 431, 452–53, 463–64, 479–82; ibid., I: xciii, cxvii. In 1882 Congress ordered the circle at the intersection of Massachusetts and Connecticut Avenues be named for Du Pont. Two years later a statue by Launt Thompson was added. It was replaced in 1921 by a fountain made by Daniel Chester French. Charles Oscar Paullin, "Samuel Francis Du Pont," *Dictionary of American Biography*, V: 533.

DAVID GLASGOW
FARRAGUT:
THE UNION'S NELSON

BY WILLIAM N. STILL, JR.

British military historian Cyril Falls described David Glasgow Farragut as "a great naval commander with something of the dash and inspiration of Nelson."[1] Farragut, however, was not so romantic a figure as the famous British admiral. His personal life was above reproach, and he was not mortally wounded during his most famous battle. Nevertheless, to the generation of naval officers that came of age during the Civil War, and to the Northern public in general, he was a genuine hero, rightfully compared to the victor of Trafalgar.

Farragut was born on 5 July 1801, at Campbell's Station, outside of Knoxville, Tennessee. His family moved to New Orleans in 1807. Following the death of his mother and the enlistment of his father in the Navy, David was taken into the family of Commander David Porter, in charge of the New Orleans Naval Station.[2] After a brief period in school, David at the age of nine and a half was appointed a midshipman in the Navy.

When Porter was given command of the frigate *Essex* in 1811, Farragut sailed with him. After war broke out with Great Britain in 1812, the *Essex* captured a number of prizes in the Pacific; and Farragut as prize master took one of them into Valparaiso. He was twelve at the time. In 1814 Farragut became a prisoner of war when the *Eseex* was taken after a long and bloody engagement with two British warships. Porter was extremely pleased with Farragut's performance during the battle and would have recommended him for promotion except for his youth.

After the war Farragut served in various ships, primarily in the Mediterranean and the West Indies. In 1821 he was promoted to lieutenant and shortly afterward he briefly commanded the *Ferret*, his first naval command. In 1823 he married Susan C. Marchant of Norfolk, Virginia. She died in 1840 after an extended period as an invalid, and three years later he married Virginia Loyall, also of Norfolk. They had one child, Loyall. From the end of the War of 1812

until the time of the Civil War, Farragut's career was varied but unspectacu-
lar. He received his first important command, the sloop *Decatur*, in 1842 and
his last, the *Brooklyn*, in 1860. In between he commanded the *Saratoga* during
the Mexican War. Of his shore assignments the most important was the period
(1854–59) that he spent in California establishing the Mare Island Navy Yard.
In September 1855 he was appointed captain. When the Civil War broke out,
he was at home in Norfolk awaiting orders. Then sixty years old, he had spent
nearly half a century in the Navy.

Career officers with the prospect of promotion on the horizon are usually
delighted with the coming of war, yet this was not generally true in 1861.
Certainly it was not true for Farragut. His residence was Norfolk when
Virginia seceded in mid-April; he then moved his family to New York. There
he remained, cooling his heels for nearly four months. As an officer of Southern
descent he was under suspicion. In September, he was made a member of a
naval board to select incapacitated officers for retirement. Farragut's chances
for active employment were not promising. He was close to retirement age,
had been passed over three times for squadron commander, and had spent very
little time at sea since the Mexican War. In fact his greatest accomplishment
had been the establishment of the Mare Island Navy Yard.[3] Yet, through
fortuitous circumstances, he would be given command of the most important
naval expedition to be mounted during the war, the opening of the Mississippi
River and the capture of the port of New Orleans.

Secretary of the Navy Gideon Welles appointed Farragut to this prestigious
command for several reasons. Welles was impressed that Farragut had left
Norfolk when Virginia seceded and moved his family to New York. He was
also familiar with the naval officer's plan to capture a fortification at Vera Cruz
during the Mexican War. Perhaps most important was the endorsement from
Commander David Dixon Porter, the son of Farragut's guardian, who with
Assistant Secretary of the Navy Gustavus Fox and Welles strongly urged
Farragut's selection. Finally, Farragut was the most likely candidate in order
of seniority not already assigned to an important command.[4] At times Welles
would ignore strict seniority, but in this case he decided to adhere to it.
According to the Secretary's most recent biographer, Welles believed that
President Lincoln would insist on giving the command to Commander John
Dahlgren, in charge of the Washington Navy Yard and a favorite of the
President, unless seniority were followed. A number of officers consulted by
the Secretary had reservations concerning Farragut's ability to command a
large force. Nevertheless, Welles decided to appoint him. "All who knew him
gave him credit of being a good officer, of good sense," Welles wrote.[5]

On 21 December 1861, Farragut journeyed to Washington where he met
with Fox and Welles. That night he elatedly wrote his wife the news of his
appointment: "I am to have a flag in the Gulf and the rest depends upon
myself."[6] Two days later he received his official orders to the command with

David G. Farragut. Though a flag officer, Farragut was wearing a captain's uniform when this photograph was taken in New Orleans in 1862. *Courtesy of the Naval Academy Museum.*

the *Hartford* as his flagship. Within a month, on 19 January 1862, the *Hartford* was commissioned and left Philadelphia for the Gulf of Mexico.[7]

A month later the *Hartford* arrived at Ship Island, an islet lying approximately thirty miles to the south of Biloxi, Mississippi. Here Flag Officer W. W. McKean transferred to Farragut thirty vessels that would comprise the nucleus of his force, the West Gulf Blockading Squadron. Farragut would need far more ships, however, to carry out his responsibilities, which included not only the capture of New Orleans, but the blockade of the Gulf region from

St. Andrews Bay in the east to the Rio Grande in the west. Fox had already written him that "we are crowding everything into your hands so as to give you enough to make sure work." This would include additional shallow-draft steamers, mortar boats to be commanded by David D. Porter, and even the recently completed revolutionary warship, the *Monitor*.[8]

By the beginning of April, Farragut commanded a heavily increased squadron. He had forty-seven warships, not counting mortar boats, with which to carry out the Mississippi River operation while enforcing the blockade throughout his station. A military force of some 18,000 men under Major General Benjamin F. Butler had arrived to cooperate in the attack.[9] Throughout March, Farragut had concentrated on getting his heavier ships over the bar at Southwest Pass and into the Mississippi River. He had reluctantly delayed the attack until the larger vessels were in the river. There is little doubt that he would have attacked with only his smaller ships and avoided several weeks' delay had the choice been his, but it was not. The Navy Department expected him to mount the attack not only with his larger vessels, but with the support of Porter's mortar boat flotilla as well.

The department's orders called for him to reduce the two forts, Saint Philip and Jackson, using Porter's mortar boats as long as necessary, and then to place New Orleans under his guns until troops could arrive and assault the city. On 18 April, the mortar boats, in position below the forts, opened fire, supported by the gunboats. Almost immediately, Farragut realized that he did not have enough ammunition for a lengthy bombardment. On the 20th, at a conference of officers, he informed them of his decision to run past the forts, even though they had not been rendered ineffective. To the assembled officers, many of whom had strong reservations about his plan, including Porter, he replied, "something must be done immediately. I believe in celerity."[10]

At 2:00 A.M. on 24 April, red lanterns hoisted to the mizzen peak in the *Hartford* signaled the fleet to get under way. Detachments from two of the smaller gunboats had already cleared an opening in a barrier of dismantled hulks across the river between the forts. Farragut's original plan called for the sortie to be in two columns with the lighter gunboats shielded by the heavier ones, but the passageway in the barrier was too narrow for ships to pass through two abreast—the advance instead would have to be in one long single column of three groups. The first group, under the command of Captain Theodorus Bailey, consisted of six gunboats and two sloops of war. The second was led by the *Hartford*, followed by the *Brooklyn* and the *Richmond*. Six gunboats brought up the rear. The battle began immediately after the second vessel, the *Pensacola*, passed through the barrier. As both forts opened fire, and the Union ships replied, Confederate vessels joined in the fight.

The small Confederate naval force above the forts consisted of four wooden gunboats and one ironclad ram, the *Manassas*. Only the *McRae* and the *Manassas* posed a serious threat to Farragut's ships. The Confederates had hoped to reinforce this flotilla with two large armored vessels, the *Mississippi* and the *Louisiana*, but both were still under construction when Farragut attacked, with only the *Louisiana* far enough along to be used. On the day that the mortar boats opened fire on the forts, she was towed down the river and moored to the bank above Fort Saint Philip. The day before Farragut's attack, six guns were mounted on her gundeck facing the river.[11]

As with so many plans, Farragut's soon collapsed during the smoke and confusion of battle. Most of the ships got through the barrier safely although the *Brooklyn* strayed into a hulk, then into a raft of logs, before emerging in front of Fort Saint Philip. The *Kennebec*, one of the smaller gunboats, leading the third division, fouled the barrier, and along with two others in this division, the *Winona* and the *Itasca*, remained below it. Some of the vessels passed the others, firing on one fort and then the other, before finally emerging from the smoke above the forts. There the Confederate vessels added to the confusion by entering the fray. The *Manassas* rammed the *Brooklyn*; the *Hartford* was set ablaze by a fire raft; first the *McRae* and then the *Manassas* attacked the *Iroquois*. The *Cayuga*, challenged by three of the Confederate vessels, escaped unharmed; but the *Varuna* was not so fortunate—seven miles above the forts the *Governor Moore* sank her after a running fight. Shortly afterward the *Governor Moore* was herself disabled and run aground by several Union ships. The fleet, less the three vessels that remained below the barrier and the sunken *Varuna*, assembled at Quarantine Station, seven miles above the forts.

Farragut had won his first major engagement as a fleet commander. Since observing French warships in action against a Mexican fort in 1838, he had been convinced that ships with sufficient speed could bypass forts without sustaining appreciable damage. This laid the basis for his plan of action, and the results justified his expectations. He lost only one ship, with minor damage to the others, and he suffered only 37 killed and 146 wounded. The forts were isolated, and with their line of communication cut, it would be only a matter of time before they must surrender. New Orleans was next.[12]

Shortly after noon on 25 April, Farragut's fleet rounded the last bend in a drizzling rain and appeared within sight of New Orleans. The spectacle appalled the flag officer: "the levee of New Orleans was one scene of desolation; ships, steamers, cotton, coal, etc., were all in one common blaze and our ingenuity much taxed to avoid the floating conflagration. . . ."[13] Shortly after anchoring, Farragut sent his second in command to demand the city's surrender. After some defiance by Confederate military and civil officials, New Orleans surrendered to the Navy. Farragut then ordered a detachment of marines to raise the American flag over the U.S. Mint. Although the citizens remained hostile, with curses and threats following the U.S. uniforms, the city was taken. That night Farragut wrote his wife and son: "I am so agitated that I can scarcely write and shall only tell you that it has pleased almighty God to preserve my life and limb. . . . I took the city at Meridian today."[14]

Farragut's haste to take New Orleans without waiting for Butler's troops had one unfortunate consequence: it allowed the Confederates to remove most of their stores, railroad rolling stock, and dismantle factories. The flag officer's decision may have been for personal achievement and a race for glory, as Butler hinted in a letter to his wife, but more than likely it was simply a product of Farragut's aggressiveness, self-confidence, and impatience. Farragut's victory clearly was important, but just how important it is difficult to say. A recent study has concluded that "without question the capture of New Orleans was the most important Union conquest of the war—strangling Southern commerce on the river and along the Gulf coast." Another author, in obvious agreement, entitled his book-length study of the campaign *The Night the War was Lost*.[15] It is doubtful, however, that the battle and capture of New Orleans were that decisive, certainly in terms of the war's outcome. Southern morale was shaken by the fall of the largest city and most important port in the Confederacy; trade virtually ceased to flow on the Mississippi River. But Confederate morale was still resilient, and it would be another year and a half before it would begin to collapse. Also, closing the Mississippi had little affect on trade elsewhere along the Gulf Coast. Yet, Liddell Hart correctly maintained that running past the forts and thereby gaining "the bloodless surrender of New Orleans . . . was the thin end of a strategical wedge which split the Confederacy up the vital line of this great river." It was the capture of the lower Mississippi along with Port Hudson and Vicksburg that proved decisive. James D. Bulloch, a Confederate naval officer, wrote years after the war, "I have always thought that the consequences which resulted from the operations of [the Union Navy] . . . in the waters of the Mississippi were more fatal to the Confederacy than any of the military campaigns."[16]

After New Orleans what next? Farragut's original instructions had stressed that he reduce the forts, capture New Orleans, continue up the river possibly as far as Memphis, link up with Union forces descending the river, and finally seize Mobile. With New Orleans in Union hands, Farragut initially decided to attack the forts guarding Mobile Bay, but informed of Farragut's plan, the Navy Department reacted very negatively. Although the capture of Mobile had been in Farragut's instructions, the evidence is clear that the Navy Department expected him to complete the river campaign before attacking Mobile. On 17 May, Fox wrote to Porter: "Somebody had made a most serious blunder in persuading the Flag Officer to go at Mobile instead of obeying his instructions to go up the Mississippi. . . . It seems extraordinary how Farragut could have committed this terrible mistake. . . . Mobile and the whole Gulf will fall at any time, but the Mississippi is a golden opportunity that I fear is fast slipping through our fingers."[17]

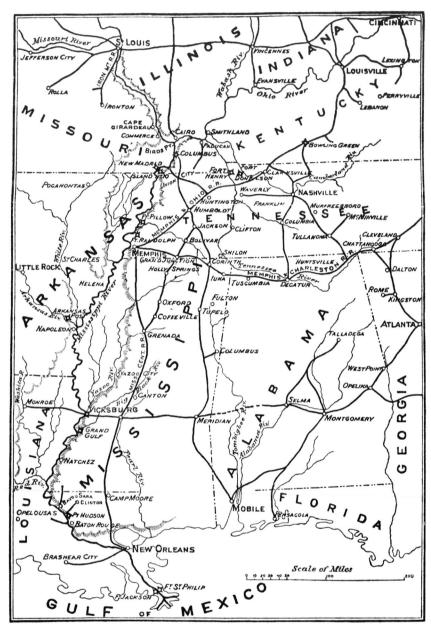

The western theatre of war, 1862–63. From Francis Vinton Green, *The Army in the Civil War*, vol 8: *The Mississippi* (1885).

Before Fox could communicate his concerns to Farragut, the flag officer had already changed his mind and ordered vessels up the river "to keep up the panic as far as possible." Why had Farragut reconsidered? One biographer suggests that the flag officer had second thoughts about his orders and realized the priority of moving up the river. Rowena Reed in *Combined Operations in the Civil War* argues that Butler persuaded the flag officer to change his mind. On 29 April, he wrote to the Secretary of War that he hoped to convince Farragut "to pass up the River as far as the mouth of Red River if possible, so as to cut off [the Confederates] supplies," and added that he believed Mobile was not so important as this.[18] Whatever the reason, the decision was correct. Opening the Mississippi was far more vital to ultimate victory than the capture of Mobile.

On 7 May, Farragut left New Orleans with the *Hartford*, two large steamers, and eight small gunboats, arriving below Vicksburg on 24 May. Some 2,000 men under the command of General Thomas Williams accompanied the naval force. Convinced that more troops were needed to attack Vicksburg successfully, Farragut awaited reinforcements. When no additional troops materialized, the flag officer left for New Orleans determined to begin the Mobile campaign. Within a few weeks, however, a reluctant Farragut returned upstream under orders to pass Vicksburg and take Memphis if possible.

By the time Farragut reached Vicksburg, Memphis had fallen, and the Union Mississippi Squadron was approaching Vicksburg from upstream. Farragut determined to link up with the descending squadron. On 28 June, his vessels, once again in two columns, got under way and under the cover of fire from mortar boats made their way slowly past the fort. Although several vessels were hit, none was seriously damaged, and all but the *Brooklyn* and two gunboats made it past the city. Farragut's conviction that ships could run past forts and fortifications without receiving serious damage again proved correct.[19] On the last day of June, the Union river squadron under Flag Officer Charles Davis joined Farragut at anchor above Vicksburg.

Farragut wanted to return downstream as quickly as possible. Additional troops were still unavailable, the river was begining to fall, and he feared for the health of his crews in the unhealthy river lowlands. On 4 July he wrote his wife, "If I can retain my health and get out of this river . . . I shall be most thankful."[20] He felt that he had accomplished the department's major objectives with the exception of capturing Vicksburg, and it could not be taken without more troops. His officers and men overwhelmingly concurred. Lieutenant George H. Preble, commanding the *Katahdin*, complained that the "Squadron has no business up the river at all . . . and for once President Lincoln made a mistake in ordering it."[21] Farragut delayed his decision, however, partly because of news of a Confederate ship under construction up the Yazoo River. On 15 July, a small reconnaissance force was sent up that stream. A few miles above the river's mouth the Union ships encountered the Confederate ironclad *Arkansas*. In a running fight back downstream, one of the Union vessels ran ashore while the other two fled toward the anchored fleets.

Approximately halfway between Vicksburg and the mouth of the Yazoo, the thirty-odd vessels that made up the squadrons of Davis and Farragut were anchored generally in two lines, one on each side of the river. At 7:15 A.M. the two Union ships were observed rounding a bend, followed by the *Arkansas*. The Confederate ironclad fired broadsides at the anchored Union vessels as she steamed slowly between the lines. Some of the ships returned the fire; others did not. Aroused by the cannonade, Farragut appeared on the flagship's deck in his nightgown and "seemed much surprised."[22] After running the union gauntlet, the *Arkansas* successfully reached the protection of the Vicksburg batteries.

The presence of the ironclad between his squadron and the Gulf prompted Farragut to end his indecision and take his vessels back downstream. They would attack and destroy the *Arkansas* in their descent. "No one will do wrong who lays his vessel alongside of an enemy or tackles the ram," Farragut said in orders reminiscent of Nelson.[23] The attack failed; by the time the vessels got under way, it was twilight and the ironclad could not be seen. Thus ended what was probably the most humiliating day in Farragut's career.

On 22 July, a final and futile effort was made to destroy the Confederate ship. The Union warships *Essex* and *Queen of the West* attempted to ram the *Arkansas*, moored below Vicksburg, but heavy fire from the Confederate ironclad and the land batteries forced the two ships to retire, leaving the Southern vessel battered but seaworthy. This failure was the last straw. Two days after the abortive attack, the entire fleet was standing down the river. Farragut went all the way to New Orleans but left several vessels at Baton Rouge to watch for the *Arkansas* in case she came down. On 6 August, the Confederate ironclad approached Baton Rouge but broke down and was destroyed by her crew.[24]

Arriving in New Orleans on 10 August, Farragut received official word that he had been promoted to rear admiral, the first in terms of seniority and the first admiral in the U.S. Navy. According to one officer, "a prouder or a happier or more boy like exhilarated little man you never saw." The following day the admiral wrote to his wife, "yesterday I hoisted my flag on the main, and the whole fleet cheered."[25] On 13 August, as the *Hartford* got under way for the Gulf, the squadron recognized his promotion with a fifteen-gun salute.

Farragut went to Pensacola for a period of rest, and during the following weeks, devoted much of his time to improving the blockade. Prior to this time, he had generally neglected this responsibility, though the neglect was not altogether his fault. The Navy Department had made it clear that as important as the blockade was, he was to concentrate his energies on the Mississippi River campaign. In April Farragut had deployed the bulk of his steamers on the Mississippi, leaving five steamers plus a dozen or so sailers to blockade the Gulf from Pensacola to the Rio Grande. By the end of the year his squadron had increased to nearly seventy vessels. A third of them, however, were still sailing vessels, of little use in chasing fast blockade runners. During the fall of 1862 and early 1863, Farragut had between twenty-five and thirty steamers on blockade station, approximately half stationed off Mobile and Galveston, with the remainder scattered throughout the Gulf.[26]

The Union blockade in the Gulf was not effective, at least not until late 1864. According to one authority in 1862, 65 percent of the vessels attempting to run through the blockade of the Gulf ports succeeded.[27] Like blockaders on the Atlantic coast, those in the Gulf were frustrated by their apparent inability to stop blockade runners. In October 1862, one officer wrote, from a ship patrolling off Mobile, "two steamers and seven schooners have run through the blockade last month, and it is a shame." He blamed Farragut: "It makes me feel cross . . . that our Commodore does not keep up the blockade more strictly." Although Farragut would insist that few blockade runners were getting through, one British observer thought otherwise. In May 1863, he noted: "Blockade running goes on very regularly at Mobile, the steamers nearly always succeed, but the schooners are generally captured."[28]

Farragut was not solely to blame for his squadron's problems with blockade running; there simply were not enough vessels available. Nevertheless, he had little faith in an outside blockade. Quite early in the war he had advocated blockading ports from inside a harbor, bar, or inlet. In a letter to his wife written before his ships crossed the bar into the Mississippi River the first time, Farragut wrote: "I shall endeavor to keep at the Head of the Passes a sufficient force to hold it against the Rebels without Blockading outside. You know my idea was always to Blockade inside, not outside and when I show the example I feel satisfied that others will follow."[29]

Farragut hoped to employ this tactic at the other Confederate Gulf ports, particularly Mobile and Galveston. In September, Sabine Pass fell to Union forces, and early in October four gunboats under Commander W. B. Renshaw closed Galveston by capturing the harbor's entrance. The Galveston blockade was effective—that is, until Confederates on New Year's Eve defeated Renshaw's flotilla, capturing one vessel, destroying another, and forcing the remaining Union ships to retire outside the bar. Although Farragut immediately reinforced his force off Galveston, the port remained in Confederate hands. To add to the admiral's distress, one of his ships off Galveston, the *Hatteras*, gave chase to a suspicious-looking craft and paid the penalty for failing to identify her as the raider *Alabama* until it was too late. After a brief engagement, the Union vessel was sunk, and the *Alabama* escaped.[30]

Farragut was also deeply concerned about another Confederate raider that had entered his area. In September, the *Florida* slipped past the blockaders and entered Mobile Bay. When Welles dismissed the officer in command of the ship nearest the *Florida*, Farragut protested to his wife that "almost any man would have been deceived by a vessel coming right down to him with the English flag flying." The admiral, however, was not so understanding when the *Florida* again successfully eluded his vessels and escaped from the bay, in January 1863. Farragut's son, Loyall, who was acting as his father's secretary at this time, wrote his mother: "Pa has been very much worried at these things but still he bears it like a philosopher. He knows that he has done all in his power to avert it with the vessels he has; if the government had only let him take Mobile when he wished to, the [*Florida*] would never have run out."[31]

Farragut was in New Orleans preparing to deploy again up the Mississippi when the incidents at Galveston and Mobile Bay occurred. Jim Dan Hill, in his excellent biographical essay of the admiral, suggests that Farragut decided to return to the river because his ships had been overhauled; the winter was far healthier than the summer along the river; and, most important, a combined expedition was again threatening Vicksburg from upriver.[32] Farragut certainly recognized these changes, but given the choice he would have preferred to concentrate on Mobile. The problem was that the Army would not commit troops to attack Mobile. Late in November 1862, Farragut had written to Captain Henry H. Bell: "I will not take another place without troops to hold it. . . . As to Mobile I have but little hopes of getting troops for the attack."[33] A few days later he informed Bell, "by the indications of [General] Butler's letters [the next operation] will be in the River," adding that "they appear to be anxious for us to keep the River open up to Red River." Then on 15 December, he informed Bell that "Porter is knocking at the open door to Vicksburg and we must go to work at the lower door—Port Hudson."[34]

In mid-December, Major General Nathaniel Banks replaced Butler. Bank's orders were vague and conflicting, but Farragut was convinced that he was to cooperate with the general in attacking Port Hudson.[35] During the winter months Farragut assembled his fleet at New Orleans for the movement upriver, but Banks continued to vacillate. Unknown to the admiral, Banks had decided not to attack Port Hudson because of its supposed strength.

As Farragut waited, passing his time in social activities, Rear Admiral Porter, in command of the Mississippi Squadron, ran two of his vessels past the Vicksburg batteries to secure the river between there and Port Hudson. The apparent Union success was mitigated in less than a month when the Confederates captured one of the vessels. Hearing the news, Farragut informed his flag captain: "the time has come; there can be no more delay. I must go, army or no army."[36]

Early in March, Farragut led his fleet of eight warships and a flotilla of mortar boats some 135 miles upstream to Port Hudson. There the Confederates had heavily fortified the bluffs overlooking the river with light field pieces and heavy guns, and the garrison numbered more than 6,000 men. Banks had promised to provide troops to make a diversion while Farragut's ships ran by the fortifications, but unfortunately the "diversion" consisted of some 15,000 troops bivouacking a few miles outside of the Confederate stronghold. Banks had been convinced by a deserter that more than 30,000 troops occupied Port Hudson.[37]

On 13 March, Farragut arrived below Port Hudson intending to take his fleet past the fortifications the following night. As Mahan in his biography of Farragut points out, it was at Port Hudson that the admiral for the first time experimented with "a somewhat novel tactical arrangement," lashing his weaker vessel to the protected side (the side away from the fortifications) of the more powerful warships. Not only would this protect the lighter gunboats, but it gave each pair of ships the maneuverability of a twin-screw steamer. If one vessel were damaged, the other hopefully could carry it on upstream out of danger.[38]

It was nearly 10:00 P.M. when Farragut got his vessels in a column and under way. The *Hartford* led the line with the *Albatross* lashed to her side, followed in order by the *Richmond* and the *Genessee*, the *Kineo* and the *Monongahela*, and the old side-wheeler *Mississippi* bringing up the rear. The Confederates were expecting the Union vessels to attempt to pass Port Hudson and opened fire as soon as the leading vessels got in range. The Union guns thundered in reply. Gunners on board the ships and in the land batteries had difficulty in spotting targets because of smoke from several hours of mortar fire. Port Hudson was built on a ninety-degree turn in the river, so the admiral feared that poor visibility would result in one or more of his vessels missing the turn and running aground directly under the batteries. The *Hartford* and her consort barely made the turn; the following ships did not. The *Richmond*'s machinery was put out of action by a lucky shot, and she drifted back downstream with the *Genessee* lashed to her side. The smaller gunboat with her single screw was unable to stem the current. The *Monongahela* did run aground; and in breaking free, damaged her machinery, a mishap that forced her and the *Kineo* back downstream. The *Mississippi* also ran aground and had to be abandoned under fire from several batteries. She burst into flames and was destroyed with heavy loss of life—64 killed out of a complement of nearly 300 men.

Although the Confederates achieved something of a victory at Port Hudson, it was certainly a mixed one. Farragut was able to get only his flagship and one other ship above the fortified town, but they were sufficient to control the river south of Vicksburg and blockade the mouth of the Red River. Much to his relief, the Navy Department did not censure him for what happened at Port Hudson, although Fox apparently referred to it as a disaster in a letter to Du Pont. Du Pont, himself, mentioned Farragut's "repulse," and later wrote, "I am worried about Farragut; he did not know, poor fellow, the difference between running forts and engaging them direct."[39]

Farragut was unusually depressed by what happened at Port Hudson. "Oh,

Farragut's fleet engaging the Confederate batteries at Port Hudson. On 14 March 1863 the *Hartford* led the attack on Port Hudson. In the background the side-wheeler USS *Mississippi* is aground and burning. Currier & Ives lithograph. *From a private collection.*

how I feel the failure of my ships to get past," he wrote to his wife, and added, "but it was God's will and I must submit and be happy that it was no worse." He wrote to Du Pont the same day, admitting that he had had some "sad disasters, but as the Frenchman said, 'you can't make an omelet without breaking eggs.'"[40]

Farragut would remain above Port Hudson for nearly two months patrolling the river before returning to New Orleans. He had hoped that Porter would send one or two ironclads below Vicksburg to reinforce him, but the Mississippi Squadron commander refused, stressing that he had none "fit for service." Nevertheless, two of the Army's "Ram Fleet" did attempt to run the Vicksburg batteries and join Farragut. The *Lancaster* was sunk, but the *Switzerland* under Lt. Colonel Ellet was successful. Although Ellet wrote that "Farragut and all his officers have treated me with the utmost kindness and cordiality," he was not happy when the admiral ordered him to blockade the Red River.[41]

On 6 April, the Navy Department instructed Porter to "occupy the river below Vicksburg" so that Farragut could return to the Gulf. Ten days later his fleet ran the batteries. This move not only carried out the department's wishes, but it fitted Grant's plan of attacking Vicksburg from below.[42] On 4 May, Porter conferred with Farragut; and four days later Farragut left for New Orleans, turning over command of the *Hartford* to Captain James S. Palmer.

The admiral was not free of the river campaign, however. For two months longer he remained at New Orleans, keeping close watch over the river up to Port Hudson. Porter's squadron was concentrated near Vicksburg, cooperating with Grant's army. Banks was laying siege to Port Hudson, and Farragut's vessels had to support him until either Vicksburg or Port Hudson fell. Vicksburg's surrender on 4 July finally freed his vessels to return to the Gulf.

Early in August, Farragut, whose health had deteriorated, obtained leave and sailed with the *Hartford* for New York. During the fall months while the admiral recuperated, his flagship was overhauled. On 30 December, a telegram from the Navy Department brought Farragut the intelligence that the Confederate naval force in Mobile planned to attack the blockaders off the Bay in the near future. Farragut was urged to expedite his departure. Within a week he sailed south, with Mobile, finally, his major objective.

While in the East, Farragut requested that monitors be assigned to his squadron. Ironically, he preferred wooden to iron-armored ships, including monitors. It was not altogether because of "ignorance" or "inexperience," as a Confederate naval officer later wrote, but because he considered monitors undependable, unseaworthy, and frequently inoperable. Less than a month before the Battle of Mobile Bay he wrote to his wife, "Monitors and Rifled Guns are in my opinion demoralizers to men—they make them think that men should only fight in Iron cases or at 3 or 4 miles distance."[43] He preferred ships with broadside guns, "high speed, and all good fighting men." Although he wanted monitors, they were primarily to be used against the forts guarding the bay; against enemy warships, including ironclads, he was quite willing to hazard his wooden ships. "I am tired of watching Buchanan and Page, and wish from the bottom of my heart that Buchanan would come out and try his hand upon us," he wrote his son. "This question has to be settled, iron *versus* wood; and there never was a better chance to settle the question." Farragut's opinion of ironclads was common knowledge, but not accepted, in the Navy. His friend Du Pont wrote, "Farragut will [have to learn] that iron vessels are required to meet iron vessels."[44]

Farragut returned to his squadron expecting to attack Mobile within the next month or so, as soon as troops and the monitors arrived. However, the troops were tied up in Banks's Red River expedition, and it would be more than six months before the first monitor joined his force off Mobile. The admiral's queries to the Navy Department about ironclads for his squadron finally brought a response from Fox in late March: "I have three letters from you. . . . I have held on to the last moment . . . in hopes to be able to say exactly what we can do for you about iron-clads." The Assistant Secretary then went on to say that Grant's campaign just getting under way in Virginia would determine when monitors could be assigned to the Gulf. "If [Grant] goes to James River, of course we shall have to keep a force of iron-clads to keep his communications open," Fox wrote. Finally, in what must have been a bitter pill for Farragut, Fox mentioned, "We have the summer before us and I trust you will not act until you oblige us to give you everything you require."[45] Once again the Mobile attack was to be delayed.

The Confederate States Navy's growing strength in the Mobile area finally persuaded the Navy Department to order monitors to the Gulf. The Confederates there had four ironclads either completed or under construction. On 18 May, they succeeded in getting the *Tennessee* over the bar and into Mobile Bay. From then until a monitor finally arrived, Farragut was worried about the possibility of a surprise attack. Every night half the crew of each ship remained at battle stations with the batteries cast loose. On 10 May, he informed his ship commanders that leave would no longer be granted "for the next two months." Later that month he wrote his wife, "My life is now one of anxiety—I cannot leave here to go beyond a few miles."[46] When the news that the *Tennessee* was in Mobile Bay reached Washington, Welles ordered the monitor *Manhattan* at New York to "proceed with all possible dispatch" to the Gulf, and instructed Porter to send the double-turreted monitors *Chickasaw* and *Winnebago* from his squadron immediately.[47]

Even if ironclads had been available earlier in the year, it is doubtful that Farragut would have attempted to enter Mobile Bay without the support of troops. The Army did not consider Mobile Bay to be a priority until the Red River campaign had ended, and Sherman's movement on Atlanta was under way. In June, Grant, who favored an attack on Mobile, ordered that troops be

Farragut and staff on the poop deck of the USS *Hartford. Courtesy of the Naval Historical Center.*

assigned to cooperate with Farragut. However, the first contingent of 2,400 men did not arrive from New Orleans until 3 August.[48]

In July with the *Manhattan* at Pensacola, Farragut received word that a second ironclad, the *Tecumseh*, was en route, and that the two river monitors from Porter's squadron had reached New Orleans. On 31 July, the admiral wrote his wife, "my monitors are all here now so that I am the one to attack, and no longer expect to be attacked."[49] On 3 August, the various ship commanders assembled in the *Hartford* for final instructions. Farragut planned to use the same tactics employed at Port Hudson—each large wooden ship would have a smaller gunboat secured to her disengaged side, while the monitors would move past the forts in a separate column, on the starboard side of the wooden ships. As the channel approached the bay at right angles to Mobile Point where Fort Morgan was situated, the wooden vessels firing broadsides would be unable to fire until nearly opposite the fort. Monitors, with their uninhibited field of fire, would be able to open fire much sooner.

The main channel into the bay, approximately three miles wide, ran between Mobile Point to the east and Dauphin Island to the west. Fort Morgan on the end of Mobile Point and Fort Gaines on the eastern end of Dauphin Island guarded the channel. To the west of Dauphin Island was Grant's Pass, a smaller shallower channel used only by light-draft vessels, and guarded by Fort Powell, a small earthwork fortification. The main channel was partially obstructed by pilings jutting eastward from Fort Gaines and a mine or torpedo

Battle of Mobile Bay. Farragut in the USS *Hartford* is exchanging fire with the CSS *Tennessee* in this print based on sketches by Robert Weir. *Courtesy of the Naval Institute.*

field extending an additional 400 yards into the channel. The narrowed channel forced ships to pass within relatively close range of Fort Morgan's powerful batteries. Because of the "configuration of the bottom" Farragut believed he would have to stay in the main channel. He hoped to make the attack on a flood tide going into the bay, which would help the vessels pass through the channel as swiftly as possible.[50]

On 3 August, the ships were readied for action. One young officer, flushed with the anticipation of battle, wrote in his diary, "this has been the most exciting day on the blockade . . . sand bags have been piled up around the machinery, guns shifted to the starboard side, shot and shell rooms and magazines placed in readiness." Anchor chains were ranged along the exposed side of the larger vessels to protect their machinery. These preparations continued after sunset while heavy rains accompanied by fierce lightning covered the area.[51]

During the night Farragut postponed the attack because the *Tecumseh* had not arrived from Pensacola. The attack on Dauphin Island to invest Fort Gaines went ahead, however. Under the protection of gunboats, 1,500 soldiers were landed on the island and began a fifteen-mile march to the fort. In the afternoon, while another squall was blowing in, the *Tecumseh* arrived. The attack would be made the following morning.

The fifth of August dawned beautiful and cloudless, with ideal conditions for the attacking force. An early morning flood tide would carry damaged vessels past the fort and into the bay, and a breeze blowing out of the southwest would carry the smoke of battle toward Fort Morgan. At 5:30 A.M. the fleet got under way in two columns. The main column consisted of seven large ships, each with a gunboat lashed to her port side; to starboard of these ships a second parallel column was formed, with the *Tecumseh* in the lead, followed by the *Manhattan, Winnebago,* and *Chickasaw.* Farragut had relinquished the lead position in the main column to the *Brooklyn*—the only vessel with bow chasers and a minesweeping device on her bow. After the *Brooklyn,* with the *Octorara* lashed to her side, came the *Hartford* and the *Metacomet,* the *Richmond* and the *Port Royal,* the *Lackawanna* and the *Seminole,* the *Monongahela* and the *Kennebec,* the *Ossipee* and the *Itasca,* and at the end of the column the *Oneida* and the *Galena.*

At 6:30 the battle began when the *Tecumseh* fired a 15-inch shell in the direction of Fort Morgan. The fort's guns replied, and by 7:00 the engagement had become general—each vessel firing as she came within effective range. After firing twice at the fort, the *Tecumseh* turned toward the Confederate ironclad *Tennessee,* which was moving slowly into the bend in the channel just clear of the mine field. The monitor crossed the main column about 300 yards in front of the *Brooklyn* on a collision course with the enemy ironclad. Farragut's instructions required the vessels to pass east of buoys marking the end of the mine field, but the *Tecumseh,* turning to port, penetrated the field.

At 7:30 she struck a mine, reeled to port, and went down within two minutes, bow first. Commander Thomas H. Stevens, in command of the *Winnebago*, wrote that as his ship steamed by the spot where the *Tecumseh* had sunk, all that could be seen was "the top of the smoke stack and the seathing water beneath which she had gone down."[52] The crews of the flagship *Hartford* and the *Metacomet* cheered as they observed the three remaining monitors steaming unhesitatingly by the sunken monitor into the bay.

Meanwhile a lookout on board the *Brooklyn* sighted suspicious objects in the water ahead. Her captain immediately backed his engines to avoid them. Earlier, Farragut had climbed into the rigging for better visibility, where he was lashed to the after shroud by a piece of line fastened around him, and upon seeing his lead ship apparently backing down, he ordered the flagship to pass her and take the van. As the *Hartford* steamed by the port side of the *Brooklyn*, the flagship's captain informed Farragut that there was a "heavy line of torpedoes ahead." The admiral is then supposed to have shouted "Damn the torpedoes!" or something to that effect, and the *Hartford* followed by the rest of the column steamed directly across the mine field and into the bay. As most authorities rightly imply, this was the decisive moment in the battle, for the admiral's courageous decision to ignore the mines—a calculated risk, for he had earlier suspected that if there were any, they were inactive from long immersion—prevented the development of a chaotic situation that might have caused the attack to fail.

As Farragut's ships entered the bay, they engaged a small Confederate naval force under the command of Rear Admiral Franklin Buchanan. In the ensuing battle, they captured or destroyed every Confederate warship, with the exception of one small wooden gunboat. The ironclad *Tennessee* continued to fight until rammed by three Union ships, and, with the *Chickasaw* pounding her mercilessly, she surrendered. By noon the battle was over, and Farragut's fleet was at anchor in the bay.

Alfred Mahan, an admirer and biographer of Farragut, wrote that "the Battle of Mobile Bay was to the career of Farragut what the Battle of Copenhagen was to that of Nelson." Mahan was right. As Jim Dan Hill said: "Farragut's public was not even academically critical. It considered Farragut greater than Nelson." And yet Hill himself wrote that the battle was "void of major strategic significance."[53] It had little or no effect on the war's outcome.

Farragut's plan of attack was carefully thought out. The decision to place the ironclads in a column nearest to Fort Morgan generally worked as expected despite the *Tecumseh*'s unfortunate move and demise. The monitors did attract most of the fort's fire. The tactic of lashing two vessels together had not worked well at Port Hudson; yet Farragut had adopted the same plan again, and in this instance it was far more successful. All of his warships except the *Tecumseh* made it into the bay.

There has been some criticism of Farragut's tactics. Hill suggests that it was a mistake to have rammed the *Tennessee* with wooden vessels: "this repeated ramming injured the cruisers much more than they did the hostile armored craft." Carroll S. Alden wrote: "certain English tacticians asserted, and with some show of reason, that Farragut had placed his fleet in an untenable position. For so long as three Confederate forts controlled the approaches to Mobile Bay, the fleet could not be reached by the transports and was cut off from supplies."[54] This criticism is unfounded. Farragut was aware that Grant's Pass was guarded by a small earthwork fort, and on 4 August an amphibious force was landed to take it. The fort was captured the same afternoon as the Battle of Mobile Bay. Supply ships used this entrance until the forts guarding the main channel were taken. Fort Gaines surrendered on 7 August, but it was not until Union troops invested Fort Morgan from the landward side, with a heavy bombardment from both siege artillery and ships' guns, that the fort finally yielded on 23 August.

Farragut's victory at Mobile Bay created something of a dilemma for the Navy Department. Fox was urging Welles to place the admiral in command of a naval force to take Wilmington, North Carolina. On 18 August, the Assistant Secretary wrote Farragut, "I do not see the necessity of you remaining to blockade," and added, "Wilmington . . . is the most important point remaining." Welles, however, resisted, convinced that the city of Mobile should be taken as soon as possible. Farragut was opposed to taking Mobile, considering it unnecessary "except for the morale effect."[55] Finally, Welles gave in to Fox's insistence and ordered Farragut to take command of the Wilmington attack force.

Farragut accepted these orders, but requested leave to return to the North before assuming the new command. In fact, the admiral was most reluctant to undertake the Wilmington operation. He questioned the suitability of a naval attack up the shallow Cape Fear River, and he also felt that the season was far too advanced to begin such a campaign. Perhaps his greatest reservation, however, was himself. He was physically and emotionally worn out. He recognized this and so did his officers. On 24 August, Lieutenant George Perkins wrote: "I was talking to the Admiral today . . . when, all at once, he fainted away. He is not very well, and is all tired out." In September Percival Drayton wrote to Du Pont that Farragut "has not been well."[56] Farragut finally informed the department that he had to have an extended leave of "four or five months," and Welles assigned the Wilmington operation to Porter.

With the *Hartford* Farragut arrived in New York on 13 December. Ten days later President Lincoln signed a bill creating the office of vice-admiral, and Farragut was immediately named to fill it.[57] The admiral would not command an active naval force again during the war. During the final months he served as president of an officers promotion board. After the war ended, he continued to head the board but spent most of his time at home in New York City. In July 1866 Congress established the rank of admiral, and he was appointed to this office. Early in 1867 he assumed command of the European Squadron.[58]

Farragut's appointment to this command surprised many. He was sixty-six years old, a full admiral, and not in good health. Welles does not say in his diary why he appointed Farragut, but the reasons seem obvious: he was the most prestigious officer; the European Squadron was at that time the most important peacetime command; it was a traditional appointment for a senior officer about to retire; and Farragut clearly wanted it. On Bastille Day, 14 July 1867, Farragut arrived in Cherbourg, France, in the flagship *Franklin*. The following day he relieved Rear Admiral Louis Goldsborough of the command.[59] During Farragut's seventeen-month tour with the European Squadron, no serious problems required attention; in fact, it was one triumphal visit after the other to various countries. On 18 October 1868, the *Franklin* left for the United States, and for all practical purposes Farragut's active service in the Navy came to an end.

While Farragut was in Europe, U.S. Grant won the presidency.[60] The admiral, however, would have little to do with the new administration. He was displeased with the new Secretary of the Navy, Adolph Borie, as well as the influence that Porter had with both Grant and the Secretary. He was also ill during the spring of 1869; in fact, his health, which had been poor since the river campaign in 1863, would continue to be delicate for the remainder of his life. In May 1869, Mrs. Farragut wrote that "the Admiral continues very miserable and I can scarcely leave his side. . . . I am very much discouraged about him."[61] He recovered and visited the Mare Island Navy Yard, which he had started some eleven years before. On the way home, however, he had a heart attack. He again recovered, but in August 1870, while visiting the Portsmouth Navy Yard in New Hampshire, he died. Farragut had a premonition of his approaching death, and when Mrs. Farragut protested his activities, he said that "he would just as well die in harness as any other way."[62]

Farragut was the most competent naval officer on either side during the Civil War. He was, as Bern Anderson wrote, "head and shoulders above them all." He had all the attributes of a great commander: intelligence, knowledge, self-confidence, enormous energy, and courage. "Farragut has always been my ideal of the naval officer," Admiral George Dewey related in his autobiography. Other officers would reiterate this sentiment. Alfred T. Mahan and Winfield Scott Schley would favorably compare him to Nelson. Army officers and even former Confederates would voice their admiration. Major George C. Strong, who met the admiral in New Orleans, wrote "Farragut is as gallant a man as ever walked a ship's deck." James Bulloch agreed that "Farragut showed that he had the qualities . . . which make a great naval commander."[63]

Senior officers in the Navy, Farragut's peers, Du Pont, Goldsborough, Davis, Dahlgren, and others, generally admired and liked him. Even Porter, who was clearly envious of Farragut, had a grudging respect for "his half brother." Farragut had no particular enmity for Porter although he was aware of his jealousy. Rear Admiral Charles Davis mentioned in a conversation with Farragut that Porter would give him trouble, and Farragut replied, "of course he will."[64]

S. Phillips Lee is the only Civil War flag officer who is known to have been critical of Farragut's abilities and performance, but according to one authority, Lee was at times hypercritical of all the senior officers. On 28 May 1862, Lee wrote his wife that Farragut "is a worthy man and gallant officer but deficient in judgment." Less than two weeks later he declared to her that "for [Farragut's] want of military mind and knowledge we shall earn some dear experience." Then in July he wrote that "Dr. [Jonathan] Foltz who is on good terms with the Flag Officer says to me *privately*, that he has served . . . under 3 Flag Officers . . . and that [Farragut] . . . has less mind than either of the others. That Farragut is wholly unstable, not having the same opinion from hour to hour . . . ."[65] Farragut and Lee developed an intense dislike for each other that would continue throughout the war. Farragut blamed Lee for the *Florida*'s success in slipping through the blockade into Mobile Bay in September 1862. Nevertheless, Lee would be promoted to captain and shortly afterward acting rear admiral in command of the South Atlantic Blockading Squadron.

Farragut had complete confidence in his own judgment, in his opinion of naval officers, operations, tactics, and just about anything else related to naval affairs. Before the Battle of New Orleans he wrote: "As to being prepared for defeat, I certainly am not. Any man who is prepared for defeat, would be half defeated before he commenced." Mahan mentions in his biography that Farragut admitted his "unusual self-esteem"—a characteristic that at times irritated both his superiors and subordinates. Irritated or not, they valued his advice, as is demonstrated by the impact on Welles of his recommendation of Porter to command the Mississippi Squadron. Samuel Eliot Morison, in his biography of Matthew C. Perry, suggests that Farragut "had an irascible side [and that he] disliked being subordinated to anybody."[66] It is true that Farragut was impatient with anyone questioning his judgment and became angry when they persisted. At the same time he did not get along with Perry, but there is no evidence that any of his other commanding officers considered him insubordinate. This "supreme self-confidence" possibly explains why he failed at times to award credit to his subordinates; at least many of Farragut's officers, who otherwise admired him, believed this.[67]

Farragut's self-confidence was perhaps partly a natural trait, but it also evolved from his intelligence, knowledge, and penchant for careful and thorough planning. Even before the war he was noted for his organizational ability. John M. Brooke, who would head the Confederate Bureau of Ordnance and Hydrography, served with Farragut in the *Delaware*. Brooke later recalled "that he never saw greater skill in administering affairs than Farragut displayed." Mahan mentions that before Mobile Bay, Farragut "spent hours with his flag lieutenant, studying by the aid of little wooden models, the different positions in which the ships might be placed. Afterwards he had the squadron get underway several times to practice keeping close order, and changing formation and course . . . ."[68]

The tactics that he employed at New Orleans, Port Hudson, Mobile, and elsewhere were carefully worked out, based on an analysis of his weaknesses and those of his opponent. The lashing of weak vessels to the sides of more powerful warships was a brilliant innovation. He grasped the limitations of land fortifications in naval actions, and on the Mississippi River and in Mobile Bay utilized this tactical understanding successfully. He also believed very strongly in maximum fire power: "the best protection against the enemy's fire is a well-directed fire from our own guns."[69]

Finally, he had an extremely energetic and aggressive nature, which is absolutely essential for a successful military commander. Farragut's mental and physical energy was indeed prodigious, particulary during the Civil War years when the strain of conflict seemed to tap new reservoirs of strength. Although in his sixties, he enjoyed demonstrating his physical strength and agility by running up the ratlines or doing handstands before astonished junior officers. His mental vigor was apparent and remarked on by various observers. Nor was it confined to work or professional matters. He was a very social person and took considerable pleasure in conversations. Lord Paget wrote that Farragut was "a great but very agreeable talker." Commodore Schley agreed that the admiral was an "animated and interesting talker," and added that "his information and experience were general, and upon almost all subjects."[70]

Farragut was an aggressive commander—in the opinion of Admiral George Dewey, perhaps too aggressive at times. J. C. Watson, the admiral's flag lieutenant at Mobile Bay, told his son in later years that when the *Tennessee* "was reported underway and *standing out*, Farragut at once said to [Percival] Drayton, 'Get underway and follow him (Buchanan) out' . . . . Never was an order more unwelcomed. Coming over the minefield was enough. They (none of them in the fleet) wished to go out over them."[71] Farragut's personal courage undoubtedly influenced his aggressive nature. Mahan and Schley, among others, attribute his extraordinary courage to his strong religious beliefs. Yet, his devoutness does not adequately explain his boldness, his willingness to "Damn the torpedoes." A more acceptable explanation was his sense of duty and his unusually strong desire to succeed in the Navy. Rear Admiral Bradley Fiske wrote, "Duty, in whatever form it came was sacred" to a naval officer.

And Farragut himself said that "He who dies in doing his duty . . . has played out the drama of life to the best advantage."[72]

Comparing Farragut to Nelson is probably a meaningless exercise. They were products of their time. Nelson was a brilliant tactician in utilizing sailing ships-of-the-line; Farragut was equally successful in using steam warships. Yet, they both stand out in their chosen profession. As Bern Anderson wrote, the Navy would not produce another officer as gifted as Farragut until the naval leaders of World War II.

FURTHER READING

Although David Glasgow Farragut is one of the best known and most successful admirals of the U.S. Navy, few full-length biographies have been written about him. The first, Phineas C. Headley, *The Life and Naval Career of Vice-Admiral David Glascoe* [sic] *Farragut*, was published in 1865, and the last, Christopher Martin, *Damn the Torpedoes: The Story of America's First Admiral, David Glasgow Farragut*, appeared in 1970. In between were a half dozen or more. Only two are worthy of attention: Alfred T. Mahan, *Admiral Farragut*, and Charles Lee Lewis, *David Glasgow Farragut*, 2 vols. Loyall Farragut's biography of his father, *The Life and Letters of Admiral Farragut, First Admiral of the United States Navy*, published in 1879, should be mentioned because it is the primary source for Mahan's study and most of the other biographies published before Lewis's.

Mahan was embarrassed by his biography, considering it mediocre. "The great defect in my *Farragut*," he later wrote, "was that I had no data with which to depict the *man*."[*] Historians have generally agreed with this assessment. Despite the overall quality of the book and Mahan's assertion, his characterization of Farragut is the most perceptive of any to date.

Lewis's two-volume work is the most comprehensive. Although deficient in analysis, it is impressively researched and well written. No attempt has been made to duplicate his exhaustive research for this essay. Rather, an effort has been made to supplement Lewis's work by locating relevant manuscripts that were not available when he did his work. Few were found. Perhaps the most important are the Farragut Collection on loan to the Naval Historical Foundation and located at the foundation's office in the Washington Navy Yard; and a number of Farragut letters acquired in recent years by the Henry P. Huntington Library. Lewis's bibliography is thorough, but should be supplemented by works written since its publication in 1943.

There are a large number of biographical sketches of Farragut, the best of these being the ones in the *Dictionary of American Biography* and in Jim Dan

---

[*]Quoted in Robert Seager II, *Alfred Thayer Mahan: The Man and His Letters*, 234.

Hills's *Sea Dogs of the Sixties*. Although brief, Hill's essay may well be the most balanced analysis of Farragut's Civil War campaigns.

NOTES

1. Cyril Falls, *A Hundred Years of War*, 104.
2. For Farragut's early life and career see Charles Lee Lewis, *David Glasgow Farragut*; and David F. Long, *Nothing Too Daring: A Biography of Commodore David Porter, 1780–1843*.
3. Howard K. Beale, ed., *The Diary of Gideon Welles*, II: 116, 134; John Niven, *Gideon Welles: Lincoln's Secretary of the Navy*, 383.
4. Bern Anderson, *By Sea and by River*, 118; Charles Lee Lewis, *David Glasgow Farragut: Our First Admiral*, 8–9.
5. Niven, *Welles*, 383–84.
6. Quoted in Lewis, *Our First Admiral*, 13.
7. Farragut to his wife, 23 December 1861, David G. Farragut Papers, Henry P. Huntington Library (hereafter cited as Farragut Papers, HPH).
8. Fox to Farragut, 11 February 1862, David G. Farragut Collection, Naval Historical Foundation (hereafter cited as Farragut Col., NHF).
9. Hans L. Trefousse, *Ben Butler: The South Called Him Beast*, 101–2; Robert S. Holzman, *Stormy Ben Butler*, 74–75.
10. Quoted in Lewis, *Our First Admiral*, 47.
11. William N. Still, Jr., *Iron Afloat: The Story of the Confederate Armorclads*, 55.
12. Anderson, *By Sea and by River*, 124.
13. Quoted in Still, *Iron Afloat*, 58.
14. Farragut to his wife and son, 25 April 1862, Farragut Col., NHF.
15. Clark Reynolds, *Command of the Sea*, 386. Charles L. Dufour, *The Night the War Was Lost*, 246, 284–85. Rowena Reed is critical of the decision in her *Combined Operations in the Civil War*, 195. In a letter to his wife written on 25 April, Farragut makes a statement that suggests his intense ambition to take the city: "God has permitted me to make a name for my Dear Boy's inheritance as well as for my own comfort. . . ." Farragut Collection, NHF.
16. James D. Bulloch, *The Secret Service of The Confederate States in Europe*, II: 193–94.
17. R. M. Thompson and R. Wainwright, eds., *Confidential Correspondence of Gustavus Vasa Fox, Assistant Secretary of the Navy 1861–1865*, II: 101–2. See also Lewis, *Our First Admiral*, 78.
18. Reed, *Combined Operations*, 196.
19. Lewis, *Our First Admiral*, 102–4. Farragut relieved the *Brooklyn's* commanding officer, T. T. Craven, for his failure to pass the batteries. Farragut wrote his wife a detailed account of the incident, reminding her, "I always told you I knew T. T. Craven." 4 July 1862, Farragut Col., NHF.
20. Farragut Col., NHF.

21. George H. Preble to Molley, 11 July 1862, George H. Preble Papers, Massachusetts Historical Society. See also Reed, Combined Operations, 211–12.

22. Still, *Iron Afloat*, 70.

23. Still, *Iron Afloat*, 72.

24. Still, *Iron Afloat*, 76–78.

25. Farragut to his wife, 11 August 1862, Farragut Col., NHF. See also Preble to his niece, 19 August 1862, Preble Papers.

26. Diary of H. H. Bell, entry 12 April 1862, *Official Records of the Union and Confederate Navies in the War of the Rebellion* (hereinafter cited as *ORN*), Series I, vol. 18, 690. See also Farragut to Welles, 1 January 1863, *ORN*, I, 19: 478.

27. Marcus Price, "Ships that tested the blockade of the Gulf Ports, 1861–1865," *American Neptune* XI (1951): 262–97; Stephen R. Wise, "Lifeline of the Confederacy: Blockade Running During the Civil War," 370–435.

28. Walter Lord, ed., *The Fremantle Diary*, 105–6; Carroll S. Alden, *George Hamilton Perkins, Commodore, U.S.N., His Life and Letters*, 106.

29. Farragut to his wife, 15 March 1862, Farragut Papers, HPH.

30. Farragut was extremely critical of Renshaw, writing to his wife that none of the blockaders were where they were supposed to be: "I cannot make people do their duty when they are demoralized. . . . I suppose that must have been the case with Renshaw." 1 February 1863, Farragut Col., NHF. He placed H. H. Bell in charge of the Texas blockade: "don't have any other disaster if possible for they are abusing us enough at home," he wrote Bell. 6 February 1863, Farragut Col., NHF.

31. Quoted in Lewis, *Our First Admiral*, 161.

32. Jim Dan Hill, *Sea Dogs of the Sixties*, 41.

33. Farragut to Henry N. Bell, 30 November 1862, Farragut Col., NHF.

34. Farragut to Henry N. Bell, 15 December 1862, Farragut Col., NHF.

35. Reed, *Combined Operations*, 241; Farragut to Bell, 30 January 1863, Farragut Col., NHF.

36. Quoted in Lewis, *Our First Admiral*, 168.

37. Reed, *Combined Operations*, 246. The most detailed account of the battle of Port Hudson is David C. Edmonds, *The Guns of Port Hudson*. Volume One: *The River Campaign (February–May, 1863)*.

38. Alfred T. Mahan, *Admiral Farragut*, 212; Hill, *Sea Dogs*, 43.

39. Du Pont to his wife, 23 March 1863, John D. Hayes, ed., *Samuel Francis Du Pont: A Selection from His Civil War Letters*, II: 508. See also Fox to Du Pont, 18 March 1863, Hayes, ed., *Du Pont Letters*, II: 507.

40. Farragut to his wife, 20 April 1863, Farragut Papers, HPH; Farragut to Du Pont, 20 April 1863, Hayes, ed., *Du Pont Letters*, III: 47–48.

41. Ellet to cousin, 3 May 1863, William D. Cabell Papers, University of Virginia Library.

42. Reed, *Combined Operations*, 250.

43. 12 July 1864, Farragut Papers, HPH; Bulloch, *Confederate States in Europe*, II: 205–6.

44. Loyall Farragut, *The Life and Letters of Admiral Farragut, First Admiral of the United States Navy*, 402. Franklin Buchanan, former captain in the U.S. Navy, was in command of Confederate naval forces, Mobile. Richard L. Page, formerly of the U.S. Navy, was in command of Fort Morgan. Du Pont to Davis, 29 March 1864. Hayes, ed., *Du Pont Letters*, III: 324–25.

45. Fox to Farragut, 24 March 1864, Farragut Col., NHF.

46. Farragut to his wife, 30 May 1864, Farragut papers, HPH. See also Farragut to Jenkins, 10 May 1864, Farragut Papers, HPH, and Still, *Iron Afloat*, 204.

47. Lewis, *Our First Admiral*, 246. There is an unsigned letter in the Farragut Col., NHF, dated 24 June 1864, apparently from a naval officer intimately associated with the construction of these ships. The writer assured Farragut of their seaworthiness and that he had convinced Welles of this.

48. Still, *Iron Afloat*, 204.

49. Naval History Collection, Naval War College.

50. Bartholomew Diggins, "Recollections of the War Cruise of the USS *Hartford*, January to December, 1862–1864," New York Public Library. See also G. M. Brady, "Damn the torpedoes, Full Speed Ahead," *Manuscripts*, XXXI (1979): 86–96.

51. Still, *Iron Afloat*, 204.

52. Thomas Stevens to F. A. Parker, 24 April 1877, Thomas Stevens Papers, Private Collection.

53. Mahan, *Farragut*, 239–40; Hill, *Sea Dogs*, 61.

54. Hill, *Sea Dogs*, 61.

55. Quoted in Lewis, *Our First Admiral*, 298. See also Fox to Farragut, 18 August 1864, Farragut Papers, HPH.

56. Alden, *Perkins*, 149–50; Drayton to Du Pont, 8 September 1864, Hayes, ed., *Du Pont Letters*, III: 380; Drayton to Mrs. Farragut, 20 October 1864, Farragut Papers HPH.

57. On 14 December, Welles had written to Farragut suggesting that he hold off visiting Washington as Congress was considering "a new naval grade" that would affect him. Welles to Farragut, 14 December 1865, Farragut Col., NHF.

58. Farragut to Jenkins, Farragut Papers, HPH.

59. William N. Still, Jr., *American Sea Power in the Old World: The United States Navy in European and Near Eastern Waters, 1865–1917*.

60. While in Europe, Farragut was approached as a possible Democratic Party candidate in the 1868 presidential election, but the admiral was not interested. See John Cisco to Mrs. Farragut, 7 March 1868, Farragut Papers, HPH: R. H. Kern to Samuel Jackson Randall, 7 April, 26 May, 3 June, 6

June 1868, Samuel Jackson Randall Papers, Van Pelt Library, University of Pennsylvania, Philadelphia. There is a brief note on the back cover of a small red notebook or diary belonging to Jonathan M. Foltz, naval surgeon in the *Hartford* during the war years and in the *Franklin* during the European cruise, that says, "Mr. Sisco writes to the Admiral in relation to Presidency. Answer No." Jonathan M. Foltz papers, Library of Franklin and Marshall College, Lancaster, Pennsylvania. Harold D. Langley, Curator of Naval History at the National Museum of American History, brought to my attention the Randall and Foltz items.

61. Mrs. Farragut to Thomas Welles, 17 May 1869, Thomas C. Welles Papers, Duke University.

62. Mrs. Farragut to Welles, 19 January 1870, Welles Papers, Duke University. See also Lewis, *Our First Admiral*, 374–75.

63. George Dewey, *Autobiography of George Dewey, Admiral of the Navy*, 49; Winfield Scott Schley, *Forty-five Years under the Flag*, 28, 50–51; Strong to ———, 20 May 1862, Gratz Collection, Historical Society of Pennsylvania, Philadelphia; Bulloch, *Secret Service*, II: 192.

64. 5 March 1864, Hayes, ed., *Du Pont Letters*, III: 435.

65. Lee to Elizabeth Lee, 28 May, 10 June, 12 July 1862, in the Blair–Lee Papers, Princeton University Library. These letters were brought to the author's attention by Dudley T. Cornish, whose biography of Lee is to be published by the University of Kansas Press. For Farragut's attitude toward Lee, see letter to his wife, 10 October 1862, Farragut papers, HPH. Foltz is not critical of Farragut in his autobiography, *Surgeon of the Seas: the Adventurous Life of Surgeon General Jonathan M. Foltz in the Days of Wooden Ships*.

66. Farragut, *Life and Letters*, 218; Samuel E. Morison, *"Old Bruin": Commodore Matthew C. Perry*, 240.

67. T. Bailey to his nephew, 22 May 1869, Theodorus Bailey Papers, Duke University; Mrs. Farragut to Welles, Welles Papers, Duke University; Paulding to Dahlgren, 12 May 1868, John Dahlgren Papers, Duke University.

68. George M. Brooke, Jr., *John M. Brooke: Naval Scientist and Educator*, 12. Mahan, *Farragut*, 327.

69. Robert S. Browning III, *Two if by Sea: The Development of American Coastal Defense Policy*, 116; Lewis, *Our First Admiral*, 316; Henry N. Sulivan, ed., *Life and Letters of the Late Admiral Bartholomew James Sulivan*, 428; Farragut to Du Pont, 20 April 1863, Hayes, ed., *Du Pont Letters*, III: 47.

70. Sir Arthur Otway, ed., *Autobiography and Journals of Admiral Lord Clarence E. Paget*, 306–7; Schley, *Forty-five Years*, 50–51.

71. Edward Watson to William Rodgers, 14 March 1901, Rodgers Family Papers, Library of Congress.

72. Quoted in Peter Karsten, *The Naval Aristocracy*, 250, 261.

RAPHAEL SEMMES:
CONFEDERATE RAIDER

BY WARREN F. SPENCER

During the Civil War, Confederate Admiral Raphael Semmes was the most successful practitioner of the traditional American naval strategy of commerce raiding. At sea for a total of twenty-five months on board the CSS *Sumter* and the CSS *Alabama*, Semmes destroyed or bonded seventy-six U.S. commercial ships.[1] As early as November 1862 cargo owners began to ship by neutral vessels, and this "flight from the flag" as it continued throughout the war crippled the U.S. merchant fleet permanently.[2] Semmes's wide-ranging cruises—from the West Indies into the North and South Atlantic oceans, across the Indian Ocean to the China Sea and back—made him world-renowned. Newspapers in the Americas, London, Paris, Cape Town, and Singapore traced his movements and reported his victims. He became a romantic figure to millions throughout the world, a national hero to Southerners, but in the United States he was castigated as a pirate and a beast.

Aware of his fame and infamy, Semmes nonetheless was only fulfilling instructions from his superior, Confederate Secretary of the Navy Stephen R. Mallory. To compensate for the superior Northern naval power, Mallory developed a twofold policy: draw Union ships from blockade duty by striking at Northern commercial ships with privateers and regularly commissioned naval vessels, then force the weakened blockade by warships purchased or built in Europe. His strategy anticipated cooperation of the European maritime powers, but in the spring and early summer of 1861 a series of international proclamations appeared from both sides of the ocean that affected both Mallory's naval strategy and Semmes's career as a commerce raider.[3]

On 17 April 1861 President Jefferson Davis announced that in "accordance with international law" his government would issue letters of marque for privateers to prey on Northern commercial shipping, and two days later President Abraham Lincoln proclaimed a blockade of Southern ports and further stipulated that if any person should molest a U.S. vessel or a cargo on board her, he would be held under U.S. laws of piracy. The European maritime powers accepted Lincoln's threat against possible Confederate privateers because in the Declaration of Paris (1856) they had outlawed privateers. If Lincoln simply had closed Southern ports as a sovereign act, other governments could have accepted that also without response. But a blockade of a port is an act that affects other nations, and the same Declaration of Paris had established international law concerning blockades. The British and French governments had already adopted a common policy to pursue toward the American secession crisis, and Lincoln's blockade proclamation elicited from them proclamations of neutrality, the British on 14 May 1861 and the French on 10 June 1861. Other European nations soon issued similar proclamations.

The neutrality proclamations forbade belligerents from recruiting neutral subjects, equipping or arming warships on neutral territory or in neutral territorial waters, or in any way enhancing the war-making powers of such vessels. Belligerent use of neutral dock facilities was limited to repairing damage that resulted from "acts of God." To discourage privateering, the domestic laws also forbade subjects from adjudicating belligerent prizes.[4]

These proclamations both enhanced and hindered the South's war-making efforts. The neutrality proclamations gave de facto recognition to the Confederate States as a belligerent engaged in legitimate warfare, extending to them the same belligerent rights enjoyed by the United States. Confederate warships, but not privateers, could purchase coal and food in neutral ports and use neutral shipyards to repair damage to their ships caused by nature. But neither belligerent could purchase warships from the neutrals, as Mallory had expected to do, or take prizes for adjudication into a neutral port, as Mallory had expected his commerce raiders to do.[5] This latter provision forced Semmes to remain at sea for over two years and to destroy his captures, an act he regretted.

The U.S. government, maintaining that the Civil War was a rebellion and not legitimate warfare, never officially accepted the neutrality proclamations. That is why Northern officials constantly referred to Semmes as a pirate or privateer.[6]

Thus before the first shot was fired at Manassas (21 July 1861), the Southern secession, based primarily on anticipated naval activities, had become a worldwide event. Before Appomattox, people in the West Indies, Brazil, Australia, South Africa, Indochina, as well as Europe, would be drawn into the American conflict because ships flying the Confederate flag would sail in their adjoining waters. The man whose ships touched most of these people was Raphael Semmes, commander (1861), captain (1862), then admiral (1865) of the Confederate States Navy. What kind of man was he?

The circumstances of his youth foreshadowed the introspective and self-reliant captain of the *Alabama*. Born in Piscataway, Charles County, Mary-

Raphael Semmes. Photograph taken in London in 1863. *Courtesy of the Naval Historical Center.*

land, on 27 September 1809, into a Roman Catholic family, Semmes on his father's side descended from an early (1640) French settler and on his mother's from a signer of the Declaration of Independence (Arthur Middleton of South Carolina). Ophaned at an early age, he grew up in the Georgetown home of his uncle, Raphael Semmes. He had some formal education in private schools and with tutors, where he learned Latin and natural history.

When he was about fifteen years old, young Raphael decided to pursue two careers, those of lawyer and naval officer. The influence to study law undoubtedly came from his brother and intense family discussions on the nature of the U.S. Constitution. The reasons for his attraction to a naval career are not so clear, but perhaps he viewed it as one of travel, excitement, and learning. At any rate, his congressman uncle obtained for him an appointment as midshipman in the U.S. Navy from President John Quincy Adams, dated 1 April 1826.

A second career was almost a necessity in the old navy because there were more officers than officer-slots. A young officer could expect many enforced and long leaves of absence during his slow rise through the ranks. For five years Raphael Semmes served as a trainee-officer in five different ships, sailing the Caribbean Sea, the Gulf of Mexico, and the Mediterranean Sea. He spent much time studying navigation and naval regulations and developing an appreciation for the varieties of tropical nature—different plants, sunsets, and sudden storms. Finally, on 28 April 1832, having passed at the head of his class, he was promoted to passed midshipman and placed on extended leave.[7]

Interspersed with the long leaves, Semmes's naval career developed slowly in the years prior to the Mexican War. For a year and a half he was acting mate on board the USS *Constellation*, a ship that decades later would pursue the CSS *Alabama*. He was promoted to lieutenant on 9 February 1837, eleven years after his appointment as midshipman. His longest continuous duty was from May 1841 to April 1845 as a surveyor of the Gulf Coast, based at the Pensacola Navy Yard in Florida. In performance of that duty he sailed in the USS *Warren* and commanded the USS *Poinsett* (1843–45), one of the few steamers in the U.S. Navy. Survey duty was not demanding, and the Navy used officers and ships for occasional duties such as transporting diplomats. On one such journey to Mexico, Semmes navigated the treacherous waters of the approaches to Vera Cruz and accompanied his passenger to the Mexican capital, thereby gaining two types of knowledge he would use during the Mexican War.[8]

Semmes's personal life developed more rapidly than his military career. During a two-and-a-half-year leave after his promotion to passed midshipman, he read law in his brother's office, and in early 1835 he passed the Maryland bar examination. Later he established a law practice in Cincinnati, Ohio, where he met and married Ann Elizabeth Spencer (1837). She was Protestant and of New Jersey origins, "a stately, handsome woman with regular chiseled features, brilliant brunette complexion and hazel eyes."[9] In a move indicative of their strong mutual bonds, or perhaps Raphael Semmes's strong personality, or both, Ann Spencer joined the Catholic Church prior to the wedding, and later she adopted Semmes's ardent Southern sentiments. Their marriage, marred only by his absences at sea, was a happy and long one, blessed with three sons and three daughters.

Raphael Semmes moved his family to be near him while he served at Pensacola Navy Yard, buying property just across the Perdido River in the state of Alabama. It was a symbol of passing because afterward he considered himself a citizen of Alabama, and Ann followed him. His commitment to the Southern cause was both intellectual and emotional.

Semmes's experiences in the Mexican War seem almost to have been a dress rehearsal for his later duties during the Civil War. As flag-lieutenant to the commander of the Home Squadron, he was privy to the U.S. government's policies and close to the fleet commander's interpretations and applications of the government's directives. Later, as commander of the USS *Somers* on blockade assignment of Vera Cruz harbor, he experienced first-hand the intricacies of neutral and belligerent rights as well as the boredom, frustrations, and dangers of blockade duty. More important, he learned how a blockader must think, and exploited that knowledge later during the Civil War when he escaped two federal blockades on board the CSS *Sumter*. He dealt with problems, both real and potential, of Mexican privateers, whom he condemned as nothing more "than licensed pirates."[10]

The few months of blockade duty led Semmes to complain that the conflict had become "a war, for the navy, of toils and vigils, without the prospect of either excitement or glory."[11] But excitement seemed to attract Raphael Semmes, and it inspired in him an eloquence that characterized his writing ever after. He was commanding officer of the brig *Somers*, on blockade duty, which he so detested, when he lost his ship to a gale. Semmes's report to his superior officer candidly recounted the loss of thirty-nine men, re-creating as well the excitement of the life-and-death struggle, the necessity of making split-second decisions to save lives, and the ability to discern the moment when nature had won and man had lost: "I gave the order 'Every man save himself who can!'" His report, so filled with heroic imagery, completely overshadowed any question that Semmes might have contributed to the fate of his ship by failing to provide proper ballast or to order the correct sails carried. Semmes was not simply "rather lucky," as another officer put it, that the court of inquiry found for him; he had, unconsciously, manipulated it by the force of rhetoric.[12] He would later, in June 1864, swim off from another sinking ship under his command and be promoted to admiral.

Semmes was reassigned as flag-lieutenant to the fleet commander, a duty he considered boring. But within six months—after General Winfield Scott's successful landing at Vera Cruz and march to Jalapa on the road to Mexico City—excitement once again beckoned. Semmes was assigned to take a message from Washington through the military lines to the Mexican government. He was delighted: "There was romance in the idea!" On 28 April 1847 he left the Home Squadron to spend the remainder of the war with the Army.[13] His account of the journey is spiced with vivid word-pictures of the Mexican landscape and of the plant and animal life.[14]

General Scott was jealous of civilian interference in the war, and took out his resentment on Semmes. Only after a sharp exchange of letters did the general finally permit the persistent Semmes, who could write more convincingly, to remain with the Army.[15] When his mission "was suddenly brought to a close," Semmes "had no thought of returning to the squadron" because the Army was "on the eve of commencing our glorious campaign."[16] To fight with the Army was much more exciting than blockade duty.

Semmes was, as he said, an onlooker. He observed, he took notes—his memoirs are based more on these notes than on memory—and ever inquisitive, he described and characterized all that he saw. As a Catholic, Semmes was drawn to the Cathedral in Puebla, and his description reveals a clear understanding of architecture and its symbolism. In Mexico he seemed to discern social inequities more clearly than he did in Alabama, and he deplored the squalor of Mexican poverty which he blamed on the government and the country's socio-racial history. But his favorite topic was people—beautiful women, leaders of men, and even the common sailor and soldier. A product of the age of romanticism and nationalism, he firmly believed in the superiority of the Anglo-Saxon race and the great-man theory of history.[17] From all these observations, Semmes developed a view of history and of man's role in it based on a concept of the proper order-of-things in which the higher element had the responsibility to protect and nourish the lower element, but not the power to coerce it. By the end of the Mexican War his mind-set had matured; he was the man who in thought and action would become the world-renowned captain of the CSS *Sumter* and the CSS *Alabama*. Although his was not a unique attitude in the mid–nineteenth century— he shared it with English aristocrats, French notables, and thousands of Americans, North and South—his age of preparation was complete, and the stage for greatness was set.

In 1849 the peacetime Navy placed Lieutenant Raphael Semmes on extended leave. He moved his family to Mobile and settled into a quiet practice of law and reflection upon his Mexican experiences. Using his wartime notes and adding long digressions that grew from his reflections, in 1851 he published *Service Afloat and Ashore during the Mexican War*. It became a best seller, as much perhaps because of its flowing and flowery language as for its revelations of Americans at war.

The U.S. Navy seemed to have forgotten Semmes. But his name gradually rose on the promotion list, and on 8 October 1855 he was promoted to commander effective 14 September 1855.[18] Recalled to duty the following month, Semmes began the longest continuous stretch of active naval service of his career. For ten months he commanded the mail steamer *Illinois*, the last U.S. ship to which he was assigned. In December 1856, Commander Semmes became lighthouse inspector of the 3rd District, conveniently based in Mobile. From 1858 into 1861 Semmes served as secretary to the Lighthouse Board in Washington, D.C.[19]

Viewing the developing secession crisis from the nation's capital as it moved to its climax, Semmes rejected the arguments of early advocates of secession. Although he considered the tariff to be economic suppression of the South and the abolition movement a violation of states' rights, he expected a solution to be reached, and he believed Stephen A. Douglas's popular sovereignty theory was the best possible solution. In the election of 1860 he was a Douglas man, regarding the election of Abraham Lincoln as President as the final blow to the Union. Semmes thus became a secessionist; his "*Alabama*" mind-set was complete.

If his change of mind about secession was difficult, his personal break with the U.S. Navy was even more soul-wrenching. "Civil war," he wrote, "is a terrible crucible through which to pass character."[20] Loyalty to the flag, love of country, old friendships, career advancement and security, care of family—all of these practical factors shouted for Semmes to remain in the U.S. Navy and loyal to the United States. But his personal psychology demanded allegiance to his state, and during the congressional session of 1860–61 Semmes informed members from Alabama of his "intention of retiring from the Federal Navy, and of taking service with the South" should the state of Alabama join other Southern states in secession. Although the Alabama secession vote passed on 11 January 1861, Semmes waited over a month to resign his position.

During that interlude Semmes was promoted from secretary of the Lighthouse Board to membership on the board, which he accepted on 12 February 1861. Only two days later, he received a telegram from the Committee on Naval Affairs of the Provisional Government in Montgomery, Alabama, requesting him to "repair to this place at your earliest convenience." Semmes replied on the same day, "I will be with you immediately." The next day he resigned his commission in the U.S. Navy and informed the new secretary of the Lighthouse Board that because of that resignation he was "no longer a member" of the board. All official commitment to the U.S. government thus dissolved, on 16 February Mr. Raphael Semmes took a sorrowful leave from his wife and children, and embarked by train for Montgomery.

Semmes arrived in the provisional capital on 19 February 1861, consulted with the chairman of the Committee on Naval Affairs and with provisional President Jefferson Davis, and departed for New York on 21 February. His first duty for the Confederacy, on Davis's request, was a shopping trip in the North. En route he stopped in Washington to inspect machinery in the U.S. Arsenal and to recruit skilled machinists, so scarce in the South. In New York City, where he arrived on 5 March, he purchased "large quantities of percussions caps," which he sent without disguise to Montgomery, "made contracts for batteries of light artillery, powder, and other munitions," and purchased a complete set of machinery for rifling cannon. Although he found no ships suitable for conversion to warships, he did manage to visit his eldest son, who was a cadet at West Point.[21]

Semmes returned by ship to Savannah, and thence by train to Montgomery where he arrived on 4 April 1861, just eight days prior to the firing on Fort Sumter. It had been a whirlwind trip and more successful than those of other Southern agents sent on similar missions.[22]

In Montgomery Semmes found the Confederate government to be organized on a regular basis. Stephen R. Mallory, a former chairman of the U.S. Senate Committee on Naval Affairs, was Secretary of the Navy. He was one of only two of the original Davis cabinet appointees to serve throughout the war, and he directed the Confederacy's Navy and naval policy with a firm hand.[23] He and Semmes worked well together, and Mallory had the good sense to allow Semmes complete freedom during the cruises of the *Sumter* and the *Alabama*. Mallory immediately appointed Semmes a commander in the Confederate States Navy and chief of the Lighthouse Bureau.

With the firing on Fort Sumter (12 April 1861), Semmes realized it was "time to leave the things of peace to the future." He went immediately to Mallory and urged the use of privateers to strike at the enemy's commerce. Semmes saw no contradiction in recommending the use of "licensed pirates," as he had called privateers early in the Mexican War, because now his country was the weak naval power fighting an enemy with an established navy. Mallory agreed fully with the commander, and on 17 April 1861 President Davis announced his intentions to issue letters of marque. But Semmes did not intend to serve as a privateer; he asked Mallory at the same time for command of a regularly commissioned Confederate naval vessel suitable for commerce raiding. Mallory despondently showed him a file on a ship examined by a naval board in New Orleans and condemned as unfit for commerce raiding. Examining the file, Semmes saw that with modifications the ship could be converted into a suitable raider. "Give me that ship," he said to the Secretary; "I think I can make her answer the purpose." Thus was conceived the CSS *Sumter*, the first war vessel of the Confederate Navy.[24]

Semmes arrived in New Orleans on 22 April 1861, immediately taking possession of his new ship. He found her to be "as unlike a ship of war as possible . . . . Still, . . . her lines were easy and graceful, and she had a sort of saucy air about her . . . ."[25] It took two months of hard work to convert the ship. Semmes removed the superstructure, provided crew and officer quarters, acquired ordnance from as far away as the Norfolk Navy Yard, designed new gun carriages, bought clothing, and recruited a crew.

The officers, all natives of Confederate states, received their assignments to the *Sumter* from Mallory's office, and all except the marine officer had experience in the U.S. Navy. The enlisted crew consisted of seventy-two seamen and twenty marines. The seamen, as was the custom in most navies, were recruited from among sailors who were between voyages and happened to be in the New Orleans port. Only about half a dozen were native Southerners, a situation that reflected the scarcity of seafaring men in the South and imposed upon Semmes special problems of discipline and constant recruiting in neutral ports. Most of those recruited in New Orleans were English and Irish whom Semmes considered generally to be good sailors.[26]

Finally, on 3 June 1861, Semmes formally commissioned the converted packet-ship as the CSS *Sumter*, named after the fort in Charleston harbor. She was a small screw steamer of 499 tons, length only 152 feet, beam 27 feet, and draft 12 feet. She had a coal capacity for only eight days, and her propeller was stationary and therefore a drag when she was under sail only; her top speed under sail and steam was from ten to twelve knots.

After some trial runs, Semmes dropped the *Sumter* down river where he put

Semmes in the CSS *Sumter* running the blockade of the Pass à l'Outre. *Courtesy of the Naval Historical Center.*

the crew through training exercises and awaited an opportune moment to run the Union blockade. Drawing on his own blockading experiences, he knew the Union blockader had large stretches of water to watch. Given a few miles distance, Semmes calculated that the *Sumter* could make a fairly safe run for the open waters. So he stationed a small boat just beyond Pass à l'Outre to signal the location of the blockader. On 30 June 1861, with a little luck and superior seamanship, he narrowly escaped the faster and larger USS *Brooklyn*.

In the evening as the sun was setting, Semmes stood on the poop deck, and mused about the past few months—how "hurried and confused" they had been, how "family ties were severed," and how war was "arraying a household against itself." He thought of the American flag flying on board the *Brooklyn* and was startled to realize how he "now hated that flag!"[27] Nonetheless he slept soundly that night.

Free of the USS *Brooklyn*, Semmes was beginning a new naval career for which his previous naval experience had little prepared him. He knew that destruction of the enemy's merchant fleet was common naval duty, and he knew the glory it had brought to his predecessors during the American Revolution and the War of 1812; he also knew that he had no open home ports where he could take his prizes for adjudication, and that neutral nations prohibited the adjudication of prizes taken by either belligerent. That was a problem he would have to solve in his own way. There were other problems: to develop a technique of prize taking; financing and provisioning his own ships and crew; dealing with neutral port authorities; sailing in strange seas. He was fully aware of the dangers implicit in Mallory's twofold strategy. If he succeeded in destroying Northern merchant ships and in luring federal vessels from blockade duty, he risked his own destruction by those faster and larger warships. The success of his mission and the safety of his ship and crew depended more on Semmes's seamanship, cunning, and innovation than it did on his naval experiences.

The study of law was Semmes's most useful prewar experience for his career as a commerce raider. It enabled him to master the intricacies of international law concerning belligerent and neutral maritime rights and obligations. At sea during the war, he consulted his ever-handy copy of Phillimore, *Commentaries upon International Law*, and presented legal briefs to neutral port authorities, successfully arguing that as a belligerent he had rights to buy coal and provisions and to repair his vessel. Otherwise he could never have kept constantly at sea for over two years.

But legal knowledge was not enough. Semmes was also an excellent naval strategist who possessed the nautical knowledge necessary to execute that strategy. He knew that prevailing winds and currents created crossroads-at-sea for merchantmen carrying goods between certain markets and the fishing and whaling grounds where other ships congregated. The crossroads-at-sea just off the south end of Cuba served Semmes in the same strategic sense that Marye's Heights above the Rappahannock River served General Lee in December 1862. In two days off Cuba, Semmes in the CSS *Sumter* captured seven Northern merchantmen. When Semmes commissioned the *Alabama* off the Azores in September 1862, he immediately sought out the New England whaling fleet, whose Azores season ended about 1 October. Within three weeks he destroyed eight whalers that sat low in the water, heavy with the season's catch. Then he changed his hunting grounds to the Newfoundland fishing banks. He followed the strategy of sea-position throughout his career as a commerce raider.

Semmes's strategy was successful, and was adopted by other Confederate commerce raiders. The total number of Northern merchant vessels destroyed by Confederate ships was about 200.[28] On board the *Sumter* and the *Alabama*, Semmes captured eighty-seven ships, of which he burned sixty-two, converted one into a Confederate raider (the *Conrad* into the *Tuscaloosa*, June 1863), and sold another (the *Sea Bride*, August 1863). Thus Semmes accounted for about 32 percent of all Union commercial ships lost during the war. However, that is not the full story. Semmes captured 85 percent of his total prizes during the first year of his twenty-two-month cruise in the *Alabama*;[29] and the *Florida*'s thirty-three and the *Georgia*'s five prizes after August 1863 were mostly coastal ships. Thus by early fall of 1863 Semmes had driven the bulk of the U.S. merchant ships from the busiest sea lanes. Many that he did not capture were sold to neutrals, and those still flying the Stars and Stripes were old or worthless craft used in coastal service.[30] Marine insurance rates increased by a factor of three between 1861 and 1863. Cargo owners naturally shipped by neutral vessels, so much so that in November 1862, only 20 of 150 vessels loading in New York for European ports were under the U.S. flag; by 1864 neutral flags were "almost monopolizing European trade." More than half of the U.S. merchant fleet was lost during the Civil War, either directly to Confederate raiders (110,000 tons) or indirectly by sale to neutrals (800,000 tons).[31] Semmes was mostly responsible for the success of one part of Mallory's strategy—drive the Northern merchant fleet from the seas.

For the other half of that same strategy—lure Union naval vessels from their blockading stations—Semmes was notably less successful. Counting both the *Sumter* and the *Alabama* voyages, records reveal that from July 1861 to June 1864 Semmes encountered at most only ten to fifteen U.S. naval vessels, and none of these was from the blockading fleet. This was true partly because Semmes's mission was to sink commercial ships, not fight naval battles. Despite these orders, Semmes did challenge and sink the USS *Hatteras* in January 1863. He searched for the USS *Wyoming* which was seeking him in the China Seas in October 1863, but the two never met.[32] Finally, in a kind of death wish, he sailed from Cherbourg, France, precisely to fight the *Kearsarge* (21 June 1864). But none of the Northern naval vessels was on blockade duty. Semmes's failure to help lift the Union blockade was more a failure of Mallory's strategy and of Confederate diplomacy, and particularly of Union naval policies, than of Semmes. Rapid expansion permitted the U.S. Navy, without weakening the blockade, to create the West Indies Fleet that guarded the Gulf area and occasionally sent ships to search the Brazilian coast for Confederate raiders; individual ships were dispatched to foreign stations such as the China Sea and, especially, to European waters. Union strategy against Confederate raiders, however, was to chase and destroy them, not to escort or defend Northern merchant ships, and this strategy failed as completely as did Mallory's. The Union Navy did not capture even one Confederate raider on the open high seas. Civil War naval strategy concerning commerce raiders was a failure on both sides because the North did not protect its commerce, nor did the South lure the blockaders away from the Confederacy.

The cruises of the *Sumter* and the *Alabama* have been detailed completely,[33] but no account explains how Semmes—a naval officer with much more sea time on coastal waters than on the high seas—could convert himself into the most proficient of commerce-destroying sea captains. In fact, his experiences on board the *Sumter* served as training for his much longer and more varied *Alabama* cruise.

First, he had to develop a method of disposing of his prizes. Despite restraints imposed upon him by the Union blockade of Southern ports and the refusal of neutrals to adjudicate belligerent prizes, Semmes did not want to destroy his captures. His first victim was the *Golden Rocket*, taken off the southeastern tip of Cuba on 3 July 1861 and burned. In the log he recorded simply that "she made a beautiful bonfire," but the moment was so etched in his mind that seven years later he recounted every vivid detail. Despite the thrill of his first capture, he found his duty "a painful one to destroy so noble a ship," and his officers felt badly enough about the burning ship to take up a collection for the *Golden Rocket*'s captain.[34] Semmes refused to destroy any of his next ten captures. Instead, he tested the neutrality prohibitions against adjudicating prizes. He took six into a Cuban harbor, hoping the Spanish colonial officials would intern them until a Confederate court of admiralty could adjudicate them, and he took one to Venezuela hoping to impose his will on a weak neutral. In both places he submitted a lawyer's brief claiming that the neutral's position was, in fact, unneutral because Confederate captains had no ports to take their prizes, whereas the federal captains had their own open ports. His pleas, however, fell on deaf ears, and he claimed the United States "not only bullied the little South American republics, but the whole world besides."[35] Semmes had learned his lesson. Thereafter he constituted himself to be a Confederate court of admiralty, and he tried, condemned, bonded, or released all merchant ships he hailed, in accordance with the rules established by the Declaration of Paris in 1856: neutral cargo, except contraband, is free from seizure even when in an enemy ship; and enemy cargo, except contraband, is free from seizure when in a neutral ship. Of course not all cases were as clear-cut as the Paris Declaration would have them be—cargoes of mixed ownership and falsified papers gave Semmes difficulty. Without the leisure of contemplative time, Semmes made some debatable decisions. But he never again took a captured vessel into a neutral port; and although he regretted the necessity of burning ships, he performed his duty unhesitatingly, and his officers never took up a collection for another victim's captain.

In order to bring cases before his floating court of admiralty, Semmes developed his own techniques of capture. Seagoing merchant and war vessels were unmarked and similar in configuration. Only the flag indicated nationality. When Semmes sighted a sail, he gave chase flying a British, French, or U.S. flag. If the merchantman did not haul to, Semmes fired a round or two across her bow, then hailed her captain to ask the ship's name and nationality. Only then did he raise the Confederate flag and order the ship to receive a boarding party. The boarding officer, usually a lieutenant, was ordered to bring the merchant captain with his ship's papers to Semmes's cabin. After an examination of the papers, Semmes questioned the captain, and rendered his decision. If he condemned the ship, the crew and passengers, if any, were transferred to the *Sumter*, as were any usable supplies such as food, fuel, clothing, and rigging. For all condemned ships, Semmes meticulously wrote a legal decision setting forth the evidence and the law.

Semmes's very success created problems of adjudication. Out of fear of the *Sumter* and the *Alabama*, shippers began to use false papers of registry or of cargo ownership. In such a case Semmes consulted legal references such as Phillimore, carefully detailed the circumstances, and then recorded his decision. Here is an excerpt from Semmes's *Alabama* journal, dated 6 July 1863: " . . . at 3:30 AM hove to a ship with a shot, she having disregarded two blank cartridges. She proves to be the *Express*, of Boston, from Callao to Antwerp . . . . Captured her . . . fired her at about 10:30 AM and filled away on our course." Noting that the French chargé d'affaires at Lima had certified the cargo to be neutral property, Semmes wrote the following legal justification for having destroyed the cargo:

> This certificate fails to be of any value as proof, for two reasons: First it is not sworn to, and secondly, it simply avers the property to be neutral . . . instead of pointing out the owner or owners. First, a consul may authenticate evidence by his seal, but when he departs from the usual functions of a consul and becomes a witness he must give his testimony under oath like other witnesses . . . . Now, the presumption of law being that goods found in an enemy's ship belong to the enemy, unless a distinct neutral character be given to them by pointing out the real owner by proper documentary proof, and as neither the bill of lading nor the certificate . . . amounts to proper documentary proof, the ship and cargo are both condemned . . . as a distinct neutral character is not impressed upon the property by proper evidence. I must act under the presumption of law. (See 3^d Phillimore, 596.)[36]

This tactic of enforcing international law strictly, even in the face of cleverly falsified documents, led Northern ship owners to sell their vessels legitimately to neutral nationals, thus reducing Union commercial shipping.

Not all cases were as easily accepted by the victims as was the case of the *Express*. Later, on his return trip from Singapore, just off the Strait of Malacca, on 24 December 1864, Semmes hove to "an American-looking bark, under English colors, with the name *Martaban*."[37] Semmes ordered Master's Mate George Fullam, an Englishman, to board her. Fullam considered the bark to be "suspicious looking," and soon ascertained that she was originally the *Texan Star* out of Houston. The captain, Samuel B. Pike, who spoke with a Maine accent, refused to board the *Alabama* because he claimed to be a British subject. So, for the only time, Semmes boarded a victim. From all appearances—freshly repainted name, ship's design, American captain, officers, and even "a black, greasy cook"—the transfer was recent and probably fraudulent. Although Captain Pike claimed the cargo to be neutral-owned, there was no bill of sale and only the ordinary cargo bill of lading. The ship's papers were freshly written in the same handwriting, even to the crews' signatures. That was enough for Semmes. "I had no doubt," he noted in the log, "that the transfer was fraudulent and captured and burned her." But there was some lingering doubt, especially because of the claim that the cargo was British-owned. So he called Captain Pike into his cabin (Semmes typically getting in the last word on a cabin visit), placed him under oath, and asked if the transfer of the ship were bona fide. Pike admitted, then, that out of fear of the *Alabama* he had arranged "a sham sale in hopes of saving" his ship. Upon the "answer being recorded," Semmes wrote, "the court adjourned." Since the ship was American and there existed no legal evidence that the cargo was British-owned, then, as in the *Express* case, Semmes had not violated a neutral's rights. But if Semmes had closed the case by adjourning the court, British public and official opinion was not satisfied.

The *Martaban* incident aroused adverse feelings among the English in Singapore.[38] The Chamber of Commerce of the Straits Settlement put the issue clearly when it petitioned the governor, asking "whether the capture and destruction of a vessel possessed of a certificate of British Registry is legal or justified because suspicions may be entertained that she is not *bona fide* the property of a British subject."[39] This outcry from the commercial circles of Singapore, despite the U.S. consul's belief that the registry transfer was "a 'bogus' sale," reflected their concern for the safety of investments in merchant ships acquired by transferring the registry from the United States to Great Britain. Captain David McDougal of the USS *Wyoming* wrote to Washington that "nearly all of the American vessels in the China Seas have changed flags." When the *Alabama* had approached the Eastern waters, "fourteen American ships were sold in Calcutta in short order."[40] British concern spread from Singapore to England and on to Sir James Hope, vice-admiral of the English Atlantic Fleet. Citing the case of the *Martaban*, Sir James instructed officers under his command "to capture and send to England for adjudication in the admiralty court every vessel by which a British vessel, *i.e.*, with legal British papers, is burned at sea."[41]

This naval interpretation of the British Proclamation of Neutrality, according to the records, was never applied, but it reflected growing British concern over the *Alabama*'s destruction of ships on the high seas, and, perhaps, the South's failing fortunes of war as well. The fact that Semmes was legally correct in the *Martaban* case, as he had been in the *Express* incident, illustrates the difference between dealing with a weak neutral state (Belgian ownership of the *Express* cargo) and a strong one.

Semmes seems never to have known of Sir James Hope's instruction because he never mentioned it in the *Alabama*'s log or in his memoirs. He did, however, know the difference between dealing with a weak as opposed to a strong neutral state—he learned it at the end of the *Sumter* cruise. After a rough and long Atlantic crossing, the little *Sumter* was leaking badly, food and provisions were low, and Semmes had left but a thousand of his ten-thousand-dollar cruising fund. She limped into the harbor of Cadiz, Spain, on 4 January 1862, seeking repair facilities, food and provisions, and time to receive funds from Confederate Commissioner William L. Yancy in London. The harbor officials received him coolly, forced him to justify every request by legal brief, and delayed responses while they consulted Madrid. Finally, after allowing

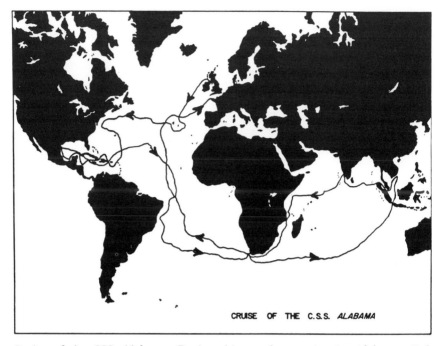

CRUISE OF THE C.S.S. *ALABAMA*

Cruise of the CSS *Alabama*. During this year-long cruise the *Alabama* sailed approximately 75,000 miles and took sixty-four prizes. From Charles G. Summersell, *The Journal of Charles Townley Fullam*, xliv.

him to repair the *Sumter'*s hull in a government-owned dry dock, they refused to allow him to remain in the harbor while awaiting funds from London. Disgusted with the Spanish treatment, Semmes blamed it on their fear of the United States and later noted "that all of the weak powers were timid, and henceforth, I rarely entered any but an English or French port."[42]

The Spanish officials' delays in responding to Semmes's request allowed him time to read and write. In January in Cadiz he read a copy of U.S. Secretary of the Navy Gideon Welles's report to Congress, which prompted him on 9 January 1862 to write a long letter to the *Times* of London.[43] In it he identified Welles as "the Secretary of the Northern fragment of what was formerly known as the United States of America," and noted that Welles wrote that the *Sumter* and Confederate privateers were engaged in "piratical warfare." Enraged, the *Sumter* commander with logic and a cool head set out to refute Welles's accusation of piracy, and did so in a manner designed to appeal to English readers of the *Times*.

"Mr. Welles . . . calls me a privateer. He knows better than this." Privateers sail under a letter of marque, but "he knows that I have been regularly commissioned as a ship of war of the Confederate States." If Welles insists on calling all Confederates rebels, "then he might criticize me as a rebel man of war." But "if I am this, so were all the ships of the American colonies commissioned by that Virginian, George Washington."

In referring to the *Sumter*, Welles listed those U.S. ships assigned to search for her. Among them was the USS *San Jacinto* which violated English neutral rights by stopping HMS *Trent* on the high seas and forcibly removing John Slidell and James Mason. European pressure and British preparation for war forced the federal government to release the two Confederate diplomatic commissioners, and news of their release had reached Europe just days before Semmes was writing. "I feel honored," Semmes wrote, "to have been pursued by six frigates, and one of them caught Messrs. Mason and Slidell instead of catching me." This was an effective stroke of Semmes's pen because it placed him and the English on the same side against the United States.

Also at Cadiz, twelve enlisted seamen deserted the *Sumter*, seduced, Semmes claimed, by the "agents, spies, and pimps" of the U.S. consul. But such problems were common to most ships in his day. Seamen signed on for a particular voyage, and most of them left the ship on completion of their contract. At any given time there were unemployed seamen in port cities throughout the world ready to sign on board any ship. They had no allegiance to any flag. Semmes had a constant problem with his foreign seamen.

Although the *Sumter*'s crew were mostly non-Americans, they were homogeneous compared to those of the *Alabama*. By midcruise, there were English, Irish, French, Portugese, Spanish, and Oriental sailors on board the *Alabama*, and they were controlled only by strict discipline. Semmes read the Confederate Articles of War to the full crew every Sunday morning. Even so, he had to suppress a mutiny on 19 November 1862 while at Fort de France in Martinique.[44] Semmes nevertheless developed a strong attachment to his crew and often moderated discipline with mercy. His crew in return respected the captain and affectionately referred to him as "Old Beeswax." Semmes was particularly proud of the fact that of the 2,500 persons—officers, seamen, and prisoners—under his command from time to time, on board both ships, he "had not lost a single man by disease."[45]

On 17 January 1862, after the Cadiz governor, "a bull-head, stupid official," refused to allow him to stay any longer, Semmes sailed out of the port and turned the *Sumter*'s bow toward the British base at Gibraltar. En route the *Sumter* made her last captures, bonding one and burning the other,[46] and she anchored in Gibraltar Bay early the next evening. This was the effective end of the *Sumter* cruise. From 30 June 1861 to 18 January 1862, she had captured eighteen enemy merchant vessels, burned seven, bonded two, lost eight to Cuban internment and had two recaptured by the enemy, and overhauled thirty-four neutral ships. Unable to procure coal or repair the *Sumter*'s boilers, and blockaded variously by three or four U.S. warships including the *Kear-*

sarge, Semmes finally abandoned the ship. In mid-April 1862 Semmes and several officers boarded a passenger steamer for England.

Semmes and John MacIntosh Kell, his first lieutenant, took rooms together in Euston Square, London, where they remained through May. Semmes appreciated the "relaxation and ease" of London living compared to the past six months on board ship. Through James Mason, Semmes met many distinguished men—cotton brokers, shippers, shipbuilders—who had an economic interest in the Confederate cause. Normally a sharp judge of character, he misread their genial entertainment, flattery, and expressions of support for the Confederacy as reflecting British government policy. More important, he also conferred with James D. Bulloch and James North, Confederate naval purchasing agents, and learned of the recent sailing of the CSS *Florida* and the near-readiness of the future CSS *Alabama*. Persuaded, however, that no ship was available to him, Semmes decided to return immediately to the Confederate States and arrived at Nassau on 8 June 1862.[47]

By pure coincidence, Semmes met another officer fresh from Richmond with copies of letters from Secretary Mallory, who thought Semmes was still in England. From the letters he learned that Mallory had nominated him for promotion to captain and appointed him to command the *Alabama*.[48] Fearful that the British would seize the ship before he could return to England, Semmes wrote to Bulloch suggesting that the *Alabama* be sent to some rendezvous point to await her newly assigned captain. Not knowing whether Bulloch received his letter, Semmes spent "several very anxious weeks" before securing passage back to England.

Meanwhile, Commodore Bulloch received the letters of Mallory and Semmes at the same time, and put into effect a plan to evade British neutrality laws. He sent the *Alabama* under British colors and a British captain to the Azores Islands to await her captain, crew, munitions, and supplies. Both Bulloch and Semmes expended great effort to prove that the building, equipping, arming, and manning of the *Alabama* was done within the boundaries of the British neutrality laws. But neither ever understood that England had adopted a strict policy of neutrality, found her own domestic laws inadequate, and acted thereafter on policy and not on law. Semmes covered thirty-two pages of a tightly written and logical argument in his *Memoirs* to prove that the *Alabama* was a legitimate warship of the Confederate Navy, operating in an accepted mode of naval warfare. The postwar negotiations between London and Washington, however, concerned not the ship herself, but her origins and the British obligation to prevent a ship intended for war use—regardless of how or where she might later be armed, manned, and equipped—from leaving their territory. As a matter of principle, the British government accepted in 1861 its own responsibility for preventing a ship from leaving British territory if it were built in England by a belligerent power and intended to war on an enemy. That principle, incorporated into the Treaty of Washington (1871), served as the basis for the 1873 Geneva Tribunal's decision that Great Britain must pay an indemnity of $15,500,000 to the United States.[49] Semmes, writing in 1867–68, of course, could not have known of the diplomatic principle accepted by England, or that Great Britain, not the *Alabama*, was to be put on trial. Unfortunately, the writings of Semmes and Bulloch have influenced many scholars and still serve to cloud the origins and nature of the ship on whose decks Semmes would rise to greatness.

The *Alabama* sailed from England (30 July 1862) several days before Semmes returned from Nassau (8 August 1862). He spent about a week gathering his *Sumter* officers and making financial arrangements for a cruise fund. Recalling his embarrassments in Cadiz, Semmes obtained a cruising fund, and there is evidence that he also had a "considerable sum of gold" in the ship thoughout the cruise.[50] At no time while on board the *Alabama* did Semmes ever mention the need for money.

Bulloch had designed the ship, nursed her to completion, and now turned her over to Semmes, who saw her afloat for the first time on 20 August 1862 when he, his officers, and Bulloch arrived in the Azores. Semmes paid his great debt to Bulloch when he described the ship in words that convey across a hundred years his thrill and excitement: "Her model was of the most perfect symmetry, and she sat upon the water with the lightness and grace of a swan. She was barkentine rigged, with long lower masts, which enabled her to carry large fore- and aft-sails . . . . Her sticks were of the best yellow pine, that would bend in the gale like a willow wand, without breaking, and her rigging was of the best Swedish iron wire." She had a lifting device to raise her propeller out of water to prevent drag when under sail. "She was a perfect steamer and a perfect sailing ship at the same time. . . . ."[51] Semmes saw the *Alabama* as a love-partner, a home, and once he took possession of her he was pleased and legitimatized their affair. "I had surveyed my new ship as we approached with no little interest, as she was to be not only my home, *but my bride*, as it were, for the next few years, and I was quite satisfied with her external appearance." Once on board her, Semmes "was as much pleased with her internal appearance, and arrangements, as . . . with her externally."[52] The union was complete between man and ship, for that night Semmes slept in her bosom, a sound, restful, and peaceful sleep. It was a union that over the next twenty-two months would become ever more intimate as each learned more about the other, and they responded to each other's demands.

By Saturday night, 23 August 1862, all supplies were transferred to the *Alabama*, and on Sunday, 24 August 1862, in international waters where no nation had jurisdiction, Semmes commissioned the *Alabama* as a regular warship of the Confederate States Navy. He read to the assembled officers and seamen his commission as a captain and his orders. The seamen who had signed on as merchant seamen had no obligation to the *Alabama*. So Semmes spoke to them in terms of fighting the "battles of the oppressed" and a cruise of "excitement and adventure." And then he offered them contracts at twice the going wage and "lots of prize money." Aroused by the ceremony they had just witnessed and greedy for the double wages and prize money, eighty of the assembled ninety sailors—English, Dutch, Irish, French, Italian, and Spanish—signed on. Semmes "felt much relieved in consequence."[53]

The next few days Semmes exercised his crew and gave them gunnery practice. Then he turned to his task, and on 5 September 1862 the *Alabama* made her first capture, a whaling vessel off the Azores, the first of the 54 ships she would capture and of the 447 she would speak or board.[54] Thus the *Alabama* began her career as the most destructive commerce raider in history.

Her captain, however, had greater ambitions for her. Even on board the *Sumter*, Semmes resented the reputation that he "never fights, only plunders." When he first had seen the *Alabama* in England, still in the shipyard, he thought her to be "quite equal to encounter any of the enemy's steam sloops." Four months into the cruise he deliberately sought a battle with an enemy war vessel. Having learned from captured Northern papers that the United States was planning a combined operation under General N. P. Banks against Galveston, Texas, Semmes decided "to strike a blow" against the expedition in the Gulf of Mexico. Accordingly, after recoaling and resting his crew at an island 100 miles east of Vera Cruz, waters familiar to him from his Mexican War days, Semmes approached the Texas coast. On 11 January 1863, as he timed his speed to arrive before Galveston after dark, the *Alabama*-turned-huntress flushed the enemy. Semmes soon realized he had come upon three warships, not the Banks expedition. He tacked off, and when one of the enemy ships got up steam to investigate, he tried to lure the enemy vessel away from her sister ships and to gain time for darkness to arrive. Semmes had an advantage because he knew the ship was an enemy, but his antagonist proved to be the USS *Hatteras*, an eighteen-month-old iron-steamer of 1,100 tons, with airtight compartments. Still, the *Alabama* met her captain's demands as the two ships, standing from 30 to 100 yards apart, exchanged fire. The close distance offset the effect of the *Hatteras*'s light cannon; but the *Alabama*'s shells "entered the *Hatteras* at the waterline tearing off entire sheets of iron," the water rushed in, and the *Hatteras* struck her flag. Within forty-five minutes, the first battle on the high seas between Confederate and federal warships was a victory for Semmes and his ship.[55]

Neither Semmes nor H. G. Blake, captain of the *Hatteras*, made special comment on the fact that the *Alabama*'s shells tore off "sheets of iron" at the waterline of the *Hatteras*. Yet the impact of the new ironclad ships on naval warfare was a constant topic among maritime people, especially after March 1862 when the ironclad CSS *Virginia* inflicted destruction upon the wooden Union warships in Hampton Roads and then fought the USS *Monitor* to a draw. Eleven months later the wooden *Alabama* destroyed an iron federal warship in an exchange of shots at close range! It was a remarkable feat, yet

Semmes made no remark on it; why not? His omission is a mystery unless one suspects that he did not want to cloud his later argument that the *Kearsarge*'s captain surreptitiously armored his ship by covering the vertical chains that hung from deck to waterline.

After the battle with the *Hatteras*, Semmes could find no prey in American waters; so in compliance with Mallory's suggestion he decided to head for the East Indies. The life of a commerce raider was not easy. The loneliness of a sea captain, the strains of imposing discipline on a motley crew of several nationalities who depended on him for food and clothing, the challenges of rough seas, the thrills of the chase and the climax of the capture, all had a psychological effect on the introspective Semmes. He never confided in his men, but wrote in his ship's journal. In June 1863, frustrated by bad weather, Semmes noted that his two years afloat had "produced a constant tension of the nervous system, and a wear and tear of body that . . . , no doubt, would be quite obvious to my friends at home." The introspection continued. On 8 September 1863 as he complained of the rolling and pitching in the sea, he confessed to his journal: "I am supremely disgusted with the sea and all its belongings. The fact is, I am past the age when men ought to be subjected to the hardships and discomforts of the sea."[56]

The man and the ship both needed rest and refurbishing. On 16 September 1863, they entered the anchorage at Simon's Town, South Africa, where they spent eight days. The *Alabama* took on a full provision of coal, repaired her copper hull sheathings, and refitted her fore-topmast. Semmes strolled into the countryside beyond Simon's Town, attended mass in the small Catholic Church, and dined with British officers. Thus refreshed they sailed from Simon's Town on 24 September, rounded the Cape of Good Hope, and headed into the Indian Ocean.[57] Semmes chose the southern route to avoid U.S. warships. The constant rain squalls and gale winds imposed a dull routine on the man that tested his spirit, and a stress on the ship that tested her timbers.

On the return voyage from the Far East, the chase that led to his last capture momentarily lifted the spirit of the still-despondent captain. The weather was good: the moon bright, the breeze gentle, and the sea smooth. "The Yankee worked like a good fellow to get away, piling clouds of canvas upon his ship . . . , but it was no use," Semmes wrote. "When the day dawned we were within a couple of miles of him. It was the old spectacle of the panting, breathless fawn, and the inexorable stag-hound." But the thrill of the kill soon turned to despair as Semmes read of Northern victories in recent New York newspapers he captured. "Might it not be," Semmes mused, "that after all our trials and sacrifices, the cause for which we were struggling would be lost? . . . The thought was hard to bear."

The ugly mood persisted, and as he recrossed the equator northward toward Cherbourg, Semmes fell into a deep depression. Detached, he referred to himself in the third person—no longer the bright-eyed seaman who "gloated upon the spectacle" of the burning *Golden Rocket*, his first victim two and a half years earlier, and saw in those leaping flames the bright promise of a war easily won, but now only a man upon whom stress and strain "had laid, in the three years of war he had been afloat, a load of a dozen years on his shoulders." And he saw his ship just as clearly. She was no longer the "inexorable stag-hound," but only a "wearied foxhound, limping back after a long chase, footsore and longing for quiet and repose." And above his visions of man and ship, he saw "shadows of a sorrowful future," and knew that his cruise on board the *Alabama* was "drawing to a close" in defeat. The man and ship were beaten not by the enemy on the high seas, but by the seas themselves and by the enemy armies on land.[58]

The bent and beaten seaman had pushed his ship, his sea bride, too hard for too long. She had answered his every demand. She had fought and defeated a U.S. war vessel; she had braved the storms of the Antarctic; she had survived the tropical waters of the East Indies. She had not been in dry dock since her launching into the River Mersey that 15th of May so many nautical miles ago in 1862. As she approached Cherbourg, on 10 June 1864, she complained that her boilers were rusted and leaky, her copper sheathing was broken and dragging in the water, and her timbers—so tested by raging seas infested with icebergs—were wearied by her long journeys. Her captain, too, was exhausted, not only from the "vigils by night and by day," but even more by a new mental attitude: the lost cause for which he had "so struggled," "the shadows of a sorrowful future," his beloved *Alabama*'s cruise "drawing to a close."

It was in this depth of depression that on 11 June 1864 Semmes in his well-worn ship dropped anchor in Cherbourg. Two days later he learned that Commodore Samuel Barron was in Paris. He immediately wrote to his superior officer: "my health has suffered so much from a constant and harassing service of three years almost continuously at sea, that I shall have to ask for relief [from command of the *Alabama*]."[59] Semmes makes no mention of this request in any of his writings because the USS *Kearsarge*'s arrival in Cherbourg harbor (14 June 1864) changed the situation. He had to reassess the *Alabama*'s role in the new circumstances, and, having done so, realized the necessity for quick action. His depression left him as he prepared for the task at hand.

The *Kearsarge*, he knew, had been guarding Calais where the CSS *Rappahannock*, held by the French government, was slowly rotting away.[60] Semmes could not permit his gallant staghound, tail between her legs, to be bottled up in Cherbourg as the *Rappahannock* was in Calais. What an inglorious end to a glorious cruise that would be! No, better that once again she ride the waves like a swan. She might win against the *Kearsarge*: the U.S. vessel possessed no obvious overwhelming advantage over the *Alabama*; and if she failed, she would die as she had lived—gloriously. But Semmes was a realist as well as a romantic. He knew other U.S. warships would soon appear and confine him to Cherbourg harbor as they had done at Gibraltar Bay. The *Alabama*'s only chance to get to sea ever again was to risk battle with the *Kearsarge* before they arrived. It was a naval captain's decision to take the proper action at the proper moment in order to keep his ship afloat and in service against the enemy.

Departing from custom, Semmes summoned his first lieutenant and announced: "Kell, I'm going to fight the *Kearsarge*. What do you think of it?"Kell dutifully reminded his captain that in target practice a few weeks earlier the gunpowder appeared to be weak and that one in three shells had failed to explode because of the defective fuses. Semmes replied, "I will take my chances of one in three."[61]

Semmes required four days to take on 150 tons of coal. Sailors holystoned the *Alabama*'s decks, polished brass, repaired or replaced the sails and riggings. In the meantime, word of the impending battle spread, and the curious and concerned took the train from Paris to Cherbourg. The artist Edouard Manet came and painted the *Alabama* in her death throes; photographers and newspaper reporters arrived to record the event. Confederate naval officers from Paris tried to join the crew, but were denied by the French officials who were enforcing their neutrality obligations. On Sunday morning, 19 June 1864, the *Alabama*, with her officers and crew in dress uniform, sailed out of Cherbourg harbor as if en route to a gala naval review. The crowds on the quays, housetops and hills, boats, and even the breakwater cheered as the proud ship steamed toward the waiting *Kearsarge*. The *Alabama* responded to the occasion, once again riding the water with the grace of a swan.

About three miles out of Cherbourg Semmes called his crew together to hear a rousing speech, reminiscent of Napoleon's First Order to his army in Italy: "The name of your ship has become a household word wherever civilization extends. Shall that name be tarnished by defeat? The thing is impossible." And the sailors, aroused, at the word "defeat" answered, "Never! Never!" But Semmes himself was not so sure. Just earlier he asked his fifth lieutenant, "How do you think it will turn out today, Mr. Sinclair?" Surprised to be asked his opinion, the lieutenant replied, "I cannot answer the question, Sir, but can assure you the crew will do their full duty, and follow you to the death." Turning away, Semmes responded, "Yes, that's true." Did Semmes mean that the crew would literally, that day, "follow him to the death"?[62]

The story of the battle has been repeated often, from that day to this, by eyewitnesses, participants, popular writers, and scholars.[63] The plain facts— the "whats" of the battle—are clear: the two ships met about seven miles at sea, still in view of the spectators; Semmes opened fire about a mile from the *Kearsarge*, and the force of the fight threw the two ships into a circular pattern; after about sixty-five minutes of intense and continuous firing, the *Alabama*

Fight between the CSS *Alabama* and the USS *Kearsarge*. The wood engraving by Smyth is a fairly accurate depiction of the ships. *Courtesy of the Naval Historical Center.*

was foundering, and she sank stern first at 12:24 P.M. The "whys" of the battle are disputed still because eyewitnesses and participants recounted the events from their own scope of vision, personal allegiance, and mental conditions.

Depression struck Semmes early in the battle because he could see that the *Alabama*'s shot and shell did little damage to the *Kearsarge*. He ordered his gunners to aim low so the shots would ricochet off the water into the enemy hull. Finally, about thirty minutes into the fight, a lucky shot embedded a shell into the *Kearsarge*'s sternpost. A cheer went up from the *Alabama*'s crew, but the shell failed to explode. As Semmes later wrote, that shell "was the only trophy they ever got of the *Alabama*! We fought her until she could no longer swim, and then we gave her to the waves." As the ship began to settle stern first and the water engulfed the taffrails, Semmes and Kell prepared to abandon ship. Once again, Semmes identified with his ship. At almost the last moment, in a gesture of defiance against the Yankee victor, Semmes cast his sword—symbol of command—into the sea. Then he and Kell jumped, and side by side swam away to avoid the vortex of the waters.

It was an emotional moment for the two men as they swam in the water and saw their ship go down. Gallant losers often gain more renown than the winners. Whose name do we remember from the Battle of Thermopylae? And whose name comes to mind when we hear the word "Waterloo"? Who remembers the name of the *Kearsarge*'s captain? It is from such stuff that legends grow.

Semmes later blamed his defeat on weak gunpowder and faulty percussion caps. But a sailor on board the *Kearsarge* claimed that the *Alabama*'s shells failed to explode because the gunners had not removed the lead caps, which exposed the time fuses that in turn caused the shells to explode.[64] If that were true, then the blame should be placed on the gunners, not the gunpowder. Only about 8.5 percent of the 370 shots fired by his gunners even touched the *Kearsarge*, and of these more hit the rigging than the hull. Commander Bulloch, analyzing the loss, wrote that the *Alabama* crew had not been trained at judging distance, nor had they practiced "firing at a visible target and noting effect," and concluded that "the results of the action was determined by the superior accuracy of the firing from the *Kearsarge*."[65] Semmes refused to criticize or lay blame on any of his officers or crew. Despite his earlier criticism of Jack Tar and the stern discipline he imposed during the cruise, after the battle Semmes wrote of them with sentiments he had never before expressed:

> When I looked upon my gory deck, toward the close of the action, and saw so many manly forms stretched upon it, with the glazed eye of death, or agonizing with terrible wounds, I felt as a father feels who has lost his children.[66]

It is true that of the twenty-one men who died in the action and in the waters, thirteen had served from the start of the cruise. It is also true that such a scene as the "gory deck" would impress itself on Semmes's mind as indelibly as that of his sinking ship. And Semmes's memoirs are impressionistic, but do his impressions convey any less truth than Edouard Manet's impressionistic painting of the end of the *Alabama*? No. Semmes could not blame his crew any more than he could blame his ship:

> No one who is not a seaman can realize the blow that falls upon the heart of a commander, upon the sinking of his ship. It is not merely the loss of a battle—it is the overwhelming of his household, as it were, in a great catastrophe. The *Alabama* had not only been my battlefield, but my home, in which I had lived two long years, and in which I had experienced many vicissitudes of pain and pleasure, sickness and health.[67]

And so Semmes sought other causes for the catastrophe. Just two days after the event, from Southampton, England, Semmes composed his official report to Commodore Barron. In it he referred to the slight damage done by shells exploding against the *Kearsarge*'s hull, but only in the context of his order to use shot alternately with shells; he did not mention weak gunpowder. Two paragraphs later, simply as a matter of information, he noted that his officers who went alongside the enemy's ship reported that "her midship section on both sides was thoroughly iron-coated" by perpendicular chains covered by a thin outer planking. But he made no critical comment about the iron coating. Ten days later, on 1 July, he wrote: "My defeat is due to two circumstances— the very thorough manner in which the enemy's ship was protected by her chain armor and the deterioration . . . of my powder and fuses." On 5 July, he placed the loss on the condition of the powder and referred to the *Kearsarge*'s chain armor only by indirection. In neither letter did he criticize Captain Winslow for applying the chain armor or for covering it with planking. He did comment in the letters that he was "overwhelmed" and "oppressed" with "mortification" for the defeat. His humiliation grew with the passing years, so that he wrote in his memoirs: "The plain fact is, without any varnish, the *Kearsarge*, though as effectively protected as if she had been armored with the best of iron plates, was to all appearance a wooden ship of war." She really had "concealed armor."[68] The battle, then, had been unfair, won by deceit and trickery. The Semmes who wrote those words was not the naval officer who took the *Sumter* through the Union blockade in 1861, who destroyed more Northern merchantmen than any other raider captain in history, who guided and molded a motley crew of replacements and various nationalities into fighting men who, despite defeat, left him glory; no, it was not Captain Raphael Semmes of the CSS *Alabama*, but a broken man whose pride and, perhaps, self-respect had been destroyed on that Sunday off Cherbourg in 1864.

Although his years of greatness ended when the *Alabama* sank, excitement still beckoned Semmes. After several weeks paying off the crew and settling the *Alabama*'s affairs, he regained his self-confidence. He was feted by several pro-South British societies, one of which presented him with a new sword. Recovered from the ordeal of battle, his health restored, Semmes embarked on 3 October 1864 on his return journey to the Confederate States. Wartime necessity imposed upon him a circuitous route: by ship to Matamoros, Mexico, thence to Brownsville, Texas, and by coach with a military escort to Shreveport, Louisiana, where he rested a few days and visited his son, whom he had last seen at West Point before the war. Traveling by horseback, eluding U.S. troops by sleeping in swamps and swimming rivers, the fifty-six-year-old Semmes in good health and high spirits greeted his wife and daughters in Mobile on 19 December.[69] Given the circumstances, a seven-and-a-half-week trip from England to Mobile was rather remarkable.

Semmes left his family on 2 January 1865 to report to Secretary Mallory in Richmond. For two weeks he traveled in the wake of war, shocked at the "scene of havoc and destruction." In Richmond he was received by President Davis and both houses of Congress, promoted to admiral, and given command of the James River Fleet. The breakdown of Confederate society was almost more than Semmes could bear. His concepts of social structure, privilege and responsibility, honesty, loyalty, were shaken. "The *Alabama* had gone to her grave none too soon. If she had not been buried with honors at war, with the howling winds of the British Channel to sing her requiem, she might soon be handed over to the exultant Yankee, to be exhibited at Boston as a trophy of war."[70] Time had stopped for the *Alabama*; now safe in her grave, she remained in her proper place in Semmes's concept of the order-of-things. It was a notion that along with his family sustained him during those last, horrible days of the war.

Semmes had to destroy his own fleet as Grant turned Lee's right flank, and flee with his officers and sailors to Danville, Virginia, where President Davis appointed him a brigadier general in the Confederate Army. At the end he was with General Joseph E. Johnston in North Carolina, and accepted that unusual military convention General William T. Sherman offered to Johnston's troops. Later, he used its particular terms to refute charges of piracy and, after a four-month imprisonment, gain a pardon from President Johnson. Forbidden from practicing law during the period of reconstruction, Semmes sustained himself and his family by teaching in an academy that later became Louisiana State University, editing a newspaper in Memphis, and lecturing on his wartime experiences. He also wrote the 833-page *Memoirs of Service Afloat during the War Between the States* (1869). He completed his life in Mobile as a lawyer, appropriately specializing in international law and maritime affairs. In 1877, short by a month of being sixty-eight years old, he died at Point Clear, in his second residence, on the east side of Mobile Bay. The citizens of Mobile declared a full day of mourning, during which cannon sounded every half-hour. After a military burial in the Catholic cemetery, Semmes had rejoined the *Alabama*.

What kind of man was Raphael Semmes? In one sense he was very ordinary, a typical product of his time. But he was also an extraordinary man because he tempered romanticism with the discipline of a naval career, and balanced nationalism with the logic of a legal mind. He accepted the decisions of the battlefield and adjusted to life-after-the-Confederacy, but he always remained convinced that the South was constitutionally right. He also managed to retain, despite the Civil War, the mind-set about the proper order-of-things that he developed during the Mexican War.

As commanding officer of the *Sumter* and the *Alabama* he gained world renown as a romantic sea raider, but he also applied imagination and resourcefulness to the unpleasant job that wartime circumstances assigned him. Whatever the task, he threw himself into it with conviction and intelligence. Imagery dominated his moods, reinforcing his aloofness as a sea captain and fostering occasional mental depressions that led him to identify with his ship so as to become one with her. If history associates "Semmes and the CSS *Alabama*," it is right; and if historians have romanticized the man and the ship, they are also right because that is the way Semmes imagined himself—as one with her on a great adventure.

FURTHER READING

The best sources for the life of Raphael Semmes are the two memoirs he wrote. *Service Afloat and Ashore during the Mexican War* (1851) and *Memoirs of Service Afloat during the War Between the States* (1869) are autobiographical accounts that are self-serving but at the same time contain some documents, relate actual facts, and, most important, reveal Semmes's acute observations and inner thoughts. When compared with the logs of the CSS *Sumter* and the CSS *Alabama*, Semmes proves to be quite accurate, and even his acidulous comments about Northern leaders and issues of the Civil War cast much light on his mental attitudes. They are indispensable in reaching an understanding of the man.

In 1864 a London house published *The Cruise of the Alabama and the Sumter* (2 vols.) based on the "Private Journals and Other Papers of Commander R. Semmes, C.S.N. and other Officers," which Semmes considered to be only "a meagre and barren record." A very helpful book on Semmes as captain of the CSS *Sumter* is *Rebel Raider* (1948), composed of extracts from Semmes's *Memoirs* with comments by Harper Allen Gosnell on points of international law and seamanship. In 1962 Indiana University Press published in its Civil War Centennial Series *The Confederate Raider Alabama*, which consisted of selections from Semmes's *Memoirs*, edited with an introduction by Philip Van Doren Stern. Stern gives a sketch of Semmes's life and attempts a characterization of him as a person and ship commander. Perhaps the most valuable and straightforward memoir of Confederate naval activity in Europe, including Semmes's role there, is James D. Bulloch's *The Secret Service of the Confederate States in*

Europe: or How the Confederate Cruisers Were Equipped (2 vols., 1883). It contains the full story of the *Alabama* from design to commissioning at sea.

Other essential sources are those in *Official Records of the Union and Confederate Navies in the War of the Rebellion*, Series I, vols. 1 and 2. They contain the logs of Semmes's ships and correspondence pertaining to the ships' cruises. Series II, vols. 1–3 contain correspondence between the Secretary of the Confederate Navy and his various agents and officers. For Semmes's personnel service record in the U.S. Navy, the listing of assignments and extended leaves is in the National Archives, Washington, Record Group 24, Records of the Bureau of Naval Personnel, rolls 4–7, and also in the National Archives, Publication #19, "Treasury Department Collection of Confederate Records."

Two of Semmes's close associates in the Confederate Navy published memoirs. John McIntosh Kell's *Recollections of a Naval Life* (1900) and Arthur Sinclair's *Two Years on the Alabama* (3rd ed., 1896), although containing errors of fact, reveal attitudes about Semmes held by his subordinates. Both authors, however, ardently admired Semmes, and their accounts are uncritical and nonanalytical.

Biographers have all based their works on Semmes's own writings, and they are equally uncritical. The two best ones are W. Adolphe Roberts, *Semmes of the Alabama* (1938), which romanticizes Semmes's life and career, and Edward Boykin, *Ghost Ship of the Confederacy: The Story of the Alabama and Her Captain, Raphael Semmes* (1957). Boykin presents his account of Semmes as "the best out-and-out adventure story of the Civil War," and that theme characterizes the whole book. The most recent biographical treatment is in Charles Grayson Summersell, *CSS Alabama: Builder, Captain, and Plans* (1985). It also contains an account of Bulloch and the construction of the *Alabama*, including the building contract, specifications, and plans, and a detailed record of the *Alabama*'s cruise.

Recently, some very good, scholarly works have appeared on Confederate naval officers who were associated with Semmes. Norman C. Delaney's *John McIntosh Kell of the Raider Alabama* (1973) is an excellent study and clarifies the relationship between Semmes and his executive officer on board both raiders. Charles Grayson Summersell, *The Cruise of the C.S.S. Sumter* (1965) reveals a good understanding of Semmes and details the full story of the ship. The same scholar had edited *The Journal of George Townley Fullam* (1973), the English master's mate on the *Alabama*, and annotated it with invaluable detail gleaned from various other sources. This book, without doubt, provides more factual detail about the cruise of the *Alabama* than any other. William Stanley Hoole wrote *Four Years in the Confederate Navy: The Career of Captain John Low on the C.S.S. Fingal, Florida, Alabama, Tuscaloosa, and Ajax* (1964). Low was fourth lieutenant in the *Alabama* until Semmes made him commanding officer of the *Tuscaloosa*. Hoole has also edited *The Logs of the C.S.S. Alabama and C.S.S. Tuscaloosa 1862–1863* (1972), with an introduction.

For an excellent study of Confederate naval activity in England, see Frank J. Merli, *Great Britain and the Confederate Navy, 1861–1865* (1970), and for the diplomatic implications of Southern naval activities, see my own *The Confederate Navy in Europe* (1983).

NOTES

1. W. Adolphe Roberts, *Semmes of the Alabama*, 282–84.

2. George W. Dalzell, *The Flight from the Flag*, 237–48.

3. United States, Department of the Navy, *Official Records of the Union and Confederate Navies in the War of the Rebellion* (hereinafter cited as *ORN*) series II, 2: 151, Mallory to Davis, first annual report, 27 February 1862. See Warren F. Spencer. *The Confederate Navy in Europe*, 1–4, for the circumstances that necessitated Mallory's naval policy.

4. The Davis proclamation is in *ORN*, II, 3: 96–97; the Lincoln proclamation is in Richardson, comp., *A Compilation of Messages and Papers of the Presidents, 1789–1897*, 7: 3215. For the early French–English consultation, see Lynn M. Case and Warren F. Spencer, *The United States and France: Civil War Diplomacy*, 50–57, and 59 for the French proclamation of neutrality. The British proclamation of neutrality is in Ephraim Douglas Adams, *Great Britain and the American Civil War*, 1: 94–95.

5. For a more detailed discussion of the European neutrality proclamations and their effects on the Confederate Navy, see Spencer, *Confederate Navy in Europe*, 8–10, 212–16.

6. For Seward's reactions to the neutrality proclamation see Norman B. Ferris, *Desperate Diplomacy*, 33–54, *passim*, and Case and Spencer, *Civil War Diplomacy*, 71–72.

7. For Semmes's early life, see Roberts, *Semmes*, 11–27 and John McIntosh Kell, *Recollections of a Naval Life*, 278–79. For his naval assignments, see Records of the Bureau of Naval Personnel, rolls 4, 5, 6, 7, 9.

8. For Semmes's naval leaves and promotion, see Records of Naval Personnel, rolls 5 and 6. For his *Poinsett* services, see Harper Allen Gosnell, *Rebel Raider*, 4–5.

9. Roberts, *Semmes*, 18.

10. These quotes are from Raphael Semmes, *Service Afloat and Ashore during the Mexican War*, 80–82. For the Mexican War and the Navy's role in it, see K. Jack Bauer, *The Mexican War, 1846–1848*, esp. Chapter 7; Robert Selph Henry, *The Story of the Mexican War*; Charles L. Dufour, *The Mexican War*, esp. Chapter 23. All of these authors cite Semmes, *Service Afloat and Ashore*, as an eyewitness account. It is difficult to discern whether Semmes reflects his ideas as of the time of the events or as of the time he wrote (1849–50). Even in the latter case, this work reflects his ideas as a result of the Mexican War, and as he held them prior to secession.

11. Semmes, *Service Afloat and Ashore*, 76.

12. Semmes's report is in *Service Afloat and Ashore*, 93–99. The critical comment is by Gosnell, *Rebel Raider*, 6.

13. Semmes, *Service Afloat and Ashore*, 158–96, *passim*. The quote is on 159, and the letters are on 159–61. Semmes's duty with the Army is also covered in Edward S. Wallace, *General William Jenkins Worth*, 136–49, *passim*. Wallace cites Semmes's work frequently, but supplements his accounts of Semmes with other original sources.

14. Semmes, *Service Afloat and Ashore*, 168, 169.

15. For the exchange of letters, see Semmes, *Service Afloat and Ashore*, 198–202.

16. Ibid., 302.

17. See in order ibid., 255, 256, 379, 281, 282–83, 379.

18. This and the following information are in Records of the Bureau of Naval Personnel, roll 7 and "Treasury Department Collection of Confederate Records."

19. "Treasury Department Collection of Confederate Records." The U.S. Government took over the lighthouses from private owners in 1787; the Lighthouse Board, established in 1852, was under the Treasury Department; the Lighthouse Service, established in 1910 in the Department of Commerce, was transferred to the U.S. Coast Guard in 1939.

20. Raphael Semmes, *Memoirs of Service Afloat during the War Between the States*, 72.

21. Ibid., 86–88. The younger Semmes later served as a major in the Confederate army.

22. For the purchasing mission of Lieutenant James North and for the travels of James D. Bulloch, see Spencer, *Confederate Navy in Europe*, 16–17, 19–20.

23. The best historical treatment of Mallory is J. T. Durkin, *Stephen R. Mallory: Confederate Navy Chief*.

24. The story of the birth, conversion, and fate of the CSS *Sumter* has been thoroughly detailed in Charles Grayson Summersell, *The Cruise of the C.S.S. Sumter*, and need not be repeated in this essay.

25. The quotes in this section all come from Semmes, *Memoirs*, 96–118, *passim*.

26. Ibid., 123–25.

27. Ibid., 121.

28. Dalzell, *Flight from the Flag*, 240.

29. Ibid., 137; Roberts, *Semmes*, Appendix II, 282–84.

30. Dalzell, *Flight from the Flag*, 247.

31. Ibid., 241, 247 (". . . the only business American bottoms got consisted of evil-smelling, offensive cargoes that neutral vessels did not want").

32. *ORN*, I, 2: 777–79.

33. For the CSS *Sumter* cruise see: Summersell, *Cruise of the C.S.S. Sumter* and Gosnell, *Rebel Raider*; for the two best secondary accounts of the CSS *Alabama*, see Norman C. Delaney, *John McIntosh Kell of the Raider Alabama* and *The Journal of George Townley Fullam*, edited and annotated by Charles G. Summersell. See also William Stanley Hoole, *The Career of Captain John Low* and W. Stanley Hoole, *The Logs of the C.S.S. Alabama and the C.S.S. Tuscaloosa 1862–1863*.

34. *Sumter* log, *ORN* I, 1: 695: Semmes, *Memoirs*, 128–29 and Kell, *Recollections*, 150.

35. Semmes, *Memoirs*, 161–62. Summersell, *Cruise of C.S.S. Sumter*, 60–71 and 80–82 details these two incidents.

36. *Alabama* log. *ORN*, I, 2: 755.

37. Semmes's actions and reasons for his decision in this famous *Martaban* case are taken from the *Alabama* log, ibid., 792 and Semmes, *Memoirs*, 717–19, where he acknowledges the cargo to have been neutral-owned, but without legal evidence. The case is presented fully in Summersell, ed., *Journal of George T. Fullam*, 166–69. The accuracy of Semmes's *Memoirs* account is confirmed in "Statement of Samuel B. Pike . . . ," 30 December 1863, Governor's Papers: Miscellaneous Letters, Public Records Office (hereafter cited as PRO), Singapore. I am indebted to my former colleague at Old Dominion University, Harold S. Wilson, for sharing with me his research notes from the Public Records Office, Singapore, and the *Straits Times*, Singapore.

38. *Straits Times*, 2 January 1864.

39. Chamber of Commerce to Captain Burn, 30 December 1863, Governor's Papers: Misc. Letters, PRO, Singapore.

40. In order, U.S. consul to U.S. State Department, 8 January 1864, R.G. 59: Despatches from the U.S. Consuls in Singapore, M-464, r. 2, National Archives; McDougal to Welles, 22 October 1863, *ORN*, I, 2: 474; U.S. Consul to Seward, 10 January 1864, R.G. 59: Despatches from the U.S. Consuls in Calcutta, M-464, n. 3, National Archives.

41. Sir James Hope to Charles M. Morris (commanding officer of the CSS *Florida*), undated, enclosed in Morris to Mallory, St. George, Bermuda, 21 June 1864, *ORN*, I, 3: 616.

42. Semmes, *Memoirs*, 304. Semmes never entered a port in England, only colonial English ports. Summersell, *Cruise of the C.S.S. Sumter*, 146–51, details Semmes's experiences while at Cadiz. See also, log of the *Sumter*, *ORN*, I, 1: 734–37 and Semmes's correspondence while at Cadiz, *ORN*, I, 1: 638–53. The Spanish did revoke the leave order, but Semmes in his fury refused to read it.

43. The letter is in *ORN*, I, 1: 640–43 and appeared in the *Times* (London) of 17 January 1862.

44. Summersell, ed., *Journal of George T. Fullam*, 54; Delaney, *John Kell*,

137–38; Semmes, *Memoirs*, 511–13.

45. Semmes, *Memoirs*, 750–51, 763–64; Delaney, *John Kell*, 174.

46. *Sumter* log, *ORN*, I, 1: 747–45; Semmes, *Memoirs*, 306–46. The best secondary account of the *Sumter* at Gibraltar and of her later fate is Summersell, *Cruise of the C.S.S. Sumter*, 152–78; see also Spencer, *Confederate Navy in Europe*, 34–37, for the *Sumter*'s role in Confederate naval affairs in Europe.

47. Semmes, *Memoirs*, 375–81. For additional information on activities of Bulloch and North, see Spencer, *Confederate Navy in Europe*.

48. Semmes, *Memoirs*, 351–53. For Confederate confusion concerning *Alabama* command assignment, see Spencer, *Confederate Navy in Europe*, 48–55, and for the ship's preparation and sailing, 55–58. For an evaluation of Semmes's officer roster, see ibid., 58–60. Spencer's account is based largely on James D. Bulloch, *The Secret Service of the Confederate States in Europe: or How the Confederate Cruisers were Equipped* (2 vols.), Frank J. Merli, *Great Britain and the Confederate Navy*, and various documents in *ORN*, I, 1 and *ORN*, II, 2.

49. Spencer, *The Confederate Navy in Europe*, 8–10, 212–16 and *passim*.

50. Bulloch to Mallory, 21 July 1862, *ORN* II, 2: 336; Arthur Sinclair, *Two Years on the Alabama*, 127.

51. Semmes, *Memoirs*, 402–5. I use Semmes's dimensions of the ship, which are given in round figures. It is through his eyes that we must meet the *Alabama*.

52. Ibid., 408–13.

53. Bulloch's report to Mallory, *ORN* I, 1: 777 and Semmes, *Memoirs*, 413.

54. Summersell, ed., *Journal of George T. Fullam*, Appendix, 197–98.

55. The battle is described by Lieutenant Commander N. G. Blake, U.S.N., in his report to Secretary Welles, *ORN*, I, 2; 19–21; Semmes's first-hand account is in ibid., 721–22, and his later one in his *Memoirs*, 545–52. The two captains differed on the distance between the ships during the battle, Semmes giving a range of 200 to 500 yards, while Blake gave 25 to 100 yards. A sailor from the *Hatteras* confirmed Blake's figures so I have used the shorter distance.

56. *ORN*, I, 2: 753, 764.

57. Ibid., 765–67.

58. These and subsequent quotations are from Semmes, *Memoirs*, in order, 748, 749–50 and 746, 756, 765.

59. Semmes to Samuel Barron, Commodore, C.S.N., 13 June 1864, *ORN*, I, 3: 651; Barron to Semmes, draft, 14 June 1864, Whittle Papers, Norfolk Public Library, folder X, no. 7. The commodore had already selected Commander Thomas J. Page to succeed Semmes.

60. Spencer, *Confederate Navy in Europe*, 191–92.

61. Kell, *Recollections*, 245. In 1883, Kell in a newspaper report was quoted as saying that Semmes had told him: "I have sent for you to discuss the

advisability of fighting the *Kearsarge*" [Alfred I. Branham, reporter, reprinted (1930) in booklet form as '*290*' *Story of the Sinking of the Alabama*]. Either version could be correct although Semmes was not in the habit of *discussing* ship operations with the officers.

62. Sinclair, *Two Years*, 275–76.

63. The best accounts remain those by participants and by Bulloch. Captain Semmes rendered an impressionistic report, *ORN*, I, 3: 649–51: and an even more subjective account in his *Memoirs*, 751–65; Captain Winslow's reports were matter-of-fact, *ORN*, I, 3: 59–82, especially 79–81; Lieutenant Arthur Sinclair of the *Alabama*, writing almost thirty years after Semmes, gave a subjective yet amazingly honest account in Sinclair, *Two Years*, 259–91; Commander Bulloch, writing with the aid of documents including the two captain's reports, presented an analytical and balanced account, *Secret Service*, 1: 277–93. For accounts of eyewitnesses, see George T. Sinclair to Barron, Cherbourg, 20 June 1864, Whittle Papers, folder X, no. 9, and William M. Leary, Jr., "The Alabama vs. the *Kearsarge*," *American Neptune* 29, no. 3 (1969), 167–68 ff. Excellent illustrations are in Norman C. Delaney, "Showdown at Cherbourg," *Civil War Times Illustrated* 15, no. 3 (June 1976), 16–21. The best secondary accounts are Delaney, *John Kell*, 164–68 and Summersell, ed., *Journal of George T. Fullam*, 190–96. Other good secondary accounts are Roberts, *Semmes*, 195–211, and Edward Boykin, *Ghost Ship of the Confederacy. The Story of the Alabama and Her Captain, Raphael Semmes*, 344–84. For the diplomacy of the pre- and postbattle days, see Case and Spencer, *Civil War Diplomacy*, 509–15.

64. Delaney, *John Kell*, 170, citing a newspaper report of the battle.

65. Bulloch, *Secret Service*, 1: 279.

66. Semmes, *Memoirs*, 763.

67. Ibid.

68. In order: Semmes to Barron, 21 June 1864, *ORN*, I, 3: 650; Semmes to Slidell, 1 July 1864 and to Barron, 5 July 1864, ibid., 663, 664; Semmes, *Memoirs*, 754, 761, 762.

69. The story of the journey is based on Semmes, *Memoirs*, 790–98.

70. Ibid., 801.

DAVID DIXON PORTER: FIGHTING SAILOR

BY TAMARA MOSER MELIA

David Dixon Porter lived in the shadow of his famous father, Commodore David Porter, an adventurous, independent officer, whose annhilation of the British whaling fleet in the War of 1812 made him both a popular national hero and the most successful member of an old naval family. Commodore Porter, who had gone to sea with his own father at an early age, wanted sons to carry on the family tradition. His foster son, David G. Farragut, won the Navy's first admiralcy. Of the commodore's six natural sons, David Dixon, neither the eldest nor his father's favorite, became the second admiral of the Navy, both because of his father and despite him. From the first, he had to struggle to be noticed.

David Dixon, born while his father sailed the Pacific in the *Essex*, retained an idealized memory of his childhood. Commodore Porter was his greatest hero. Stimulated by his father's war stories and constantly aware of his heritage, Porter lived secure in the childlike belief that his father, a member of the Board of Navy Commissioners, literally ran the Navy. The commodore returned to sea duty in the West Indies in 1823, and on one cruise, in 1824, took along the entire family. David Dixon's first voyage lasted only a few months. He was away at school when, at Fajardo, Puerto Rico, Commodore Porter overstepped his authority by demanding an apology for disrespect to an American warship, was court-martialed, and received a six-month suspension. Incensed, David Porter resigned his commission and entered the service of the Mexican Navy, taking with him David Dixon, age twelve; his favorite son, Thomas, age ten; and a nephew.

David Dixon watched his father sternly mold the Mexican seamen into a fighting unit and saw more action in a few months with the Mexican Navy than in the next thirty-five years. On board his cousin David H. Porter's ship the *Guerrero*, in close combat with the Spanish frigate *Lealtad*, David Dixon received his first war wound, and he was captured and imprisoned in Havana

227

David Dixon Porter. Photograph taken circa 1863. *Courtesy of the Naval Historical Center.*

Harbor. When paroled, he returned to the United States where his maternal grandfather, Congressman William Anderson, wrangled him a midshipman's appointment in the U.S. Navy. His brother Thomas died in Mexico, and his other brothers distanced themselves from their father. Only David Dixon pleased his father, who, by the time of his death in 1843, found life and family disappointing. David Dixon Porter fought for naval distinction to earn his father's love and to restore his father's tarnished image.[1]

Porter's midshipman career was fairly routine. His father had taught him tradition, discipline, and seamanship; the Navy, technical skills and leadership. Porter became an expert channel surveyor and pilot in the Coast Survey and the Hydrography Department. He learned quickly and became known as a man who thought on his feet and who could be trusted with special operations. Detached to State Department service, he secretly surveyed Santo Domingo to determine its suitability as a naval base.

Porter participated in several major naval engagements of the Mexican War. His operational experiences, although totaling only a few hours of battle, demonstrated his inventiveness and courage. He planned and helped execute the naval bombardment on the defenses of Vera Cruz and led a sailors' charge on the fort at Tabasco, capturing the works and earning command of his first steamship, the *Spitfire*. After the war, Porter sought to captain a modern steamer, but the peacetime Navy could afford only sail craft, and he was reassigned to the Coast Survey. Like many other young officers, Porter, anticipating a lifetime as lieutenant with little chance of advancement in rank or duty, chose a safe, attractive alternative: he obtained leave and captained mail vessels between New York and San Francisco, gaining valuable experience commanding large ocean steamships. On board the *Panama*, *Georgia*, and *Crescent City*, Porter tried to instill naval discipline into civilian crews. Although he was a formalist like his father, Porter's disciplinary methods were less punitive than paternal. He also gained popular notice by nearly re-creating his father's Fajardo incident when, at Havana in 1852, he refused to accept the closure of the port to his mail vessel, almost provoking war between the United States and Spain.

Porter soon gained a reputation for speed, even at the expense of his mail route. He set new world records in the remarkable *Golden Age*, cutting the voyage from England to Australia by a third, and the Melbourne–Sydney run in half. Porter's Australian adventures netted him something more valuable than money and experience: fame made him a national figure and raised him from the ranks of "one of the Porters." He became known in his own right for his energy, perseverance, and clever direction of "unusual enterprises."[2]

Porter returned to naval duty in the spring of 1855 to command the storeship *Supply*, ferrying camels from the Mediterranean to Texas for the War Department, and later served as executive officer of the Portsmouth, New Hampshire, Navy Yard. After three years' administration of inert peacetime shipbuilding, he negotiated for a return to civilian duty. At the age of forty-seven, having spent twenty years as a lieutenant, Porter was fully aware that his childhood heroes had made their careers at nearly half his age. As he debated between captaining another mail vessel or a Coast Survey schooner, Abraham Lincoln won the presidency, and the Southern states began to secede. Members of the Navy Department eyed each other with distrust as more Southern ports fell into Confederate hands, and officers resigned to go south.

Porter seized the moment. Along with his neighbor, Army Captain Montgomery C. Meigs, Porter formulated plans to reinforce Fort Pickens and recapture Pensacola, Florida. Secretary of State William H. Seward took their plans to the President. Lincoln agreed that Pickens, like Fort Sumter, should be saved if at all possible, and he allowed Porter and Meigs to write their own orders and attempt the mission without the knowledge of their superiors. In addition, Porter wrote a cryptic order over Lincoln's signature attempting to restructure civilian control of naval policy by effectively reorganizing personnel detailing within the Navy Department.[3]

Porter charged off to New York and quickly fitted out his ship, the *Powhatan*. The President had second thoughts and had Secretary of the Navy Gideon Welles order Porter to give up the *Powhatan* to her assigned duty with Gustavus V. Fox's expedition to relieve Sumter, but neither Porter nor Meigs was willing to let his chance for action and advancement go by. Proclaiming Welles's telegram "bogus," they stalled by wiring Seward to confirm the order while they went to sea. By the time Seward's terse reply reached Porter, he had left the harbor and would not put back. Rationalizing that presidential orders outweighed cabinet ones, he politely refused to comply. With his experience of short wars and stalled promotions, this chance, he feared, might be his only one.[4]

Porter steamed toward Pensacola in an unsound ship with an untrained crew. Organizing en route, he drilled the men at the guns and disguised the ship as a mail steamer. Arriving near Pickens on 17 April 1861, Porter prepared to steam straight in and retake Pensacola by surprise, but Meigs stopped him. The Army was unwilling to provoke a battle before ensuring their own invulnerability, and the commanders wavered at disobeying presidential orders calling for strictly defensive operations. Frustrated, Porter raged up and down the harbor, surveyed the bay for shelling positions, and planned a night attack at the Army's convenience. It never happened. The Union Army retained Fort Pickens and gave up any attempt to retake Pensacola, a decision that Porter later called "the great disappointment of my life."[5]

The *Powhatan* incident had several repercussions. Lincoln learned to confide in his cabinet officers, Seward to keep his hands off naval affairs, and Welles to watch Porter. Although Lincoln assumed all responsibility for the diversion of the *Powhatan* from Sumter, Welles never forgave Porter. He did recognize, however, that in Porter he had an asset, a brash, ambitious officer who would prove aggressive in battle. As for Porter, his inability to control events in Pensacola Harbor taught him that he must command more than a ship to effect a victory; the single-ship actions of his father's day would not suffice. Subsequent ineffectual blockading duty at the mouth of the Mississippi convinced him of the need to capture New Orleans.

The campaign for New Orleans was both a victory and a defeat for Porter, who overconfidently projected that a fleet of boats firing properly aimed army mortars could reduce the strong forts below within forty-eight hours, allowing ships to run up and capture the city. The Union desperately needed a victory in the spring of 1862, particularly at New Orleans. Porter recommended that his foster brother Farragut lead the expedition. Porter, who received independent command of the mortar flotilla over the heads of senior officers, did not impress the rest of Farragut's command, who looked down on his ragtag fleet and his use of merchant marine captains. Farragut himself had almost no faith in the mortar fleet, but accepted it along with the assignment.[6]

Despite scientific placement of the mortars and highly accurate fire, the forts withstood six days of heavy bombardment. Farragut changed strategy and ran past the forts at night. Porter covered the attempt with mortar fire and received the forts' surrender three days after Farragut took New Orleans. The mortar boats failed to destroy the forts, but Porter's plan to capture New Orleans succeeded by adaption. The mortars kept Confederate gunners under cover, helped the fleet to pass the forts, and disabled several of the enemy's best guns. More important, the psychological effect of Porter's relentless attack caused the men in Fort Jackson to mutiny.[7] After the surrender, the forts were found to be as strong as ever; Porter won by perseverance. Lincoln recommended Porter for the thanks of Congress, both as a member of Farragut's command, and separately, for "distinguished services in the conception and preparation of the means used for the capture of the Forts below New Orleans, and for highly meritorious conduct in the management of the Mortar Flotilla . . . ."[8]

Following up the victory proved more difficult. Porter pushed for an attack on Mobile Bay, but the Navy Department ordered the fleet to Vicksburg. The city's defending river guns were placed high on terraces, and Porter, minus his survey ship, had to aim his mortars by trial and error. It proved another futile effort. Farragut's fleet successfully ran the Vicksburg batteries, but several vessels were badly damaged, and Porter's flotilla suffered heavy casualties covering him. Low water and low morale led to dissension, as Farragut's captains and Army Major General Benjamin F. Butler warred with Porter over credit for the New Orleans expedition. Soon Porter wanted release from the Gulf Squadron so badly, he swore he would even prefer "to serve any where else in a yawl boat."[9]

As politics played an increasing role in the war effort, Porter's distaste for civilian meddling grew. He loathed political generals like Butler, yet used politics to advance his own career. He cultivated congressmen and developed close ties in the Navy Department with Assistant Secretary Fox, a trusted member of the Lincoln administration. When he angered Welles with outspoken criticism of the Union high command, the Secretary reassigned him to obscurity inspecting gunboats under construction at Cincinnati. Faced with exile, Porter the politician went over his superior's head to Lincoln.

Lincoln twice before had given Porter major commands beyond his rank, the *Powhatan* and the mortar flotilla, with only partial success. Still, Porter had qualities Lincoln could use. His persuasiveness and determination, along with Fox's influence, convinced Lincoln that Porter was exactly the fighter he needed, for he gave him command of the Mississippi Squadron, the fleet above Vicksburg. Welles made the assignment grudgingly, noting that recklessness and energy were Porter's primary qualifications. [10]

Porter's new assignment had its good and bad points. Given the temporary and local rank of acting rear admiral, he controlled nearly all the naval forces on the upper Mississippi, truly a partner with Farragut this time. Porter saw his elevation to rank and command over the heads of some eighty senior officers as retribution for his father's suspension. [11] To uphold his father's image, and to attain permanent rank, Porter had to succeed on the Mississippi. But Porter's orders required him to cooperate in the capture of Vicksburg with Major General John A. McClernand, a distinctly political general with whom few people got along. The upper Mississippi was, moreover, the dumping ground for unpredictable commanders: Porter's disreputable elder brother, William, was there, with a ship he named the *Essex* in memory of their father.

With funds, authority, and amenable subordinates, Porter reorganized his command and worked quickly to bring the fleet up to the Navy's standards. Hearing nothing from McClernand, recruiting in Illinois, Porter offered his services to Major Generals Ulysses S. Grant and William T. Sherman. Almost immediate affinity marked their relations. [12] All three were professionals in a war of volunteers, disliking civilian interference, and their personalities, although distinctly different, meshed. Grant, the taciturn commander, worked well with Sherman, whose fiery, outspoken leadership complemented Grant's more methodical style. Porter and Sherman were of the same mold: emotional, temperamental fighters, considered brilliant yet difficult; both unrelentingly energetic, they were impatient with slower men.

Nevertheless, their combination did not thrive from the start. Porter and Sherman assaulted the bluffs north of Vicksburg near Chickasaw Bayou. The loss of Grant's supply line kept him from supporting Sherman, whose defeat in December 1862 proved that route to Vicksburg impossible. Porter, energetically supporting Sherman's advance and worrying Confederate troops in the northern rivers, could do little more to effect a victory. McClernand's arrival to command after the battle did not help.

McClernand brought to the field raw troops, a political appointment, a drive for personal fame, and a new bride. Porter disliked McClernand, but agreed to support him in capturing Arkansas Post, where Sherman had planned to secure their supply line and achieve a victory. So determined was Porter to win that, when McClernand's green troops left the post's Fort Hindman in retreat, Porter boarded troops and prepared to take the fort himself. The surrender of the fort to Porter earned him Lincoln's gratitude and another vote of thanks from Congress. [13] Grant soon supplanted McClernand on the river and sought other routes through the swollen wintry swamps to Vicksburg.

In an effort to circumvent the batteries at Vicksburg, Grant's army dug canals while Porter and Sherman unsuccessfully attempted to turn the northern flank of Vicksburg at Yazoo Pass and Steele's Bayou. While Porter was upriver, two important vessels were captured by Confederates. Having nothing to send down to save them, Porter and his men rigged up a dummy monitor from an old barge and pork barrels. As it floated by in the dark, the monster frightened Vicksburg, stampeding the Confederates into destroying the *Indianola* to prevent recapture. The effect of this ruse delighted Porter, and he later used another dummy monitor to draw fire at Wilmington, North Carolina. The Navy Department fully appreciated Porter's often unusual attempts to recover something from every loss.[14]

On 16 April 1863, Porter, under cover of darkness, ran part of his fleet safely past the Vicksburg batteries. While Sherman feinted north to Haynes' Bluff, Porter bombarded Grand Gulf and covered Grant's crossing at Bruinsburg. With three days' rations and no supply line, Grant set out overland to take Vicksburg. Porter, eager for action, destroyed the abandoned Grand Gulf, then assisted Farragut in a run up the Confederate supply line of Red River, capturing Fort De Russy and Alexandria, Louisiana. Grant and Porter opened a concentrated attack on Vicksburg on 22 May before settling into a siege. Porter maintained Grant's supply line, fired steadily on the city, fought guerrillas, and kept communications open to Washington. His passage of the Vicksburg batteries signaled the beginning of the end for the South. Confederate agents in London credited Porter with depressing their loan rate overseas. Porter's achievement and the anticipated fall of Vicksburg dominated all conversation in Washington, with most observers believing that success at Vicksburg would decide the war.[15] All Porter had to do for his coveted promotion was to support Grant, but he was too much of a fighter to wait patiently.

Within six weeks, Porter's forces captured fourteen Confederate forts above Vicksburg, destroyed over two million dollars' worth of Confederate naval stores and ships building on the Yazoo, and assisted in demoralizing Vicksburg with desertion propaganda and constant shelling. The city surrendered on 4 July 1863, and Porter immediately followed up the victory with a series of raids on inland waterways to Yazoo City, and up the Red and White rivers. Lincoln shared the spoils of victory with those most responsible, promoting Porter to permanent rear admiral to date from the fall of Vicksburg.[16]

Porter's last major campaign in the west, up the Red River in the spring of 1864, was the fiasco he expected it to be.[17] Ordered to command the naval arm of the attack toward Shreveport, Louisiana, in cooperation with Major General Nathaniel P. Banks, Porter doubted that the river would provide sufficient draft for his vessels and that he would want to attempt operations with another

Battle of Vicksburg. On the night of 16 April 1863 Porter led his Mississippi Squadron on a dash past Confederate guns at Vicksburg. Currier & Ives lithograph. *From a private collection.*

political general. He was right on both counts. There was little coordination between the two commands. When Banks finally arrived at the rendezvous point over a week late, he found Porter and the Navy chasing prize cotton on the river. Once operations began, Porter sent his largest vessel upriver first, and she grounded, further delaying cooperation. The water fell rapidly, and Banks abandoned the Navy after his repulse at Sabine Crossroads.

Porter's fleet had to fight its way downriver, but it was not the sort of fight he liked. Confederates with artillery ambushed the unprotected naval vessels. Porter got his fleet safely down to Alexandria, only to be stranded above the city in less than four feet of water. Without the support of regular army officers and an ingenious army dam to float the boats over the bar, Porter would have been unable to extricate his command. The Army, the Navy, and his own men condemned Banks for his incompetency, preserving Porter's reputation despite his costly errors of judgment.[18]

Porter, ordered from one disaster to another, had no time to make up for this defeat. Welles brought him east to command the North Atlantic Blockading Squadron off North Carolina, where the only remaining port supplying General Robert E. Lee's army remained open at Wilmington. Porter used every stratagem he had learned in the war to tighten the blockade. He built up a powerful naval force, tightened cordon lines, and decoyed in two million dollars' worth of prizes, but only the capture of strategic Fort Fisher would close the port. Porter asked Grant for troops, and he agreed; but when the Army finally appeared, Butler led it. Porter, livid, treated Butler cordially, while privately damning Grant unfairly for sending the politician.[19]

Porter's and Butler's attack on Fort Fisher in December 1864 failed primarily because of distrust between the two commanders. Butler planned to destroy the fort by exploding an old ship loaded with gunpowder. Neither naval nor army engineers believed it would work, but Butler pressed, and Porter acquiesced. Butler kept most of his plans secret, leading to a long string of misunderstandings. The explosion failed, as expected. Porter bombarded the fort to cover Butler's landing, but Butler chose not to assault, as Porter hoped he would, or to entrench, as Grant ordered him to, but instead retreated, leaving behind several hundred men. Lincoln relieved Butler of command, and Brevet Major General Alfred H. Terry replaced him in a second attempt at the fort.

The stakes were high. Lee believed that Union capture of Forts Fisher and Caswell would force the evacuation of Richmond. A second failure would sustain Butler. As insurance, in case the Army should fail him again, Porter drilled a landing party of 1,600 sailors and 400 marines to storm the fort. Porter and Terry cooperated fully. Between the two men there were no secrets, and their determination effected a true combination.[20]

The attack of the naval landing party failed, but it diverted the fort's defenders from the army landing. Seven difficult hours later, the fort surren-

On board the USS *Malvern*. Admiral Porter as commander of the North Atlantic Blockading Squadron with his staff in Hampton Roads, December 1864. Photograph by Matthew Brady. *Courtesy of the Naval Historical Center.*

dered to Terry. The Confederates, forced to evacuate Caswell, fell back on Wilmington; pursued by Porter and Terry, they abandoned the last port in the Confederacy in January 1865. There was little left for the Navy to do. Porter went up the James River to Grant's headquarters at City Point, where his final war duties included attending strategy conferences on board the *River Queen* with Lincoln, Grant, and Sherman, and escorting the President around captured Petersburg and Richmond.

Most of Porter's fame stems from his actions in combined operations. While he was strategically clearsighted, his tactical plans as first conceived rarely worked. Luckily, he directed most maneuvers with enough personal autonomy to change course halfway and push the object through to success, at times by sheer force of will. Porter's strength was in special operations, and his fighting personality accentuated his ability to follow up nearly every setback with a victory.

Porter's campaigns depended on army operations for success. At Chickasaw Bayou and the Yazoo Pass expedition, complete military cooperation would not overcome the barriers of geography, weather, and Confederate strength. Lack of coordination of forces up the Red River and in the first attack on Fort Fisher doomed the efforts from the start. Porter's successes, notably at Arkansas Post, Vicksburg, and the second attempt at Fort Fisher, were due in no small part to the personalities of the commanders involved. Porter worked well with those who fought, poorly with those who hesitated.

The war made Porter both famous and controversial. His ambition, hunger for publicity and prize money, and swift advancement offended many he had surpassed. Peace brought a new set of problems for Gideon Welles, among them the question of what to do with Porter. He could not be sent to sea: his oft-stated belief that those countries that had supported the Confederacy should pay, particularly Great Britain, might lead him to provoke a foreign war. Porter never made any secret of his wish to command the U.S. Naval Academy and "get the right set of officers into the Navy."[21] His wide fame and belief in strong discipline could only help the troubled institution, which, although removed north, had barely survived the war intact.

The wartime Naval Academy took little notice of changing technology and encouraged no physical activities. Drinking sprees were the prime extracurricular recreation, and an antiquated demerit system proved ineffectual in controlling student abuses. The academy was, in fact, little more than a secondary school, and taught midshipmen little they could use to command ships.[22] Porter believed the academy's purpose was to train officers for naval war. Installed as superintendent in 1865, he imprinted the academy with his own philosophy of practicality and professionalism, and was determined to make it the rival of West Point, whose graduates had impressed him with just those qualities.[23]

Porter began his tenure by strictly enforcing discipline. Common infractions included hazing, drinking, and taking "French leave," none of which Porter took lightly. "The first duty of an officer," he taught, "is to obey."[24] He proved to the midshipmen that he was serious. On one day in October 1865, Porter issued orders requiring regular small arm drills, dress parades, an oath of allegiance, and an eight-year service obligation. Further, he repealed all upperclass privileges for those forced to repeat a year, and organized recreation times, cleverly keyed to begin as soon as drill obligations were properly completed. Porter supplemented the demerit system with practical punishments, as at West Point, with guard duty and drill, assigned by severity of the offense, used to enforce discipline.[25]

Before Porter's arrival, few extracurricular activities were organized to keep midshipmen out of trouble. Porter realistically decided that sports would give the young men an outlet for their frustrations. He built a gymnasium and especially encouraged fencing, boxing, bowling, shooting, and baseball. One never knew when Superintendent Porter might enter the ring to box the first classmen, and he especially hated losing a game of baseball. Porter encouraged competition within the academy and took his midshipmen to West Point for intercollegiate athletic trials.[26]

Porter also insisted on an honor system "to send honorable men from this institution into the Navy."[27] He designed uniforms, fostered music and drama clubs, invited midshipmen to test their gentlemanly behavior at tea, and led regular dancing parties. Lying and drinking earned his severest reproof, and he worked to close Annapolis brothels. He exhorted the midshipmen to act like officers and not "common sailors." Unashamedly elitist, Porter even recommended denying admission to candidates who were cross-eyed, "common looking," or too old. If he interfered with every aspect of the midshipmen's private lives, at least he stood by them, occasionally directing a redress in grades or accepting an apology in lieu of punishment.[28]

Porter redesigned the academy curriculum, emphasizing lectures over textbooks and requiring courses in seamanship, gunnery, naval construction, practical navigation, and steam engineering. Midshipmen learned to operate fully rigged ship models, drill with mortars, run and repair steam engines, strip sails on ships in record time, and give exhibitions of steam tactics and seamanship. He enlarged the department of steam engineering with a new building housing a working engine and several boilers, and required three years of courses and a practical knowledge of steam engines of each graduate.

Porter successfully dabbled in politics to keep the academy afloat. Seeking support for a growing school during intense fiscal retrenchment, Porter invited politicians to review dress parades and exhibitions of naval tactics, never failing to publicize the academy or impress visitors. As a result of his political influence and the growing prestige of the academy under his direction, appropriations increased despite national budget cuts. With ideological renewal, congressional appropriations, and stringent economy, Porter physically rebuilt the academy, spending $225,000 in buildings and alterations and purchasing over 130 acres of adjacent land.[29]

Despite Porter's fame as an operational commander, his most enduring legacy was his whole philosophy of naval discipline and leadership, embedded in the academy and learned, he would say, from his father. By strictly charging the midshipmen themselves with responsibility for their actions and the future of their institution, he made them aware of their elite status as naval leaders. Although Porter may indeed have "set the tone" for the modern-day Naval Academy, he did so by pinning that obligation on the midshipmen themselves, particularly upon the first class.[30]

Porter restored pride to the academy. Grant and Sherman convinced him by their own examples that despite West Point's reputation as the premier engineering school in America, it did not necessarily turn out only engineers and theoreticians, but men trained in the basics of the military profession: discipline, duty, honor, obedience, command—principles transcending service divisions. Such basic officer training also suited Porter's daily expectations of foreign war.

Americans in peacetime have rarely supported a standing army or navy; the aftermath of the Civil War was no exception. Four years of expensive warfare

The U.S. Naval Academy. This photograph was taken from the cupola of the New Quarters during Porter's superintendency. From the left in the foreground are the chemistry, physics, and steam buildings, which were built in 1866. In the river, from left are the USS *Tonawanda,* the USS *Dale,* and the USS *Santee. Courtesy of the Naval Historical Center.*

put the United States ahead of its contemporaries in technology. Much of the rest of the world took America's advances and improved upon them. Naval vessels of the war period were soon outdated, and few Americans supported their replacement. The naval stagnation following the Civil War probably could not have been avoided short of the war Porter anticipated. And Americans, if anything, were sick of war, believing peace to be permanent.

The Army fared better than the Navy in the postwar world. Battlefield brevet and volunteer rankings faded away with war's end, leaving in the service only those who had earned regular army promotions. The Army also had posts to maintain in the South and Indians to fight in the West. Sherman, as lieutenant general and general, retained some active control over operations. Porter had no such power in his corresponding roles as vice admiral and admiral. With no offensive mission, the Navy had no role for ranking officers.

Congressmen, unwilling to fund advanced naval technology in peace, got only what they paid for—the U.S. Navy of their fathers, not that of their sons. Demobilization forced the Navy into a limited world mission until the 1890s, a rational approach to economic reality. Congress wanted a floating police force and saw no need to compete with European technology. Naval officers disagreed over the process of inevitable retrenchment, seeking to protect their own definitions of a peacetime navy.[31]

Welles, proud of his success in directing the naval war, did not take kindly to any suggestions to share power in peace. Welles's burgeoning naval bureaucracy greatly expanded the powers of the Navy's bureau system. His raises in relative rankings and prerogatives for staff officers in support positions and his recall of retired officers at high rank bloated the officer class. Postwar retrenchment hit ranking line officers hardest, or so they perceived. With their ships laid up and promotion stagnant, staff officers and the bureau system, not Welles, bore the brunt of line officers' blame. The line/staff controversy, renewed and confused by technological issues, and exacerbated by Welles's intransigence, erupted into war within the Navy. Behind the battles lay the real issue: who should control the Navy?

Porter's role in the naval controversies created his image as an operational progressive and a technological reactionary, while his fighting personality defined his perception of the naval establishment. Porter believed the Navy's mission was war, and preparation for future wars was its peacetime occupation. Offensive purpose defined his view of naval administration, which he believed should remain strictly in the hands of experienced operational officers. "The Navy," he declared, "will be dead for many years to come unless we have another war . . . ."[32]

Technology, particularly steam engineering, was an important side issue in the controversy over control of the Navy. Neither Congress nor the American public would pay for advanced military technology. Between 1865 and 1869 the Navy's budget declined 84 percent. A great portion of that budget went to the Bureau of Steam Engineering, where Benjamin Franklin Isherwood still spent money at wartime levels.[33] Isherwood further offended line officers by seemingly placing the interests of machines over those of men. The attacks of Porter and the line officers on the status quo reflected the real anxieties of men who feared replacement by technology or by men of different abilities.

Porter did not hate engineers; he hated theoreticians, impractical, inflexible, wasteful men who built vessels but never sailed them—who understood machines, but could not make them run. Isherwood's prize ship, the *Wampanoag*, was Porter's pet peeve, the symbol of technological inefficiency—the fastest ship in the world, built at an exorbitant cost, with insufficient room to house the men needed to run her, let alone those needed for naval maneuvers. That Isherwood, entrenched in the bureau, had sufficient power to control the direction of naval shipbuilding policy reaffirmed Porter's belief that the bureau system was faulty. But despite Porter's lengthy campaign to remove Isherwood and restore line supremacy, the two men remained friends, supporting each other professionally in later years.[34] Porter never hated Isherwood; his attacks were a means to an end. Porter wanted to revive and lead his father's old Navy Board and made several unsuccessful attempts to have Congress restore it. His insistence on the importance of line officers controlling the Navy had led him to replace staff with line officers in teaching positions at the academy.

In 1869, when Grant assumed the presidency, he appointed Adolph E. Borie as Secretary of the Navy, assigning Porter to special duty as his assistant, a rudimentary chief of naval operations. Porter took personal control of the Navy Department at the most visible levels and immediately issued a blizzard of sweeping general orders, twelve in one day, over Borie's signature. He reduced staff prerogatives and defined those of the line, redesigning uniforms to reflect the staff's lower status and ranking. Further orders limited the power of the bureaus to internal matters, consolidated squadrons, renamed vessels, and organized a line board of ship examiners. Porter's most controversial orders were among his last. He delayed reducing the relative rankings of the staff officers to pre-Welles levels until a legal basis for it could be found. His orders requiring full sail power in all naval ships and strictly limiting the use of coal, along with the condemnation of Isherwood's ships by a board of line officers, were the parting shots of Porter's short administration.[35]

Behind Porter's attempted reforms of 1869 lay the threat of war with Great Britain. American diplomats were then negotiating reparations due the United States for Britain's assistance to the Confederacy. Porter wanted war, especially with Great Britain, and he wanted a navy prepared for war. At the Naval Academy he prepared men for command and for war; in the department he attempted to do the same. He endeavored to restore unity to a fragmented command structure, returning control to the Secretary and removing it from the bureaus. The Secretary, or his assistant, Porter, would command the naval forces in any coming war. Unfortunately for Porter, his war did not materialize. His reputation was the major casualty of his own administration.

Porter knew the U.S. Navy could not match the Royal Navy, but he insisted on strengthening all natural advantages. General Orders 128 and 131 did no more than adopt international naval policies. British regulations requiring sails and restricting coal use were far harsher than Porter's—coal was expensive, and engines were inefficient in 1869. In declaring steam auxiliary to full sail power, Porter capitalized on the natural resources of men and wind, while directly overturning Welles's emphasis on steam over sails. Porter's orders prescribed readiness and constant exercise. He wanted the Navy to be ready for immediate action with maximum efficiency. A master at improvising, Porter convinced Congress to fund Naval Academy expansion through a combination of politics, prestige, and stringent recycling. He hoped, by using similar tactics, to convince Congress to fund a real naval fighting force.

Borie never wanted to run the Navy and was happy to sign over full authority to Porter, who issued orders in Borie's name until the furor over Porter's arbitrariness, impatience, and highhandedness made Borie's life miserable. After three months Borie resigned, and Grant replaced him with George Robeson, who eased Porter from his position of power. Within one year Porter's influence had so declined that he claimed he did not enter the Navy Department's headquarters more than four times between 1870 and 1876.[36]

Despite strong political opposition, Porter, promoted to admiral in 1870, remained on active duty until his death in 1891. In those last twenty-one years he wrote regular advisory reports, sat on inspection boards, and worked to develop naval higher education. The few duties he had were unimportant, and his opinions were generally ignored. Unhappy with semi-retirement, he still sought to influence naval policy and continued to send in an unwanted yearly report.[37] Despite Porter's advocacy of a stronger coastal defense, he retained his vision of offensive naval purpose. His reports, in the form of incomplete, repetitive letters addressed to successive secretaries, sought immediate, effective answers to contemporary problems. Read as statements of policy, they seem foolish today; in the context of their intent, they are extremely revealing.

Porter, the product of a maritime nation, lived in an emerging industrial age. The Civil War destroyed America's commercial shipping industry while it strengthened the British carrying trade. The United States failed to recover its oceanic trade or its maritime reserve in Porter's lifetime. From 1870 until 1889, Porter fought a losing battle to restore U.S. maritime eminence, enhancing his image as a reactionary against industrialization. He appreciated new technology but thought the training of men as important as the building of ships. Nothing in Porter's experience prepared him for an age when the needs of ships would outweigh those of men.

Machine dominance was by no means certain until after his death. Science and technology advanced slowly, and not until 1880 were the first and second laws of thermodynamics usable in creating efficient steam engines. By 1884, steam predominated, leading the Navy to reduce sail power, and by 1889 to begin establishing the international fuel depots Porter believed were necessary for a steam navy. Only as technology and foreign policy changed did Porter's advocacy of coastal defense and commerce raiding appear outdated; even Alfred Thayer Mahan supported such a program in 1885. Until instant obsolescence of naval vessels was controlled, the Navy remained transitional.[38]

What Porter advocated was naval diversification. He wanted improved forts, rams and monitors for defense, fast commerce raiders to cripple future enemy shipping, advanced submarine torpedo-firing boats for both offense and defense, and, ultimately, steel ships.[39] He opposed rebuilding the Navy around only one type of ship. Rather than returning the Navy to the age of sail, he sought to keep it flexible, advocating constant exercise of existing ships and squadrons, development of new vessels, education of all naval personnel, modernization of armament, and subsidization of a new merchant marine. The 1874 sea trials in the West Indies following the *Virginius* crisis forced Porter into a more defensive position, convincing him that what little navy Congress allowed would be destroyed in the inevitable war; but by 1881 he spoke of planning "a navy for *home defense*, but, of course, in time of war we should not be willing to rest quietly guarding our coast."[40]

On the eve of the "New Navy," Porter reargued diversity, defense, and dedication, and reasserted the necessity of rebuilding America's lost prestige as a maritime nation. He urged officers to exchange ideas about the new types of strategy and tactics needed for the battles of the future at the struggling Naval War College. Porter decried Congress's attempts to rebuild the Navy overnight with a quote from Mirabeau expressing his own naval philosophy: "You cannot have a navy without sailors, and sailors are made through the dangers of the deep, from father to son, until their home is on the wave. You cannot build up a navy at once by a simple act of legislation."[41]

Despite his high rank, Porter had no voice in the Navy. Embittered, he turned to writing to gain an audience. His first and best work, *Memoir of Commodore David Porter* (1875), attempted to justify his father's career as well as his own. His later works, particularly his *Incidents and Anecdotes of the Civil War* (1885) and *Naval History of the Civil War* (1886), rank with some of his personal correspondence in the magnitude of their inaccuracy. Porter fired words like grapeshot, indiscriminately and in haste, often regretting rash comments.

The deaths of Porter and Sherman, one day apart, ended an era. Of the Union heroes of the Civil War, they were the last of the high command. Porter, excoriated by navalists of an expansionist, steam-powered world for advocating sails and a defensive strategy, by surviving political generals for his hatred of them, and by the many men he argued with in print in the pages of the various naval and maritime journals, was either damned in print for his personality or mentioned only for his operational victories.

Commodore Porter's sons never escaped their father. William David Porter, disinherited by his family, named his ship the *Essex*, and at his death was buried next to his father, who had actively loathed him.[42] David Dixon never saw the restoration of the maritime splendor of his father's age, but he surrounded himself with mementos of the commodore, and retained many of his sociable habits. He easily eclipsed his father in the happiness of his relationships with his friends, his wife, and his children, but the Porter name advanced his career when his own actions failed to; so despite his rank and achievements, he never quite believed that his career was more successful than his father's.

One of Porter's subordinates said that it was a naval tradition that "the Porters were all brave and all braggarts," and David Dixon Porter was no exception.[43] He organized chaos into order, executed seemingly impossible tasks, cooperated well with anyone who respected him and gave him sufficient credit, and implacably hated those who did not. His boundless energy and pursuit of knowledge invigorated the Naval Academy. He helped found the U.S. Naval Institute and an experimental torpedo school (the progenitor of the Naval Underwater Systems Center), and influenced Stephen B. Luce's determination to make the Naval War College the home for the study of the art of war at sea.[44] Porter lived in the ages of both sail and steam, wooden ships and steel, and appreciated the qualities of each. His fighting spirit, the legacy of David Porter, for better or worse, affected all that he did.

FURTHER READING

David Dixon Porter has always provoked much comment in print. His associations with many of the nineteenth-century military and political figures have caused much speculation, and opinions concerning each facet of his life are often conflicting. The best and standard biography of Porter is Richard Sedgewick West, Jr.'s *The Second Admiral*, which, although favorable, is realistic about many of his shortcomings through the Civil War period. James Russell Soley's *Admiral Porter* and Paul Lewis's *Yankee Admiral: A Biography of David Dixon Porter* provide interesting insights but lack documentation. Porter's childhood is best illustrated in David F. Long's *Nothing Too Daring: A Biography of Commodore David Porter, 1780–1843.* The "Camel Corps" of the 1850s has been the subject of several short books and articles, and as it pertains to Porter is outlined in Malcolm W. Cagle's "Lieutenant David Dixon Porter and His Camels," U.S. Naval Institute *Proceedings.*

Studies of the war period abound with references to Porter's activities, but West's *Second Admiral* remains the best source for the war as it relates to Porter. Porter's war career is ably related in several articles, particularly William N. Still's "'Porter . . . is the Best Man': This was Gideon Welles's View of the Man He Chose to Command the Mississippi Squadron," *Civil War Times Illustrated*; a chapter of Caroll Storrs Alden and Ralph Earle's *Makers of Naval Tradition*; and Richard West's "The Relations between Farragut and Porter," U.S. Naval Institute *Proceedings*. Ludwell H. Johnson's *Red River Campaign: Politics and Cotton in the Civil War* goes beyond the normal campaign history to describe the outside influences that affected this operation, particularly as they relate to individuals, and ably describes Porter's errors of judgment.

Porter's postwar career is best discussed in Kenneth J. Hagan's *American Gunboat Diplomacy and the Old Navy, 1877–1889* and "Admiral David Dixon Porter: Strategist for a Navy in Transition," U.S. Naval Institute *Proceedings*; Charles O. Paullin's "A Half Century of Naval Administration in America, 1861–1911: Part IV. The Navy Department Under Grant and Hayes, 1869–1881," U.S. Naval Institute *Proceedings*; Lance C. Buhl's "Mariners and Machines: Resistance to Technological Change in the American Navy, 1865–1869," *Journal of American History*; Park Benjamin's *The United States Naval Academy*; and Edward William Sloan III's *Benjamin Franklin Isherwood, Naval Engineer: The Years as Engineer in Chief, 1861–1869.* Porter's own writings, written mostly in reaction to his postwar inactivity, should not be relied on for specific facts, although they reveal clearly his personality.

Manuscript sources for the study of Porter have never been scarce. In addition to holdings still in private hands, the Gustavus Vasa Fox Collection at the New-York Historical Society, the David Dixon Porter and Porter Family Papers at the Library of Congress, the David Dixon Porter Papers at the Henry E. Huntington Library, and army and naval sources in the National Archives are the most significant collections; but Porter letters appear in hundreds of other collections. *War of the Rebellion: A Compilation of the Official Records of the Union and Confederate Armies,* the *Official Records of the Union and Confederate Navies in the War of the Rebellion,* the *Confidential Correspondence of Gustavus Vasa Fox, The Sherman Letters,* and the *Papers of Ulysses S. Grant* have printed many, although hardly most, of these. The sheer mass of extant Porter letters and the constant controversy he so loved to generate have affected any accurate portrait of Porter, and a thorough, scholarly biography covering all portions of his life has yet to be written.

NOTES

1. The chaotic Porter family relationships are best described in David F. Long, *Nothing Too Daring: A Biography of Commodore David Porter, 1780–1843* and Richard Sedgewick West, Jr., *The Second Admiral: A Life of David Dixon Porter.* For David Dixon Porter's idealized view of his father, see his *Memoir of Commodore David Porter, of the United States Navy.*

2. West, *Second Admiral,* 63.

3. Lincoln to Porter, 1 April 1861, *Official Records of the Union and Confederate Navies in the War of the Rebellion* (hereafter cited as *ORN*), Series I, vol. 4: 108; ibid., 108–9; Lincoln to Welles, 1 April 1861, Roy P. Basler, ed., *Collected Works of Abraham Lincoln,* 4: 318–19. The appointment, over Lincoln's signature, of Samuel Barron to head the Office of Detail received much attention after the war by anti-Porter factions, who saw in it an attempt by Porter to place a Southerner, and one who ultimately sided with the Confederacy, in a place of importance in the Navy Department. In reality, both Lincoln and Welles were also in the process of appointing to responsible commands men who would later turn Confederate. Welles certainly detested Porter's attempt to alter Navy Department policy, but he made a public issue of Porter's selection of Barron only after the war, when politics intervened. Porter had as many Southern connections as most officers in this war, but even Welles admitted Porter proved his loyalty to the Union cause in action. Barron's appointment, in Meigs's handwriting, with Porter's postscript, had the approval of Secretary of State Seward. For Welles's postwar view, see Howard K. Beale, ed., *Diary of Gideon Welles, Secretary of the Navy Under Lincoln and Johnson,* I: 16–21, and Gideon Welles, "Facts in Relation to the Expedition Ordered by the Administration of President Lincoln for the Relief of the Garrison in Fort Sumter," *The Galaxy,* 10 (November, 1870), reprinted in *Selected Essays by Gideon Welles: Civil War and Reconstruction,* compiled by Albert Mordell.

4. Porter to [A. H. Foote], [5 April 1861], *ORN*, 1, 4: 111–12; Seward to Porter, 6 April 1861, ibid., p. 112; Porter to Seward, 6 April 1861, ibid.

5. Porter to [Captain H. A. Adams], 24 August 1862, ibid., 130.

6. West, *Second Admiral*, 114; Richard West, "Relations between Farragut and Porter," U.S. Naval Institute *Proceedings*, 61 (1935): 989; Loyall Farragut, *The Life and Letters of Admiral Farragut, First Admiral of the United States Navy*, 210.

7. Lt. Col. Edmund Higgins, CSA, to Lt. William M. Bridges, CSA, 30 April 1862, David Dixon Porter Papers, Library of Congress (hereafter cited as DDP, DLC).

8. Lincoln to Senate and House of Representatives, 14 May 1862, Basler, ed., *Lincoln Works*, 5: 215n and 11 July 1862, ibid., 315–16.

9. Porter to Fox, 22 June 1862, DDP, DLC.

10. David Dixon Porter, *Incidents and Anecdotes of the Civil War*, 120–22; *Diary of Gideon Welles*, 1 October 1862, 1: 157–58; ibid., 10 October 1862, 1: 167. Welles glumly recorded his advancement of Porter in his diary, noting many more of Porter's negative than his positive qualities, and questioning Porter's ability to succeed, sighing, "If he does well I shall get no credit; if he fails I shall be blamed. No thanks in any event will be mine." Ibid., 1: 157–58. Given his negativism and Porter's distinct mission to assist Lincoln's special forces under McClernand, it is more likely that Fox and Lincoln decided on Porter's assignment, and Welles acquiesced. Welles was later able to impress Lincoln with the first news of the fall of Vicksburg, making Welles briefly Porter's strong supporter.

11. William N. Still, "'Porter . . . is the Best Man': This Was Gideon Welles's View of the Man He Chose to Command the Mississippi Squadron," *Civil War Times Illustrated* 16 (1977): 5.

12. Porter to Fox, 17 October 1862, Robert Means Thompson and Richard Wainwright, eds., *Confidential Correspondence of Gustavus Vasa Fox, Assistant Secretary of the Navy, 1861–1865*, 2: 140; Porter to Fox, 21 October 1862, ibid., 2: 143; Sherman to [John Sherman], 14 December 1862, Rachel Sherman Thorndike, ed., *The Sherman Letters: Correspondence Between General Sherman and Senator Sherman from 1837 to 1891*, 174–75.

13. William T. Sherman, *Memoir of William T. Sherman*, 1: 297; Lloyd Lewis, *Sherman, Fighting Prophet*, 257–61; West, *Second Admiral*, 199; Fox to Porter, 6 February 1863, Thompson and Wainwright, eds., *Fox Correspondence*, 2: 156; Lincoln to Congress, 28 January 1863, Basler, ed., *Lincoln Works*, 6: 82; Lincoln to Congress, 19 February 1863, ibid., 111–12.

14. Porter to Welles, 10 March 1863, *War of the Rebellion: A Compilation of the Official Records of the Union and Confederate Armies* (hereafter cited as *OR*), Series 1, vol. 24, Part 3: 97–98; Porter to Fox, 19 February 1864, Thompson and Wainwright, eds., *Fox Correspondence*, 2: 200–201; Fox to Porter, 16 July 1863, ibid., 2: 185.

15. Henry Hotze to Judah P. Benjamin, 9 May 1863, *ORN*, 2, 3: 760; Hotze to Benjamin, 14 May 1863, ibid., 768; West, *Second Admiral*, 229–30.

16. West, *Second Admiral*, 231–32; Lincoln to the Senate, 8 December 1863, Basler, ed., *Lincoln Works*, 7: 56–57.

17. Porter anticipated problems with the water level before the expedition. See Sherman to Grant, 4 January 1864, John Y. Simon, ed., *Papers of Ulysses S. Grant*, (hereafter cited as *PUSG*), 10: 20. Porter also knew Banks, and had previously noted his unwillingness to assist other commands. See, for example, Porter to Grant, 14 May 1863, *OR*, 1, 24, Part 3: 309 and Porter to Grant, 10 June 1863, *PUSG* 8: 335.

18. Ludwell H. Johnson, *Red River Campaign: Politics and Cotton in the Civil War*, 241; Porter to Sherman, 14 April 1864, *OR*, 1, 34, Part 3: 153–54. Examples of army opinions on Banks are printed in *PUSG* 10: 340, 351–52, and 429.

19. Porter's condemnation of Grant, soon regretted, was printed in newspapers and an anti-Porter tract in 1876. See Porter to Welles, 24 January 1865, in F. Colburn Adams, *High Old Salts: Stories Intended for the Marines, but Told before an Enlightened Committee of Congress*, 32–36.

20. West, *Second Admiral*, 288; Grant to Terry, 3 January 1865, *PUSG* 13: 219; Porter to Grant, 14 January 1865, ibid., 227.

21. Porter to Fox, 28 March 1862, Thompson and Wainwright, eds., *Fox Correspondence* 2: 95.

22. Park Benjamin, *The United States Naval Academy*, 266–71. See also Charles Todorich, *The Spirited Years: A History of the Antebellum Naval Academy*.

23. Porter to Welles, 25 September 1866, U.S. Navy Department, *Annual Report of the Secretary of the Navy* (hereafter cited as *Annual Report*), 1866, 76; James Russell Soley, "Eulogy," in *A Memorial of David Dixon Porter from the City of Boston*, 63.

24. Porter Order, 14 October 1865, National Archives, R.G. 405, #48, Press Copies of Orders Issued by the Superintendent, 1865–69 (hereafter cited as DNA, RG 405, #48), 1: 19–20.

25. Porter to Welles, 18 October 1865, National Archives, R.G. 45, #34, Letters from Commandants of Navy Yards and Shore Stations, Naval Academy (hereafter cited as DNA, RG 45, Naval Academy Letters), 246: 48; Porter Order, 24 October 1865, DNA, RG 405, #48, 1: 43; Porter Order, undated, ibid., 52.

26. Benjamin, *Naval Academy*, 266–67; Todorich, *Spirited Years*, 39; Walter Aamold, "Athletic Training at the Naval Academy," United States Naval Institute *Proceedings*, 61 (1935): 1562.

27. Porter Order, 21 November 1865, DNA, RG 405, #48, 1: 82–83.

28. Porter Order, 11 January 1866, DNA, RG 405, #48, 1: 125–26; Porter Order, 2 June 1867, ibid., 540–42; Porter to Welles, 19 December 1865, DNA, RG 45, Naval Academy Letters, 246: 110; Porter Special Order,

24 October 1865, DNA, RG 405, #48, 1: 45; Porter Order, 21 November 1865, ibid., 82–83.

29. Report of Board of Visitors, 4 June 1869, *Annual Report*, 1869, 137.

30. Porter Order, [30] September 1867, DNA, RG 405, #48, 1: 582–88.

31. Lance C. Buhl, "Maintaining 'An American Navy,' 1865–1889," in Kenneth J. Hagan, ed., *In Peace and War: Interpretations of American Naval History, 1775–1984*, 145–70.

32. Porter to John Barnes, 25 February 1869, quoted in Peter Karsten, *The Naval Aristocracy: The Golden Age of Annapolis and the Emergence of Modern American Navalism*, 266.

33. Charles O. Paullin, "A Half Century of Naval Administration in America, 1861–1911: Part IV. The Navy Department under Grant and Hayes, 1869–1881," U.S. Naval Institute *Proceedings* 39 (1913): 744; Edward William Sloan III, *Benjamin Franklin Isherwood, Naval Engineer: The Years as Engineer in Chief, 1861–1869*, 199.

34. Sloan, *Benjamin Frankin Isherwood*, 240.

35. General Order No. 89, 10 March 1869; General Orders Nos. 90, 91, 94, 95, 96, 97, and 99, 11 March 1869; General Order No. 105, 13 March 1869; General Orders Nos. 108 and 109, 15 March 1869; General Order No. 124, 15 May 1869; General Order No. 130, 15 June 1869; and Circular, "Duties of Bureaus to Commence May 15, 1869," DNA, RG 45, #43, "Directives."

36. Although later navalists, notably Harold and Margaret Sprout (in *The Rise of American Naval Power, 1776–1918*) and Samuel W. Bryant (in *The Sea and the States: A Maritime History of the American People*) claimed Porter controlled naval policies under Robeson, there is no evidence to support this. Porter's lack of influence in naval matters is reported in Paullin, "A Half Century of Naval Administration," U.S. Naval Institute *Proceedings* 39: 750, and is mentioned in Porter to William C. Whitney, 30 November 1885, *Annual Report*, 1885, 280.

37. Porter to William H. Hunt, 19 June 1881, *Annual Report*, 1881, 95.

38. Lance C. Buhl, "Mariners and Machines: Resistance to Technological Change in the American Navy, 1865–1869," *Journal of American History*, 61 (1974): 709; Kenneth J. Hagan, *American Gunboat Diplomacy and the Old Navy, 1877–1889*, 19–27; Karsten, *Naval Aristocracy*, 312, 334.

39. Porter to Hunt, 19 June 1881, *Annual Report*, 1881, 102, 216; Porter to William E. Chandler, 19 November 1883, *Annual Report*, 1883, 390–405. Porter early advocated abandonment of wood for all-metal shipbuilding. See "Lecture delivered before the 2nd Class of Midshipmen at the U.S. Naval Academy, January 22nd., 1870," DDP, DLC.

40. Porter to Hunt, 19 June 1881, *Annual Report, 1881*, 103.

41. Porter to the Secretary of the Navy, 6 July 1887, *Annual Report*, 1887, 53.

42. Dana M. Wegner, "Commodore William D. 'Dirty Bill' Porter," U.S. Naval Institute *Proceedings*, 103 (1977): 44, 49.

43. Typescript, "Autobiography of Joseph Smith Harris," 12 August 1908, Naval Historical Foundation, Washington, DC.

44. John B. Hattendorf, B. Mitchell Simpson III, and John R. Wadleigh, *Sailors and Scholars: The Centennial History of the U.S. Naval War College*, 5–6, 17; Ronald Spector, *Professors of War: The Naval War College and the Development of the Naval Profession*, 21.

TWILIGHT OF THE OLD NAVY

JOHN RODGERS: THE QUINTESSENTIAL NINETEENTH CENTURY NAVAL OFFICER

BY ROBERT ERWIN JOHNSON

Few U.S. naval officers of the nineteenth century had more active careers than the Navy's second John Rodgers, and few were more fortunately placed for such a career. Fourth son of Commodore John Rodgers and Minerva Denison Rodgers, the second John Rodgers was born at Havre de Grace, Maryland, on 4 August 1812, while the squadron commanded by his father was cruising against British commerce. Despite a rather lackluster performance in the War of 1812, the senior John Rodgers became the first president of the Board of Navy Commissioners, established in 1815 to advise the Secretary of the Navy, and he held that position for the next twenty-two years with the exception of the period 1825–27, when he commanded the Mediterranean Squadron. The commodore's younger brother was also a naval officer, as were two of his brothers-in-law and a number of others related to him by marriage.[1] Thus, the younger John Rodgers entered a service in whose upper ranks his family was well represented.

Rodgers received his appointment as acting midshipman in April 1828, a few days before Midshipman Frederick Rodgers, his elder brother, was drowned when a small boat capsized in Norfolk harbor. That tragedy may explain the delay of John Rodgers's formal entry into the Navy until February 1829.[2] The following June brought orders to the frigate *Constellation*, probably chosen because she was commanded by Captain Alexander S. Wadsworth, the commodore's brother-in-law, who could be relied on to begin his nephew's naval education properly. The *Constellation* spent two years with the Mediterranean Squadron, and before she returned to the United States, Rodgers was transferred to the sloop of war *Concord* under Master Commandant Matthew Calbraith Perry, a kinsman by marriage and a sometime protege of Commodore Rodgers.

Unlike some commanding officers, both Wadsworth and Perry paid a good deal of attention to the training of the midshipmen assigned to their vessels,

John **Rodgers**. Photograph taken by E. Anthony in New York City in 1863. *Courtesy of the National Archives.*

nor did Rodgers's education terminate when he left the *Concord* late in 1832. He attended the school for midshipmen conducted in the frigate *Java*, in ordinary at the Norfolk Navy Yard, and after passing his examination for promotion to lieutenant in the spring of 1834, he received a year's leave of absence to attend the University of Virginia.[3] Promotion was by seniority and so slow in the antebellum Navy that Rodgers spent nearly six years awaiting a vacancy in the rank of lieutenant. The six months that Passed Midshipman Rodgers spent in the survey schooner *Jersey* under Lieutenant Thomas R. Gedney in 1836 might also be considered a part of his education, for this period of working in New York bay was his introduction to hydrographic surveying.

After a two-year cruise on the Brazil Station in the brigantine *Dolphin* and the razee-frigate *Independence*, during which he received news of his father's death, Rodgers was appointed to command the centerboard schooner *Wave* in November 1839. She was assigned to the "mosquito fleet" composed of small schooners and barges—large open boats—that cooperated with army forces in the Second Seminole War. On passage to the Florida keys in January 1840, the *Wave* lost her mainmast, but her captain's seamanship was equal to the occasion, winning him a commendation from the Secretary of the Navy.[4] Rodgers learned of his promotion to lieutenant while his vessel was refitting at Indian Key.

The war in Florida was an ignoble affair in which several thousand soldiers, sailors, and marines pursued many fewer Seminoles and fugitive slaves into the Everglades, an area little known to white men. The invaders seldom sighted their elusive opponents and made war by burning villages and destroying crops and stores of foods.[5] Lieutenant John T. McLaughlin, commanding the naval force, and Lieutenant Rodgers, his second in command, led expeditions into the Everglades repeatedly, enduring the enervating climate and the hardships of life in small canoes for weeks at a time in the hope of cutting off sizable parties of Seminoles, a feat that they were never able to accomplish. Four somewhat larger vessels were added to McLaughlin's squadron in 1841— John Rodgers assuming command of the former revenue cutter *Jefferson*—but the enlarged force brought no significant result.

By the beginning of 1842, the American public, including the residents of northern Florida, was tiring of the apparently interminable campaign against the Seminoles, whose numbers had been reduced to a few hundred, and Secretary of the Navy Abel P. Upshur concluded that the "mosquito fleet" had outlived its usefulness. Leaving two schooners to support army forces as necessary, the squadron sailed northward in June. The homeward passage was not without incident—off Cape Canaveral, a violent squall carried the *Jefferson*'s fore and main topmasts away, and her sister *Madison*, closing to offer assistance, then collided with the crippled schooner. No lives were lost, and the damage, while extensive, was not serious; the vessels reached Norfolk without further mishap.[6]

On arrival at Norfolk, a marine officer charged Lieutenant Rodgers with cruel and improper punishment, citing five occasions in 1841 when Rodgers had ordered men flogged with more than thirty lashes despite the regulation that only a court-martial could sentence a man to more than twelve lashes. One of them had died subsequently, but the charge that Rodgers had been responsible for his death was withdrawn when the surgeon at Indian Key stated that the flogging had not hastened the man's demise—he had died of tuberculosis. In response, the naval officer informed the Secretary of the Navy that he had indeed ordered between thirty and forty-two lashes for four men who had become intoxicated during Florida expeditions, capsizing two canoes with the loss of arms, ammunition, and provisions, and endangering themselves and their fellows. Only prompt, severe punishment could prevent a recurrence of the theft of whiskey provided for the statutory spirit ration, and courts-martial were impossible; therefore, he had seen no alternative. Although Secretary Upshur was not satisfied with this explanation, he dismissed the charges on the rather surprising ground that Rodgers had not understood the regulation and so had not violated it intentionally.[7] One may wonder whether Upshur would have been so generous had the lieutenant not been a member of the "naval aristocracy's" leading family.

Rodgers next spent a year as first lieutenant of the Home Squadron's brig *Boxer*, during which time he seems to have become interested in steam propulsion. Early in 1844, he asked to be assigned to superintend the construction of a steam warship, and within a few weeks he received orders to Pittsburgh, where the steam frigate *Allegheny* was being built. This vessel was unusual in two respects: she was the U.S. Navy's first iron warship, and she was propelled by the submerged horizontal paddle wheels invented by Lieutenant William W. Hunter, who was overseeing her construction.

Like a number of other naval officers and engineers, Rodgers saw no reason to doubt the practicability of the Hunter wheels, which nonetheless were to prove a failure in every ship in which they were installed, but he was perhaps more impressed by the fact that the inventor received a royalty based on the size of each of the naval vessels so fitted.[8] Could he invent something useful to the Navy, he might expect a similar reward. Accordingly, he spent some of his plentiful leisure time in Pittsburgh designing a "cycloidal" vessel that promised to be superior in sailing qualities to those built on conventional lines.[9] The Navy Department, however, showed no interest in arranging the tests he desired.

Having failed as an inventor, the lieutenant turned to the field of geographic exploration, obviously prompted by publication of the five volumes in which Lieutenant Charles Wilkes described the four-year cruise of the U.S. Exploring Expedition. Rodgers proposed to investigate possible water routes between Lake Superior and the headwaters of the Columbia River and thereafter to survey the Rio Grande. With Anglo–American and Mexican–American relations tense because of the Oregon and Texas situations, the potential military usefulness of the proposed surveys was obvious. Nonetheless, Secretary of the Navy George Bancroft responded regretfully that his department had no funds with which to support them.[10]

By the spring of 1846, life in Pittsburgh had ceased to hold any attraction for Rodgers, and the prospect of war with Mexico led him to seek employment in the Gulf of Mexico. But the Home Squadron had no need for another lieutenant, so he accepted orders to the frigate *United States*, fitting out for a cruise on the unpopular Africa Station. Duty as watch officer in a large warship cannot have been rewarding to one who had spent most of his career in small vessels; thus, Rodgers welcomed transfer to the sloop of war *Marion* as second lieutenant soon after reaching the station.

Cruising between the squadron's base in the Cape Verde Islands and its patrol area off Africa's "Slave Coast" provided little excitement; as Rodgers wrote his brother, "This is a d___l of a coast for want of interest and if Jimmy Polk and the Mexicans had not fallen out so that we have bloody wars to speculate upon I do not know what we should do."[11] His speculation led to a plan for the capture of San Juan de Ulua, the principal fortification guarding Veracruz, Mexico's major port. Briefly, the lieutenant proposed to use an especially fitted merchant steamer that would run close under the fort's walls, release iron shafts to fix herself in position, and direct a stream of scalding water from her boiler on the defenders. Congreve rockets would add to the confusion, which should enable 200 armed men concealed in the vessel to take the fort with relative ease. As Rodgers summed it up:

> . . . I will run alongside and pin the steamer into her position, scald every man upon the ramparts, wrap them in a new shirt of Nessus—sprinkle impartial agony on every mother's son of them—Terrify them with Congrieve rockets which will sweep through their rank scattering fire smoke horror and roaring of death. Surprised confused with an unknown force of resolute steel, without a knowledge of what more is in store for them what can they do— . . . there will be a tall getting down stairs—I shall board the deserted ramparts and take all like rabbits in a trap—[12]

He sought support for this proposal from a number of prominent officials, including the secretaries of state and the Navy, the superintendent of the Coast Survey, and senior military and naval officers, but the desired orders to the Gulf of Mexico failed to materialize. Finally Rodgers concluded that his government had no taste for "Boiled Mexican," which was probably just as well. San Juan de Ulua fell five months later without resort to methods that would have been denounced as barbarous.

So John Rodgers spent the period of the Mexican War thousands of miles from the theaters of operations, but at least the latter part of his cruise took him to the more interesting waters of the Mediterranean Sea. Commodore George C. Read was transferred to command the Mediterranean Squadron with the *United States* and the *Marion* in 1847; so he and his subordinates had the opportunity to witness the political disturbances in the Italian peninsula and Sicily. Although American sentiments were generally with those rebelling against the established order, Read was able to maintain a discreet impartiality between the opposing factions so that the failure of the revolutionary movement did not affect his country's interests adversely.

In 1848, Lieutenant Commanding William F. Lynch of the USS *Supply* carried out the first modern survey of the Dead Sea, which probably aroused Lieutenant Rodgers's interest in survey activity. Returning to the United States early in 1849, he applied for assignment to the Coast Survey, which was required to utilize officers of the Army and the Navy to conduct its topographic and hydrographic surveys. Naval lieutenants found such service attractive, for it offered early command, and while the actual work of surveying was arduous, they spent the inclement months of each year compiling the results of the season's work at the Survey's Washington office.

An interview with Professor Alexander Dallas Bache, the able superintendent of the Coast Survey, brought Rodgers orders to command the hydrographic party working in Section VI, the coast of Florida including the reefs and keys. He spent three and one-half years on this assignment, commanding the schooner *Petrel* and the steamers *Hetzel and Legare*, winning Bache's praise for salving the *Hetzel* when she grounded on Cape Canaveral after her anchor chain parted in February 1850. Gales and heavy surf drove the sidewheeler farther onto the beach, but Rodgers persisted, and after two weeks of unremitting labor, his ship was hauled off to her anchors. On the way to Key West, however, she began to leak so badly that he had to run her aground at Indian River Inlet for recaulking before continuing southward for repairs.[13]

In the course of his service with the Coast Survey, John Rodgers directed the hydrographic work for the chart of Key West Harbor and surveyed the Florida Reefs from Key Biscayne to Triumph Reef. Reconnoitering Rebecca Shoals, midway between the Dry Tortugas and the Marquesas Keys, he discovered another bank in that vicinity, which he named Isaac Shoal. His sketches of Boca Grande and Mosquito Inlet and of the shoals off St. Andrew's Sound and Cape Canaveral were published as the first charts of each. Nor had this service been unimportant in his own career. Combining experience in command of both sidewheel and screw steamers with a thorough education in hydrographic surveying, it was excellent preparation for his next assignment.

In the autumn of 1852, Lieutenant Rodgers was ordered to report to Commander Cadwalader Ringgold "for duty connected with the survey of Behring's Straits, North Pacific & China seas."[14] This North Pacific Surveying Expedition had been authorized earlier in 1852 as a hydrographic counterpart to Commodore Matthew Calbraith Perry's Japan mission—charts and sailing directions for Japanese waters were necessary if American vessels were to avail themselves of the ports of refuge that Perry was to open to them. It might also emulate in the northern and western Pacific the work done by Charles Wilkes's U.S. Exploring Expedition in the southern and eastern waters of that ocean. Rodgers was attracted to this service from its beginning, reading everything about Japan that he could acquire. Indeed, it became something of an obsession with him, leading a brother to observe that he had "Japanese fever."[15]

Ringgold, ten years Rodgers's senior, had commanded the brig *Porpoise* under Wilkes, a fact that may explain his selection to command the North Pacific expedition. He had his broad pennant in the sloop of war *Vincennes*, earlier Wilkes's flagship, with the screw-steamer *John Hancock*, the *Porpoise*, the pilot schooner *Fenimore Cooper*, and the sailing storeship *John P. Kennedy* also under his command. Lieutenant Rodgers, the second-ranking officer, was captain of the *Hancock*.

The North Pacific Surveying Expedition sailed from Hampton Roads on 11 June 1853 and proceeded to Simonstown, South Africa, whence a month after its arrival the steamer and the schooner stood out for the Netherlands East Indies to undertake a survey of the Gaspar and Karimata straits. The storeship joined them later, while Ringgold with the *Vincennes* and the *Porpoise* visited Australia, from which the two vessels would steer divergent courses northward through the Coral Sea and the Caroline Islands before joining their consorts at Hong Kong in the spring of 1854.

After four months of strenuous activity surveying the straits, through which nine-tenths of the world's commerce with China passed, one of Rodgers's subordinates summarized the results: "We found *some* parts of *some* charts correct; but generally speaking, they were all woefully out. We found dozens of rocks and shoals where all the charts gave safe water, and we found blue water where all the charts located rocks and shoals."[16]

When Rodgers's vessels reached Hong Kong, they found that the survey had been abandoned temporarily in favor of protecting American interests apparently endangered by the Taiping Rebellion, then raging in southern China. Ringgold's orders specified that nothing was to interfere with the survey, but Perry, whose East India Squadron was charged with protection of such interests, had taken all of his ships to Japan to conclude the negotiations leading to the Treaty of Kanagawa, leaving only Lieutenant Alfred Taylor in a chartered steamer at Canton. Considering the situation one that the Secretary of the Navy could not have foreseen, Ringgold divided his force between Canton, Whampoa, and Hong Kong. The commander himself was suffering from intermittent fever, so Taylor was the senior officer at Canton.

In mid-July, the American vice-consul asked Rodgers to accompany him upstream to Fatshan, a rebel stronghold besieged by imperial forces, to seek information as to the state of affairs. Ringgold's doctor would not permit him to be disturbed, but Taylor gave his permission, so the consul and Rodgers pulled up the river in two armed boats. Having gained the desired intelligence, the boats were retiring when a rebel shot grazed the consul's cheek. Riflemen in both boats returned the fire before they pulled out of range.

Learning of this incident, Commander Ringgold charged Rodgers with having disobeyed his orders to observe strict neutrality, deserted his post of duty, and endangered the lives of his men and of Americans resident in Canton.[17] There were too few officers to form a court-martial, however; so no further action could be taken until Commodore Perry's squadron returned.

By this time, it seemed doubtful that the survey would ever be resumed. Much money had been expended in repairs to the *Porpoise*, and Ringgold planned to have extensive repairs and alterations made to the other vessels, which would almost exhaust the expedition's funds and would require a further detention of several months. Liquor and disease were demoralizing the ships' companies, condemned to idleness by the commander's departure from his orders, and a number of officers were awaiting courts-martial on the charges filed by Ringgold or their fellows. The commander's behavior had become increasingly erratic even before his illness, causing some to question his competence, and by midsummer the squadron surgeon suspected that he was mentally deranged.[18]

Thus, when Commodore Perry reached Hong Kong, he received Ringgold's recommendation that Rodgers and several others be tried by courts-martial, and Rodgers's request that a board of medical survey be convened to investigate the commander's mental condition. The commodore ordered the medical survey, and after a cursory examination, three doctors found Cadwalader Ringgold incapable of holding command by reason of insanity due to his illness. Perry thereupon dismissed the charges against Rodgers and ordered him to assume command of the North Pacific Surveying Expedition pending action by the Secretary of the Navy.[19]

The circumstances of Ringgold's relief and Rodgers's relationship to Perry, which was the closer since the latter's daughter had married the lieutenant's elder brother, led inevitably to suspicion that the commodore had acted out of nepotism. Ringgold's subsequent complete recovery—he would receive the thanks of Congress and a gold medal after his frigate *Sabine* rescued the marine battalion from the foundering steamer *Governor* in 1861—heightened this suspicion, which cannot definitely be disproved. Whatever Perry's reasons, however, his course of action was undoubtedly correct. Unlike his second in command, Ringgold seems to have had little knowledge of marine surveying—most of the surveys made before his relief were carried out under Rodgers's direction—and the expedition was on the verge of dissolution by July 1854.[20] Thus, new leadership was practically mandatory, and Lieutenant Rodgers had the ability and experience to provide it.

The new senior officer reorganized his command thoroughly, no easy task because both squadrons were short of officers and few of Perry's subordinates wished to join the surveying expedition. Rodgers himself left his slow, cranky steamer to take command of the *Vincennes*, and transferred the *Kennedy*, too rotten for active service, to Perry for use as guardship at Canton. Ringgold had promised vessels to ferry a diplomatic mission from Shanghai to the mouth of the Peiho in north China; so his successor sent the *Hancock* and the *Cooper* on this mission in September 1854, ordering them to reconnoiter the Yellow Sea and to survey adjoining bays and river mouths when possible, while he took the *Vincennes* and the *Porpoise* to work among the islands south of Japan. In the course of this cruise, the last went missing with all hands, probably the victim of an October typhoon.

The squadron rendezvoused at Hong Kong early in 1855, and Rodgers learned that Secretary of the Navy James C. Dobbin had confirmed him in command and approved his plans for the expedition's employment. The vessels then searched in vain for survivors or information of the *Porpoise* while surveying islands in the vicinity of Formosa before undertaking a running survey of the Japanese coast and detailed surveys of Shimoda and Hakodate, the ports opened by Perry's Treaty of Kanagawa.

At the former, Rodgers found a party of Americans who wished to establish a ship chandlery business at Hakodate to serve whalers expected to touch there. They had been permitted to land at Shimoda so that their schooner could repatriate the company of a Russian frigate that had foundered in a seismic disturbance, but Japanese authorities would not permit them to go to Hakodate. Rodgers thought their purpose legitimate, but when his efforts on their behalf brought no result, he advised them to leave Japan, explaining, "It is not admissible for any mere casual man-of-war to expound without instructions an interpretation of a formal treaty at the cannon's mouth."[21]

Cutting up a whale. Native half-breeds and a marine guard from the USS *Vincennes*, landed to protect a surveying party from the North Pacific Surveying Expedition in 1855. Contemporary oil painting by Edward Kern. *Courtesy of the Naval Academy Museum.*

From Shimoda, the three vessels proceeded to Hakodate, leaving Lieutenant John M. Brooke, the expedition astronomer, to reconnoiter the 450 miles
of irregular and foggy coastline between the treaty ports in the *Vincennes's*
32-foot launch. Thereafter, the *John Hancock* was ordered to the Sea of Okhotsk
while the *Vincennes* and the *Fenimore Cooper* stood northeastward, touching at
Petropavlovsk before the flagship entered the Arctic Ocean to confirm the
existence of land reported by British and Russian explorers, and the schooner
sought survivors of a wrecked whaler in the Aleutians. Completing their
various assignments, the vessels headed for San Francisco, whence Rodgers
planned to investigate potential steamship routes across the Pacific. When the
squadron was reunited in October 1855, however, he learned that the funds
appropriated for its work had been exhausted. Thus, he returned to the
Atlantic coast by way of Cape Horn in the *Vincennes*, leaving the other two
ships at Mare Island.

Duty at the Japan Expedition Office in Washington followed Rodgers's
arrival in New York, duty none the more pleasant because Commanders
Ringgold and Rodgers—the latter had been promoted in September 1855—
had to work in close proximity compiling the results of the squadron's
activities. The work was interrupted by the Civil War, and while the expedition's charts and sailing directions were ultimately published, no detailed
report ever appeared. Thus, the North Pacific Surveying Expedition attracted
little notice at the time or later. From private and official letters and records,
however, it is clear that its achievements were considerable and that most of
them can be attributed to John Rodgers's ability as hydrographer and leader. [22]

The years of duty in Washington brought Rodgers an unusual opportunity
to enlarge his interests, which he did by paying court to Ann Elizabeth
Hodge, the daughter of a former assistant secretary of the treasury. The
forty-five-year-old commander and Miss Hodge, eleven years his junior, were
married in November 1857. [23] They would become the parents of three
children, a son—the future Vice Admiral William L. Rodgers—and two
daughters.

The coming of the Civil War was the more painful for John Rodgers because
some of his closest friends elected to "go South," but his own devotion to the
Union seems never to have wavered in spite of the likelihood that his native
Maryland would secede. In April 1861, the commander participated in the
evacuation of the Norfolk Navy Yard, attempting unsuccessfully to blow up
the dry dock, an action that led to his capture by the Virginians. Soon released,
Rodgers returned to Washington, and in May he was ordered to duty with the
Army in Cincinnati to create a gunboat force for the Ohio and Mississippi
rivers. This assignment was logical; in addition to his service in Pittsburgh
and in steamers, Rodgers had two army officer brothers-in-law, one of whom,
Montgomery C. Meigs, would soon become quartermaster general of the
Union Army, whose department was responsible for providing river gunboats.

In the four months that he spent with the Army, Rodgers directed the conversion of three river steamers to "timberclad" gunboats, overseeing almost every detail of their fitting out and manning. While commanding this force in modest offensive operations, he worked with Naval Constructor Samuel H. Pook to develop the design for the first ironclad gunboats, which were built at St. Louis by James B. Eads under the commander's distant supervision. Perhaps he tried to do too much, for in August Major General John C. Fremont asked that Rodgers be relieved, ostensibly because he was not devoting enough attention to the ironclad gunboats under construction, perhaps because of his relationship to Meigs, who had found a good deal to criticize in Fremont's conduct of affairs.[24]

Flag Officer Andrew H. Foote, who superseded Rodgers in September, made St. Louis his headquarters, leaving his subordinates to handle the wooden gunboats. Foote publicized his difficulties and accomplishments so effectively that many at the time and later considered him the true creator of the river gunboat flotilla. He was the first to lead the ironclads into combat in 1862; unfortunately, he preferred tactics that emphasized the gunboats' vulnerability, leading to their repulse at Fort Donelson and his own subsequent relief due to a wound suffered there.

Returning to Washington, Commander Rodgers sought a command in the expedition preparing to sail against Port Royal, South Carolina. He had to be satisfied with the *Flag*, a converted screw-steamer then blockading Charleston, but Flag Officer Samuel Francis Du Pont invited him to take passage in the flagship *Wabash* as an acting member of the flag officer's staff, which also included Chief of Staff Charles H. Davis and C. R. P. Rodgers, John's cousin who commanded the *Wabash*. Du Pont, who characterized John Rodgers privately as "a peculiar man but of great ability in various ways," asked him to remain in the *Wabash* until after the Port Royal attack.[25]

On 5 November 1861, Rodgers led gunboats in a reconnaissance of the forts on either side of the entrance to Port Royal Sound: "It was beautiful firing on both sides—we put a number of 11 inch shells into their camp and a number of their shot fell so near that one could scarcely have put a knife between the vessels and the shot. Some of the rigging was cut—I found the excitement not unpleasant and when a shot splashed up close alongside I involuntarily exclaimed 'well done rebel'—."[26] Returning to the *Wabash*, Rodgers took part in Du Pont's attack on the fortifications two days later, braving enemy fire with an unnamed seaman to secure damaged spars and rigging, some of which might have fouled the ship's screw. He wrote his wife later that "I have come to the conclusion that I am a good man in a battle."[27]

With Port Royal secured, the commander joined Davis and his cousin leading gunboat forces attempting to find a water route that would enable Du Pont's squadron to bypass Fort Pulaski, which guarded the approach to Savannah. Little came of their efforts except discontent among the squadron's other commanding officers, who resented the distinction gained by the flag officer's favorites while they endured the monotony of blockade duty.[28] While blockading off Savannah in the *Flag*, however, John Rodgers ascertained that the Confederates had evacuated Tybee Island, within artillery range of Fort Pulaski. He anticipated that batteries on the island could force the fort to surrender, which they did in April 1862, effectively closing Savannah as a blockade-running port.[29]

By that time, the *Flag* had been ordered to Baltimore for repairs, and her captain sought command of an ironclad. Awaiting orders, he spent several days with Major General George B. McClellan's Army of the Potomac involved in the Peninsula Campaign. Rodgers then took command of the new ironclad gunboat *Galena*, which joined Flag Officer Louis M. Goldsborough's squadron in Hampton Roads. McClellan wished the commander to ascend the James River with gunboats to support his advance toward Richmond, but Goldsborough refused because the Confederate ram *Virginia* at Norfolk might interdict their supply line. Early in May, Rodgers took advantage of a chance encounter with President Abraham Lincoln at Fortress Monroe to urge such a movement, and Goldsborough agreed reluctantly that he should take the *Galena* and two smaller vessels up the river.[30] The Confederates evacuated Norfolk two days later, necessitating the destruction of the *Virginia*; so the *Monitor* and the experimental *Naugatuck* joined Rodgers's force, which was ordered to destroy the batteries on the way to Richmond and to shell the Confederate capital to surrender, if possible.

On 15 May, the five vessels reached Drewry's Bluff, eight miles below Richmond, at which point obstructions blocked the river. These could not be removed while Confederate forces held Fort Darling, atop the bluff. Had

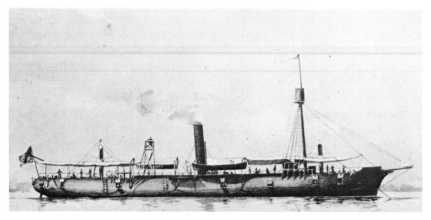

The ironclad USS *Galena*. Rodgers's flagship while commanding the James River Squadron, April to November 1862. *Courtesy of The Mariners Museum.*

Rodgers's ascent of the James been coordinated with McClellan, troops from the latter's army might have taken the fort with relative ease. In their absence, the naval vessels did their best, and it was too little. The *Monitor*'s guns could not be elevated enough to reach the fort at effective range, the *Naugatuck*'s one large gun burst early in the action, and the wooden gunboats could not withstand the Confederate fire, which was the more effective because sailors from the late *Virginia* manned many of the guns. The *Galena* bore the brunt of the action, fighting at anchor because of the restricted waters. So long as she had shells to fire, she held her own; when they were exhausted, her gun crews had to use much less effective solid shot. With the supply of these running low, his vessel's armor holed repeatedly, and thirty-three men killed or wounded, Rodgers broke off the action and retired downstream to City Point, intending at least to hold the river as a supply route for McClellan's army.[31]

Secretary of the Navy Gideon Welles expressed contemporary opinion regarding the battle at Drewry's Bluff: "It was impossible to do more. [Rodgers] did all that could possibly be done."[32] Responsibility for the repulse clearly rested with Lincoln and Goldsborough, neither of whom seems to have considered whether the advance up the James River should be a joint military–naval endeavor. Yet one must note that Rodgers, its instigator, made no mention of army support in his record of his conversation with the President. Had he done so, the outcome might have been different.

General McClellan decided that his army must have a base on the James, and it was Rodgers who selected the easily defended Harrison's Landing below City Point. Following the Battle of Malvern Hill, during which Rodgers's gunboats contributed fire support, the Union Army fell back to Harrison's Landing, where Confederate General Robert E. Lee declined to attack it so long as gunboats were guarding its flanks.[33] Thereafter, Captain Charles Wilkes assumed command of a greatly enlarged James River Flotilla, with which Rodgers, promoted to captain in July, remained until McClellan's army was withdrawn to Fortress Monroe. With little prospect of further action there, he requested assignment to one of the monitors then building.

The *Passaic*-class monitor *Weehawken*, Rodgers's new command, sailed from New York under tow in January 1863, not long after the original *Monitor* had foundered off Cape Hatteras. Deteriorating weather forced the towing steamer to seek shelter in Delaware Bay, but Captain Rodgers was determined to prove the monitors seaworthy and kept his ship on the course for Chesapeake Bay. She too nearly foundered in a gale the next morning, surviving mainly because her engineers were able to free her of water by the use of steam pumps and the bilge injection. The Navy Department, which had committed itself heavily to monitor construction, was greatly relieved when the *Weehawken* weathered the gale, Secretary Welles noting that "No man but John Rogers would have pushed on his vessel in that terrific storm."[34]

The *Weehawken* was one of the armored vessels—seven monitors, the experimental *Keokuk*, and the broadside ironclad *New Ironsides*—with which Rear Admiral S. F. Du Pont was to attack Charleston in the spring of 1863. Although Du Pont had little faith in the ability of monitors to reduce fortifications, he was not willing to entrust the attack to another, and his reservations made no impression on the Navy Department. The extent of Charleston's defensive works rendered inapplicable the proven tactics of running past the forts to capture the city; so his battle plan required the reduction of the fortifications in turn as the ironclads stood upstream in single line ahead, with Fort Sumter as the first target. Incredibly, Du Pont seems to have made little effort to ascertain either the exact strength of the defenses or the nature of the obstructions that the Confederates had placed in the channel.[35] To cope with the obstructions, John Ericsson had devised a minesweeping raft with a 700-pound torpedo suspended beneath it. Captain Rodgers, the most ardent of the monitor advocates, volunteered to push it ahead of the *Weehawken*—without the explosive charge because "that folly would rise into crime which should carry loaded torpedoes in a rapid tideway in a somewhat narrow channel, without known buoys, under fire, and with attention divided, among a friendly fleet."[36]

When the Union force attacked Charleston during the afternoon of 7 April 1863, Rodgers considered the obstructions too extensive to be cleared by the raft; so the battle was fought at greater range than anticipated. After two hours of fighting, in which the unwieldy *New Ironsides* could take little part, the approach of evening caused the admiral to discontinue the action. All of his smaller vessels had been battered considerably by the rapid and accurate Confederate fire—the *Keokuk* sank the next morning—but they had lost only one man killed and twenty-two wounded.

The slow-firing monitors had failed to damage Fort Sumter seriously, and their commanding officers recommended that the attack not be renewed the next day. As John Rodgers wrote Secretary Welles: "No one can say what would have been the result of a renewal of the fight—but if after a renewal we had been driven out, and left a single monitor to fall into the enemies['] hands then the whole character of the war would have been changed. The wooden blockade would have been at an end—as far at least as Charleston is concerned as far indeed as she could get along the coast."[37] If he spoke for his fellows, which seems likely, this statement reveals a strange attitude; most of them had scant regard for their vessels' offensive qualities, yet they assumed that a single monitor under Confederate command would be an invincible adversary! They were correct, however, in opposing a renewal of the attack, for Charleston's defenses were too formidable to be reduced by a naval attack alone, as the following months would demonstrate.

Du Pont's unwillingness to renew the attack and his subordinates' loyal support of the admiral led the Navy Department to suspect the existence of a

"Du Pont clique" and to order his relief. Before that occurred, intelligence that the ironclad ram *Atlanta* at Savannah was ready for sea reached the admiral, who ordered Rodgers with the monitors *Weehawken* and *Nahant* to Wassaw Sound to meet her. The *Atlanta* appeared early on 17 June, ran aground, and fired six shots, all of which missed. The *Weehawken* opened fire at 300 yards, and two solid shots from her 15-inch Dahlgren smoothbore brought the ram's surrender before the *Nahant* fired a shot.[38]

The capture of a grounded vessel manned almost entirely by landsmen was hardly a notable feat, but it was the first undeniable monitor victory over a ram and as such brought Rodgers the thanks of Congress, promotion to commodore, and orders to command a larger monitor. It also ended his active participation in the Civil War, for he spent the remainder of the conflict attempting vainly to overcome the numerous defects of the big *Dictator*.

At the war's end, shore duty was long overdue for Commodore Rodgers, yet he accepted with alacrity when offered command of a special service squadron composed of three wooden warships and the double-turret monitor *Monadnock*, bound to the Pacific coast by way of the Strait of Magellan. En route, the squadron was to maintain strict neutrality in the struggle between a Spanish fleet and the forces of Chile, Peru, and Ecuador. On arrival at Valparaiso in 1866, however, Rodgers decided to join British warships in preventing a bombardment of the defenseless city. First, he attempted to mediate between the Spanish admiral and the Chilean government, and when that effort failed, the British admiral unexpectedly declined to act on his own authority. Thus, the American squadron merely looked on during the bombardment on 31 May 1866, sending fire and rescue parties ashore when the Spanish warships withdrew. A month later, Rodgers witnessed the attack on Callao, Peru. Fortifications there proved more than a match for the Spanish fleet, which returned to Spain not long after its repulse. Thereupon, the commodore's flagship accompanied the *Monadnock* to San Francisco, whence he returned to Washington overland, satisfied that the cruise had removed any doubts as to the monitors' seagoing ability.[39]

After three years as commandant of the Boston Navy Yard, Rodgers was promoted to rear admiral and ordered to command the Asiatic Squadron in the screw-frigate *Colorado*. In this assignment, he joined Frederick F. Low, the U.S. minister to China, in an effort to secure a treaty with Korea, the "Hermit Kingdom," to provide for the safety of shipwrecked seamen.[40]

Low and Rodgers sailed from Nagasaki with five vessels in May 1871, and on arrival at Inchon, Low informed local officials of his mission and asked that boats sent to survey the riverine approaches to Seoul not be molested. Steam launches supported by the gunboats *Monocacy* and *Palos* began the survey on 1 June, and as they came abreast of the principal Korean battery on Kanghwa Island, it opened a rapid and inaccurate fire, which was immediately returned by the vessels. Although the Korean garrison soon fled, the launches had expended most of their ammunition, and the *Monocacy* was leaking badly after striking a rock; so the surveyors returned to Inchon.

Minister and admiral agreed that punitive action would probably be necessary, but they decided to wait until more favorable tidal conditions prevailed. During the ten-day interlude, Low continued his efforts to open negotiations with the Korean government while Rodgers and his subordinates prepared the landing force and made plans for its attack on the Kanghwa fortifications. On 10 June, 651 sailors and marines landed on the island while the *Monocacy* provided gunfire support, the *Palos* having run aground after towing the small boats to the point of disembarkation. The first battery was occupied that evening after the gunboat's fire caused its garrison to evacuate. The next morning, sailors and marines, their assault supported by field guns and the *Monocacy*, carried the remainder of the fortifications, losing three men

Rodgers off Korea, 1871. Admiral John Rodgers, his staff, and captains confer on board the USS *Colorado* prior to the attack on the Korean forts. Seated left to right are Captain Edward T. Nichols, Rodgers's chief of staff, Captain George H. Cooper, commander of the *Colorado,* and Commander Edward P. McCrea, commander of the *Monocacy*. Rodgers is standing at the left leaning on the table. *Courtesy of the Naval Institute.*

killed and ten wounded, while the Korean loss probably exceeded 300. The Americans held the forts overnight to demonstrate their ability to do so, after which they returned to their ships to receive Admiral Rodgers's thanks for an operation that had been conducted very efficiently.[41]

The military success notwithstanding, the killing of hundreds of Koreans obviously made a successful outcome to the Korean mission very improbable. Rodgers believed that nothing short of the occupation of Seoul would lead the Korean government to negotiate. With 5,000 soldiers "such as our army furnished at the conclusion of the late war," he thought that Korea's capital might be captured, but his country's taste for military adventure had been sated by "the late war."[42] The Asiatic Squadron departed Korean waters early in July, leaving the "Hermit Kingdom" to retain its solitude until Japan forced a treaty of commerce and amity on its government in 1876.

With affairs on the remainder of his station tranquil, Admiral Rodgers requested relief in the autumn of 1871, and his twenty-six years of sea duty came to an end when his flag was hauled down in the *Colorado* at Yokohama in May 1872. Returning to the United States, he became commandant of the Mare Island Navy Yard in 1873, relinquishing that position to become superintendent of the Naval Observatory four years later.

During the five years he spent in this, his last assignment, Rodgers helped to prevent the observatory's transfer to civilian management under another department, and he was instrumental in obtaining the present site, its original location near the Potomac River having become unsuitable because of the prevalence of malaria and its atmospheric and spatial limitations. He also served as chairman of the Lighthouse Board, the interservice group that supervised the nation's system of aids to navigation under the Treasury Department, and headed the first Naval Advisory Board.

The latter was established by Secretary of the Navy William H. Hunt in 1881 to recommend a program for restoring the Navy from the neglect of the depression-ridden 1870s. Fifteen officers, ranging from flag rank to lieutenant and including three engineers and as many naval constructors, served on this board, which met in Washington in July 1881. After preliminary meetings in which the members agreed that unarmored cruisers for peacetime duties were the Navy's most immediate need, the board recessed to obtain information on the nation's metallurgical and shipbuilding capabilities. Convening again in October, the officers found themselves disagreeing on a number of points, and a month later they produced a majority report signed by the line officers and two engineers and a minority report presenting the views of Chief Engineer Benjamin F. Isherwood and the constructors. Both groups agreed that the Navy should have seventy cruising vessels and that thirty-two of the sixty-one it had were worth retaining. Thus, thirty-eight cruisers and gunboats should be built. Neither group recommended the construction of armored capital ships, although both recognized that they would be necessary in event of war.

In their place, the majority desired a coast defense force composed of torpedo boats and rams. The minority doubted the value of rams and thought that only one should be built for experimental purposes. More important, its members urged that the larger vessels be built of iron instead of steel, as the majority wished, because American industry could not yet produce the necessary amount of steel.[43]

Secretary Hunt sent the two reports to the Congress with a strong statement of support for the majority's recommendations, but the board's belief that the Congress would appropriate $30,000,000 to carry out its program proved to be wildly optimistic. Not until August 1882 did that body authorize the construction of two steel cruisers, and they were to be paid for from funds appropriated for the repair of existing warships. The board's work had not been entirely in vain, however, for its reports helped to focus public attention on the Navy's plight. The building of the "new" Navy of the 1890s is properly held to have begun with the work of the first Naval Advisory Board.

Rodgers did not live to see even the first modest result of the board's deliberations. He had enjoyed robust good health until 1881, when he contracted malaria which developed into Bright's disease. The admiral died on 5 May 1882 and was buried in Washington's Oak Hill Cemetery.

John Rodgers's contemporaries were impressed by his scientific bent—he had been made a corporator of the National Academy of Sciences when it was founded in 1863 in recognition of his attainments as a hydrographer—and by his attitude toward technological change. As a younger officer noted, "Perhaps none of the older class of naval officers had a better right by reason of length of service and family traditions to be prejudiced against the introduction of the new form of war-ship to the disadvantage of the old than had John Rodgers . . . ,"[44] yet he welcomed innovations—somewhat uncritically, to be sure, as witness his support of such mistaken concepts as the Hunter wheels, the monitors, and the rams. One suspects that he would have approved the decision of his great-nephew and namesake to become one of the Navy's pioneer aviators.[45]

Above all, however, he was known as a naval officer per se. Assistant Secretary of the Navy Gustavus V. Fox, perhaps influenced by Rodgers's support of the monitor program, thought him "the best captain in the service,"[46] and after receiving the Korea expedition reports, Admiral David Dixon Porter wrote: "Your squadron seems to be the most efficient afloat. I cannot pay you a higher compliment."[47] A member of the first Naval Advisory Board told the admiral's widow that "[Rodgers] bossed us all; I did not think there was a man living could do it, but he kept us all in, and kept us quiet and we did not feel the reins either."[48]

John Rodgers expressed his own opinion when he disclaimed any desire to become a bureau chief after the Civil War: "I think my forte *if I have one* is in commanding ships and men—"[49] Two years earlier, he had explained his reputed popularity as senior officer of the James River squadron in a letter to his wife:

> I am fair, I think, I have no humbug—I prefer to let the commanders know what I am doing and what they are doing instead of making automatons of them. I think by this more intelligent service is rendered—and more willing service—and I love to give credit where credit is due—at the same time I do not think that I neglect any points necessary to be observed—I do not care for popularity—and I make no effort to attain it—; as I am amiable, fair, and I hope efficient enough to command respect popularity has come I think as a matter of course.[50]

And in 1854 he had assured the Secretary of the Navy of his ability to command the North Pacific Surveying Expedition: "While I have never had serious trouble with officer or man under my command, nor troubled the Department with courts, nor complaints, I have always I believe preserved a proper measure of discipline and good order."[51] With the exception of the ill-advised floggings during the Seminole War, which he understandably neglected to mention, this was true of Rodgers's entire career.

The obituary notice appearing in the *Proceedings* of the U.S. Naval Institute, of which Rear Admiral John Rodgers was president from January 1879 to January 1882, concluded: "The purpose of this Institute is to elevate the character of the Naval Service, and this cannot better be done than by lessons learned from a life so useful, so honorable, so grand in simplicity, and so complete."[52] With due allowance for the hyperbole expected on such occasions, this seems a fair evaluation. John Rodgers was in most regards the quintessential nineteenth-century naval officer.

FURTHER READING

John Rodgers enjoyed a considerable reputation in his own time and for almost thirty years thereafter, but the publication of his father's biography, *Commodore John Rodgers . . . 1773–1838*, by Charles Oscar Paullin in 1910 led to a partial eclipse. Thus, the official publication *Ships' Data: U.S. Naval Vessels* listed a lighthouse tender and a torpedo boat named for the son as honoring his father. The younger Rodgers's only full-scale biography, *Rear Admiral John Rodgers, 1812–1882*, by Robert Erwin Johnson, was published in 1967. It is based mainly on the collections of John Rodgers Letters and Papers and Rodgers Family Papers held for the Naval Historical Foundation by the Library of Congress Manuscript Division.

John K. Mahon's *History of the Second Seminole War, 1835–1842* has relatively little on the Navy's role; George H. Preble's diary account "A Canoe Expedition into the Everglades in 1842," originally published in 1883 and reprinted in *Tequesta* in 1945, is invaluable. Clark G. Reynolds, "The Great Experiment: Hunter's Horizontal Wheel," in *The American Neptune* (January

1964) describes that fiasco, and for the refloating of the *Hetzel*, see Robert Erwin Johnson, "The Stranding and Salving of *Hetzel*," in *Steamboat Bill of Facts* (Fall 1960). Allan B. Cole's superbly edited *Yankee Surveyors in the Shogun's Seas* contains the records of the North Pacific Surveying Expedition under Rodgers's command. Lieutenant Alexander W. Habersham, who sailed in the *Kennedy* and the *Hancock*, described his experiences in *My Last Cruise; or, Where We Went and What We Saw*; and interesting accounts may be found in Robert V. Hine, *Edward Kern and American Expansion*—Kern was the expedition artist—and George M. Brooke, Jr., *John M. Brooke: Naval Scientist and Educator*. Samuel Eliot Morison's biography of Matthew C. Perry, *"Old Bruin,"* surprisingly has no mention of Ringgold's relief; the commander gave his side of the controversy in a pamphlet entitled *Defense of Commander Cadwalader Ringgold, before Court of Inquiry No. 2 Convened at Washington City*.

Rodgers's Civil War service is summarized in interesting fashion by Jim Dan Hill in *Sea Dogs of the Sixties*, which has some minor errors. John D. Milligan, *Gunboats Down the Mississippi*, is perhaps the best account of the river gunboats, although Rodgers's relief is not explained adequately. The capture of Port Royal and subsequent operations on the South Carolina and Georgia coasts are described by participants in *Samuel Francis Du Pont: Selections from his Civil War Letters*, three volumes edited by John D. Hayes, while Craig L. Symonds, ed., *Charleston Blockade*, contains the journals of John B. Marchand, one of those who envied Du Pont's favorites. Rowena Reed failed to use all of the available naval material for her account of the James River campaign in *Combined Operations*. James M. Morgan, who was in the Fort Darling garrison, described the repulse at Drewry's Bluff in his *Recollections of a Rebel Reefer*, as did Robert W. Daly in *How the "Merrimac" Won*. There is no adequate work on the Civil War monitors; their characteristics and more important operations are summarized in Frank M. Bennett, *The Steam Navy of the United States*.

Charles E. Clark has an amusing account of Commodore Rodgers and the special service squadron in *My Fifty Years in the Navy*, and William C. Davis, *The Last Conquistadores: The Spanish Intervention in Peru and Chile, 1863–1866*, is an excellent account of that episode. For a recent description of Rodgers's command of the Asiatic Squadron, see Robert Erwin Johnson, *Far China Station: The U.S. Navy in Asian Waters, 1800–1898*. The work of the first Naval Advisory Board is evaluated briefly by Lance C. Buhl in "Maintaining 'An American Navy,' 1865–1889," in Kenneth J. Hagan, ed., *In Peace and War: Interpretations of American Naval History, 1775–1978*.

NOTES

1. Charles O. Paullin, *Commodore John Rodgers*, 18, 84.
2. Ibid., 382–84.
3. University of Virginia Matriculation Book, Non-Resident Students, 11th Session, Alderman Library, University of Virginia.
4. Secretary of the Navy James K. Paulding to Lieutenant John T.

McLaughlin, 2 December 1839, Letters Sent by the Secretary of the Navy to Officers, 1798–1868, R.G. 45, National Archives. Henceforth cited as Letters to Editors.

5. John K. Mahon, *History of the Second Seminole War, 1835–1842, passim*; Robert E. Johnson, *Rear Admiral John Rodgers, 1812–1882*, Chapter IV.

6. George H. Preble, "A Canoe Expedition into the Everglades in 1842," 30–51.

7. Upshur to Rodgers, 13 August 1842, John Rodgers Letters and Papers, Library of Congress. Henceforth cited as Rodgers Papers.

8. Rodgers to Bancroft, 18 January 1846, Letters Received by the Secretary of the Navy from Officers below the rank of Commander, 1802–1886, R.G. 45. Henceforth cited as Officers' Letters.

9. Rodgers to Secretary of the Navy John Y. Mason, with enclosure, 16 February 1845, ibid.

10. Bancroft to Rodgers, 4 March 1846, Letters to Officers.

11. Rodgers to brother, 22 October 1846, Rodgers Papers.

12. Ibid.

13. Entries in *Hetzel* Log Book, February and March 1850, copy in General Correspondence of A. D. Bache, Superintendent of the Coast Survey, 1850, R.G. 23, National Archives.

14. Bache to Rodgers, 15 October 1852, ibid.

15. William P. Rodgers to brother, 12 July 1852, Commodore John Rodgers Papers, Historical Society of Pennsylvania.

16. Alexander W. Habersham, *My Last Cruise*, 74–75.

17. Report of Com. C. Ringgold, Movements and Operations of Surveying Exp. under his Com. & Circumstances Attendant upon his Removal by Commodore Perry, 1855, 28–35, Letters from Officers Commanding Expeditions, R.G. 45.

18. Dr. William Grier to Rodgers, 1 August 1854, ibid.

19. Perry to Secretary of the Navy James C. Dobbin, 9 August 1854, copy in ibid.

20. For Ringgold's ability as a surveyor, see William Stanton, *The Great United States Exploring Expedition of 1838–1842*, 253, 322.

21. Quoted in Allen B. Cole, ed., *Yankee Surveyors in the Shogun's Seas*, 119.

22. Ibid., *passim*; Dudley W. Knox, *A History of the United States Navy*, p. 182.

23. Johnson, *Rodgers*, 143–45.

24. John D. Milligan, *Gunboats Down the Mississippi*, 19; Russell F. Weigley, *Quartermaster General of the Union Army*, 186–94.

25. Du Pont to Mrs. Sophie Du Pont, 25 October 1861, Samuel Francis Du Pont Papers, Eleutherian Mills Historical Library.

26. Rodgers to Mrs. Ann Rodgers, 5 November 1861, Rodgers Papers.

27. Rodgers to Ann, 10 October [actually November] 1861, ibid.

28. Craig L. Symonds, ed., *Charleston Blockade*, 85, 90, 101–3.

29. Rodgers to William L. Hodge [?], 6 December 1861, Rodgers Papers.

30. Rodgers to Ann, 6 and 8 May 1862, ibid.

31. Rodgers to Goldsborough, 25 May 1862, John Rodgers Letter Book, *Galena,* Letter Books of Officers of the United States Navy at Sea, March 1778–July 1908, R.G. 45.

32. Quoted in Ann to Rodgers, 20 May 1862, Rodgers Papers.

33. *Civil War Naval Chronology, 1861–1865,* II: 77–80.

34. Entry for 22 January 1863, Gideon Welles Diary, November 1862– April 1863, Library of Congress.

35. This impression is based on a perusal of Du Pont's correspondence before the attack; e.g., he had little idea of the number of guns in the Confederate defenses or the nature of the channel obstructions. John D. Hayes, ed., *Samuel Francis Du Pont: A Selection from his Civil War Letters,* 2: *passim.*

36. Rodgers to Du Pont, 20 April 1863, *Official Records of the Union and Confederate Navies in the War of the Rebellion,* Series 1, 14: 44.

37. Rodgers to Welles, 2 May 1863, Huntington Library Manuscripts. This idea probably originated with the pessimistic Captain Percival Drayton of the monitor *Passaic.* See Du Pont to Mrs. Du Pont, 31 March 1863, Hayes, ed., *Du Pont Letters,* 2: 530.

38. Rodgers to Ann, 18 June 1863; Rodgers to William L. Hodge [?], same date, Rodgers Papers.

39. Frank M. Bennett, *The Steam Navy of the United States,* p. 587.

40. Secretary of State Hamilton Fish to Low, 20 April 1870, Diplomatic Instructions of the Department of State, 1801–1906—China, R.G. 59, National Archives.

41. Robert E. Johnson, *Far China Station,* 155–66.

42. Rodgers to Secretary of the Navy George M. Robeson, 5 July 1871, Letters from Offices Commanding Squadrons, 1841–1886, Asiatic Squadron, R.G. 45.

43. *Report of the Secretary of the Navy, 1881–1882,* Appendix.

44. Bennett, *Steam Navy,* 584.

45. Lieutenant John Rodgers became Naval Aviator No. 2 in 1911; he was a commander when killed in an airplane crash in 1926.

46. Quoted in Fletcher Pratt, *The Navy: A History,* 314.

47. Quoted in Rodgers to Ann, 26 October 1871, Rodgers Papers.

48. Quoted in Ann to William L. Rodgers, 7 May 1882, ibid.

49. Rodgers to William L. Hodge, 8 August 1865, ibid.

50. Rodgers to Ann, 7 September 1862, ibid.

51. Rodgers to Dobbin, August 1854, quoted in Cole, ed., *Yankee Surveyors,* 25.

52. Quoted in Johnson, *Rodgers,* viii.

ROBERT WILSON SHUFELDT: THE NAVAL OFFICER AS COMMERCIAL EXPANSIONIST AND DIPLOMAT

BY FREDERICK C. DRAKE

Robert Wilson Shufeldt was one of the foremost nineteenth-century expo-nents of using the U.S. Navy to further commercial expansion. He was especially adept at conveying his theories to the politically powerful in order to influence policy. In addition, he desired to implement those theories himself in various areas of the world. His reflections upon the role of the Navy in the Pacific, on the desirability of cutting an isthmian canal, on improving the commercial strength of the nation, on developing connections with indepen-dent African and Asian kingdoms, and in participating around the world as a diplomatic and a moral force place him among the leading thinkers on the Navy in national life in the nineteenth century. As a treaty-maker in Madagas-car, Johanna, Zanzibar, and Asia in the late 1870s and early 1880s, especially with the opening of Korea to U.S. trade in 1882, he was proficient in extending U.S. diplomatic and political influence. Because he also advocated an efficient navy to stimulate commercial ventures in a period of post–Civil War retrenchment, his contributions to the twilight of the old navy were instrumental in heralding the birth of the new, particularly when he served as chairman of the Second Naval Advisory Board, which superintended the designs and awarded the contracts for the White Squadron of the 1880s, the Navy's first all-steel vessels.

Shufeldt had two naval careers, the first of which was, in effect, a naval apprenticeship lasting from 1839 to 1854, with the second, and more influen-tial, stretching from midway through the Civil War until 1884. Sandwiched between the two was a period of time when he left the Navy and attempted to earn his living, first as a merchant marine captain and, second, as a consul general in Havana, Cuba during the first two years of the Civil War. Both the early naval career and the period between 1854 and 1863 were important for shaping the style and character of the naval-diplomat of the later career. During the antebellum years he began to develop theories and visions that he later tried to implement in the various parts of the world he visited on commercial and diplomatic missions. Whereas in the early years he tended to focus on the Caribbean area, in the later career he looked more extensively at Africa and Asia.

Shufeldt was born in 1822 in Red Hook, Dutchess County, New York, of German Palatine extraction. He was educated at the local Red Hook school and at Middlebury College in Vermont. He left the college after two years, without graduating, and joined the Navy in 1839. His father, George Adam Shufeldt, a prominent lawyer, wanted his son to follow in his footsteps, but a maternal uncle, Commander Steven Bayard Wilson, U.S.N., probably influenced his decision to enter the Navy.[1]

His early naval career was probably typical of that era. During his first decade in the Navy, Shufeldt cruised in the Home squadron (1839–40), the Brazil squadron (1840–43), and the African station (1846–48), which pa-

Robert Wilson Shufeldt. Photograph taken in Portland, Maine in 1870. *From a private collection.*

trolled the West African slave trade jointly with a Royal Naval squadron under the terms of the Webster–Ashburton treaty of 1842. In 1845 he attended the Naval School in Philadelphia, the predecessor of the United States Naval Academy, and was commissioned a passed midshipman in June 1845. Between 1846 and 1854 he gained experience in a variety of naval tasks, assigned at times to the Coast Survey (1845–46, 1849), and then employed by the Navy Department in 1850–51 as an acting lieutenant working to gain experience of steam propulsion on board Edward Knight Collins's steamship *Atlantic*—vying, with the remainder of Collins's ocean-named vessels, with the British Cunard company for control of the Atlantic passenger trade in the early 1850s. In 1854, after a prolonged period of furloughs (1851–53), he terminated his first naval career when he resigned from the Navy to become a merchant steamship captain on the Havana–New York–New Orleans run, working for such companies as George Law's New York and Alabama steamship line, the Tehuantepec Transit company, and, finally, the Louisiana Tehuantepec Company until 1860.[2]

After 1856 Shufeldt became associated with several prominent New Orleans business visionaries (and future leaders of the Confederacy), U.S. Senators Judah P. Benjamin and John Slidell, and Emile La Sère, president of the Louisiana Tehuantepec Company, all leading lights in the company's bid to extract a concession from the Mexican government for transisthmian transit rights. The object of the company, heavily subsidized by the New York business brothers Peter A. and Louis E. Hargous, was to breach the Mexican isthmus of Tehuantepec with a transit road and bring the commerce of San Francisco and Asia to New Orleans.[3] Shufeldt, who captained the company's main steamer, the *Quaker City*, from 1857 to 1860, later accused Benjamin and Slidell of wrecking the company, in the interests of the future Confederacy, even though Benjamin also lost heavily in the company's collapse. Shufeldt acquired a strong dislike of Slidell that carried over into his wartime diplomatic experiences when he aided Captain Charles Wilkes in the capture of Slidell and his fellow Confederate Commissioner James M. Mason of Virginia in the *Trent* affair. As the outbreak of the Civil War ended any hopes of the Southern community making a success of a southern-Mexican transit route, the collapse of the Louisiana Tehuantepec company left Shufeldt nurturing a private dream of straddling the isthmus, first with a railroad and then by canal, and he retained an interest in the southern-Mexican transit route for the rest of his life.[4]

Shufeldt gained considerable diplomatic experience in the first two years of the Civil War when he was appointed by Secretary of State William H. Seward and President Lincoln as consul general to Havana.[5] He maintained close contact with visiting naval commanders and reported the movement of Southern blockade runners. This work reached a timely climax when he returned in September 1861 from a visit to the United States—occasioned by the need to convalesce from a bout of yellow fever—in time to participate in a major incident of the Civil War, the *Trent* affair. Shufeldt consulted with Charles Wilkes, captain of the USS *San Jacinto*, then searching the consulate law books for precedents in international law to justify the dramatic seizure of James M. Mason and John Slidell from on board the Royal Mail packet *Trent*. These Confederate commissioners to London and Paris were then en route from Havana to St. Thomas and England. In addition, he arranged with Wilkes to forward to him news of the *Trent*'s time and route of sailing, a connection that broke when Wilkes's boats left the beach area too soon for Shufeldt's messenger, Charles Horner, consul at Saugua la Grande, to bring the message to the officers. The fame that Wilkes achieved for his seizure of Mason and Slidell did not embrace Shufeldt, who had played an important advisory role in the events prior to the capture.[6]

As a part of his consular task, Shufeldt watched and reported to Washington on events in Havana that might impinge upon the course of the Civil War in the United States. He spent considerable time observing the activities of Confederate agents trying to win recognition for the Confederacy from the Spanish government in Cuba. He wrote regularly to Seward about the machinations in Havana of such Confederate agents as Charles Helm, the former U.S. consul in Havana. On one occasion he barely missed assassination by a Southern sympathizer.[7] In addition, he reported on the build-up of men and supplies in late 1861 for the combined British, Spanish, and French expedition to Mexico, which sought to force the Mexicans to repay debts contracted in their capitals. He sent twice-weekly reports to Seward and his Assistant Secretary of State, Frederick W. Seward, on forces, vessels, and manpower, and the arrival of the leaders of the expedition preparing for the invasion of Mexico early in 1862.

Impressed by Shufeldt's excellent news-gathering ability, Seward decided to send him on a secret mission to Mexico to report on the condition and ability of the Mexican government to resist the tripartite expedition. At the culmination of his visit to Mexico City, Shufeldt consulted with the foreign minister of Mexico, Manuel Doblado, on the possibilities of an eight-point scheme to colonize on the isthmus of Tehuantepec the American slaves seized during the Civil War as "contraband" of war, and to provide secret service funds for the Mexican government. In these discussions, Shufeldt overstepped his authority. Seward had sent him only as an observer and had not credited him with diplomatic powers. Thus when Seward received Shufeldt's dispatches on the subject of his settlement scheme, the Secretary reprimanded him for overstepping the mark, and, later, rapped him sharply over the knuckles for persisting in attempting to justify his conduct.[8] It was probably this reprimand, and Lincoln's private disapprobation of his actions, that led Shufeldt to think again of reentering the Navy, which was just then finding a dearth of experienced officers to command blockading vessels in the newly swollen wartime squadrons. Despite the protests of some naval officers directed at the Secretary of the Navy and Congress for employing former officers at the ranks they would have held had they not left the Navy, Shufeldt successfully reentered the Navy in 1863. He did not leave his second naval career until he retired in 1884.[9]

This second naval career was interwoven with special diplomatic interests. From his early consular work in Havana, Shufeldt had gained considerable political support, which stood him in good stead in his later naval and diplomatic careers. Chief among his early political contacts before the Civil War was former Whig Senator Truman Smith of Connecticut. Shufeldt wrote Smith a long exposé of the slave trade practices in West Africa, on the middle passage, and into the island of Cuba in 1859.[10] Four years later, Smith used his influence to assist Shufeldt in reentering the Navy. Secretary of State Seward proved to be another especially helpful contact, despite the reprimand over Mexico. Gideon Welles, Lincoln's Secretary of State, thought Shufeldt "an officer of more than ordinary ability" in the South Atlantic squadron, and later gave him a quasi-independent command in the USS *Proteus* to intercept blockade runners operating outside the orbit of the normal blockading squadrons but within the overall limits of Theodorus Bailey's East Gulf Squadron.[11] In addition to these influential politicians in Lincoln's Civil War cabinet, Governor William Buckingham of Connecticut and Representative Benjamin F. Butler and Senator Charles Sumner of Massachusetts provided significant political endorsements at various stages of Shufeldt's career. Sumner, especially, discussed the question of emancipated blacks in the United States with Shufeldt, and, with Buckingham and Butler, mustered political backing in the Senate, the House of Representatives, and the Navy for a survey Shufeldt wished to make of Tehuantepec as a possible canal route in 1870–71. Shufeldt also won the support of the powerful Admiral David Dixon Porter, with whom he had served on board the steamship *Georgia*, on the New York to New Orleans run in 1851.

Shufeldt displayed a remarkable facility for maintaining close contact with the inner councils of political power through changing administrations when he received the patronage of Ulysses S. Grant's Secretary of the Navy, George M. Robeson, and that of William Maxwell Evarts and Richard Wigginton Thompson, Secretaries of State and Navy, respectively, in the Rutherford B. Hayes administration. Even later, Shufeldt acquired help from the "Plumed Knight," James G. Blaine of Maine, Garfield's Secretary of State, who sent him detailed instructions in November 1881 relating to the opening of Korea, and who offered him the post of minister to China in 1889. After Shufeldt visited William H. Hunt, James A. Garfield's Secretary of the Navy, Hunt selected him for a posting to the U.S. legation in China as a naval attaché in 1881, so that he might negotiate the Korean treaty through Chinese intermediaries. Lastly, William E. Chandler, Chester Arthur's Secretary of the Navy, protected him from criticism over his handling of the Korean treaty by appointing him to superintend the designs of the Navy's new steel vessels, the *Atlanta, Boston, Chicago,* and *Dolphin.* Shufeldt's close contacts with such major political figures from the 1860s to the late 1880s reveal that he was well known and respected in the inner circles of the post–Civil War Republican Party. [12]

Immediately after the Civil War ended, Shufeldt was posted as flag captain of the USS *Hartford* when Admiral Henry Haywood Bell's newly created Asiatic squadron resumed patrols off the China coast. His two-year service under Bell presented him with opportunities to observe the activities of American vessels operating in the opium and coolie trades and to command the USS *Wachusett* on a voyage up the Yangtze river, during which he learned at first hand the attractive possibilities of opening up "the Child of the Ocean" to American trade. At the same time he returned U.S. Consul Colton Salter to his consulate at Hankow following Chinese riots against foreigners. [13] In the wake of that task, he prepared a report for Thornton Jenkins, chief of the Navy Department's Bureau of Navigation, urging a survey of the Yangtze, the west coast of Korea, and Japanese seas with their "10,000 islands still comparatively unknown, tho' each successive year increasing in interest & importance," to stimulate American commerce. In 1867, he was ordered to investigate the loss of an American trading schooner, the *General Sherman,* which had vanished in one of the northwest rivers of Korea. When he discovered that the crew of the vessel had been massacred by villagers—who had been fired on by the captain and crew of the *Sherman* while they were trying to steal village horses to tow their vessel back over Crow rapids—Shufeldt, seconded by Rear Admiral Bell, called for punitive action or seizure of the Nan Hoo islands (Port Hamilton) off the southern coast of Korea. [14] The government wisely refrained from such action for a period before authorizing a punitive expedition, the Low–Rodgers expedition in 1871.

Following his return from the Far East in 1868, Shufeldt toyed with thoughts of rejoining the consular service and serving again in Havana. After the Cuban Revolution of 1868–73 broke out, he wrote several long articles for the press on the unfitness of the Cuban creoles to rule themselves. However, this interest in Cuban affairs proved only a temporary distraction. Shufeldt remained in the Navy and served a number of billets, including ones at the New York naval rendezvous (1868–69), at the Portsmouth Navy Yard (1870), and in the USS *Miantonomoh* in charge of funeral arrangements in the return from Great Britain of the body of George Peabody to Portland, Maine (February 1870). These routine duties were scarcely stimulating to a mind that had already been awakened to postwar diplomatic and commercial opportunities in Cuba and Asia, and Shufeldt worked assiduously for a chance to lead an expedition to survey and explore the commercial possibilities of a transit route across the isthmus of Tehuantepec in southern Mexico.

The 1870–71 Tehuantepec expedition was one of a number of surveys of isthmian crossings authorized by the U.S. government in the 1870s.[15] Shufeldt strongly believed that Tehuantepec was a viable route; and he was assisted in gaining the leadership of this expedition by congressmen who were instrumental in passage of the bill authorizing the expedition and by Admiral David Dixon Porter, who urged President Ulysses S. Grant to appoint Shufeldt to lead it.[16]

Assisted by the civilian engineer Estevan Fuertes, Commander Norman Farquhar, who surveyed the eastern coast and the mouth of the Coatzacoalcos river, and Commander Alfred Hopkins, who surveyed the Pacific lagoons for a possible terminus, Shufeldt's surveying team found water at a high enough level in the mountains to maintain a feeder canal that would supply sufficient water for a canal with a breadth at the top of 162 feet and at the bottom of 60 feet and a depth of 22 feet. This canal would have accommodated nine-tenths of the world's shipping of the time, would have required 140 locks in a 144-mile length, and would have cost, according to Fuertes's estimates in 1872 for the American Society of Civil Engineers, between $69 million and $109 million.[17] For a number of reasons, President Grant's Inter-Oceanic Canal Commission, headed by Rear Admiral Daniel Ammen, decided against Tehuantepec and in favor of a Nicaraguan canal in 1876.

In the early 1870s Shufeldt fought hard for a canal at Tehuantepec on two grounds. One was its strategic location, close to the United States. Shufeldt assumed the Gulf could be held against any naval power because the channel between Cuba and Florida in the north and Cuba and Yucatan in the south "could always be effectively closed by our Navy holding Key West and Tortugas as a base of operations." No other isthmus possessed this military advantage, and he doubted that the United States could maintain control over any other in time of war—a rueful acknowledgment of the superiority of British sea power in the Caribbean area. Second, Tehuantepec was the shortest route between New Orleans and San Francisco, shorter than Panama by 1,350 nautical miles, and therefore cheaper to cross for commercial reasons. He wanted the canal to be American-controlled and, later in his life, in the 1880s, when other routes were proposed, he objected to them because of the possibility that the United States would not control them, and because they would also undercut the railroad monopoly across the continent. What he wanted, therefore, was American commercial domination of the Gulf and the transcontinental routes of commerce. In 1871 he thought that he could gain this with a canal through Tehuantepec; in 1886, he rejected the canal because the transcontinental railroads already gave the United States such a monopoly, and such a distant canal would require a huge navy for its defense. Later still, in 1887, when he advocated a larger navy, his views on a canal began to return once more to his 1871 position. Behind all of his shifts of opinion on the canal, he retained the consistent attitude that, if it were built, it must be controlled and organized by the U.S. government, and that strategic and commercial reasons should dictate its site. For example, he noted in April 1870:

> The Pacific Ocean, with its long swell & gentle breezes lies waiting for the American flag. Alaska & the Aleutian isles form the arm which America is stretching out to embrace the Nations & the commerce of the East. A recent cruise of three years in China & Japan—has imparted to me the full conviction—that we in accord with the laws of progress—are destined to civilize & control those nations. A Canal somewhere between the Atlantic & the Pacific is for this purpose—an absolute & an inevitable necessity.

He added to this opinion later, in making his report:

> it is here . . . upon this [Pacific] sea . . . the ocean bride of America, that the East & West will join hands & the great circle of civilization will be complete— . . . . This canal is within the compass of modern science—within easy reach of our resources—it is demanded by the times & is worthy of the Nation. The Pacific Ocean is to be hereafter the field of our commercial triumphs—we have been driven from the Atlantic by superior weight of metal. Let us see that no rival flag floats upon its Pacific bosom. It is upon these shores that our ambition must cease—for it is here that our Empire terminates. The Pacific Ocean is & must be essentially American. Through it & by us China and Japan must acquire a new civilization & adopt a new creed—for it is in this sense that "Westward still, the Star of Empire takes its way."[18]

In the 1870s, apart from cruises in the European squadron (1871–73), Shufeldt turned toward reflecting upon the state of the postwar Navy while he held a number of administrative positions, the most important of which was chief of the Bureau of Equipment and Recruiting from 1875 to 1878. A reform leader, he worked to increase the Navy's efficiency by improving living conditions for sailors. To do so, he proposed relaxing the Navy's harsh punishment code, advocated better pay and working conditions for sailors, diminished desertion rates by introducing a more humane policy into the manning of vessels, and encouraged the development of a merchant training school and recruitment of American boys as apprentices for an American navy. This last scheme is usually associated with Stephen B. Luce, who picked up Shufeldt's work in the Bureau of Equipment and Recruiting and developed it further.[19]

Equally important, in 1877 and 1878 the impact of the depression of 1875–78 on the nation's economic health made Shufeldt reflect considerably upon the role of the Navy in American commercial life. In a letter on that subject, which was published under the title *The Relation of the Navy to the Commerce of the United States*, Shufeldt asserted that "No country can be really great without an external commerce."[20] He feared that the United States, with an immense internal trade, was losing much of its benefit to others by not trading under its own flag. Commercial power was to him an indication of a nation's strength and greatness. "We are sowing the seeds while others gather the fruit," he declared, adding that:

> We surrender our commercial power on our very coasts to our commercial rivals, thereby courting the contempt of nations and cultivating our own insignificance. But, in addition to this fact, which is true as a matter of political economy, we are urged imperatively to the recreation of our commerce through the absolute necessity of procuring a market for our surplus products. At least one-third of our mechanical and agricultural products are now in excess of our own wants, and we must *export* these products or *deport* the people who are creating them. *It is a question of starving millions.*

To induce capital investment in American shipping, he wanted the government to guarantee such investments against loss for ten years. That way, he assumed, shipping would increase, commerce would be reestablished, and the country would be relieved of its surplus products. He considered steamship lines to be "as essential to the commercial prosperity of the country and our real greatness as a nation." The fast steamers that he pressed for could be converted into warships for the Navy if necessary, to back up the more ponderous ships of war—a reaffirmation of the dual role for nineteenth-century naval vessels.

Shufeldt envisioned the U.S. Navy as a leader and "pioneer of commerce." "Are we to hire some belligerent to fight our battles? Is the boundless empire of the oceans, is the sceptre of the sea, to pass entirely from our hands under a policy which fears to risk a dollar for the chance of gaining a thousand?" he lectured Morse. "Are the United States and China to be joint apostles of inertness and consequent insignificance upon the world's great battlefield—the mighty deep?" The Navy could also deal with "barbarous tribes and with men who appreciate only the argument of physical force." At times he waxed eloquent in his descriptions of the advantages of the Navy to commerce, as when he told Morse:

> The man of war precedes the merchantman and impresses rude people with the sense of power of the flag which covers the one and the other . . . . Travel where you may over the boundless sea, you will find the American flag has been there before you, and the American Navy has left its imprint on every shore—no less in peace than in war . . . . Nor has this mission ended, nor will it ever end, unless Congress cripples this arm of the national defense . . . . I, for one, however, still believe in the inherent greatness of our people. I believe that our merchant marine and our Navy are joint apostles, destined to carry all over the world the creed upon which its institutions are founded, and under which its marvellous growth in a century of existence has been assured.[21]

Shufeldt himself undertook to spread that gospel to the "barbarous tribes" when he lobbied for and received permission to mount a national expedition around the world to stimulate American commercial opportunities. He was fortunate, also, that others were preparing to spread the same message, and were willing to support him in urging the government to join the scramble.

One such was Colonel Henry Shelton Sanford, an ex-diplomat who promoted the advantages of American trade with the Congo, and pressed President Rutherford B. Hayes to get involved in Africa. In addition, Aaron A. Sargent, chairman of the Senate naval committee, pushed the Navy and State Departments for a treaty to open Korea to American commerce. In consequence, Secretary of the Navy Richard Wigginton Thompson authorized a two-year around-the-world cruise for Shufeldt in the steam corvette USS *Ticonderoga*. On 29 October 1878, Thompson ordered Shufeldt to visit Africa, Asia, the islands of the Indian Ocean, and the adjacent seas "with a view to the encouragement and extension of American Commerce."

Shufeldt was also assigned a number of special tasks to perform by both the State and Navy Departments.[22] He was expected to report on the exports and imports and the commercial facilities afforded by the laws of the countries that he visited. In addition, he also possessed treaty-making powers and was urged to encourage and extend American commerce by visiting countries such as Liberia, where the United States had treaty relations, and Muscat and Zanzibar, where treaties needed revising. He was expected to make contact with tribes in Africa not under the control of European powers and to bring to their attention the benefits of trade and commerce with the United States. Following reports to the State Department about the possible maltreatment of American citizens in Madagascar and Burma, he was ordered to visit and uphold the rights of American citizens in those places, and to visit Borneo, as well as some port of "the Corea" to negotiate a treaty for the protection of shipwrecked mariners. On his pilgrimage he was to make surveys and corrections to maps and charts. He was to report upon the consular services of the United States in the various ports visited and to suggest desirable locations for adding new consulates. Lastly, he was appointed to replace Commander Richard Bradford, returning from the European squadron, who had been nominated as the U.S. arbitrator to settle a boundary dispute between the British colony of Sierra Leone and Liberia in 1879, following negotiations between the British and American governments.[23]

Under such orders the cruise of the *Ticonderoga* lasted two years. Following his instructions Shufeldt visited the west and east coasts of Africa, including Sierra Leone, Liberia, Gabon, the oil rivers of West Africa, the Congo, St. Helena (to restore the crew from coast sickness) and Angola, Cape Town, Madagascar, Zanzibar, and Muscat, as well as Aden, Persia and the Persian Gulf, India, Brunei in Borneo, Java, Spain's colonies of the Philippine Islands, Japan, China, and Korea. The *Ticonderoga* sailed and steamed 35,000 miles, dropped anchor in fifty-three ports, and visited the imperial holdings of the

The USS *Ticonderoga* at Table Bay, South Africa, in 1879. *Courtesy of the Library of Congress.*

English, Dutch, Portuguese, Spanish, and French, as well as numerous independent kingdoms, sheikdoms, and tribal areas.[24]

In Liberia, Shufeldt, now a commodore, never did arbitrate the boundary dispute, partly because of his refusal to accept the British view of his role, which would be to arbitrate disputed points, if there were any, rather than sit as umpire in the tribunal for all points under discussion. Consequently, he spent part of his time visiting old acquaintances from a previous visit in 1873 in the USS *Plymouth*, and the remainder attempting to help the republic assert its taxation laws on the tribes to the south, encouraged to defy the republic by traders operating near the Liberian garrison of Harper. He considered Liberia to be the "Garden of Africa," and the objective point of American commerce in Africa from which he hoped to see light railroads extended through the country into the interior. When he left Liberia and took his flagship farther south, he called for a greatly expanded consulate service for the coasts of Africa—one of his more notable contributions to increasing the awareness of the State Department to trade advantages on the continent.[25] He was excited by the railroads when he visited the British colony of South Africa, though he deplored the colonial policies towards the black African.

Once he rounded the Cape of Good Hope, Shufeldt negotiated new treaties for American commerce in Madagascar, with Kings Balambé and Lamarese, chiefs of the Malagasy and Sakalava tribes, effectively reinforcing their resistance to domination by the central government of Queen Ranavalona II and the Hova peoples of the island. He also negotiated a treaty with the Sultan of Johanna (Comorro islands) and urged the United States to maintain its old treaty with the Sultan of Zanzibar, negotiated in 1833, because its terms contained a preferential tariff clause allowing Americans to import into Zanzibar at a tariff rate lower than that obtained by other nations in subsequent treaties with the Sultan. The commodore wrote detailed reports on Madagascar, Johanna, and Zanzibar, and he took the *Ticonderoga* into the Persian Gulf, where she became the first American man-of-war, and the largest warship up to that time in the Karun River. Shufeldt waxed eloquent on the occasion:

> The spirit of civilization cradled in the valley of Mesopotamia has gone abroad throughout the world and in the process of time America has been born, the instrument perhaps, though the youngest of the nations—to bring back to the Euphrates—the blessings of a liberal religion and a free Government . . . . In almost a moral and religious sense therefore the display of the American flag, in these sacred waters and over the cradle of civilization, is a duty we owe to mankind—as well as to ourselves . . . . The Government of the United States is the product of ages of experiment. Its flag represents the result up to the 19th century of the Christian era. It is a sign and symbol of modern civilization—it involves a responsibility and dictates a course of action.

In the Navy Department Records in the National Archives and in Shufeldt's papers at the Library of Congress there are duplicate copies of two volumes of a journal of the cruise that he edited for publication but which was never funded by Congress. It contains a distillation of all of his experiences in showing the flag in most of the world's countries and to "barbarous tribes," when following his orders from the State and Navy Departments.[26]

When Shufeldt arrived in the Far East in the spring of 1880, he had in mind the opening of Korea to American commerce, an idea that he had held since his 1867 visit. Following Shufeldt's sojourn to the west coast rivers of Korea in 1867 seeking information on the *General Sherman*'s crew, the government did authorize a military and naval expedition, the Low–Rodgers expedition, of five ships and 1,200 men, which entered the Han River in 1871 and was fired on by the Koreans. In the ensuing fight, American forces destroyed the forts guarding the entrance to the Han River and killed 800 Koreans.[27] Yet the Low–Rodgers expedition was a failure, for it produced no opening of Korea, deeply increased the suspicions of foreign powers by the Korean government, led that government to assume that a state of war existed between the United States and Korea, and reinforced the conservative elements in the country, the *ajon* (nobles) and *yangban* (gentry), to protect their Chinese cultural heritage and their isolation even more fervently.[28]

When Shufeldt had visited the west coast in 1867, he sent a letter to the king of Korea asking about the fate of the crew of the *General Sherman*. After he had left the area, a letter was forwarded to him from the king, by Captain

Febiger of the USS *Shenandoah*, and Shufeldt was later to use this contact from the monarch as a means of introduction to persuade the Koreans that they had already made contact with him, and should therefore open the door for discussions with him. But before that, he was to encounter difficulties in his desires to open Korea.

After the *Ticonderoga* arrived at Nagasaki in March 1880, Shufeldt contacted John A. Bingham, U.S. minister to Japan, for aid in approaching Korea through the Japanese government, which had negotiated a treaty of commerce with Korea and opened the ports of Fusan (Pusan) and Gensen to Japanese trade in the treaty of Kanghwa of 1876. Under that treaty a Japanese minister resided at Seoul. As Shufeldt was arriving in Japan, the State Department authorized Bingham to apply to the Japanese minister for foreign affairs, Inouye Kaoru, for letters of introduction for Shufeldt to present to the Korean authorities. Despite the support of the Japanese cabinet, given at a meeting of 24 May 1880, the gift of nine charts of the coast of Korea to help Shufeldt navigate the waters, a covering letter from Inouye Kaoru to the Korean government pointing out that conditions in the world had changed and urging the government to meet with Shufeldt, and a visit by the *Ticonderoga* to Fusan, Shufeldt failed to gain entrance. The Korean Minister of Ceremony brusquely refused to forward any letter from Shufeldt to the monarch and inquired if "Melikan" was the country whose vessels had fired on the Han River forts in the bay of Kokwa (Han River). When told that it was the same country, he angrily informed the messenger that the Koreans would never consent to a treaty with the country that had made war. Shufeldt's first approach to Korea had failed.[29]

He tried another approach. While at Yokohama, awaiting a reply from Korea to the covering letter sent with his first approach to that country, he met Ü Tsing, the Chinese consul at Nagasaki and a representative for Li Hung-chang, the powerful Viceroy of Chihli, and guardian of the northern provinces of China. After the failure of the first attempt to get to Korea, Li issued a formal invitation to Shufeldt to visit the summer palace at Tientsin, and the commodore took the *Ticonderoga* to that port in August 1880. Shufeldt arrived just as the Japanese–Chinese struggle to control Korea was beginning to intensify.

In August 1880 the threat of war between Russia and China loomed following Chinese dissatisfaction with the disastrous Treaty of Livadia, which had led to a large section of northern China being annexed by Russia. A twenty-two-ship Russian fleet was sighted in the northern waters off the Chinese coast. Li Hung-chang wanted the views of visiting naval officers on the results of a war between Russia and China, and concurred in Shufeldt's view that it would be disastrous to China. So did the Chinese court. Shufeldt's advice pleased Li, who used it as ammunition in counseling peace. After this visit, Shufeldt took the *Ticonderoga* to San Francisco via the Sandwich Islands (Hawaii) in November 1880, and completed his cruise. It was obvious, however, that he had failed, initially, to move the Korean authorities.[30]

Three forces aided the commodore in pursuing his ambitions to open Korea. First, Li Hung-chang had contacted Charles L. Fisher, U.S. consul at Tientsin, to solicit Fisher's aid in urging Shufeldt to return to the Orient and complete the task of opening Korea. Li dangled before the commodore the prospects of a position as Grand Admiral in the Chinese Navy. When Fisher relayed the message, the commodore jumped at the chance. Second, the accession to office of James A. Garfield brought into office a Secretary of State, James G. Blaine, who, like his predecessor Evarts, was sensitive to the needs to extend American commerce. From Blaine, Shufeldt received instructions authorizing him to proceed to Korea to negotiate a treaty. Third, Secretary of the Navy William H. Hunt of Louisiana was sympathetic to Shufeldt's plans. Hunt instructed Shufeldt temporarily to join the U.S. legation in Peking as a naval attaché.[31]

The difficulties of concluding a treaty had increased considerably since the summer of 1880. Shufeldt was caught between the competing pressures of the Chinese and Japanese attempts to control Korea. Li Hung-chang was somewhat reluctant to push for a treaty because the diplomatic and military tension of the preceding summer and fall had been eased somewhat by the conclusion of a Russian–Chinese treaty restoring some of the previously annexed northern territory. He also expressed annoyance at what he thought was an attempt to make a treaty through Japan, which John A. Bingham had apparently attempted after Shufeldt had left Japan to return to the United States in November 1880. Finally, the domestic opposition within Korea to any movement to open the country was still very powerful, strong enough to deadlock the court decision.[32]

Unknown to Shufeldt, Li Hung-chang himself was kept waiting for the struggle in the Korean court to be resolved between three groups: the pro-Chinese Confucians, including the more reactionary forces backing the former regent; the Tai Wün Kun, the forces of the Queen Min's family; and the pro-Japanese progressives. Shufeldt assumed the delays were occasioned by Li's desire that he remain dependent upon Li. However, once the shifting factions in Korea finally resolved the debate over opening the country, when the king intervened in favor of the event, an envoy was appointed to negotiate at Tientsin and to lead a seventy-man-strong trading mission to Tientsin. In fairness to Li Hung-chang, who was a master at procrastination when it served his ends, he had not only to wait until the struggle in the Korean court circles had been resolved, but he was also acting under instructions from the Chinese Tsungli Yamen ("the Office for the General Management of Affairs Concerning the Various Countries"). Shufeldt did not discover this until a critical stage of the negotiations, in February 1882.

Shufeldt in China. Commodore Robert W. Shufeldt (third from left) with Li Hung-chang, viceroy of Hopei (center), and mandarins of Li's Yamen in 1881. *From a private collection.*

Shufeldt knew little of these difficulties in Korea. He had been kept waiting and was sensitive to the charge he suspected others were leveling at him, that he was a hanger-on at Li's Yamen. Both James B. Angell, U.S. minister to China, and Chester Holcombe, the chargé d'affaires who replaced Angell when he left in October 1881, urged Shufeldt to leave China, or at least Tientsin, while Li was still there. Shufeldt decided to wait for instructions from Blaine, or until he heard who had been appointed as the commissioner to negotiate any treaty. The commodore had a fortunate break when the dowager Chinese Empress Tsu An died. Li retired to the winter palace at Pao Ting Fu for court mourning, and Shufeldt was able to remain detached in Tientsin.[33]

His persistence finally paid off. A reply eventually came from Korea on 15 December 1881 that the anti-foreign party headed by the former regent had lost the struggle, and that the king and the court party in favor of opening the country had triumphed. New instructions also came through from Blaine, who drew them up in the last few days of office just before President Garfield died. His successor, Vice-President Chester Arthur, chose as his Secretary of State Frederick T. Frelinghuysen of New Jersey, a "Stalwart" feuding in the ranks of the Republican Party with Blaine's "Half-Breeds," who was not likely to be sympathetic to any of his predecessor's policies. Frelinghuysen modified, but did not abrogate, Blaine's original instructions.[34]

The United States–Korean treaty was negotiated entirely at Li's Yamen in four main sessions between 22 March and 10 April 1882. Each side presented an initial draft and points for discussion. The main contention in the Chinese drafts was that Li Hung-chang and the Chinese Tsungli Yamen wanted an article inserted in the treaty that Chosen, the Chinese name for Korea, was a dependency of China, an obvious diplomatic bargaining chip for dealing with the Japanese. Shufeldt could not agree to that, and the negotiations stalled over that clause.[35] An appeal by Shufeldt to Frelinghuysen to indicate his sentiments on the "dependency" clause was met by silence, probably out of embarrassment arising from the publication of a private letter by Shufeldt, written to Senator Aaron A. Sargent in California. When eventually signed, the treaty omitted the "dependency clause." It was taken to Korea for signing on 22 May 1882, despite being negotiated entirely in China, and was ratified in the United States on 9 January 1883. The Korean court ratified it on 19 May 1883, and it was proclaimed on 4 June 1883. The treaty permitted American citizens to trade in the open ports of Korea and to erect residences and warehouses; set a tariff of 10 percent on necessities, 30 percent on luxuries, and 5 percent export duties; established privileges for victims of shipwrecks; provided for diplomatic and consular representatives; prohibited the opium trade; granted American consuls extraterritorial jurisdiction; and guaranteed the United States most-favored-nation privileges.[36]

Shufeldt received nothing from his government for his tenacious efforts over the Korean treaty, unlike Matthew Calbraith Perry, who opened Japan in 1854 and was granted $20,000 plus costs for publishing the narrative of his cruise. Chester Arthur ignored the Korean treaty, and it was attacked in the Senate for being negotiated by an "executive agent" who had been appointed without the advice and consent of the Senate. In fact, the Korean treaty was the last treaty negotiated exclusively by a naval officer posted to a legation at a foreign court by the Secretary of the Navy and acting under instructions from the Secretary of State.[37]

The main reason for the oversights, which distressed him considerably, lay at Shufeldt's own door. In the winter of 1881, as he waited in China for news from Korea and instructions from Washington, his impatience over the long delays made Shufeldt deeply pessimistic. In January he wrote three letters, all expressing a similar view of China, that he sent to Frelinghuysen, Chester Holcombe, and Aaron A. Sargent (believing the last-named would be Chester Arthur's Secretary of the Interior). The Sargent letter, the longest and most detailed, was highly critical of China, its armed forces, Li Hung-chang, and the Empress of China. In it Shufeldt damned China as a decadent land, and argued that force was the only solution to use in dealing with it. He called the Empress "an ignorant, capricious and immoral woman"—scarcely adequate diplomatic language for a representative to use, even one delegated as a naval attaché to his legation. Shufeldt sent the letter, on which he had written the words "open letter" to a cousin in San Francisco, Albert Dibblee, expecting Dibblee to give it to Sargent and explain it was "open" for Sargent's immediate political friends in the anticipated cabinet posting. Dibblee took the letter to Sargent's hotel, and, finding him absent, left it there for him. Sargent read the letter and realized its importance (in the politics of Chinese exclusion in California, for example), but he misread (or perhaps ignored) the concept of the "open letter" and gave it to the press. It was published in the San Francisco

Evening Bulletin of 20 March 1882, while the diplomatic negotiations were still under way in Tientsin.[38]

The contents, if not the full format of the Sargent letter, were known to Li Hung-chang. During the last meeting in his Yamen, which finalized the draft before the treaty was taken to Korea for signing, Li mentioned that a friend in America had telegraphed him that Shufeldt had advocated force "was the only argument to use in Corea," and asked Shufeldt if this were true and if he had written so to his government. Bristling at this revelation, Shufeldt counterattacked:

> I then said to H. E. that since he had broached the subject outside of the matter under discussion, I wished him to understand that I appreciated the studied indignity with which I had been treated by him for four months—That I had on two or three occasions sought an interview & it had been denied me—That his manner had been more or less reflected by the mandarins surrounding him until the foreign residents in Tientsin had come to consider me an adventurer seeking office in China. . . . it was so marked, that my own Minister had on two occasions advised me to leave Tientsin rather than submit to it. . . . I then said to H. Ex. that I did not wish any further discussion to this subject & that I respectfully desired him to understand that our intercourse here after must be of an official character.[39]

Li obviously did not use his knowledge of the contents of the Sargent letter to terminate the treaty negotiations that he and China wanted to succeed.

The official American reaction to the Sargent letter was one of embarrassed silence. Shufeldt was recalled from Japan, where he was relaxing after the signing ceremonies in Korea. The President did not draw attention to the letter or the treaty in his annual message to Congress. Frelinghuysen speculated that Shufeldt's appointment for a diplomatic post might have put him out of the Navy, but, when protests were mounted, declared he was only offering a private opinion and did not intend to act upon it. In San Francisco, Shufeldt slid into deep depression and entered the Mare Island naval hospital following his return. Yet his naval friends congratulated him on his success, and they successfully deflected the opposition to his remaining in the Navy. The new Secretary of the Navy, William E. Chandler, allowed him to recuperate over the summer of 1882 in San Francisco and then appointed him to be president of the Second Naval Advisory Board, which eventually produced the plans for the construction of the White Squadron, the first all-steel vessels in the Navy. Although the designs for these vessels, the *Atlanta, Boston, Chicago,* and *Dolphin,* were later attacked, and the role of the government in awarding contracts to a staunch Republican, John Roach, for all four vessels, was condemned by the Democratic press, Shufeldt himself did not come under fire for his role on the board.[40]

The opening of Korea and the presidency of the Second Naval Advisory Board were the crowning achievements of Shufeldt's diplomatic and naval careers, but were deeply tinged with personal regret. His was a career that was interesting and significant in merging the role of the naval officer as diplomat, thinker, and man of action. The treaty was the high point for him of a life spent in reasoning and examining what the role of the Navy should be in the nation's diplomatic, commercial, and national life. He preached the gospel of commercial expansion for American business in Africa and Asia, and he was instrumental in creating opportunities for others to apply this doctrine, both with his world cruise and with his opening of the hermit kingdom. His views on the necessity of an isthmian canal showed that he placed American abilities to defend and control that canal, and commercial nearness to America, above all other considerations; and he became involved in the great debate of the 1880s on the desirability of a canal. He displayed an ability to think through problems and to see how they affected American society and security and the future of the Pacific. He urged the taking of the Sandwich (Hawaii) islands once a canal was built.

Yet, as far as the most important event of his career was concerned, the negotiating of the Korean treaty, he never received any official thanks from his government similar to what Perry had received—an omission that embittered the admiral and his adopted daughter, Molly Miller Shufeldt. His marvelously detailed journal of the cruise of the *Ticonderoga* still awaits a publisher, when, in fact, less significant journals have been published. Shufeldt retired to Japan after serving as president of the Naval Advisory Board, but he returned to the United States in 1889, when the Republicans regained office. Offered the position of minister to China by James G. Blaine, he declined, preferring to live out a relatively quiet retirement in Washington and Virginia, cared for by his niece and adopted daughter, Molly. His last years were ones of increasing bitterness toward his three sons, who had been estranged from him after the death of their mother in 1871, and by his preference for Molly's company not theirs.

That he possessed racial views in accordance with the social Darwinism of the late nineteenth century was apparent. In his eyes the United States was not only the epitome of civilization and democracy up to the nineteenth century, whose task was the uplifting of "inferior" races in Africa and the Far East, but he actively counseled his government to commence the task. He was far ahead of most of his contemporaries in stressing the need for increased commerce, better diplomacy, a better consular service, and stronger commercial and naval power. As a diplomat he helped the United States to compete openly in the arena of Far Eastern tensions in the crucial rivalry of competing empires in the last two decades of the nineteenth century.

Shufeldt was determined to overhaul the Navy, his work at the Bureau of Equipment and Repair revealed considerable organizational talents, and he instituted reforms that improved working conditions for servicemen and lowered desertion rates. Finally, as a naval theorist Shufeldt recognized that the United States needed an efficient—and toward the end of his life he would have said a larger—navy to spread the nation's message throughout the world.

Seldom remembered today, his explorations, surveys, cruises, naval reforms, and diplomatic efforts were noted by contemporaries, especially prominently situated politicians, and it is certain that his life and work helped to create, by thought and action, the intellectual fomulation of the pre– and post–Civil War expansionist schools that he so effectively links.

FURTHER READING

Compared with other nineteenth-century naval officers, works on Robert W. Shufeldt were sparse until the 1950s and 1960s. Contemporary accounts relating to Korea, including the 1881 study "Corea," *Cyclopedia of Political Science* and "Corea The Hermit Nation," *Bulletin of the American Geographical Society*, did not mention him. From shortly after his death in 1895 until the 1950s, the few writings on him, however, tended to concentrate on the opening of Korea. See, in particular, James S. Gale, "The Fate of the *General Sherman*: From an Eye Witness Account" and William E. Griffis's two works, "The Opening of Korea" and the longer study *Corea: The Hermit Nation*. Four short articles appeared between 1892 and 1917, including one by the missionary Henry G. Appenzeller, which contained a summary of Shufeldt's own recollections in "The Opening of Korea: Admiral Shufeldt's Account of It," in 1892; one article upon "The Opening of Korea by Commodore Shufeldt," which surveyed Shufeldt's diplomacy but misjudged his attitude towards Japanese help over Korea, presented in three different sources between 1910 and 1912 by Charles Oscar Paullin (which influenced Tyler Dennett's 1922 publication *Americans in Eastern Asia*); and the short studies in 1917, F. M. Beck's "Interpreting for Captain Shufeldt," and (Anon.) "Admiral Shufeldt's Visits to Korea." In 1938 Captain A. S. Hickey wrote the first balanced study of Shufeldt as a naval officer and diplomat, "Rear Admiral Robert Wilson Shufeldt, United States Navy, Gentleman and Diplomat."

During the 1950s and 1970s interest in Shufeldt began to grow, and a number of master's theses and doctoral dissertations on Shufeldt explored his role in diplomacy and in the Navy, and his biographical–naval–diplomatic career. They include: the pioneer study of diplomacy by Russell W. Smith, "The Opening of Korea by Commodore Robert W. Shufeldt"; the routine survey by William J. Brinker, "Robert W. Shufeldt and the Changing Navy"; and the detailed biography by Frederick C. Drake, " 'The Empire of the Seas': A Biography of Rear Admiral Robert Wilson Shufeldt, USN," a revised version of which was published under the title *The Empire of the Seas* (1984). While Shufeldt received passing mention in such works as William A. Williams's *The Roots of the Modern American Empire*; David Pletcher's *The Awkward Years*, and Milton Plesur's *America's Outward Thrust*, more detailed studies of individual aspects of his career began to be made in such works as

Kenneth J. Hagan, *American Gunboat Diplomacy and the Old Navy: 1877–1889*; Hagan's essay on Shufeldt in *America Spreads her Sails* edited by Clayton J. Barrow; and articles exploring phases of his career, such as his views on the slave trade to Cuba in Frederick C. Drake, "Secret History of the Slave Trade to Cuba Written by an American Naval Officer, Robert Wilson Shufeldt, 1861," and his role in the *Trent* affair in Frederick C. Drake, "The Cuban Background of the *Trent* affair," as well as the publication of a Shufeldt dispatch of 1879 on South Africa (previously published, see the New York *Times*, November 28, 1879) in Thomas J. Noer, "Commodore Robert W. Shufeldt and America's South African Strategy."

The major collection of Shufeldt's private and official papers is in the Manuscripts Division of the Library of Congress, a deposit of the Naval Historical Foundation, which received the papers from Mary Abercrombie (Miller) Shufeldt, Shufeldt's adopted daughter. There is a small and routine collection of letters dealing with his service in the Mediterranean squadron, 1871–73, in the New York Public Library. Many of his letters can be found in the collections of James B. Angell, William E. Chandler Papers, Stephen B. Luce Papers, William Henry Seward Collection, and Charles Wilkes Papers.

Genealogical and anecdotal material on the family can be found in H. B. Shufelt, *Our Folks: A History of the Shufelt Family* and the reminiscences by Shufeldt's eldest son, Robert W. Shufeldt, Jr., "Life History of an American Naturalist."

Material upon various aspects of Shufeldt's Civil War and post–Civil War naval service include Mark F. Boyd, "The Joint Operations of the Federal Army and Navy near St. Mark's, Florida, March 1865," and E. Mowbray Tate, "Admiral Bell and the New Asiatic Squadron 1865–1868." For his work in superintending the design of the White Squadron and his views on an enlarged navy, see "New Steam Cruisers for the United States Navy," *Annual Report of the Secretary of the Navy, 1883*, Appendix 2, and *Senate Report 161, 48th Cong., 1st Sess.*, "Report to accompany Bill S. 698 to authorize the construction of additional steel vessels for the Navy." On isthmian negotiations refer to the *Annual Reports of the Secretary of the Navy, 1871*, Appendix 14, 178–203; *1873*, Appendix 12, 164–80, Appendix 13, 180–207, Appendix 15, 260–64; *1875*, Appendix 12, 206–35 and Appendix 13, 235–69; and read Gerstle Mack, *The Land Divided*. A good article on the development of the call for an exclusive American canal is Jackson Crowell, "The United States and a Central American Canal 1869–1877."

To place Shufeldt effectively in the postwar Navy, begin with the more traditional accounts such as Walter Herrick, *The American Naval Revolution* and Donald W. Mitchell, *History of the Modern American Navy from 1883 through Pearl Harbor*. Afterward turn to the more innovative and challenging newer studies that have begun to question older interpretations. For instance, Lance C. Buhl, "Mariners and Machines: Resistance to Technological Change in the American Navy, 1865–1869," in the *Journal of American History*; Stanley Sandler, "A Navy in Decay: Some Strategic Technological Results of Disarmament, 1865–1869, in the U.S. Navy," 138–42; and Robert Seager II, "Ten Years before Mahan: The Unofficial Case for a New Navy, 1880–1890," all provide reflective alternatives to older views. Next, one can sample some of Shufeldt's naval writings, letters, and reports. Four important ones that have been published are *Report of Explorations and Surveys to ascertain the Practicability of a Ship Canal between the Atlantic and Pacific Oceans by way of the isthmus of Tehuantepec*; Shufeldt's letter to Leopold Morse, *The Relation of the Navy to the Commerce of the United States; The United States Navy in connection with the Foundation, Growth and Prosperity of the Republic of Liberia*; and the letter to Aaron A. Sargent printed originally in The San Francisco *Evening Bulletin*, 20 March 1882 and the New York *Times*, 30 March 1882, now reprinted in F. C. Drake, *The Empire of the Seas*, Appendix 1, 355–62.

On the Korean treaty-making process see Frederick F. Chien, *The Opening of Korea: A Study of Chinese Diplomacy, 1876–1885*; Hag-w'on Sunoo, "A Study of the U.S.–Korean Treaty of 1882"; Francis C. Jones, "Foreign Diplomacy in Korea, 1866–1894," Chapter 7; and David H. Kim, "Americans in Korea: The Background of the Shufeldt Treaty, 1866–1882." James Burrill Angell, *The Reminiscences of James Burrill Angell* and his "The Diplomatic Relations Between the United States and China," while not often used in diplomatic studies, have useful contemporary materials on the situation in Tientsin. The *Papers relating to the Foreign Relations of the United States, 1867 and 1870*, have short but useful materials on Korea (414–16 and 333–39 respectively).

In a modern and recent account Martina Deuchler, *Confucian Gentlemen and Barbarian Envoys: The Opening of Korea, 1875–1885* offers revised interpretations from her doctoral dissertation, and there is new material on two crucial Secretaries of State, who were instrumental in propelling the United States and Shufeldt toward Korea, in two dissertations: Gary Pennanen, "The Foreign Policy of William Maxwell Evarts," especially the chapter "Shufeldt and Grant"; and Richard C. Winchester, "James G. Blaine and the Ideology of American Expansionism."

Good secondary surveys to set Shufeldt into the diplomatic context can be found in Milton Plesur, ed., *Creating an American Empire, 1865–1914*; Gregory Henderson, *Korea: The Politics of the Vortex*; Hilary Conroy, *The Japanese Seizure of Korea: 1868–1910*; M. Frederick Nelson, *Korea and the Old Orders in Eastern Asia*; C. I. Eugene Kim and Han-Kyo Kim, *Korea and the Politics of Imperialism, 1876–1910*; and the short article by Milton Plesur, "Across the Wide Pacific." Yur-bok Lee, *Diplomatic Relations between the United States and Korea, 1866–1887* has some serious errors with regard to Shufeldt. Donald S. MacDonald, "The American Role in the Opening of Korea to the West" is somewhat naive about American intentions. Robert T. Pollard, "American Relations with Korea, 1882–1895" is a long and useful article.

NOTES

1. His ancestors, originally named Zufeld, came to New York in the German Palatine migration of 1710, moved to Rhinebeck and Red Hook, held slaves, and, later, included farmers in Livingston Manor who helped challenge the title of Robert Livingston in 1795. Henry B. Shufelt, *Our Folks: A History of the Shufelt Family*, 17–21; F. C. Drake, *The Empire of the Seas*, 4–6.

2. Drake, *The Empire of the Seas*, 6–11.

3. J. Fred Rippy, "The Diplomacy of the United States and Mexico Regarding the Isthmus of Tehuantepec, 1848–1860," *Mississippi Valley Historical Review*, VI (1920): 503–21; Judah P. Benjamin, "A Card," New Orleans *Daily Picayune*, 9 August 1851; Peter A. Hargous to James G. Bennett, "The Tehuantepec Route: Another Side," New York *Herald*, 12 August 1856.

4. Shufeldt to Seward, 21 November 1861, R.G. 59: Dispatches from U.S. Consuls in Havana (hereafter, CD, Havana), vol. 41 (3 January–31 December 1861), National Archives; "Through Mexico to the Pacific–In Search of a Canal Route," p. 26 (undated, post-1870), Robert Wilson Shufeldt Papers (hereafter RWS), Box 21, Library of Congress.

5. "Memorandum on Foreign Appointments," in R. P. Basler, ed., *The Collected Works of Abraham Lincoln*, 4: 310.

6. F. C. Drake, "The Cuban Background of the *Trent* Affair," *Civil War History*, XIX (1973): 29–49.

7. Shufeldt to Seward, nos. 75, 76, 81–87, 89, 91, 96, and 109, 25 October, 4, 15, 21, 22, 27 November, 5 and 24 December, 1861, CD, Havana, 41; nos. 4, 6, 8, 13, 20, 28, 31–37, 48, 50, and 51; 14, 17, 24 January, 6, 14, 28 February, 7, 22 March, 10, 16, and 17 April 1862, CD, Havana, 45 (12 January–31 December 1862); Shufeldt to F. W. Seward, 10 December 1861, William Henry Seward Collection, Rush-Rhees Library, University of Rochester; Shufeldt to F. W. Seward, 16 January 1862, CD, Havana, 45; on the assassination attempt, see R. W. Shufeldt, Jr., "Life History of an American Naturalist," *Medical Life*, 31 (1924): 72; Shufeldt to W. H. Seward, private letter, 24 February 1862, Seward Collection; to F. W. Seward, private letters, 20 March, 1 and 17 April 1862, CD, Havana, 45.

8. Seward to Shufeldt, two letters, 31 March 1862, R.G. 59: Instructions of the Department of State to Consuls (hereafter CI), Havana, 31: 332–34, National Archives; Shufeldt to Doblado, 16 May 1862, and Doblado to Shufeldt, 19 May 1862, CD, Havana, 45; Seward to Shufeldt, 23 May, 24 June, and 15 July 1862, CI, Havana, 31: 408–9, 437–38, and 466–68; Drake, *The Empire of the Seas*, 58–69.

9. Truman Smith to Shufeldt, 30 May and 21 November 1861, 3, 7, 17 January, 4, 14, 18 March, 16 December 1862, RWS, Box 18 (May 1861), Box 11 (November 1861), Box 12 (January and March 1862), Box 19 (October–December 1862).

10. F. C. Drake, ed., "Secret History of the Slave Trade to Cuba Written

by an American Naval Officer, Robert Wilson Shufeldt, 1861," *Journal of Negro History*, LV (1970): 218–35.

11. Howard K. Beale, ed., *Diary of Gideon Welles: Secretary of the Navy under Lincoln and Johnson*, II, entries for 15 and 17 September, 3 October 1863, 434, 466–67; Welles to Shufeldt, 6 October 1863, RWS, Box 6 (October–December 1863).

12. Shufeldt to Sumner, 17 January 1862, Sumner Collection, Harvard University, vol. 56, no. 15; W. A. Buckingham to Shufeldt, 21 May 1870, RWS, Box 13 (17–31 May 1870); Sumner's resolution amending H.R. 2165 was sent to the Committee on Appropriations, 4 July 1870, 41st Cong., 2nd Sess., copy in RWS, Box 14 (4–15 July 1870); on contacts with Buckingham, Porter, Evarts, Thompson, Blaine, and Hunt, see Drake, *The Empire of the Seas*, (Buckingham) 118, 126, 128, 153; (Porter) 11, 117–18, 123, 126, 128–29, 131, 146, 154, 158, 163; (Thompson and Evarts) 164–67, 175, 177–80, 206–7, 222–23; (Blaine) 261, 272–75; (Hunt) 261.

13. Shufeldt to Bell, nos. 11, 19, 24, and 25, 3, 30 October and 1 November 1866 and "Dispatches from the Acting Taotai at Kiu Kiang . . . to Shu [*sic*] Commander of the naval troops of the Great Country of America," 20 March 1867, Letterbook (hereafter LBK) of USS *Wachusett* 1866–1868, RWS, Box 3; Salter to Shufeldt, 20 February, 13 March 1867, RWS, Box 8; Shufeldt to Jenkins, 1867, RWS, Box 24 (China and Korea Correspondence, 1882); E. M. Tate, "Admiral Bell and the New Asiatic Squadron, 1865–1868," *American Neptune*, XXXII (1972): 130.

14. Shufeldt to Bell, after no. 43, memorandum, 25 and 30 January 1867; Shufeldt to the King of Korea, 24 January 1867; Shufeldt to His Excellency, the Presiding Officer of the district of Chang Yuen Heen, 25 January 1867; "Memorandum of an interview between Commander Shufeldt of the USS *Wachusett* and a Corean official from the district city of Hae Chow Poo on the Tai Tong river, 29 January 1867," with no. 46; and Shufeldt to Bell, no. 47, 30 January 1867, all in LBK *Wachusett*, 1866–1868, RWS, Box 3; H. G. Appenzeller, "The Opening of Korea: Admiral Shufeldt's Account of It," *Korean Repository*, I (1892): 59–60.

15. "The Annexation of Cuba," "The Independence of Cuba," and "The Future of Cuba," RWS, Box 19; "The Creole in Cuba," Philadelphia *Press*, 2 December 1868, RWS, Box 31, Newspaper clippings, 1859–99; Postings in Porter to Shufeldt, 23 May 1870, RWS, Box 13 (1–15 May 1870); M. Smith to Shufeldt, 18 December 1869; Godon to Shufeldt, 31 December 1869; Robeson to Shufeldt, 4 January and 1 February 1870, RWS, Box 9 (December 1869) (January 1870) (February 1870); United States Joint Resolution for a survey for a ship canal across the Isthmus of Tehuantepec, 41st Cong. 2nd Sess., S.R. 161, 18 March 1870, RWS, Box 13 (March 1870); "Through Mexico to the Pacific—In Search of a Canal Route," RWS, Box 21 (written reports); Shufeldt to Robeson, 26 September 1870, RWS, Box 20 (1861–September 1870).

16. Starkweather to Shufeldt, 25 June 1870; Buckingham to Shufeldt, 28 June 1870, RWS, Box 13 (20–30 June 1870); Sumner's resolution amending H.R. 2165, 4 July 1870, 41st Cong., 2nd Sess., copy in Shufeldt papers, RWS, Box 14 (4–15 July 1870); Porter to Shufeldt, 25 June 1870, RWS, Box 20 (1861–September 1870); "Through Mexico to the Pacific–In Search of a Canal Route," RWS, Box 21 (written reports).

17. Drake, *The Empire of the Seas*, Chapter 8; Fuertes to Shufeldt, 7 February 1874, RWS, Box 21 (written reports).

18. "Report of Captain R. W. Shufeldt, USN, to Hon. George M. Robeson, 11 August 1871," in *Report of Explanations and Surveys . . . by way of the Isthmus of Tehuantepec*; Shufeldt, New York *Herald*, 13 February 1874; Shufeldt to the *Nautical Gazette*, 1874, copy in RWS, Box 9 (front of box). "Admiral Shufeldt: the Veteran Officer on the Panama Canal and Coast Defenses," San Francisco *Chronicle*, 28 June 1886; reprinted New York *Times*, 6 July 1886; Washington *Post*, 3 February 1885; "Canal Question and Admiral Shufeldt," *The Nation*, 40, no. 1024 (12 February 1885), 128; two quotations from Shufeldt, rough draft of a proposal to go before Congress, and "Through Mexico to the Pacific–In Search of a Canal Route," 35, 51–52, RWS, Box 21 (written reports).

19. Drake, *The Empire of the Seas*, Chapter 9, "The Naval Theorist."

20. Shufeldt, *The Relation of the Navy to the Commerce of the United States*.

21. Ibid.

22. Evarts to Thompson, 3 February 1879, Thompson to Shufeldt, 25 February 1879, RWS, Box 22 (West Africa reports, Congo Cotton) and RWS, Box 27, Cruise MSS, pt. 2, "On the Liberian Boundary Question of 1879"; on Sargent's resolution, see U.S. *Congressional Record*, 45th Cong., 2nd Sess., 7, pt. 3: 2324 and 2600–2601; Thompson to Shufeldt, 29 October 1879, Lettercopybook of Richard Wigginton Thompson, Lilly Library, Indiana University, 190–94; Drake, *The Empire of the Seas*, 176–80.

23. Evarts to Thompson, 23 October, 9 November, and 2, 12 December 1878, R.G. 59: Domestic Letters of the Department of State (hereafter DLDS), vol. 125 (22 October–31 December 1878), vol. 23: 206–12, 437–38; Thompson to Evarts, 24 and 29 October, 15 November 1878: R.G. 59: Miscellaneous Letters of the Department of State (hereafter MLDS) (18–31 October 1878) (15–30 November 1878); Lettercopybook of Richard Wigginton Thompson, 190–94; Evarts to Sir Edward Thornton, 12 November 1878; R.G. 59: Notes to Foreign Legations in the United States from the Department of State, Great Britain, vol. 17 (28 July 1875–26 February 1879): 632; Thornton to Evarts, 13 November 1878; R.G. 59: Notes from the British Legation in the United States to the Department of State, vol. 103 (9 February 1878–12 November 1878), DNA.

24. Shufeldt to Thompson, nos. 26, 8 November 1880, RWS, Box 4, Ticonderoga LSN, 405–6, 409; "The Cruise of the Ticonderoga," *Annual Report of the Secretary of the Navy, 1880* (hereafter ARSN), 27–28.

25. Drake, *The Empire of the Seas*, 185–200.

26. Ibid., 211–12, 214–16; the unpublished MS of the cruise of the *Ticonderoga* is in RWS, Boxes 26–28 and a bound, two-volume copy is in the Navy Department Archives, R.G. 45, National Archives, Naval Records Collection of the Office of Naval Records and Library, Appendix A, entry 25, series entry 11.

27. Robert Swartout, Jr., "Cultural Conflict and Gunboat Diplomacy: The Development of the 1871 Korean American Incident," *Journal of Social Science and Humanities* [Seoul], XLIII (1976): 117–69; K. Jack Bauer, "The Korean Expedition of 1871," U.S. Naval Institute *Proceedings*, 74 (1948): 197–204; William M. Leary, Jr., "Our Other War in Korea," U.S. Naval Institute *Proceedings*, 94 (1968), and Peter Karsten and Thomas H. Patterson, "Reply to Leary, Our Other War in Korea," *ARSN, 1871.*

28. Carl F. Bartz, Jr., "The Korean Seclusion Policy, 1860–1876," 67–69; Soo B. Choi, "Political Dynamics in Hermit Korea; The Rise of Royal Power in the Decade of the Tae Wŏn Kun, 1864–1873," Chapters 3–4; Andrew C. Nahm, "Reaction and Response to the Opening of Korea, 1876–1884," *Studies on Asia*, VI (1965), 61–80, and "Korea's Response to International Rivalries: Korean Domestic Policies, 1876–1884," *Michigan Academy . . .* , L (1964): 445–65.

29. Shufeldt to the King of Korea, no. 44, 24 January 1867, RWS, Box 3, LBK *Wachusett*; Febiger to Shufeldt enclosing a letter from the King of Korea to Shufeldt, 19 May 1868, RWS, Box 28, World Cruise of USS *Ticonderoga*, 1879–1883, and undated (China and Japan); Drake, *The Empire of the Seas*, 238–44.

30. Drake, *The Empire of the Seas*, 245–49, 251–52.

31. C. L. Fisher to Shufeldt, 3 March 1881 and Blaine to Shufeldt, 9 May 1881, RWS, Box 24 (Korea Correspondence, 1880–81) and (China Correspondence, 1880–81); Appenzeller, "The Opening of Korea," 61; Shufeldt to Holcombe, January 1881, RWS, Box 4, Korean Letterbook . . . formal letters to the Secretary of the Navy and Secretary of State, 1 July 1881 to 3 August 1882 (hereafter KLBK), 26–27; Blaine to James B. Angell, no. 94, 9 May 1881, Diplomatic Instructions, China 3 (January 1879–February 1885); Hunt to Shufeldt, 18 March 1881 at back of RWS, Box 4, KLBK.

32. Shufeldt to Blaine, 1 July 1881, RWS, Box 4, KLBK, 1–4; Shufeldt to Angell, 4 July 1881, Angell MSS 7, University of Michigan Library; Angell to Shufeldt, 14 September 1881, RWS, Box 16 (July–September 1881); F. F. Chien, *The Opening of Korea: A Study of Chinese Diplomacy, 1876–1885*, 78–79.

33. Shufeldt to Angell, 15 July 1881, RWS, Box 4, KLBK, 4–6; and 2, 3, 18, 30 July, 4, 11, 18, 21, 24 August, 23 September, 1 October 1881, Angell MSS 7; Angell to Shufeldt, 19 July 1881, RWS, Box 24 (Korea Correspondence, 1880–81); to Shufeldt, 1, 12, 17, 21, 22 August, 25 September, 8 October 1881, RWS, Box 16 (July–September 1881) (Octo-

ber–December 1881); Chester Holcombe to Shufeldt, 4 February 1882, RWS, Box 24 (Korea Correspondence, January–April 1882); Holcombe to Frelinghuysen, no. 60, 4 February 1882, Diplomatic Dispatches, China, 58; Shufeldt to Frelinghuysen, nos. 2 and 4, 11 and 30 March 1882, RWS, Box 4, KLBK, 46–47, 51–52; former in DD, China 59.

34. Chien, *The Opening of Korea*, 80–81; C. I. E. Kim and H.-K. Kim, *Korea and the Politics of Imperialism, 1876–1910*, 20–21, 24, and n. 19; Appenzeller, "The Opening of Korea," 61; Blaine to Shufeldt, 14 November 1881, and Blaine to Holcombe, no. 134, 14 November 1881; Frelinghuysen to Shufeldt, 6 January 1882, RWS, Box 4, KLBK, all at back of volume; Richard C. Winchester, "James G. Blaine and the Ideology of American Expansionism," 61.

35. First American draft; Chinese draft no. 2, RWS, Box 24 (Treaties Korea) and (Korean Treaties); Shufeldt to Li Hung-chang, 4 April 1882, RWS, Box 4, KLBK, 54–55; T. C. Lin, "Li Hung-chang: His Korea Policies, 1870–1885," *Chinese Social and Political Science Review*, 19 (1935): 223–24; Kim and Kim, *Korea and the Politics of Imperialism*, 22, n. 14; Hag-w'on Sunoo, "A Study of the U.S.–Korean Treaty of 1882," *Korea Review* II (1949): 32, n. 41.

36. Treaty draft no. 3, RWS, Box 24 (Treaties, Korea); Shufeldt to Li Hung-chang, 4 April 1882, RWS, Box 4, KLBK, 54–55; Lin, "Li Hung-chang: His Korea Politics," 224–25; Shufeldt to Frelinghuysen, nos. 5 and 7, 10 and 28 April 1882; and telegrams of 12 and 19 April 1882, RWS, Box 4, KLBK, 58–59, 60, 62–63; DD, China 59; Paullin, *Diplomatic Negotiations of American Naval Officers 1778–1883*, 322; Dennett, *Americans in Eastern Asia*, 459; a copy of the final treaty is in Drake, *The Empire of the Seas*, Appendix 2, 363–68.

37. Molly Shufeldt to Mrs. A. Dibblee, 5 July 1882, RWS, Box 16 (June–August 1882); Henry M. Wriston, *Executive Agents in American Foreign Relations*, 164, n. 126, and 174.

38. Shufeldt to Sargent, January 1882; Shufeldt to Holbombe, 16 January 1882; Shufeldt to Frelinghuysen, no. 1, 23 January 1882, RWS, Box 4, KLBK, 30–41, 15–16, 22–25; Holcombe to Frelinghuysen, no. 108, 23 May 1882, DD, China 60 (15 May–30 July 1882); Dibblee to Shufeldt, 15 March 1882, RWS, Box 16 (January–April 1882) San Francisco *Evening Bulletin*, 20 March 1882; New York *Times*, 30 March 1882; P. H. Clyde, *United States Policy toward China: Diplomatic and Public Documents, 1839–1939*, 159–65.

39. Shufeldt memorandum, 6 April 1882, RWS, Box 4, KLBK, 56–57.

40. Drake, *The Empire of the Seas*, 305–19; "Secretary Whitney's Task," Washington *Post*, 13 September 1885; Bennett, *Steam Navy of the United States*, 777; ARSN, *1883*, 4, 6–7, 85–88; Shufeldt to Molly, 13 September 1885, RWS, Box 17 (General Correspondence, 1885).

BENJAMIN FRANKLIN ISHERWOOD: FATHER OF THE MODERN STEAM NAVY

BY DEAN C. ALLARD

Benjamin Franklin Isherwood was the father of the steam navy of the Civil War and a leader in the professionalization of naval engineering. He was born in New York City on 6 October 1822 into a solid middle-class family. His father was a physician who died while Isherwood was an infant. His mother later married John Green, a civil engineer who became noted for his work on the Croton Aqueduct, which carried drinking water to New York City.[1]

In 1831, at the age of eight, the young boy enrolled in the Albany Academy, a rigorous institution that included on its faculty Joseph Henry, later a famed American physicist. Isherwood studied scientific subjects with Henry, but his formal education came to an abrupt end five years later when the strong-willed youth was expelled from the academy for misconduct. Barred from the classroom, Isherwood began a series of apprenticeships that provided a basic grounding in the engineering sciences of his day. In an era when few opportunities existed for formal technical education, it was typical that aspiring engineers received their training in America's shop culture.[2] In Isherwood's case, as for other engineers of his generation, this experience promoted the suspicion of theory and devotion to practical application that characterized his lifelong approach to his profession.

Isherwood initially was employed by the Utica and Schenectady Railroad, where he worked as a civil engineer and assisted in designing and maintaining steam locomotive engines. Thereafter, he was associated with the Croton Aqueduct project, the New York and Erie Railroad, and the federal government's Lighthouse Bureau. While with the last organization, Isherwood traveled to France to oversee construction of lighthouse lenses and to prepare a report on French lighthouse practices. Upon returning to the United States, Isherwood resolved to seek a commission in the new Engineering Corps established by the U.S. Navy in 1842. To meet the practical requirements for that position, he worked briefly with the Novelty Iron Works of New York City, a well-known steam engine manufacturer.

In 1844, at the age of twenty-one, Isherwood began a forty-year association with the U.S. Navy when he received an appointment as first assistant engineer in the first group admitted to the new Engineer Corps. His first tour of duty was at the Pensacola Navy Yard, where he served as a yard engineer and engineering officer for a small yard steamer. In 1845, Isherwood returned to Washington to be examined in his field and, as a result of his poor performance, was demoted to second assistant engineer. This process revealed the determination of Charles Haswell, the Navy's engineer in chief, to maintain

Benjamin Franklin Isherwood. Photograph taken while he was chief of the Bureau of Engineering, 1811–69. *Courtesy of the Naval Institute.*

high standards for the service's emerging technical community.[3] Despite his personal disappointment in 1845, Isherwood's later career revealed that he wholeheartedly supported Haswell's ambition to professionalize the Navy's Engineer Corps.

At the outbreak of the Mexican War, Isherwood served in the war zone on board the *Princeton*, the world's first screw-propelled warship. The designer of this vessel's machinery was the eminent Swedish-American inventor John Ericsson. Despite Ericsson's prominence, however, Isherwood had no hesitation in criticizing the efficiency of Ericsson's propeller, an opinion that may have contributed to the bitter antagonism between the two engineers that became evident during the Civil War.[4] Following his detachment from the *Princeton*, Isherwood transferred to the small steamer *Spitfire*, whose executive officer and later commander was David Dixon Porter. These two leaders also were destined to become foes. But, in 1847, Porter praised Isherwood for the efficiency of his engineering crew and commended the young engineer for his personal bravery during a landing on the Mexican coast.[5]

In July 1847, Isherwood resumed his original rank as a first assistant engineer, and in the summer of 1849, he advanced to the position of chief engineer. Under the regulations of that era, this step meant that for the first time Isherwood was a commissioned officer in the Navy. Nevertheless, many line officers were reluctant to accept steam engineers of any rank as their equals. Although recognizing the value of the new technology, they tended to view engineers as little more than civilian mechanics.[6]

In 1848, Isherwood began another tour with the Treasury Department's Lighthouse Bureau and married a widow, Mrs. Anna Hansine Ragsdale. During the latter part of 1850, he served briefly as the principal assistant to the Navy's engineer in chief. Later Isherwood turned his attention to the construction of new engines for the gunboat *Allegheny*. During that vessel's trials in 1853, the foundations for the gunboat's engines broke in several places. This embarrassing failure apparently helped to influence Isherwood's later design philosophy, which stressed exceptionally heavy and durable components.[7]

Between 1855 and 1858, Isherwood was chief engineer in the screw steamer *San Jacinto*, which made an extended cruise to the Far East. Already the author of several professional articles, Isherwood took advantage of his free time on board the *San Jacinto* to continue the study of his field. Upon his return to the United States, he published a pioneering two-volume work entitled *Engineering Precedents for Steam Machinery* (New York, 1859), which demonstrated his almost insatiable curiosity in all aspects of steam technology. Drawing upon his wide reading and personal observations, Isherwood presented his findings on the distribution and loss of energy in working steam plants, the efficiency of screw propellers, the varying energies produced by different types of coal, and other professional subjects.[8]

Isherwood's scholarly interests led to his appointment to several experimental boards, including one that in 1860 investigated the engines of the *Michigan*, a Great Lakes naval steamer. Of particular interest was the hypothesis of the European engineer Mariotte that maximum economy could be achieved by introducing steam only in the early stages of a piston's movement in the engine cylinder. During the balance of the piston's stroke, the natural expansion of steam would perform the necessary work. Isherwood and his colleagues demonstrated, however, that with the poorly insulated engines of their day, which used low-pressure and low-temperature steam, a ratio of steam "expansion was soon reached beyond which an increase would cause an absolute diminution of economy."[9] Despite the theoretical merits of Mariotte's law, they concluded that optimum efficiency required the injection of new steam until a piston completed about 70 percent of its stroke.

Early in 1861, when these findings were reported, they were greeted with "astonishment" by the world of engineering.[10] They later were elaborated upon by Isherwood, who became the chief proponent of the low-expansion school, in a two-volume work entitled *Experimental Researches in Steam-Engineering* (Philadelphia, 1863 and 1865). By that time, astonishment had turned to disbelief in many circles. For example, one American journal claimed that Isherwood, who now was the Navy's senior engineer, was "ruining the Navy by his untenable steam delusions," and referred to his engines as "monuments of mechanical incapacity."[11] A British engineering journal characterized the *Michigan* trials as a "simple, obscure experiment, bearing but a remote analogy in its conditions to those under which steam should properly be employed."[12] Nevertheless, Isherwood, who rarely was daunted by criticism, remained confident that his findings were valid.

In retrospect, it appears that both Isherwood and his opponents were correct. During the decades after the Civil War, as improved engineering practices allowed the use of high steam pressures and temperatures and the application of insulation, successful engines were built using Mariotte's principle of extreme expansion. Nevertheless, given the actual technology of the 1860s, Isherwood demonstrated repeatedly that his engines were superior to other machinery of the day. These efforts also revealed once again Isherwood's philosophical approach to his profession, which "spurned the theoretical and abstract in favor of the empirical and practical."[13]

In March 1861, on the eve of the Civil War and one month after he submitted his initial report on the *Michigan* experiments, Isherwood was appointed by the new Lincoln administration to be the Navy's engineer in chief. His elevation to this position, less than seventeen years after entering the service, rested on his reputation for professional competence. It also reflected the sponsorship of Naval Constructor John Lenthall, Chief of the Bureau of Construction, Equipment, and Repairs, who was Isherwood's immediate superior until 1862 when Isherwood took charge of the newly independent Bureau of Steam Engineering. The engineer in chief's friends also referred to his deep commitment to the Union cause. It was typical that Isherwood expressed his nationalism in technological terms. Thus, at the end of the war, in commenting on the fundamental cause of the South's defeat, Isherwood noted that "our antagonists had neither engineering skill nor resources in themselves . . . and the want was fatal; they had despised the mechanical arts and sciences, and by those arts and sciences they fell."[14]

Throughout the Civil War, the still relatively young Isherwood was noted as "one of the finest-looking men at the national capital," who would attract the attention of any group.[15] His striking appearance, featuring a mane of curling, black hair, led to comparison with the poet Byron. Isherwood also was recognized as an "entertaining and instructive" conversationalist.[16] At the same time, however, he had a blunt, combative, and proud demeanor. He was impatient of incompetence, suspicious of the Navy's private contractors, and sensitive—sometimes to a fault—in defending the prerogatives of the Naval Engineering Corps. Not surprisingly, these aspects of Isherwood's personality aroused hostility in many circles.

One of the initial tasks assigned to Isherwood in the spring of 1861 demonstrated the confidence that Secretary of the Navy Gideon Welles had in the new engineer in chief. In April, as the nation entered the vortex of war, Isherwood received orders from the Navy Department to proceed to Norfolk, Virginia, to repair the engines of the USS *Merrimack*. Because of Virginia's imminent secession from the Union, it was essential to move the vessel to a place of safety. When the engineer in chief reached the Norfolk Navy Yard, he found the *Merrimack*'s engineering components almost entirely disassembled; it appeared that at least a month would elapse before the warship could get under way. Nevertheless, with typical determination and competence, Isherwood and his assistants completed repairs of the engines in less than three days. At that point, the indecisive commandant of the navy yard refused to allow the *Merrimack*'s departure, and a disgusted Isherwood returned to Washington without completing his mission. Despite this sorry outcome, one historian notes that only Isherwood "showed imagination and leadership qualities" in the unsuccessful effort to prevent a valuable ship from falling into enemy hands.[17]

Isherwood's essential mission, however, was to administer the Navy's steam engineering bureau, which was responsible for designing, constructing, maintaining, and operating the propulsion plants of the rapidly expanding Union Navy. In March 1861, the U.S. Navy had only 42 warships in commission; but, between 1861 and 1866, the federal government built no fewer than 179 new vessels. It also acquired almost 500 additional ships from the merchant fleet and other government departments. Almost all of these vessels were steam-powered, and their propulsion plants fell under the cognizance of Isherwood's bureau. The engineer in chief personally designed the steam machinery for 125 vessels and monitored the designs prepared by private contractors. In addition, the construction and overhaul of steam equipment, accomplished almost entirely by private firms, required constant supervision by representatives of his bureau.[18]

During the Civil War, the U.S. Navy had the essential strategic roles of maintaining a blockade of Southern coasts and supporting the Army by operating on inland waters. Oceanic vessels of this era still relied heavily upon their sails, owing to the relatively short range and undependability of steam plants.[19] But, the vessels used on the restricted coastal and riverine waters of the Confederacy depended primarily upon steam propulsion. As a result of these specialized requirements, which were hardly typical of the world's other major navies, Isherwood had a superb opportunity to apply his engineering art during an era in which his nation faced a supreme crisis.

The engineer in chief's participation in constructing the 90-day gunboats, which played an essential role in the Union's blockade, exemplified his skill and responsiveness. In the early summer of 1861, the government contracted for twenty-three of these screw-driven, wooden vessels. No fewer than nineteen ships in the class carried Isherwood-designed engines. These plants, which used a low measure of steam expansion, were constructed in great haste. Yet, they were exceptionally durable, especially since Isherwood recognized that many inexperienced personnel, recruited for the rapidly expanding Engineering Corps, would operate the machinery. As a result of this concern, as well as his generally conservative approach to engineering, Isherwood specified that the steam pistons and other essential parts of the 90-day gunboat engines should have almost three times their required strength. Their boilers produced 60 percent more steam than other designers thought necessary. Eleven of these gunboats were in service by the end of 1861. In addition to their value in intercepting blockade runners, they served successfully in other campaigns, including Farragut's capture of New Orleans in 1862 and the Union naval victory two years later during the Battle of Mobile Bay.[20]

Isherwood applied the same principles to the other engines that he created during the Civil War period, including those for the famous double-ender gunboats, specially designed for operations on narrow coastal and inland waters, and several classes of blockade cruisers. Isherwood's propulsion plants may not have represented the most technically advanced solutions, and they obviously reflected special adaptations to the unusual operational demands placed on the Union Navy. But, in the words of George W. Melville, another talented chief of the Bureau of Steam Engineering, the essential fact was that Isherwood's engines "did not break down and they carried our ships to victory. To my mind this was the highest proof of his talent as a sound designer."[21]

Over and above the construction of steam plants, Isherwood became responsible for the management of the Navy's Engineering Corps. Between January 1861 and the start of 1865, the number of individuals assigned to that organization grew from under 200 to almost 2,300. Of the ultimate total,

The USS *Kennebec*. In 1861 the Navy ordered twenty-three screw gunboats built as an emergency measure. Nineteen were powered by engines of Isherwood's design. *Courtesy of the Naval Historical Center.*

about 1,800 engineers were volunteers who were appointed only for the wartime emergency.[22] Considering the dramatic growth of Isherwood's corps, and the relatively primitive development of the American engineering profession, it is not surprising that on a number of occasions Isherwood needed to deal with complaints from fleet commanders regarding the competence of their engineering crews. Isherwood's comments on these occasions revealed an acerbic pen. For example, when Isherwood received the report of a total engine failure and learned that the vessel's engineer ignored clear indications that a debacle was about to occur, he accused the culprit of a "total want of common sense" in failing to shut down the propulsion plant to make repairs. On another occasion, an engineer refused to remedy minor problems; as a result, his ship was unable to participate in an attack on Confederate positions. In this instance, Isherwood concluded that the chief engineer was either "grossly incompetent or cowardly."[23]

In an attempt to maintain the professionalism of the Engineering Corps, Isherwood continued to insist upon examinations for individuals applying for appointments in the regular service. In a more positive sense, Isherwood demanded that naval engineers, who continued to be viewed by many line officers as little more than civilian artisans, be accorded a status appropriate to their growing importance in the modern steam navy. Thus, in 1863, Secretary of the Navy Gideon Welles, acting upon Isherwood's recommendation, directed that engineers be given the use of officer wardrooms. In the same year, Welles raised the relative ranks of staff officers. Previously, the equivalent ranks of those individuals could be no higher than commanders of the line. Under Welles's new directive, however, fleet engineers ranked with line captains. Isherwood, himself, as chief of the Bureau of Steam Engineering, had the equivalent rank of commodore, making him the senior staff officer in the Navy. These institutional developments clearly reflected the importance of steam technology in the Civil War navy and Isherwood's efforts to enhance the status of his fellow engineers.[24]

Despite the pressing operational demands of the Civil War, Isherwood also continued to sponsor a surprisingly ambitious experimental program. For example, in 1864, a board of nine engineers, drawn equally from the Navy, the National Academy of Sciences, and Philadelphia's Franklin Institute, studied the troublesome issue of the relative efficiency of using differing degrees of steam expansion in marine engines. Gideon Welles, reflecting Isherwood's empirical philosophy, commented at this time that the board's effort showed that "no occasion" was neglected for "experimentally determining the data necessary for correct opinion." At the same time, the Navy tested the relative value of two different types of boilers. Even more surprising, considering the exigencies of war, Chief Engineer J. W. King was sent abroad in 1864 to undertake a thorough study of engineering practices in Great Britain and France.[25]

In the longer run, Isherwood sought to develop his profession by creating the opportunities for formal education in steam engineering that largely had been denied to men of his own generation. In 1863–64, the engineer in chief and Secretary Welles recommended that Naval Academy midshipmen receive sufficient instruction in engineering to allow them to stand both engineroom and deck watches. This concept, which, in effect, involved a merger of line and engineering offices, was not adopted until 1899. But, in 1864, Congress authorized the academy to initiate a course for engineering specialists, known as cadet engineers. In the following year, the Navy created a separate Department of Steam Engineering at Annapolis, resulting in a major increase in the engineering education received by midshipmen.[26] There was no intention to make line officers into qualified engineers. But, the ambition of Isherwood and his colleagues to embed a new technology in naval institutions obviously was reaching fruition.

All of these activities were natural by-products of Isherwood's duties as the Navy's senior steam engineer. As the power of the naval technical community grew with the development of the relatively advanced fleet of the Civil War, the bureau chief also began to exert his influence in determining overall shipbuilding and strategic policy. He was joined in these efforts by John

Lenthall, chief of the Bureau of Construction and Repair, who, as the Navy's senior constructor, was responsible for designing and maintaining the hulls of naval ships. The entry by Isherwood and Lenthall into an area that many line officers considered to be beyond the competence of the engineering community would lead to continuing controversy.

There was little debate between line and staff regarding the need for gunboats capable of restricted water operations, or the requirement to build relatively speedy vessels to intercept Confederate cruisers and blockade runners. There also was substantial agreement that the new ironclad monitor, developed by John Ericsson, was well suited to defend American coasts. Nevertheless, Isherwood and Lenthall felt that the enthusiastic acceptance by line officers of the monitors, and the construction of a large number of these vessels, was unwise. In their opinion, some of the appropriations used to build vessels for coastal defense needed to be diverted to the development of a class of speedy, high-freeboard cruisers, preferably plated in iron or built entirely of that metal, that could assure the nation's "command of the open sea" against the most powerful seagoing ships of a potential enemy. In calling for these sea-control vessels, the two engineers obviously looked beyond the requirements of a conflict with the Confederacy. What they did visualize was the possibility of a campaign against the advanced navies of Great Britain and France, which in the first years of the Civil War seemed to threaten intervention on the side of the South.[27]

In the early years of the Civil War, a few large ironclads meeting the general objectives of the Navy's technical community were laid down. But, because of the enthusiasm for monitors and the limited capabilities of America's iron shipbuilding industry, this program was never fully implemented. Instead, in 1863, Isherwood and Lenthall became the primary proponents of a fundamentally different class of warships, of which the *Wampanoag* was the most famous example. The engineer in chief regretted that the large ironclad cruisers were set aside in favor of these smaller, wooden-hulled vessels. Nevertheless, he was no less enthusiastic about the *Wampanoag*s. In fact, Isherwood specified their basic hull configurations as well as their engineering plants. The strategic purpose of these cruisers was to support the classic strategy of *guerre de course*, or as Isherwood stated with typical flair, to operate along the "great tracks of commerce" and to "attack the enemy's purse" by destroying the merchant fleets of Great Britain and France in the event those nations intervened in the American civil conflict. Although they were relatively well armed, there was no expectation that the vessels could achieve "command of the open sea" in opposition to the navies of Europe. In fact, Isherwood noted that the vessels were to engage enemy warships only if "conditions were such that battle could not be avoided." But the cruisers, equipped with powerful engines and featuring remarkably long and narrow hulls, had the high speed needed to track down enemy merchantmen. In order

The USS **Wampanoag**, 1868. *Courtesy of the Naval Historical Center.*

to provide the ships with the endurance required for extended oceanic operations, they also carried a partial set of sails. Isherwood's insistence on the latter design feature revealed his recognition that even the most efficient steam engines of his day lacked long ranges.[28]

Of the five ships in this class that were completed, Isherwood concentrated his personal attention on the lead vessel, the *Wampanoag*, and a similar ship known as the *Ammonoosuc*. The remaining cruisers were built and designed to varying degrees by private contractors, two of whom were Edward N. Dickerson and John Ericsson. Since Dickerson and Ericsson were old antagonists of Isherwood as well as his competitors in shipbuilding, it was obvious that controversy between these strong-minded individuals would continue.

Dickerson was an eminent and cultured patent attorney, a political opponent of the Lincoln administration, and an amateur engineer. He had long viewed Isherwood with contempt, especially since he considered the bureau chief an uneducated upstart who had risen from his humble position as an "engine-driver" to impose his scientific ignorance on the Navy.[29] Dickerson particularly criticized Isherwood's refusal to recognize the validity of Mariotte's law and, in his own designs, insisted on making full use of the expansive properties of steam. The lawyer further accused Isherwood, who, in fact, did grow wealthy during the Civil War, of having a corrupt relationship with the principal suppliers of the Navy's boilers and condensers. This charge was denied vigorously by Isherwood, even though Secretary Welles later observed that rumors surrounding the engineer's dealings with these firms were "never fully cleared up" and were used by his opponents "with some effect against him."[30]

Dickerson attempted to prove the validity of his technical views on numerous occasions. In 1861, the sloop-of-war *Pensacola*, carrying engines of his design, had her sea trials. Naval officials later concluded that the machinery was a complete failure. In 1865–66, another example of Dickerson's engineering, represented by the steam plant of the double-ender gunboat *Algonquin*, met an identical ship powered by Isherwood engines in competitive trials. In each instance, the *Algonquin* demonstrated her inferiority in speed, reliability, and fuel efficiency. Finally, in May 1866, as even his most diehard proponents began to admit to doubts about Dickerson's engineering genius, the *Idaho*, one of the *Wampanoag* cruisers, went to sea. The vessel's specifications called for a fifteen-knot speed over a twenty-four-hour period, but Dickerson's high-expansion engines developed little more than eight knots. A naval board thereupon concluded that the *Idaho*'s machinery was worthless, a characterization that applied equally well to all of Dickerson's fumbling efforts in the field of steam engineering. Dickerson, however, had many influential friends, and his prolonged campaign of abuse against Isherwood planted doubts in the minds of a number of people regarding the competence and honesty of the engineer in chief.[31]

Isherwood and John Ericsson, the high-strung but talented Swedish-American inventor, had been opponents for many years. Contributing to the tensions between the two men in the Civil War were their differing approaches to the design of steam engines, Isherwood's technical criticism of Ericsson's *Monitor*, and the bureau chief's opposition to building an excessive number of *Monitor*-type ships.

It was against this background that Ericsson received a contract in 1863 to design the engines of the *Madawaska*, a sister ship of Isherwood's *Wampanoag*. The inventor viewed this project as an ideal means of testing the relative efficiency of his steam machinery against Isherwood's propulsion plants. As construction of the vessel proceeded, Ericsson's animosity toward the bureau chief grew, as he charged Isherwood with seeking to sabotage his efforts by requiring excessive boiler capacity, withholding progress payments, and setting unreasonable conditions for the cruiser's sea trials. Nevertheless, in January 1867, the *Madawaska* finally was ready for sea. Because of the heavy weather encountered, the results were somewhat ambiguous. During relatively brief periods of time, the *Madawaska* slightly exceeded the contract specification of fifteen-knot speed; but her overall average for forty-one hours was less than thirteen knots. Considering the adverse conditions of her trial, Ericsson claimed that the success of his engines was "so complete as to overwhelm the Bureau Chief."[32] Ericsson and his many friends now waited with impatience for the completion of the *Wampanoag*. Both publicly and privately, they assured the American naval and engineering communities that the *Wampanoag* would demonstrate the technical incompetence of Benjamin Isherwood.

The sea trials of the *Wampanoag*, held in February 1868, seemed to lead to an entirely different conclusion. During that operation, the ship logged 17.75 knots on a one-hour run and averaged 16.6 knots over the longer period of thirty-eight hours, a record that remained unmatched by any U.S. naval vessel for more than twenty years. Isherwood noted with understandable pride that this velocity was four knots greater than that of the most advanced naval or merchant steamers in the world. In his opinion, this achievement also demonstrated that the ships built by John Ericsson and Edward Dickerson were "simply insignificant."[33]

The bureau chief soon discovered, however, that his critics were not stilled by the Wampanoag's triumph, especially since many observers could not agree that a ship, which Isherwood stated was built "purely for speed," was necessarily a successful weapon of war. Among the detractors of the new cruiser were supporters of John Ericsson, including William C. Church, editor of the Army and Navy Journal, and Vice Admiral David Dixon Porter, the Navy's second-ranking officer. A board of line officers, meeting in April 1868, also expressed reservations regarding the vessel's design. Finally, in 1869, another naval board, led by Rear Admiral Louis M. Goldsborough, submitted a report that contained an outright condemnation of the Wampanoag's overall capabilities. Additionally, Goldsborough suggested drastic changes to the ship's design in order to make her of some use to the Navy.[34]

The most persistent and telling line of criticism aimed at Isherwood's masterpiece related to the enormous weight and size of the Wampanoag's engines, around which the vessel was almost literally constructed. It was acknowledged that this machinery produced exceptional speed; but, as the Goldsborough report noted, fully 84 percent of "all the weight the hull can accommodate to the load-line" was absorbed by engines, boilers, and coal supplies. As a result, only 16 percent of her usable capacity was left for "everything else to go on board—masts, rigging, sails, cables, anchors, ordnance, provisions, water, etc."[35] Under these circumstances, the members of this board and other critics argued that it was essential to create additional storage and living spaces, even if this step required the removal of part of the Wampanoag's engineering plant. Without such modification, they argued, it would be impossible for the cruiser to undertake the prolonged, oceanic operations for which she was designed.

Isherwood's foes also claimed that the ship's range was diminished by her incomplete sail plan, which became all the more ineffective because of interference of four large steam funnels and other features of the hull design. Finally, critics made the obvious point that the "main and special purpose" leading to the original construction of the Wampanoag no longer applied.[36] Instead of facing the prospect of war against the British merchant marine, the Navy of the post–Civil War era needed cruising vessels capable of extended deployments to distant stations, a task for which the Wampanoag obviously was poorly suited. In short, as Admiral Goldsborough stated, the basic problem with Isherwood's vessel was that every "substantive attribute of an efficient vessel of war for general sea purposes [had] been, to a greater or less degree, literally sacrificed" on the altar of high speed. The Goldsborough Board, which was led by line officers, also made the pointed suggestion that the important lesson to be drawn from this sorry outcome was the "expediency of consulting, instead of ignoring, experienced and intelligent naval minds as to the properties to be secured in the construction and arrangements of a vessel of war."[37]

Gideon Welles was a long-standing supporter of Isherwood; but as congressional appropriations to the Navy were cut sharply in the later 1860s, he faced the need to scale back the large navy emerging from the Civil War. As one step in that direction, he decided in May 1868 to decommission Isherwood's controversial cruiser. During the next year, by which time Isherwood no longer headed the Bureau of Steam Engineering, the new Grant administration directed modification of the vessel in accordance with the recommendations of the naval examining board of 1869. The result, in the words of Isherwood's biographer, Edward W. Sloan, was an "overhaul which removed half her boilers, loaded her down with masts and yards (to achieve full sail power), and turned her into a useless weapon of war."[38] During the same period, the Navy Department, citing the need for "strict economy," barred the *Wampanoag* and other vessels equipped with sails from using their engines "except under the most urgent circumstances."[39]

Isherwood and many later observers viewed the opposition of line officers to the *Wampanoag* as an effort to impede technical progress and to turn the Navy back to the era of sail. The engineer and his friends also perceived the hand of partisan politics, since many of the leaders in the anti-Isherwood forces were opponents of the Johnson administration, in which the bureau chief served. Finally, the engineer in chief thought that attacks on his competence were an essential part of the campaign by David Porter and other line officers to enhance their authority in the Navy. This was to be accomplished by establishing a new board of seagoing officers, known as the Board of Admiralty, charged with general oversight of the department's operations and administration. To obtain approval for this reorganization, Isherwood felt that the reformers needed to attack the Navy's current administrative system in which the technical bureaus played such a prominent role. Yet, setting aside these ulterior motivations, which certainly existed to some extent, it also is fair to note that the essential indictment of the *Wampanoag* was far from being frivolous. To be sure, her speed demonstrated that she was a monument to the art of steam engineering, at least as it was practiced in the 1860s. But her lack of endurance, an equally essential requirement for a cruising vessel, raised valid doubts about the *Wampanoag*'s effectiveness for her intended use in anti-shipping campaigns.[40]

During the acrimonious feud over the *Wampanoag*, Isherwood, who later was described by an admirer as "the 'best abused' member of the engineering profession,"[41] was locked in an angry debate with another interest group. Throughout the Civil War, the bureau chief became increasingly suspicious of the industrial firms that manufactured and repaired most of the Navy's engineering plants. Specifically, he became convinced that private entrepreneurs produced government work "at the least possible cost to themselves that will enable it to answer a temporary purpose, using of course the poorest materials and least skilled labor because the cheapest." The solution to this problem was for the Navy to develop its own industrial facilities. Using rhetoric that foreshadowed later Populist attacks on business, the bureau chief asserted that by using government plants:

> The profits now having to be paid to wealthy capitalists owning the private establishments for this kind of work would be diffused among the workmen; the government would obtain better work; and both it and they would be mutually benefitted.[42]

It was not long before some of these "wealthy capitalists" counterattacked. This was especially the case after 1866, when Congress at last agreed to provide funds for the construction of naval engineering shops. The largest of these facilities was at the Philadelphia Navy Yard, and here, as elsewhere, John Roach, a prominent New York City entrepreneur, provided the lion's share of the specialized machine tools needed for the manufacture and repair of steam engines. Not surprisingly, Roach's domination of this lucrative market aroused resentment among industrialists in the Philadelphia area. Their complaints soon were translated into a political attack on Benjamin Isherwood when a Philadelphia congressman, William D. Kelley, launched a vigorous investigation of the Navy's tool-purchase program. Kelley's inquiries of 1868–69 fully supported the contentions of his constituents that Roach's equipment was inferior in quality and exorbitant in price, and they suggested that corruption may have entered into Roach's dealings with the Bureau of Steam Engineering. Although Isherwood was cleared of these charges by another congressional report, issued in February 1869, the Kelley investigation was one more rallying point for the many enemies of Benjamin Isherwood.[43]

The final and most formidable foe faced by the engineer in chief was Vice Admiral David Dixon Porter. This famed hero of the Civil War and leader of the line officer corps valued training under sail as a means of developing seaman-like qualities. But, he was by no means a technological reactionary, as Isherwood and his steam engineering friends often charged. In fact, Porter long had been associated with steam-powered vessels, including the *Spitfire* of the Mexican War era, in which Isherwood served as his shipmate. Later, Porter expressed deep appreciation for the contributions made by the Navy's engineers during the Civil War. And, after 1865, while serving as superintendent of the Naval Academy, the admiral gave his full support to the expansion of the school's steam engineering curriculum.[44]

Porter's essential objection to Isherwood related not to technology, as such, but to the unwarranted influence of the Navy's technical community. One historian has noted that the Navy's engineers considered themselves to be the "heralds and makers" of a bold new era of American naval history, an outlook that Isherwood fully shared.[45] In fact, using language that was typically undiplomatic, and which must have been recognizable to the social Darwinians of the nineteenth century, the bureau chief once commented that the Civil War and

> the progress of the age have changed our naval tactics, naval ships, naval machinery, and naval organizations; they have swept away many of the mouldy prejudices of an effete regime. The navy is no longer what it was; it has progressed, improved, and enlarged with the times, and if it is to continue in the same path it must be by the application of new inventions in mechanism and new discoveries in science.[46]

This attitude reflected the great power accumulated by the Navy's technical bureaus during the Civil War. Although Isherwood's special field was steam

New York Navy Yard. Three experimental ships were in New York Navy Yard during the summer and fall of 1866. Left to right: the *Wampanoag,* which was fitting out with a screw gunboat of the *Kansas* or *Cayuga* class along side; the *Madawaska,* which was preparing for trials; the *Susquehanna,* outboard of the *Madawaska;* and the *Idaho,* which was laid up after unsuccessful trials. Two double-ended gunboats can be seen behind the *Idaho. Courtesy of Martin Holbrook.*

engineering, he had no hesitation in determining the overall characteristics and strategic needs of the *Wampanoag* cruisers. His representatives in navy yards had virtual autonomy from the authority of the yard commandant, and they ignored the Navy's chain of command by reporting directly to their bureau chief. Secretary Welles's order of 1863, which increased the relative rank of staff officers, had no effect on the command prerogatives of the line; but this directive gave engineers precedence over many line officers insofar as honors and administrative procedures were concerned. Despite the ill will aroused among the line by the Welles order, Isherwood in 1867 unwisely proposed a further increase in the equivalent ranks of engineers, including his own advancement in relative rank from commodore to rear admiral. Even Secretary Welles, an admirer of Isherwood, was annoyed by the staff's "clamor for rank," and he refused to support that recommendation.[47]

Isherwood's ambitions typified the efforts of America's emerging professions to achieve recognition, status, and power. In his contest with Porter, however, he had the misfortune of dealing with an equally determined representative of another professional group. The Navy's line officers represented the executive or command function of their service, yet in the mid–nineteenth century, no institution existed to allow the line to influence the shaping of overall naval policy. In seeking to correct that situation by establishing a Board of Admiralty, composed of seagoing officers, and simultaneously diminishing the authority of the Navy's technical bureaus, Porter pursued a program that was remarkably similar to a military reform movement discerned by Samuel P. Huntington in a slightly later period of the nineteenth century. It is interesting that a central naval figure in this movement was Stephen B. Luce, who served under Admiral Porter at the Naval Academy in the post–Civil War era.[48] A principal objective of Luce and his compatriots, in Huntington's view, was to crusade against "technism," and to urge officers to "focus on their 'real business,' " which was to prepare for and, if necessary, to wage war. While recognizing the need for technological advances, these leaders insisted that such institutions as the Navy's Bureau of Steam Engineering not "become ends in themselves." Instead, it was essential to subordinate these "technical-administrative units" to ensure that they supported the operational mission of the Navy.[49]

David Porter and his allies never secured their board of line officers. But, during a three-month period in the spring of 1869, the Navy's second-ranking officer personally achieved control of the Navy Department when he served as advisor to Adolph Borie, the remarkably weak Secretary of the Navy appointed by the new Grant administration. Seizing his opportunity, Porter initiated a series of general orders that implemented his views on the role of the Navy's "technical-administrative units." These directives gave all commanding and executive officers precedence over staff officers, specified that technical bureau offices in navy yards were under the exclusive authority of the yard commandants, ordered line officers to inspect warships for deficiencies, and canceled Gideon Welles's order of 1863 that elevated the equivalent ranks of the staff corps.[50] But the ultimate step in Porter's campaign to restore the authority of the Navy's line was the peremptory removal in March 1869 of Benjamin Franklin Isherwood as chief of the Bureau of Steam Engineering. In taking this step, Porter felt that he was deposing the very symbol of staff officer pretensions.

Following eight fruitful but tempestuous years as the Navy's engineer in chief, Isherwood's later career was relatively anticlimactic. It was not without satisfaction, however. In 1869–71, he returned to his love of experimentation while assigned to the Mare Island Navy Yard. Here he tested the efficiency of various types of ship screws and, according to one authority, "formed the basis of propeller design" for almost thirty years thereafter.[51] Later in the 1870s, Isherwood sat on several boards investigating the shipbuilding practices of Grant's second Secretary of the Navy, George M. Robeson. The former bureau chief must have felt personal satisfaction when he found evidence of inefficiency and possible fraud in the administration that dismissed him so abruptly in 1869. In the early 1880s, Isherwood was an unsuccessful candidate to resume his old office of engineer in chief. Surprisingly, David Dixon Porter, who had made his peace with the former bureau chief, lent his support to Isherwood's application.[52] Another indication of Isherwood's continuing prominence was his inclusion on the first Naval Advisory Board that met in 1881 to recommend a building program for the new navy. On one key issue, the wisdom of constructing ship hulls of steel, Isherwood dissented from the position of the board's line-officer majority. Those viewing the Navy's staff as technically progressive, especially in comparison to "reactionary" seagoing officers, may have been puzzled by the engineer's views. But Edward W. Sloan suggests that the engineer was entirely consistent in stating a preference for wrought iron, a metal that was both cheaper and much more familiar to American shipbuilders than steel. As had been the case in the 1860s, when Isherwood refused to use the extreme expansion principle, Sloan notes that:

> Throughout his career Isherwood had advocated only that which would work, which was of known quality rather than of unproven merit. Feasibility, reliability, economy, practicality: these were his watchwords.[53]

Following retirement from the Navy in 1884, Isherwood returned to his home in New York City. His continuing interest in the professionalization of his field was demonstrated in 1888 by his support of the newly organized American Society of Naval Engineers. In fact, Isherwood contributed the lead article in the first issue of the society's journal. Eleven years later, naval engineers were amalgamated into the line, a development that ended the long-standing tension between the two groups and brought to fruition one of Isherwood's recommendations when he served as bureau chief. In 1915, by which time Isherwood was in failing health, he received a more direct recognition when the Naval Academy's steam engineering building was named in his honor. This gesture came none too soon. Later in 1915, Benjamin Isherwood died at the advanced age of 93.[54]

In looking at his total career, Isherwood's eight years as engineer in chief stand out in bold dominance. Throughout this period, he was an unfailing champion of his beloved Engineering Corps and of the cause of steam technology. Isherwood sometimes spoke his mind "roughly and offensively," as Gideon Welles observed.[55] That personality trait, as well as a relatively narrow interest in his own profession, aroused the antagonism of some of his contemporaries. But despite the blows inflicted on the Navy's staff by David Porter, and Isherwood's own dismissal from office, the bureau chief left behind him in 1869 a naval engineering profession that was competent, self-confident, and generally respected. This was especially the case because of the undoubted contribution made by steam engineers, under the leadership of Benjamin Isherwood, in providing the motive power for the vast Union Navy that contributed significantly to the defeat of the Confederacy.

An apt summary of all of these achievements was provided by Frank M. Bennett, a distinguished historian of the nineteenth-century Navy and the bureau chief's fellow engineer. According to Bennett, Isherwood's years as engineer in chief

> were the most exacting and important in the history of the steam navy, during which time every demand made upon that office was promptly and efficiently met and the standard of naval engineering in the United States, despite the cries of those personally hostile to him, raised to an enviable height.[56]

FURTHER READING

Although Isherwood's personal papers have not survived, much official documentation on his career is available among the Navy's official records in the Navy and Old Army Branch of the National Archives. Historians also can turn with profit to Isherwood's own writings. His annual reports as chief of the Bureau of Steam Engineering (appearing in *Annual Reports of the Secretary of the Navy*) and Isherwood's article on the *Wampanoag* (*Cassier's Magazine*, August 1900) are particularly valuable.

Isherwood's important and controversial career has attracted the interest of a number of writers. Frank M. Bennett, a fellow naval engineer, provided some of the earliest coverage on the engineer in chief in *The Steam Navy of the United States*. That basic history of nineteenth-century naval engineering also allows readers to relate Isherwood to broader developments in his field. Another associate of Isherwood, R. H. Thurston, contributed an important article ("Benjamin F. Isherwood," *Cassier's Magazine*, August 1900) that gives valuable insight into Isherwood's personality. More recent biographical articles include George W. Dyson's "Benjamin Franklin Isherwood" (U.S. Naval Institute *Proceedings*, August 1941) and K. Jack Bauer's contribution in the *Dictionary of Military Biography*.

The definitive biography is Edward William Sloan III, *Benjamin Franklin Isherwood: Naval Engineer*. That volume is one of the finest biographical accounts on a nineteenth-century figure available in the naval historical literature. Sloan writes extremely well, and his research is far-ranging and thorough. Although an admirer of Isherwood, Sloan can be critical of his subject's shortcomings.

A provocative chapter on the engineer in chief appears in Elting E. Morison's *Men, Machines, and Modern Times*. Morison concentrates on the rejection of the *Wampanoag* and concludes that this step reflected an effort by line officers to halt technological progress. That contention is specifically challenged, however, in a brilliant article by Lance C. Buhl entitled "Mariners and Machines: Resistance to Technological Change in the American Navy, 1865–1869." Buhl relates the cruiser to the engineering history of the mid–nineteenth century and concludes that her propulsion plant represented transitional technology that soon would be superseded. Buhl also adds a social-history dimension to the history of the *Wampanoag* controversy by probing the origins of the rivalries between line and staff.

A useful, but old-fashioned, account of one of Isherwood's bitter rivals is John Conant Church's *The Life of John Ericsson*. Church includes a number of original letters in his volume. In addition, there is an excellent, modern biography of John Roach, another of Isherwood's contemporaries, in Leonard Alexander Swann, Jr., *John Roach: Maritime Entrepreneur*.

Works that place Isherwood in a broader perspective include Monte Calvert's *The Mechanical Engineer in America, 1830–1910*, a major contribution to the history of nineteenth-century American technology that includes fine coverage on professionalization. Samuel P. Huntington's discussion of the origins of the military profession in the years following the Civil War can be related to Isherwood's career. Despite the apparently narrow title of his work, Huntington's *The Soldier and the State* deserves continuing attention by naval historians.

NOTES

1. See the definitive biography by Edward William Sloan III, *Benjamin Franklin Isherwood: Naval Engineer*, for all aspects of Isherwood's career. See also K. Jack Bauer, "Benjamin Franklin Isherwood," in Roger J. Spiller, ed., *Dictionary of American Military Biography*, II: 512–15.

2. See Monte A. Calvert, *The Mechanical Engineer in America, 1830–1910*, 6–8, 22–23, and *passim*.

3. Sloan, *Isherwood*, 10; Calvert, *Mechanical Engineer*, 19–20.

4. Benjamin F. Isherwood, "U.S. Screw Steamship 'Princeton,'" *Journal of the Franklin Institute* (June 1853), 377–85.

5. Sloan, *Isherwood*, 11–12.

6. Lance C. Buhl, "Mariners and Machines: Resistance to Technological Change in the American Navy, 1865–1869," *Journal of American History* (December 1974), 714–15; Calvert, *Mechanical Engineer*, 247, 260.

7. Sloan, *Isherwood*, 12–15; Frank M. Bennett, *The Steam Navy of the United States*, 57.

8. Sloan, *Isherwood*, 16–19; George W. Dyson, "Benjamin Franklin Isherwood," U.S. Naval Institute *Proceedings* (August 1941), 1141.

9. Quoted in Dyson, "Benjamin Franklin Isherwood," 1142. See also Sloan, *Isherwood*, 83–88.

10. R. H. Thurston, "Benjamin F. Isherwood: A Biographical Sketch," *Cassier's Magazine* (August 1900), 349.

11. Quoted in Elting E. Morison, *Men, Machines, and Modern Times*, 110.

12. Quoted in William Conant Church, *The Life of John Ericsson*, II: 73.

13. John Niven, *Gideon Welles: Lincoln's Secretary of the Navy*, 350. For later developments in steam engineering, see Buhl, "Mariners and Machines," 709, 716.

14. Quoted in Bennett, *Steam Navy*, 200.

15. Thurston, "Benjamin F. Isherwood," 345.

16. Ibid.

17. Niven, *Gideon Welles*, 324. Isherwood's report to the Secretary of the Navy, 18 April 1861, appears in *Official Records of the Union and Confederate Navies in the War of the Rebellion*, Series I, vol. 4, 280–81 (hereafter cited as *ORN*).

18. Charles O. Paullin, *Paullin's History of Naval Administration, 1775–1911*, 280; Sloan, *Isherwood*, 33.

19. Buhl, "Mariners and Machines," 710.

20. Bennett, *Steam Navy*, 221; Dyson, "Benjamin Franklin Isherwood," 1143; K. Jack Bauer, *Ships of the Navy, 1775–1969*, 61–62.

21. Quoted in Dyson, "Benjamin Franklin Isherwood," 1143.

22. Bennett, *Steam Navy*, 201, 205.

23. Isherwood's endorsement of 30 April 1862, *ORN*, Series I, vol. 7, 295–96; Isherwood endorsement of 29 November 1864, *ORN*, Series 1, vol. 3, 383–84.

24. Calvert, *Mechanical Engineer*, 248; Sloan, *Isherwood*, 193; Bennett, *Steam Navy*, 205–6.

25. *Report of the Secretary of the Navy, 1864*, xxix–xxx (hereafter cited as *SecNav Rpt.*). Paullin, *Paullin's History of Naval Administration*, 297.

26. *SecNav Rpt. 1864*, xxxvi–xxxviii; W. D. Puleston, *Annapolis: Gateway to the Quarterdeck*, 105–7; Bennett, *Steam Navy*, 654–66.

27. Sloan, *Isherwood*, 52–59.

28. B. F. Isherwood, "The Sloop-of-War 'Wampanoag,'" *Cassier's Magazine* (August 1900), 285–87; Bauer, *Ships of the Navy*, 65–67.

29. Sloan, *Isherwood*, 105–13.

30. Gideon Welles, *Diary of Gideon Welles*, Howard K. Beale, ed., III: 552.

31. Sloan, *Isherwood*, 106–8, 120–31.

32. Quoted in Church, *Life of John Ericsson*, II: 189. See also ibid., 13, 72, and Sloan, *Isherwood*, 146–57.

33. Isherwood to Welles, 15 May 1868, 40th Cong., 2d sess., *Letter from the Secretary of the Navy . . . ,* House Executive Document 339, 11 (hereafter cited as *House Exec. Doc. 339*). See also Sloan, *Isherwood*, 178–80, 187. The *Ammonoosuc*, the other Isherwood cruiser, demonstrated similar speed during her trials in June 1868.

34. Sloan, *Isherwood*, 180–86, 205, 233–34; "Bureau of Steam Engineering," in *SecNav Rpt. 1868*, 124.

35. "Report of the Board of Steam Machinery Afloat," in *SecNav Rpt. 1869*, 143–54 (hereafter cited as *Goldsborough Board Rpt.*).

36. Commodores M. Smith and Thornton A. Jenkins to Secretary of the Navy, 21 April 1868, *House Exec. Doc. 339*, 8.

37. *Goldsborough Board Rpt*, 148, 151.

38. Sloan, *Isherwood*, 234.

39. General Order 131, 18 June 1869, Navy Department Library, Washington, D.C. See also Buhl, "Mariners and Machines," 711.

40. Sloan, *Isherwood*, 198–99, 204–6, 211; Morison, *Men, Machines, and Modern Times*, 114–16; Isherwood to Welles, 15 May 1868, *House Exec. Doc. 339*, 15. Buhl, "Mariners and Machines," 709–11, stresses that the *Wampanoag*'s engines were transitional and were superseded in the 1880s by advanced technology. He also comments that qualities important for the cruiser's mission were sacrificed for speed.

41. Thurston, "Benjamin F. Isherwood," 352.

42. "Bureau of Steam Engineering," in *SecNav Rpt. 1866*, 178.

43. Sloan, *Isherwood*, 213–20; Leonard Alexander Swann, Jr., *John Roach: Maritime Entrepreneur*, 23–31.

44. Puleston, *Annapolis*, 107; Jack Sweetman, *The U.S. Naval Academy: An Illustrated History*, 84–90.

45. Buhl, "Mariners and Machines," 725.

46. "Bureau of Steam Engineering," in *SecNav Rpt. 1867*, 180.

47. Beale, ed., *Diary of Gideon Welles*, III: 552. See also Buhl, "Mariners and Machines," 718–19; Richard S. West, Jr., *The Second Admiral: A Life of David Dixon Porter, 1813–1891*, 320–21; Sloan, *Isherwood*, 208–11.

48. Albert Gleaves, *Life and Letters of Rear Admiral Stephen B. Luce*, 103–6.

49. Samuel P. Huntington, *The Soldier and the State*, 232, 237–38, 247–48.

50. General Order 89, 10 March 1869; General Orders 91, 94, 97, and

98, 11 March 1869; General Order 120, 1 April 1869, all in Navy Department Library.

51. Quoted in Dyson, "Benjamin Franklin Isherwood," 1146.

52. Sloan, *Isherwood*, 237, 239–40; Swann, *John Roach*, 133, 145–47.

53. Edward W. Sloan III, "Progress and Paradox: Benjamin Isherwood and the Debate Over Iron vs. Steel in American Warship Design," *Naval Engineers Journal* (August 1982), 63.

54. Sloan, *Isherwood*, 240–43.

55. Beale, ed., *Diary of Gideon Welles*, III: 552.

56. Bennett, *Steam Navy*, 609.

BIBLIOGRAPHY

DOCUMENTARY SOURCES

Manuscripts

Alderman Library, University of Virginia, Charlottesville, VA
   William D. Cabell Papers
   Matriculation Book, Non-Resident Students, 11th Session
Eleutherian Mills Historical Library, Wilmington, DE
   John A. Dahlgren Papers
   Samuel Francis Du Pont Papers
Historical Society of Pennsylvania, Philadelphia, PA
   Gratz Collection
   Commodore John Rodgers Papers
Houghton Library, Harvard University, Cambridge, MA
   Charles Sumner Papers
Henry E. Huntington Library, San Marino, CA
   David G. Farragut Papers
   Huntington Library Manuscripts
   David Dixon Porter Papers
Library of Congress, Washington, DC
   William E. Chandler Papers
   John A. Dahlgren Papers
   Andrew H. Foote Papers
   Stephen B. Luce Papers
   Porter Family Papers
   David Dixon Porter Papers
   Rodgers Family Papers
   John Rodgers Letters and Papers
   William T. Sherman Papers

Robert Wilson Shufeldt Papers
Edwin M. Stanton Papers
Gideon Welles Papers
Charles Wilkes Papers
Library of Franklin and Marshall College, Lancaster, PA
Jonathan N. Foltz Papers
Lilly Library, Indiana University, Bloomington, IN
Richard W. Thompson Papers and Letterbooks
Maryland Historical Society, Baltimore, MD
Franklin Buchanan Scrapbook
Massachusetts Historical Society, Boston, MA
George Bancroft Papers
George H. Preble Papers
Missouri Historical Society, St. Louis, MO
James B. Eads Papers
S. Ledyard Phelps Papers
National Archives, Washington DC
Records of the Coast and Geodetic Survey (Record Group 23)
Records of the Bureau of Naval Personnel (Record Group 24)
Naval Records Collection of the Office of Naval Records and Library
(Record Group 45)
General Records of the Department of State (Record Group 59)
Treasury Department Collection of Confederate Records (Record Group
365)
Records of the Naval Academy (Record Group 405)
Naval Academy Museum, Annapolis, MD
Manuscript Collections
Naval Historical Center, Washington, DC
Biographical Reference Files, Operational Archives
General Orders, Navy Department Library
Naval Historical Foundation, Washington Navy Yard, Washington, DC
Autobiography of Joseph Smith Harris
David G. Farragut Papers
Naval War College, Newport, RI
Naval History Collection
New Haven Colony Historical Society, New Haven, CT
Andrew H. Foote Collection
New-York Historical Society, New York, NY
Confidential Correspondence of Gustavus Vasa Fox
New York Public Library, New York, NY
Bartholomew Diggins, "Recollections of the War Cruise of the USS *Hart-ford,* January to December, 1862–1864"

John A. Dahlgren Papers
Robert W. Shufeldt Papers
Nimitz Library, U.S. Naval Academy, Annapolis, MD
    Franklin Buchanan File
    Thomas G. Ford, "History of the Naval Academy"
Norfolk Public Library, Norfolk, VA
    Whittle Papers
William R. Perkins Library, Duke University, Durham, NC
    Theodorus Bailey Papers
    John Dahlgren Papers
    Thomas C. Welles Papers
Princeton University Library, Princeton, NJ
    Blair–Lee Papers
Public Record Office, Singapore, China
    Governor's Papers: Miscellaneous Letters
Rush-Rhees Library, University of Rochester, Rochester, NY
    William H. Seward Manuscript Collection
University of Michigan Library, Ann Arbor, MI
    James B. Angell Papers
University of North Carolina Library, Chapel Hill, NC
    Southern History Collection
Van Pelt Library, University of Pennsylvania, Philadelphia, PA
    Samuel Jackson Randall Papers
Papers in Private Hands
    Thomas Stevens Papers, Charles Peery Collection, Charleston, SC

Printed Source Materials

Allen, Gardner Weld, ed. *Papers of Isaac Hull, Commodore United States Navy.* Boston: The Boston Athenaeum, 1929.

Angell, James Burrill. *The Reminiscences of James Burrill Angell.* New York: Longmans, Green, and Co., 1911.

Basler, Roy P., Pratt, Marion D., and Dunlap, Lloyd A., eds. *Collected Works of Abraham Lincoln,* 9 vols. New Brunswick: Rutgers University Press, 1953–55.

Bauer, K. Jack, ed. *The New American State Papers: Naval Affairs,* 10 vols. Wilmington: Scholarly Resources Inc., 1981.

Beale, Howard K. and Brownsword, Alan W., eds. *Diary of Gideon Welles, Secretary of the Navy under Lincoln and Johnson,* 3 vols. New York: W. W. Norton, 1960.

Bingham, Hiram. *A Residence of Twenty-one Years in the Sandwich Islands, or the Civil, Religious and Political History of Those Islands.* Hartford: Hezekiah Huntington, 1847.

Branham, Alfred I. *'290' Story of the Sinking of the Alabama.* 1883. Booklet form, 1930.

Bulloch, James D. *Secret Service of the Confederate States in Europe: or How the Confederate Cruisers Were Equipped,* 2 vols. Liverpool, 1883. Reprint with a new introduction by Philip Van Doren Stern. New York and London: Thomas Yoseloff, 1959.

Clark, Charles E. *My Fifty Years in the Navy.* Boston: Little, Brown, 1917.

Clyde, Paul H. *United States Policy toward China: Diplomatic and Public Documents, 1839–1939.* Durham: Duke University Press, 1940.

Cole, Allan B., ed. *Yankee Surveyors in the Shogun's Seas: Records of the United States Surveying Expedition to the North Pacific Ocean, 1853–1856.* Princeton: Princeton University Press, 1947.

Congressional Globe, Containing the Debates and Proceedings, 1833–73, 109 vols. Washington, DC: n.p., 1834–73.

"Corea." *Cyclopedia of Political Science.* Chicago: 1881.

"Corea the Hermit Nation." *Bulletin of the American Geographical Society,* III. New York, 1881.

Dahlgren, John A. *A few hints to captains of the new IX. inch shell guns.* Boston: Ticknor and Fields, 1856.

———. *Maritime International Law.* Boston: B. B. Russell, 1877.

———. *Memoir of Ulric Dahlgren, By his father, Rear Admiral Dahlgren.* Philadelphia: J. B. Lippincott & Co., 1872.

———. *Shells and Shell Guns.* Philadelphia: King and Baird, 1856.

———. *The System of Boat Armament in the United States Navy.* Philadelphia: A. Hart, 1852, rev. ed. 1856.

Dahlgren, Madeleine Vinton. *Memoir of John A. Dahlgren, Rear-Admiral United States Navy.* Boston: James R. Osgood & Co., 1882.

Dewey, George. *Autobiography of George Dewey, Admiral of the Navy.* New York: Scribner, 1913.

Du Pont, Samuel F. *Official Dispatches and Letters of Rear Admiral Du Pont, U.S. Navy, 1846–'48, 1861–'63.* Wilmington: Ferris Bros., 1883.

———. *Report on National Defenses,* 3 vols. Washington, DC: Gideon & Co., 1852.

Ferrel, William. "An Essay on the Winds and the Currents of the Ocean." *Nashville Journal of Medicine and Surgery,* XI (1856).

Foltz, Jonathan M. *Surgeon of the Seas: The Adventurous Life of Surgeon General Jonathan M. Foltz in the Days of Wooden Ships,* edited by Charles S. Foltz. Indianapolis: Bobbs-Merrill, 1931.

Foote, Andrew Hull. *Africa and the American Flag.* New York: D. Appleton, 1854.

———. *The African Squadron: Ashburton Treaty: Consular Sea Letters: Reviewed in an Address by Commander A. H. Foote.* Philadelphia: W. F. Geddes [1855].

F[razer, John F.]. "The U.S. Naval Astronomical Expedition to the Southern Hemisphere, during the years 1849–1852." *Journal of the Franklin Institute,* 37 (1859), 68–70.

Grant, Ulysses S. *Papers of Ulysses S. Grant,* edited by John Y. Simon, 14 vols. to date. Carbondale: Southern Illinois University Press, 1967– .

——. *Personal Memoirs,* 2 vols. New York: Charles L. Webster, 1885–86.

Habersham, Alexander W. *My Last Cruise; or, Where We Went and What We Saw.* Philadelphia: J. B. Lippincot and Co., 1857.

H[ammond, James Henry]. "Maury in South America and Amazonia." *Southern Quarterly Review,* XXIV (1853), 412–49.

Hayes, John D., ed. *Samuel Francis Du Pont: A Selection from His Civil War Letters,* 3 vols. Ithaca: Cornell University Press, 1969.

[Holland, Henry?]. "The Physical Geography of the Sea . . . ." *Edinburgh Review,* CV (1857), 360–90.

Isherwood, Benjamin Franklin. "The Sloop-of-War 'Wampanoag': A Once Famous, but Long Forgotten, United States Cruiser." *Cassier's Magazine,* August 1900, 282–89.

——. "U.S. Screw Steamship 'Princeton.' " *Journal of the Franklin Institute,* June 1853, 377–85.

Johnson, Robert Underwood and Buel, Clarence Clough, eds. *Battles and Leaders of the Civil War: Being for the Most Part Contributions by Union and Confederate Officers,* 4 vols. New York: Century, 1887.

Kell, John McIntosh. *Recollections of a Naval Life.* Washington, DC: The Neale Company, 1900.

Lewis, Lloyd. *Sherman, Fighting Prophet.* New York: Harcourt, Brace, 1932.

Lord, Walter, ed. *The Fremantle Diary.* New York: Capricorn Books, 1954.

Low, John. *The Logs of the C.S.S. Alabama and C.S.S. Tuscaloosa,* edited with an Introduction by W. Stanley Hoole. University, AL: Confederate Publishing Co., 1972.

M[aury], M. F. "The Commercial Prospects of the South." *Southern Literary Messenger,* XVII (1851), 686–99.

——. "The Dead Sea Expedition." *Southern Literary Messenger,* XIV (1848), 547–53.

——. *A New Theoretical and Practical Treatise on Navigation . . . .* Philadelphia: Key and Biddle, 1836. Rev. ed. Philadelphia: E. C. and J. Biddle, 1845.

——. *The Physical Geography of the Sea and Its Meteorology,* edited by John Leighly. Cambridge: The Belknap Press of Harvard University Press, 1963.

——. Letter to National Institution for the Promotion of Science. National Institution for the Promotion of Science *Proceedings,* Bulletin No. 1, 17.

—— (Pseud. "Harry Bluff"). "Scraps from the Lucky Bag." *Southern Literary Messenger,* VI (1840), 233–40, 306–20, 786–800; VII (1841), 3–25, 169–70, 345–79.

————. (Pseud. "Union Jack"). "To Mr. Clay." *Southern Literary Messenger,* VII (1841), 724–29.

Milligan, John D., ed. *From the Fresh-Water Navy, 1861–64: The Letters of Acting Master's Mate Henry R. Browne and Acting Ensign Symmes E. Browne.* Annapolis: Naval Institute Press, 1970.

Morgan, James M. *Recollections of a Rebel Reefer.* Boston: Houghton Mifflin, 1917.

Newcomb, Simon. *The Reminiscences of an Astronomer.* Boston: Houghton Mifflin, 1903.

Otway, Arthur, ed. *Autobiography and Journals of Admiral Lord Clarence E. Paget.* London: Chapman & Hall, 1896.

Papers relating to the Foreign Relations of the United States, 1867 and 1870 Washington, DC: 1868 and 1871, 414–16 and 333–39.

[Perry, Matthew C.]. *Narrative of the Expedition of an American Squadron to the China Seas and Japan,* edited by F. L. Hawks, 3 vols. Washington, DC: A. O. P. Nicholson, 1856.

"The Physical Geography of the Sea." *American Journal of Science,* ser. 2, XIX (1855), 449.

"The Physical Geography of the Sea." *Southern Quarterly Review,* XXIX (1856), 151–67.

Poe, Edgar Allan. "Maury's Navigation." *Southern Literary Messenger,* II (1836), 454–55.

Porter, David Dixon. *Incidents and Anecdotes of the Civil War.* New York: D. Appleton, 1885.

————. *Memoir of Commodore David Porter of the United States Navy.* Albany: J. Munsell, 1875

Preble, George H. "A Canoe Expedition into the Everglades in 1842." *Tequesta: The Journal of the Historical Association of Southern Florida* (no. 5, 1945), 30–51.

Redfield, William C. "On Tides, and the Prevailing Currents of the Ocean and Atmosphere." American Philosophical Society *Proceedings,* 3 (1843), 86–89.

Reingold, Nathan, ed. *The Papers of Joseph Henry,* 4 vols. to date. Washington, DC: Smithsonian Institution Press, 1972– .

Reynolds, J. N. *Address on the Subject of a Surveying and Exploring Expedition to the Pacific Ocean and South Seas . . . .* New York: Harper, 1836.

Richardson, James D., comp. *A Compilation of Messages and Papers of the Presidents, 1789–1897,* 10 vols. New York: Bureau of National Literature, 1896–99.

Ringgold, Cadwalader. *Defense of Commander Ringgold before Court of Inquiry No. 2, Convened at Washington City.* Washington, DC: n.p., 1857.

Schley, Winfield Scott. *Forty-five Years under the Flag.* New York: D. Appleton and Company, 1904.

Semmes, Raphael. *Memoirs of Service Afloat during the War between the States.* Baltimore: Kelly, Piet & Co., 1869.

———. *Service Afloat and Ashore during the Mexican War.* Cincinnati: William H. More & Co., 1851.

Sherman, William T. *Memoir of William T. Sherman, Written by Himself,* 2 vols. New York: D. Appleton, 1875.

Shufeldt, Robert W. *Report of Exploration and Surveys to ascertain the Practicability of a Ship Canal between the Atlantic and Pacific Oceans by way of the Isthmus of Tehuantepec.* Washington, DC: n.p., 1872.

———. *The Relation of the Navy to the Commerce of the United States.* Washington, DC: J. Ginck, 1875.

———. *The United States Navy in connection with the Foundation, Growth and Prosperity of the Republic of Liberia.* Washington, DC: J. L. Ginck, 1877.

Sinclair, Arthur. *Two Years on the Alabama.* Boston: Lee and Shepard, 1896.

Stern, Philip Van Doren, ed. *The Confederate Raider Alabama.* Bloomington: Indiana University Press, 1962.

Sulivan, Henry N., ed. *Life and Letters of the Late Admiral Bartholomew James Sulivan.* London: John Murray, 1896.

Summersell, Charles G., ed. *The Journal of Charles Townley Fullam.* University: University of Alabama Press, 1973.

Symonds, Craig L., ed. *Charleston Blockade: The Journals of John B. Marchand, U.S. Navy, 1861–1862.* Newport: Naval War College Press, 1976.

Thompson, Robert Means and Wainright, Richard, eds. *Confidential Correspondence of Gustavus Vasa Fox, Assistant Secretary of the Navy, 1861–1865,* 2 vols. New York: DeVinne, 1920.

Thorndike, Rachel S., ed. *The Sherman Letters: Correspondence between General Sherman and Senator Sherman from 1837 to 1891.* New York: Da Capo Press, 1969 [1894].

"Thoughts on the Navy." *Naval Magazine,* II (1837), 5–42.

U.S., Congress. "Astronomical Observations." 30th Cong., 1st Sess. *H. R. Report 470.*

———. *Congressional Record, 1873– .* Washington, DC: Government Printing Office, 1873– .

———. Espy, James P. "Fourth Meterological Report." *Sen. Exec. Doc. 65,* 34th Cong., 3rd Sess. Washington, DC: Government Printing Office, 1859.

———. "Heavy Ordnance," *Report of the Joint Committee on the Conduct of the War.* 37th Cong., 1st Sess., 3 vols. Washington, DC: Government Printing Office, 1865.

———. "Heavy Ordnance," *Report of the Joint Committee on the Conduct of the War.* 38th Cong., 2nd Sess., 3 vols. Washington, DC: Government Printing Office, 1865.

————. *House Executive Document 1*, 30th Cong., 2nd Sess. Washington, DC: Government Printing Office, 1848.

————. Joint Committee on Ordnance. *Report*. Senate Report 266, 40th Cong., 3rd Sess. Washington, DC: Government Printing Office, 1869.

————. *Letter From the Secretary of Navy . . . Relative to the Trial of . . . Wampanoag and Vessels of That Class,* House Executive Document No. 339. 40th Cong., 2nd Sess. Washington, DC: Government Printing Office, 1868.

————. "Report to accompany Bill S. 698 to authorize the construction of additional steel vessels for the Navy." *Senate Report 161,* 48th Cong., 1st Sess. Washington, DC: Government Printing Office, 1884.

U.S., Department of the Navy. *Annual Reports of the Secretary of the Navy.* Washington, DC: Government Printing Office, 1821–1948.

————. *Official Records of the Union and Confederate Navies in the War of the Rebellion,* edited by Richard Rush et al., 31 vols. and index. Washington, DC: Government Printing Office, 1894–1922.

————. *Report of the Secretary of the Navy in Relation to Armored Vessels.* Washington, DC: Government Printing Office, 1864.

U.S. *Statutes at Large of the United States of America, 1789–1873,* 17 vols. Boston: Little, Brown, 1850–73.

U.S., War Department. *The War of the Rebellion: A Compilation of the Official Records of the Union and Confederate Armies,* 130 vols. Washington, DC: Government Printing Office, 1880–1901.

Walke, Henry. *Naval Scences and Reminiscences of the Civil War in the United States during the Years 1861, 1862, and 1863 . . . .* New York: F. R. Reed, 1877.

Welles, Gideon. *Diary of Gideon Welles, Secretary of the Navy Under Lincoln and Johnson,* 3 vols. Boston: Houghton Mifflin, 1911.

Welles, Gideon. *Selected Essays by Gideon Welles: Civil War and Reconstruction,* compiled by Albert Mordell. New York: Twayne Publishers, 1959.

Wilkes, Charles. *Defense of Commodore Charles Wilkes, U.S.N., Late Acting Rear Admiral, in Command of the West India Squadron, Read Before a General Court Martial.* Washington, DC: McGill and Witherow, 1856.

————. *Narrative of the United States Exploring Expedition during the Years 1838, 1839, 1840, 1841, 1842,* 5 vols. Philadelphia: C. Sherman, 1844.

SECONDARY SOURCES

Books and Dissertations

Adams, Ephraim D. *Great Britain and the American Civil War,* 2 vols. New York: Russell & Russell, 1925.

Adams, F. Colburn. *High Old Salts: Stories intended for Marines, but Told before an Enlightened Committee of Congress.* Washington, DC: Government Printing Office, 1876.

Alden, Carroll S. *George Hamilton Perkins, Commodore, U.S.N.: His Life and Letters.* Boston: Houghton Mifflin, 1914.

Alden, Carroll S. and Westcott, Allen. *The United States Navy, A History.* Chicago: Lippincott, 1943.

Alden, Carroll S. and Earle, Ralph. *Makers of Naval Tradition,* rev. ed. Boston: Ginn, 1943.

Ammen, Daniel. *The Atlantic Coast.* New York: Charles Scribner's Sons, 1883.

Anderson, Bern. *By Sea and by River: The Naval History of the Civil War.* New York: Alfred A. Knopf, 1962, and Westport: Greenwood Press, 1977.

Barrow, Clayton J., ed. *America Spreads Her Sails.* Annapolis: Naval Institute Press, 1973.

Barrows, Edward M. *The Great Commodore: The Exploits of Matthew Calbraith Perry.* Indianapolis: Bobbs-Merrill, 1935.

Bartz, Carl F., Jr. "The Korean Exclusion Policy, 1860–1876." Ph.D. dissertation, University of California, Berkeley, 1953.

Bauer, K. Jack. *The Mexican War 1846–1848.* New York: Macmillan Publishing Co., Inc., 1974.

———. *Ships of the Navy, 1775–1969.* Troy, NY: Rensselaer Polytechnic Institute, 1970.

———. *Surfboats and Horse Marines: U.S. Naval Operations in the Mexican War, 1846–1848.* Annapolis: Naval Institute Press, 1969.

Benjamin, Park. *The United States Naval Academy.* New York: G. P. Putnam, 1900.

Bennett, Frank M. *The Steam Navy of the United States.* Pittsburgh: Warren & Co., 1896.

Bernath, Stuart L. *Squall Across the Atlantic: American Civil War Prize Cases and Diplomacy.* Berkeley: University of California Press, 1970.

Billington, Ray Allen. *The Protestant Crusade, 1800–1860: A Study of the Origins of American Nativism.* New York: Macmillan, 1938.

Boorstin, Daniel J. *The Americans: The National Experience.* New York: Random House, 1965.

Boykin, Edward. *Ghost Ship of the Confederacy. The Story of the Alabama and her Captain, Raphael Semmes.* New York: Funk & Wagnalls Co., 1957.

Bryant, Samuel W. *The Sea and the States: A Maritime History of the American People.* New York: Crowell, 1947.

Brinker, William J. "Robert W. Shufeldt and the Changing Navy." Ph.D. dissertation, Indiana University, 1973.

Brooke, George M., Jr. *John M. Brooke: Naval Scientist and Educator.* Charlottesville: University Press of Virginia, 1980.

Brookes, Jean I. *International Rivalry in the Pacific Islands, 1800–1875.* Berkeley: University of California Press, 1941.

Browning, Robert S., III. *Two if by Sea: The Development of American Coastal Policy.* Westport: Greenwood Press, 1984.

Bruce, Robert V. *Lincoln and the Tools of War.* Indianapolis: Bobbs-Merrill, 1956.

Bruce, William C. *John Randolph of Roanoke, 1773–1833; A Biography Based Largely on New Materials,* 2 vols., 2nd ed. New York: Putnam's, 1922.

Buhl, Lance. "The Smooth Water Navy: American Naval Policy and Politics, 1865–1876." Ph.D. dissertation, Harvard University, 1968.

Calvert, James. *The Naval Profession.* New York: McGraw-Hill, 1965.

Calvert, Monte A. *The Mechanical Engineer in America, 1830–1910.* Baltimore: The Johns Hopkins Press, 1967.

Canfield, Eugene B. *Civil War Ordnance.* Washington, DC: Government Printing Office, 1969.

————. *Notes on Naval Ordnance of the American Civil War.* Washington, DC: American Ordnance Association, 1960.

Case, Lynn M. and Spencer, Warren F. *The United States and France: Civil War Diplomacy.* Philadelphia: The University of Pennsylvania Press, 1970.

Chien, Frederick F. *The Opening of Korea: A Study of Chinese Diplomacy, 1876–1885.* N.p., n.p., 1967.

Choi, Soo Bock. "Political Dynamics in Hermit Korea: The Rise of Royal Power in the Decade of the Tae wŏn kun, 1864–1873." Ph.D. dissertation, University of Maryland, 1963.

Church, William C. *The Life of John Ericsson,* 2 vols. New York: Charles Scribner's, 1890.

Clark, Norman H. *Deliver Us from Evil: An Interpretation of Prohibition.* New York: Norton, 1976.

Coletta, Paolo E., ed. *American Secretaries of the Navy,* 2 vols. Annapolis: Naval Institute Press, 1980.

Conroy, Hilary. *The Japanese Seizure of Korea: 1868–1910.* Philadelphia: J. B. Lippincott, 1960.

Corbin, Diana Fontaine Maury. *The Life of Matthew Fontaine Maury, U.S.N. and C.S.N.* London: S. Low, Marston, Searle, and Rivington, 1888.

Crook, David P. *The North, the South and the Powers, 1861–1865.* New York: John Wiley, 1974.

Daly, Robert W. *How the Merrimac Won: The Strategic Story of the C.S.S. Virginia.* New York: Crowell, 1957.

Dalzell, George W. *The Flight from the Flag.* Chapel Hill: University of North Carolina Press, 1940.

Daniels, George H. *Science in American Society: A Social History.* New York: A. A. Knopf, 1971.

Davenport, Charles B. *Naval Officers: Their Heredity and Development.* Washington, DC: Carnegie Institution of Washington, 1919.

Davis, George T. *A Navy Second to None: The Development of Modern American Naval Policy.* New York: Harcourt, Brace, 1910.

Davis, William C. *The Last Conquistadors: The Spanish Intervention in Peru and Chile, 1863–1866.* Athens: University of Georgia Press, 1950.

Delaney, Norman C. *John McIntosh Kell of the Raider Alabama.* University: University of Alabama Press, 1973.

Dennett, Tyler. *Americans in Eastern Asia: A Critical Study of United States' Policy in the Far East.* New York: Barnes & Noble, 1963 [1922].

Deuchler, Martina. *Confucian Gentlemen and Barbarian Envoys: The Opening of Korea, 1875–1885.* Seattle: University of Washington Press, 1977.

Drake, Frederick C. *The Empire of the Seas: A Biography of Rear Admiral Robert Wilson Shufeldt, USN.* Honolulu: University of Hawaii Press, 1984.

Du Bois, William E. B. *The Suppression of the African Slave-Trade to the United States of America, 1638–1870.* New York: Longman, Green & Co., 1896.

Dufour, Charles L. *The Mexican War. A Compact History 1846–1848.* New York: Hawthorn Books, Inc., 1968.

————. *The Night the War Was Lost.* Garden City: Doubleday, 1960.

Dumond, Dwight Lowell. *Anti-slavery: The Crusade for Freedom in America.* Ann Arbor: University of Michigan, 1961.

Du Pont, Henry A. *Rear Admiral Samuel Francis DuPont U.S. Navy: A Biography.* New York: National Americana Society, 1926.

Dupree, A. Hunter. *Science in the Federal Government, a History of Policies and Activities to 1940.* Cambridge: Harvard University Press, 1957.

Durkin, J. T. *Stephen R. Mallory: Confederate Navy Chief.* Chapel Hill: University of North Carolina Press, 1954.

Edmonds, David C. *The Guns of Port Hudson.* Volume One: *The River Campaign (February–May 1863).* Lafayette, LA: Acadiana Press, 1983.

Eliot, George F. *Daring Sea Warrior: Franklin Buchanan.* New York: Messner, 1962.

Emmons, George F. *The Navy of the United States, From the Commencement, 1775, to 1853.* Washington, DC: Gideon & Co., 1853.

Falls, Cyril. *A Hundred Years of War.* London: Gerald Duckworth & Co., 1953.

Farragut, Loyall. *The Life and Letters of Admiral Farragut, First Admiral of the United States Navy.* New York: D. Appleton, 1879.

• Ferris, Norman B. *Desperate Diplomacy: William H. Seward's Foreign Policy, 1861.* Knoxville: University of Tennessee Press, 1976.

————. *The "Trent" Affair: A Diplomatic Crisis.* Knoxville: University of Tennessee Press, 1977.

Freeman, Douglas Southall. *R. E. Lee: A Biography,* 4 vols. New York: Charles Scribner's Sons, 1945.

Gilman, Daniel C. *The Life of James Dwight Dana, Scientific Explorer, Mineralogist, Geologist, Zoologist.* New York: Harper & Brothers, 1899.

Gleaves, Albert. *Life and Letters of Rear Admiral Stephen B. Luce.* New York: G. P. Putnam, 1925.

Gosnell, H. Allen. *Rebel Raider.* Chapel Hill: University of North Carolina Press, 1948.

Griffis, William E. *Corea: The Hermit Nation.* New York: Charles Scribner's Sons, 1888.

———. *Matthew Calbraith Perry: A Typical American Naval Officer.* Boston: Capples and Hurd, 1887.

Hagan, Kenneth J. *American Gunboat Diplomacy and the Old Navy: 1877–1889.* Westport: Greenwood Press, 1973.

———, ed. *In Peace and War: Interpretations of American Naval History, 1775–1978.* Westport: Greenwood Press, 1978.

———, ed. *In Peace and War: Interpretations of American Naval History, 1775–1984,* A Second Edition. Westport: Greenwood Press, 1984.

Hattaway, Herman and Jones, Archer. *How the North Won.* Urbana: University of Illinois Press, 1983.

Hattendorf, John B., Simpson, B. Mitchell III, and Wadleigh, John R. *Sailors and Scholars: The Centennial History of the Naval War College.* Newport: Naval War College Press, 1984.

Headley, Joel T. *Farragut and Our Naval Commanders.* New York: E. B. Treat, 1867.

Headley, Phineas C. *The Life and Naval Career of Vice-Admiral David Glascoe* [sic] *Farragut.* New York: Neale, 1906.

Henderson, Daniel. *The Hidden Coasts: A Biography of Admiral Charles Wilkes.* New York: Sloane, 1953.

Henderson, Gregory. *Korea: The Politics of the Vortex.* Cambridge: Harvard University Press, 1968.

Henry, Robert Selph. *The Story of the Mexican War.* New York: Bobbs-Merrill Co., 1950.

Henson, Curtis T., Jr. *Commissioners and Commodores: The East India Squadron and American Diplomacy in China.* University: University of Alabama Press, 1982.

Herrick, Walter. *The American Naval Revolution.* Baton Rouge: Louisiana State University Press, 1966.

Hill, Jim Dan. *Sea Dogs of the Sixties: Farragut and Seven Contemporaries.* Minneapolis: University of Minnesota, 1935.

Hine, Robert V. *Edward Kern and American Expansion.* New Haven: Yale University Press, 1962.

Holzman, Robert S. *Stormy Ben Butler.* New York: Macmillan Co., 1954.

Hoole, William Stanley. *Four Years in the Confederate Navy: The Career of*

Captain John Low in the C.S.S. Fingal, Florida, Alabama, Tuscaloosa, and Ajax. Athens: University of Georgia Press, 1964.

Hoppin, James Mason. *Life of Andrew Hull Foote, Rear-Admiral United States Navy.* New York: Harper & Brothers, 1874.

Horsfield, John. *The Art of Leadership in War: The Royal Navy from the Age of Nelson to the End of World War II.* Westport: Greenwood Press, 1980.

Huntington, Samuel P. *The Soldier and the State.* Cambridge: Harvard University Press, 1957.

Hutchins, John G. B. *The American Maritime Industries and Public Policy, 1789–1914.* Cambridge: Harvard University Press, 1941.

Jahns, Patricia. *Matthew Fontaine Maury and Joseph Henry: Scientists of the Civil War.* New York: Hastings House, 1961.

Johnson, Allen and Malone, Dumas, eds. *Dictionary of American Biography,* 20 vols. New York: Charles Scribner's Sons, 1928–36.

Johnson, John. *The Defense of Charleston Harbor . . . 1863–1865.* Charleston: Walker, Evans, and Cogswell, Co., 1890.

Johnson, Ludwell H. *Red River Campaign: Politics and Cotton in the Civil War.* Baltimore: The Johns Hopkins Press, 1958.

Johnson, Robert E. *Far China Station: The U.S. Navy in Asian Waters, 1800–1898.* Annapolis: Naval Institute Press, 1979.

———. *Rear Admiral John Rodgers, 1812–1882.* Annapolis: Naval Institute, 1967.

Johnson, Robert Underwood and Buel, Clarence Clough, eds. *Battles and Leaders of the Civil War,* 4 vols. New York: The Century Co., 1887.

Jones, Francis C. "Foreign Diplomacy in Korea, 1866–1894." Ph.D. dissertation, Harvard University, 1935.

Jones, Virgil C. *The Civil War at Sea,* 3 vols. New York: Holt, Reinhart, Winston, 1960–62.

Karsten, Peter. *The Naval Aristocracy: The Golden Age of Annapolis and the Emergence of Modern American Navalism.* New York: Free Press, 1972.

Keller, Allan. *Andrew Hull Foote, Gunboat Commodore, 1806–1863.* Hartford: Civil War Centennial Commission, 1964.

Kim, C. I. Eugene and Kim, Han-Kyo. *Korea and the Politics of Imperialism, 1876–1910.* Berkeley: University of California Press, 1967.

Kim, David H. "Americans in Korea: The Background of the Shufeldt Treaty, 1866–1882." Ph.D. dissertation, Georgetown University, 1983.

Knox, Dudley W. *A History of the United States Navy.* New York: G. P. Putnam's Sons, 1936.

Kohlstedt, Sally Gregory. *The Formation of the American Scientific Community: The American Association for the Advancement of Science, 1848–1860.* Urbana: University of Illinois Press, 1976.

Langley, Harold D. *Social Reform in the United States Navy, 1798–1862.* Urbana: University of Illinois Press, 1967.

Lee, Yur-bok. *Diplomatic Relations between the United States and Korea, 1866–1887.* New York: Humanities Press, 1970.

Lewis, Charles L. *Admiral Franklin Buchanan: Fearless Man of Action.* Baltimore: Norman, Remington, 1929.

———. *David Glasgow Farragut,* 2 vols. Annapolis: Naval Institute Press, 1941–43.

———. *Matthew Fontaine Maury, the Pathfinder of the Seas.* Annapolis: Naval Institute Press, 1927.

Long, David F. *Nothing Too Daring: A Biography of Commodore David Porter, 1780–1843.* Annapolis: Naval Institute Press, 1970.

———. *Sailor-Diplomat: A Biography of Commodore James Biddle, 1783–1848.* Boston: Northeastern University Press, 1983.

Long, John D. *The New American Navy.* New York: The Outlook Co., 1903.

Macartney, Clarence Edward. *Mr. Lincoln's Admirals.* New York: Funk & Wagnalls, 1956.

Mack, Gerstle. *The Land Divided.* New York: Alfred A. Knopf. 1944.

Mackenzie, Alexander S. *Life of Commander Oliver Hazard Perry,* 2 vols. New York: Harper, 1843.

Mahan, Alfred T. *Admiral Farragut.* New York: D. Appleton, 1892.

———. *Types of Naval Officers.* London: Sampson Low, Marston & Co., 1904.

Mahon, John K. *History of the Second Seminole War, 1835–1842.* Gainesville: University of Florida Press, 1967.

Maltzahn, Baron Curt von. *Naval Warfare,* trans. by John C. Miller. London: Longmans Green & Co., 1908.

Mannix, Daniel P. *Black Cargoes: A History of the Atlantic Slave Trade, 1518–1865.* New York: Viking, 1962.

McCollum, Kenneth G., ed. *Dahlgren.* Dahlgren, VA: Naval Surface Weapons Center, 1977.

Merli, Frank J. *Great Britain and the Confederate Navy, 1861–1865.* Bloomington: Indiana University Press, 1970.

Merrill, James M. *Battle Flags South: The Story of the Civil War Navies on Western Waters.* Cranbury, NJ: Associated University Presses, 1970.

Miller, Lillian B. *The Lazzaroni: Science and Scientists in Mid-Nineteenth Century America.* Washington, DC: Smithsonian Institution Press, 1972.

Milligan, John D. *Gunboats Down the Mississippi.* Annapolis: Naval Institute Press, 1965.

Mitchell, Donald W. *History of the Modern American Navy from 1883 through Pearl Harbor.* New York: Alfred A. Knopf, 1946.

Morgan, William James, et al., eds. *Autobiography of Rear Admiral Charles Wilkes, United States Navy, 1798–1877.* Washington, DC: Naval History Division, 1978.

Morison, Elting E. *Men, Machines, and Modern Times.* Cambridge: M.I.T. Press, 1966.

Morison, Samuel E. *"Old Bruin": Commodore Matthew C. Perry, 1794–1858*. Boston: Little, Brown & Co., 1967.

Nelson, M. Frederick. *Korea and the Old Orders in Eastern Asia*. Baton Rouge: Louisiana State University, 1946.

Niven, John. *Gideon Welles: Lincoln's Secretary of the Navy*. New York: Oxford University Press, 1973.

Paullin, Charles O. *American Voyages to the Orient, 1690–1865*. Annapolis: Naval Institute Press, 1972.

————. *Commodore John Rodgers: Captain, Commodore, and Senior Officer of the American Navy, 1773–1838*. Cleveland: The Charles H. Clark Company, 1910; (reprint) Annapolis: Naval Institute Press, 1967.

————. *Diplomatic Negotiations of American Naval Officers, 1778–1883*. Baltimore: The Johns Hopkins Press, 1912.

————. *Paullin's History of Naval Administration, 1775–1911*. Annapolis: Naval Institute Press, 1968.

Peck, Taylor. *Round-Shot to Rockets: A History of the Washington Navy Yard and U. S. Naval Gun Factory*. Annapolis: Naval Institute Press, 1949.

Pennanen, Gary, "The Foreign Policy of William Maxwell Evarts." Ph.D. dissertation, University of Wisconsin, 1969.

Pletcher, David. *The Awkward Years: American Foreign Relations under Garfield and Arthur*. Columbia: University of Missouri Press, 1962.

Ponko, Vincent. *Ships, Seas, and Scientists: U. S. Naval Exploration and Discovery in the Nineteenth Century*. Annapolis: Naval Institute Press, 1974.

Porter, David Dixon. *The Naval History of the Civil War*. New York: Sherman Publishing Co., 1886.

Potter, E. B. and Nimitz, Chester W., eds. *Sea Power: A Naval History*. Englewood Cliffs: Prentice Hall, 1960.

Pratt, Fletcher. *The Navy, A History: The Story of a Service in Action*. Garden City: Garden City Publishing, 1941.

Puleston, W. D. *Annapolis: Gateway to the Quarterdeck*. New York: D. Appleton, 1942.

Ramage, Helen. "The Wilkes Exploring Expedition on the Pacific Slope, 1841." M.A. thesis, University of California, 1916.

Reed, Rowena. *Combined Operations in the Civil War*. Annapolis: Naval Institute Press, 1978.

Reingold, Nathan, ed. *Science in Nineteenth-Century America: A Documentary History*. New York: Hill and Wang, 1974.

Reynolds, Clark S. *Command of the Sea*. New York: William Morrow & Co., 1974.

Rhodes, James Ford. *History of the United States from the Compromise of 1850*, 7 vols. New York: Macmillan, 1893–1900.

————. *Lectures on the American Civil War*. New York: Macmillan, 1913.

Reisman, David, Glazer, Nathan, and Denney, Reuel. *The Lonely Crowd: A*

Study of the Changing American Character, 2nd ed. Garden City: Doubleday Anchor, 1953.

Ripley, Warren. *Artillery and Ammunition of the Civil War*. New York: Van Nostrand, 1970.

Roberts, W. Adolphe. *Semmes of the Alabama*. New York: Bobbs-Merrill Co., 1938.

Scharf, J. Thomas. *History of the Confederate States Navy from its Organization to the Surrender of its Last Vessel*. New York: Rogers and Sherwood, 1887.

Schroeder, John H. *Shaping a Maritime Empire: The Commercial and Diplomatic Role of the American Navy, 1829–1861*. Westport: Greenwood Press, 1985.

Seager, Robert, II. *Alfred Thayer Mahan: The Man and His Letters*. Annapolis: Naval Institute Press, 1977.

Shufelt, H. B. *Our Folks: A History of the Shufelt Family*. New York: Claverack, 1929.

Sloan, Edward William, III. *Benjamin Franklin Isherwood: Naval Engineer*. Annapolis: Naval Institute Press, 1965.

Smith, Bradford. *Yankees in Paradise: The New England Impact on Hawaii*. Philadelphia: Lippincott, 1956.

Smith, Russell W. "The Opening of Korea by Commodore Robert W. Shufeldt." M.A. thesis, University of Virginia, 1953.

Soley, James Russell. *The Blockade and the Cruisers*. New York: Charles Scribner's, 1883.

Soulsby, Hugh G. *The Right of Search and the Slave Trade in Anglo–American Relations, 1814–1862*. Baltimore: The Johns Hopkins Press, 1933.

Spector, Ronald. *Professors of War: The Naval War College and the Development of the Naval Profession*. Newport: Naval War College Press, 1977.

Spencer, Warren F. *The Confederate Navy in Europe*. University: University of Alabama Press, 1983.

Spiller, Roger J., et al., eds. *Dictionary of American Military Biography*, 3 vols. Westport: Greenwood Press, 1984.

Sprout, Harold and Sprout, Margaret. *The Rise of American Naval Power, 1776–1918*. Princeton: Princeton University Press, 1939.

Stanton, William. *The Great United States Exploring Expedition of 1838–1842*. Berkeley: University of California Press, 1975.

———. *The Leopard's Spots: Scientific Attitudes Toward Race in America, 1815–59*. Chicago: University of Chicago, 1960.

Still, William N., Jr. *Iron Afloat: The Story of the Confederate Armorclads*, rev. ed. Columbia: University of South Carolina Press, 1985.

———. *American Sea Power in the Old World: The United States Navy in European Waters, 1865–1917*. Westport: Greenwood Press, 1980.

Summersell, Charles Grayson. *The Cruise of the C.S.S. Sumter*. University, AL: Confederate Publishing Co., 1965.

————. *CSS Alabama: Builder, Captain, and Plans*. University: University of Alabama Press, 1985.

Swann, Leonard Alexander, Jr. *John Roach: Maritime Entrepreneur*. Annapolis: Naval Institute Press, 1965.

Sweetman, Jack. *The U.S. Naval Academy: An Illustrated History*. Annapolis: Naval Institute Press, 1979.

Tocqueville, Alexis de. *Democracy in America*. London: Saunders and Otters, c. 1835–40.

Todorich, Charles M. *The Spirited Years: A History of the Antebellum Naval Academy*. Annapolis: Naval Institute Press, 1984.

Towle, Edward L. "Science, Commerce and the Navy on the Seafaring Frontier (1842–1861): The Role of Lieutenant M. F. Maury and the U.S. Naval Hydrographic Office in Naval Exploration, Commercial Expansion and Oceanography Before the Civil War." Ph.D. dissertation, University of Rochester, 1966.

Trefousse, Hans. *Ben Butler: The South Called Him Beast!* New York: Twayne Publishers, 1957.

Tyler, David B. *The Wilkes Expedition: The First United States Exploring Expedition (1838–1842)*. Memoirs of the American Philosophical Society, vol. 73. Philadelphia: The Society, 1968.

Van Alstyne, Richard W. *The Rising American Empire*. New York: Oxford University Press, 1960.

Wallace, Edward S. *General William Jenkins Worth. Monterey's Forgotten Hero*. Dallas: Southern Methodist University Press, 1953.

Walworth, Arthur. *Black Ships off Japan: The Story of Commodore Perry's Expedition*. New York: Alfred A. Knopf, 1946.

Warner, Oliver. *Command at Sea: Great Fighting Admirals from Hawke to Nimitz*. New York: St. Martin's Press, 1976.

Warren, Gordon H. *Fountain of Discontent: The Trent Affair and Freedom of the Seas*. Boston: Northeastern University Press, 1981.

Weigley, Russell F. *Quartermaster General of the Union Army: A Biography of M. C. Meigs*. New York: Columbia University Press, 1959.

West, Richard S., Jr. *The Second Admiral: A Life of David Dixon Porter, 1813–1891*. New York: Coward-McCann, 1937.

————. *Gideon Welles: Lincoln's Navy Department*. Indianapolis: Bobbs-Merrill Co., 1943.

Williams, Frances Leigh. *Matthew Fontaine Maury: Scientist of the Sea*. New Brunswick: Rutgers University Press, 1963.

Williams, William A. *The Roots of the Modern American Empire*. New York: Random House, 1969.

Winchester, Richard C. "James G. Blaine and the Ideology of American Expansionism." Ph.D. dissertation, University of Rochester, 1966.

Wise, Stephen R. "Lifeline of the Confederacy: Blockade Running During the Civil War." Ph.D. dissertation, University of South Carolina, 1983.

Wriston, Henry M. *Executive Agents in American Foreign Relations*. Baltimore: The Johns Hopkins Press, 1929.

Articles

Aamold, Walter. "Athletic Training at the Naval Academy." U.S. Naval Institute *Proceedings*, 61 (October 1935), 1560–67.

"Admiral Shufeldt's Visits to Korea." *Korea Magazine*, I (1917), 243–48.

Angell, James Burrill. "The Diplomatic Relations Between the United States and China." *Journal of Social Sciences*, XVII (1883), 24–36.

Appenzeller, Henry G. "The Opening of Korea: Admiral Shufeldt's Account of It." *Korean Repository*, I (1892), 57–62.

Bartlett, Merrill L. "Commodore James Biddle and the First Naval Mission to Japan, 1845–1846." *American Neptune*, 61 (1981), 25–35.

Bauer, K. Jack. "Benjamin Franklin Isherwood." *Dictionary of Military Biography*, edited by R. J. Spiller, vol. 3, 512–15.

————. "The Korean Expedition of 1871." U.S. Naval Institute *Proceedings*, 74 (1948), 197–204.

Beck, F. M. "Interpreting for Captain Shufeldt." *Korean Magazine*, I (1917), 239–40.

Blue, George Verne. "The Project for a French Settlement in the Hawaiian Islands, 1824–1842." *Pacific Historical Review*, II (1933), 85–99.

Boyd, Mark F. "The Joint Operations of the Federal Army and Navy near St. Mark's Florida, March 1865." *Florida Historical Quarterly*, XXIX (1950), 96–124.

Brooke, George M., Jr. "The Role of the United States Navy in the Suppression of the African Slave Trade." *American Neptune*, XXI (1961), 28–41.

Bryan, G. S. "The Purpose, Equipment, and Personnel of the Wilkes Expedition." *Proceedings* of the American Philosophical Society, LXXXII (June 1940), 560.

Buhl, Lance C. "Maintaining an American Navy, 1865–1889," in Kenneth J. Hagan, ed. *In Peace and War: Interpretations of American Naval History, 1775–1984*. Westport: Greenwood Press, 1984, 145–73.

————. "Mariners and Machines: Resistance to Technological Change in the American Navy, 1865–1869." *Journal of American History*, 61 (1974), 703–27.

Byron, John L. "Warriors." U.S. Naval Institute *Proceedings*, 111 (June 1985), 63–68.

Cagle, Malcolm W. "Lieutenant David Dixon Porter and His Camels." U.S. Naval Institute *Proceedings*, 83 (no. 12, December 1957), 1327–33.

Campbell, James Edwin. "Recent Addresses." *Ohio Archaeological and Historical Quarterly*, XXXIV (1925), 29–62.

Crowell, Jackson. "The United States and a Central American Canal 1869–1877." *Hispanic American Historical Review*, XLIX (1969), 27–52.

Delaney, Norman C. "Showdown at Cherbourg." *Civil War Times Illustrated*, 15 (no. 3, June 1976), 16–21.

Drake, Frederick C. "The Cuban Background of the *Trent* Affair." *Civil War History*, XIX (1973), 29–49.

———. "Secret History of the Slave Trade to Cuba Written by an American Naval Officer, Robert Wilson Shufeldt, 1861." *Journal of Negro History*, LV (1970), 218–20.

Du Pont, Samuel F. "The War with Mexico: The Cruise of the U.S.S. *Cyane* during the Years 1845–48." U.S. Naval Institute *Proceedings*, VIII (1882), 419–37.

Dyson, George W. "Benjamin Franklin Isherwood." U.S. Naval Institute *Proceedings*, 67 (August 1941), 1139–46.

Foster, Carol H. "The United States Naval Academy." *Scribner's Magazine*, 64 (July 1918), 3–21.

Gale, James S. "The Fate of the *General Sherman:* From an Eye Witness Account." *Korea Review*, II (1895), 252–54.

Gordon, Arthur. "The Great Stone Fleet: Calculated Catastrophe." U.S. Naval Institute *Proceedings*, 94 (December 1968), 72–82.

Graebner, Norman A. "American Interests in California, 1845," *Pacific Historical Review*, XXII (1953), 15–27.

Griffis, William E. "The Opening of Korea." *Korea Magazine*, I (1917), 506–10.

Hagan, Kenneth J. "Admiral David Dixon Porter: Strategist for a Navy in Transition." U. S. Naval Institute *Proceedings*, 94 (July 1968), 139–43.

Hickey, A. S. "Rear Admiral Robert Wilson Shufeldt, United States Navy, Gentleman and Diplomat." U.S. Naval Institute *Proceedings*, 69 (1943), 73–80.

Johnston, James D. "The Battle of Mobile Bay." *United Service*, VI, 108.

Kirk, Neville T. "Commander Foote at the Barrier Forts." U.S. Naval Institute *Proceedings*, 81 (1955), 126–27.

Leary, William M. "The *Alabama* vs. the *Kearsarge*." *American Neptune*, 29 (1969), 167–73.

———. "Our Other War in Korea." U.S. Naval Institute *Proceedings*, 94 (1968), 46–53.

Leighly, John. Editor's Introduction to M. F. Maury. *The Physical Geography of the Sea and Its Meterology*. Cambridge: Belknap Press, 1963.

Lin, T. C. "Li Hung-chang: His Korea Policies, 1870–1885." *Chinese Social and Political Science Review*, 19 (1935), 202–33.

Lockhart, Paul D. "The Confederate Naval Squadron at Charleston and the Failure of Naval Harbor Defense." *American Neptune*, XLIV (1984), 257–75.

MacDonald, Donald S. "The American Role in the Opening of Korea to the West." *Transactions of the Korea Branch of the Royal Asiatic Society*, XXXV (1959), 51–66.

Merrill, James M. "Midshipman Du Pont and the Cruise of the *North Carolina*, 1825–1827." *American Neptune*, XL (1980), 211–25.

Milligan, John D. "From Theory to Application: The Emergence of the American Ironclad War Vessel." *Military Affairs*, XLVIII (1984), 126–32.

Molella, Arthur P. "At the Edge of Science: Joseph Henry, 'Visionary Theorizers,' and the Smithsonian Institution." *Annals of Science*, 41 (1984), 445–61.

Nahm, Andrew C. "Korea's Response to International Rivalries: Korean Domestic Policies, 1876–84." *Michigan Academy of Science, Arts, Letters, Papers*, L (1964), 445–65.

———. "Reaction and Response to the Opening of Korea, 1876–1884." *Studies on Asia*, VI (1965), 61–80.

Noer, Thomas J. "Commodore Robert W. Shufeldt and America's South African Strategy." *American Neptune*, XXXIV (1974), 81–88.

Paullin, Charles O. "Beginnings of the United States Naval Academy." U.S. Naval Institute *Proceedings*, 50 (1924), 173–94.

———. "A Half Century of Naval Administration in America, 1861–1911: Part IV. The Navy Department under Grant and Hayes, 1869–1881." U.S. Naval Institute *Proceedings*, 39 (1913): 736–60.

———. "The Opening of Korea by Commodore Shufeldt." *Political Science Quarterly*, XXV (1910), 470–99.

Plesur, Milton. "Across the Wide Pacific." *Pacific Historical Review*, XXVIII (1959), 73–80.

Pollard, Robert T. "American Relations with Korea, 1882–1895." *Chinese Social and Political Science Review*, XVI (1932–33), 425–71.

Reingold, Nathan. "Two Views of Maury . . . and a Third." *Isis*, 55 (1964), 370–72.

Reynolds, Clark G. "The Great Experiment: Hunter's Horizontal Wheel." *American Neptune*, XXIV (January 1964), 5–24.

Rippy, J. Fred. "The Diplomacy of the United States and Mexico Regarding the Isthmus of Tehuantepec, 1848–1860." *Mississippi Valley Historical Review*, VI (1920), 503–21.

Rowland, Henry A. "The Highest Aim of the Physicist." *The Physical Papers of Henry Augustus Rowland*. Baltimore: The Johns Hopkins Press, 1902.

Sandler, Stanley. "A Navy in Decay: Some Strategic Technological Results of Disarmament, 1865–1869, in the U.S. Navy." *Military Affairs*, XXXV (1971), 138–42.

Seager, Robert, II. "Ten Years Before Mahan: The Unofficial Case for a New Navy, 1880–1890." *Mississippi Valley Historical Review*, XL (1953), 491–512.

Shufeldt, Robert W., Jr. "Life History of an American Naturalist." *Medical Life*, 31 (no. 2, February 1924), 67–76; (nos. 3–5, 8, March–May and August 1924), 67–76, 105–15, 138–49, 193–203, and 307–26.

Sloan, Edward W., III. "Progress and Paradox: Benjamin Isherwood and the Debate over Iron vs. Steel in American Warship Design." *Naval Engineers Journal* (August 1982), 59–63.

Smith, Geoffrey S. "The Navy Before Darwinism: Science, Exploration, and Diplomacy in Antebellum America." *American Quarterly*, XXVIII (1976), 41–55.

Soley, James Russell. "Eulogy," in *A Memorial of David Dixon Porter from the City of Boston*. Boston: by order of the city council, 1891.

Sperber, Hans. "Fifty-four Forty or Fight; Facts and Fictions." *American Speech*, XXXII (February 1957), 5–16.

Still, William N. " 'Porter . . . is the Best Man': This Was Gideon Welles's View of the Man He Chose to Command the Mississippi Squadron." *Civil War Times Illustrated*, 16 (no. 2, 1977), 4–9, 44–47.

Sturdy, Henry Francis. "The Establishment of the Naval School at Annapolis." U.S. Naval Institute *Proceedings*, 71 (1945), 1–17.

Sunoo, Hag-w'on. "A Study of the U.S.–Korean Treaty of 1882." *Korea Review*, II (1949), 25–44.

Swartout, Robert, Jr. "Cultural Conflict and Gunboat Diplomacy: The Development of the 1871 Korean American Incident." *Journal of Social Science and Humanities* [Seoul], 43 (June 1976), 117–69.

Swartz, Oretha, D. "Franklin Buchanan: A Study in Divided Loyalties." U.S. Naval Institute *Proceedings*, 88 (no. 12, 1962) 61–71.

Swisher, Earl. "Commodore Perry's Imperialism in Relation to America's Present-day Position in the Pacific." *Pacific Historical Review*, 16 (1947), 30–40.

Tate, E. Mowbray. "Admiral Bell and the New Asiatic Squadron 1865–1868." *American Neptune*, XXXII (1972), 123–35.

Thurston, R. H. "Benjamin F. Isherwood." *Cassier's Magazine*, August 1900, 344–52.

Tisdale, Mahlon S. "A Cruise Through the First Academic Journal and Some Modern Analogies." U.S. Naval Institute *Proceedings*, 50 (March 1924), 352–72.

Wegner, Dana M. "Commodore William D. 'Dirty Bill" Porter." U.S. Naval Institute *Proceedings*, 103 (February 1977), 40–49.

West, Richard. "The Relations between Farragut and Porter." U.S. Naval Institute *Proceedings*, 61 (July 1935), 985–96.

NOTES ON CONTRIBUTORS

John H. Schroeder received his Ph.D. in history from the University of Virginia in 1971. Since then, he has been a member of the Department of History at the University of Wisconsin–Milwaukee where he is currently Associate Professor of History and Acting Vice Chancellor for Academic Affairs. He is the author of *Mr. Polk's War: American Opposition and Dissent, 1846–1848*, as well as several articles on antebellum diplomacy and politics. His essay "Stephen Decatur: Heroic Ideal of the Young Navy" appeared in *Command Under Sail: Makers of the American Naval Tradition, 1775–1850*, and he has recently published a study of antebellum naval diplomacy entitled *Shaping a Maritime Empire: The Commercial and Diplomatic Role of the American Navy, 1829–1861*.

David K. Allison is a historian in the Department of Energy, having formerly served as historian of Navy Laboratories. His Ph.D. is from Princeton University, and he is the author of *New Eye for the Navy: The Origins of Radar at the Naval Research Laboratory,* "U.S. Navy Research and Development Since World War II," in Merritt Roe Smith, ed., *Military Enterprise and Technological Change,* and "The Origins of the Naval Research Laboratory" in the U.S. Naval Institute *Proceedings.* He is currently finishing a book on the evolution of the Navy Laboratories from 1869 to the present.

William Stanton is Professor of History at the University of Pittsburgh. He received his Ph.D. from Brown University, specializes in the history of science, and is the author of *The Leopard's Spots: Scientific Attitudes Toward Race, 1815–1859* and *The Great United States Exploring Expedition of 1838–1842*.

Geoffrey S. Smith is Professor of History at Queen's University in Kingston, Canada. He received his Ph.D. from the University of California at Santa Barbara, and served as a member of the Council of the Society for Historians of

American Foreign Relations from 1983 to 1985. His many articles include "The Navy Before Darwinism: Science, Exploration, and Diplomacy in Antebellum America," and he is the author of *To Save a Nation: American Countersubversives, the New Deal, and the Coming of World War II*, which was nominated for a Pulitzer Prize. He is currently at work on a new, fourth edition of *A History of American Foreign Policy* with Alexander DeConde.

Charles M. Todorich is a graduate of the Naval Academy, earned an M.A. in history from the University of Maryland, and is a graduate of the University of Maine School of Law. He is the author of *The Spirited Years: A History of the Antebellum Naval Academy,* and currently resides in Maine.

John D. Milligan is Professor of History at the State University of New York at Buffalo. A former Army Air Corps pilot, he received his Ph.D. from the University of Michigan. He has directed both the undergraduate and graduate programs of his department and has been a visiting professor at McMaster University. The author of *Gunboats Down the Mississippi* and the editor of *From the Fresh-Water Navy, 1861–64,* Milligan has also published articles on racial attitudes and slave rebellions.

K. Jack Bauer is Professor of History at Rensselaer Polytechnic Institute. He holds an M.A. and a Ph.D. from Indiana University and is the author or editor of numerous books and articles on naval and military history, including *Surfboats and Horse Marines, Ships of the Navy, Combat Vessels, The Mexican War 1846–1848, The New American State Papers: Naval Affairs,* and *Zachary Taylor: Soldier, Planter, Statesman of the Old Southwest.* He has been the John F. Morrison Visiting Professor of Military History at the Army's Command and General Staff College, and serves on the boards of both the American Military Institute and the North American Society for Oceanic History. Dr. Bauer is currently writing a history of the U.S. Navy.

William N. Still, Jr. is Professor of History and co-director of the Program in Maritime History and Underwater Research at East Carolina University. He received his Ph.D. from the University of Alabama and has written extensively on naval aspects of the Civil War, including *Iron Afloat: The Story of the Confederate Ironclads, Confederate Shipbuilding, American Sea Power in the Old World,* and *Why the South Lost the Civil War* (co-author). His forthcoming studies include *Ironclad Captains: The Commanding Officers of the USS Monitor.* He is also completing a study of the U.S. Navy in European Waters during World War I and afterward.

Warren F. Spencer is Professor of History at the University of Georgia. He received his Ph.D. from the University of Pennsylvania and is a specialist in nineteenth-century French diplomatic history. His publications include *The United States and France: Civil War Diplomacy* (co-author), *The Confederate Navy in Europe,* and articles in various European and American journals. He is the recipient of the University of Georgia Creative Research Award and the first occupant of the Sandy Beaver Teaching Chair in History.

Tamara Moser Melia, a historian in the Research Branch at the Naval Historical Center, Washington, D.C., is Associate Editor of volume two of *The Naval War of 1812: A Documentary History*. Ms. Melia did her graduate work at Southern Illinois University at Carbondale, where she assisted in editing *The Papers of Ulysses S. Grant*. She is a visiting faculty member at Georgetown University.

Robert Erwin Johnson served in Coast Guard escort vessels during World War II and did undergraduate and graduate work at the University of Oregon before receiving his Ph.D. from the Claremont Graduate School. A member of the history faculty of the University of Alabama since 1956, he is the author of *Thence Round Cape Horn: The Story of United States Naval Forces on Pacific Station, 1818–1923, Rear Admiral John Rodger, 1812–1882,* and *Far China Station*. He is currently completing a history of the Coast Guard.

Frederick C. Drake is Professor of History at Brock University in St. Catharines, Ontario. Born in England, he was educated at the University of Manchester and Cornell University, where he received his Ph.D. He is author of *The Empire of the Seas: A Biography of Rear Admiral Robert Wilson Shufeldt, USN,* which won the John Lyman Prize in United States Naval History from the North American Society for Oceanic History. He has published articles in a variety of journals, including one on the background of the *Trent* Affair in *Civil War History*. Dr. Drake is currently working on a study of the War of 1812 on the Great Lakes and St. Lawrence River.

Dean C. Allard is a senior historian with the Naval Historial Center in Washington, D.C., and heads that organization's Operational Archives. His publications include *The United States Navy and the Vietnam Conflict* (co-author), *Spencer Fullerton Baird and the U.S. Fish Commission: A Study in the History of American Science,* and articles on naval and maritime history that have appeared in a variety of journals. Dr. Allard serves as president of the North American Society for Oceanic History and is an adjunct professor at the George Washington University, where he teaches courses in military history.

James C. Bradford, editor of this series, is Assistant Professor of History at Texas A&M University. He did undergraduate work at Michigan State University and received his Ph.D. from the University of Virginia. He is the editor of the comprehensive microfilm edition of *The Papers of John Paul Jones* and currently is preparing a select letterpress edition of Jones's correspondence. He edited, and contributed an essay on "John Paul Jones: Honor and Professionalism" to *Command Under Sail: Makers of the American Naval Tradition,* the first volume in the series.

INDEX

349